# Blue Ridge
# Mountain Pleasures

# Blue Ridge
# Mountain Pleasures

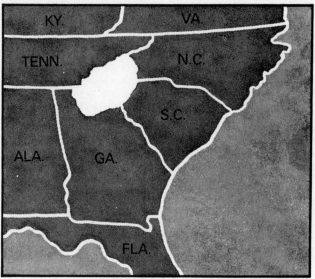

*An A — Z Guide to North Georgia,*
*Western North Carolina and the*
*Upcountry of South Carolina*

## Donald C. Wenberg

The East Woods Press
Charlotte, North Carolina

Printed in the United States of America

Library of Congress Cataloging in Publication Data

Wenberg, Donald C., 1942-
  Blue Ridge Mountain Pleasures.

  1. Blue Ridge Mountains — Description and travel — Guide-books. I. Title.
F217.B6W44   1985                    917.55'0443                    84-72967
ISBN 0-88742-051-6

Cover photograph: sunrise over Lake Lure, by Bill Tuttle. Numbered, certified prints are available from Bill Tuttle, 202 Roberta Drive, Greenville, S.C. 29615.

An East Woods Press Book
Fast & McMillan Publishers, Inc.
429 East Boulevard
Charlotte, North Carolina 28203
(704) 334-0897

# Contents

## Contents

## Contents

To those who enjoy and appreciate the many splendors of nature, the everlasting gift of God

To those who take the path less traveled and seek the adventure and excitement of exploration and discovery

To those who want to experience and enjoy the mountain culture and heritage of yesteryear

To my family — my wife, Joanne, my daughter, Kristen, my son, Todd — and their world of tomorrow

# Acknowledgments

I have traveled with my family for many enjoyable miles; met beautiful people who shared their culture, traditions and everyday lives honestly and openly with me; secured a vast amount of information by mail from the more-than-cooperative individuals who labored to answer my questions and satisfy my requests — especially the chambers of commerce; the Georgia, North Carolina and South Carolina departments of travel and tourism; and the various daily and weekly newspapers in the Blue Ridge Mountains region. To one and all a very special, heartfelt thank you.

My appreciation goes out to the persons directly involved with the preparation of the manuscript:

— Susan Cater Salisbury for her beautiful way with words in each chapter introduction . . .

— Jean Allen Kaiser for her talented sketches . . .

— Bill Tuttle for his excellent photo gracing the front cover of the book . . .

— Georgia Kagelaris for her endless hours of typing the chapters, along with the assistance of Ann McInnis and Connie Gonzalez . . .

— Sally McMillan and her staff at East Woods Press for their positive response to the manuscript . . .

— My many friends and my colleagues at South Tech. for their continuous support and positive encouragement, especially Dr. Fran. Robinson . . .

— My family (Joanne, Kristen and Todd), who after four years will no longer have to ask, "When are you going to finish the book?"

# Foreword

The mountains appear at first only as a long blue ripple on the horizon. They seem to rise above and beyond the buildings and clutter of everyday life like some fantasy world, far off and unattainable. To those who have known and loved them, the sight of those distant peaks brings a thrill of anticipation. They call up memories of many things ... of winding roads through little valleys where the houses climb upward toward the sunshine; of deep blue-green lakes and rushing mountain streams that hide themselves in tangled thickets of laurel; of long days of lying in the sunshine with nothing but the sound of crickets to break the stillness; of the crunch of a new-fallen snow underfoot as you make your way to the woodpile for another load of fuel for the hungry fire.

It is all so far from the routine of today's world that even when you live in the hills year-round there is still a sense of adventure in much of what you do. When couples gather for an evening it is like the days when pioneer families came together — for neighbors are still not so near as to be a nuisance. The lively conversation might deal with gardens, the weather or the first sign of deer tracks in the woods. It is hard to remove yourself from a sense of being very much a part of the natural world around you when the weather determines your ability to function.

This, in part, might account for the "laid back," easy-going attitude that is so much a part of the native population. Relax. If we don't get to it today, there might still be tomorrow. If the weather looks good for fishing, the inside chores can wait for rain. If it is trout season, or deer season — then everything can wait.

In the past the people of the mountains had little chance for material gain. Cash money was hard to come by. They came to value the "art of living" over that of "making a living," and much of this attitude still exists.

Perhaps it is the very nature of the mountains that invites the visitor to unwind. The beauty around you requires an unhurried attention to be truly appreciated. The scenery can become dramatic, but it is more often subtle. You must relax and begin to study the details of nature to come to the deep sense of appreciation it can give you. The world of the Blue Ridge is like a million small vignettes. Beneath the showy white blossoms of mountain laurel in the springtime, the delicate lady slipper can be found nestling in a bed of brown pinestraw; along a tiny streambank, the bell-shaped trillium stands nodding in a patchwork of light and shadows; in the deep woods, the pileated woodpecker echoes his crazy laughing call; and nothing can be more arresting than to watch a long August sunset over the mountains with the changing colors and the shadows gathering deep in the coves below.

Then there are the seasons. None is so long that you can really get tired of it. Each has a special personality. To many springtime is the best. It is hard not to find the overwhelming beauty of May appealing. May has the promise of everything good. It is new life, budding forth on the trees and swirling overhead on the wings of returning songbirds.

Summer is for the active person. There are sports to participate in, gardens to plant, places to explore, and a house full of visitors if you have a summer home. But there is also time to lie in the sun and just "go with the flow of nature."

Fall brings out the wanderlust in everyone. The spectacle of color alone is enough to send the population out to view the show. The best way to be a part of any sesaon is always to walk, and this holds true even more in Fall. Whether you're walking a mountain trail along some hog-backed ridge or simply strolling into a nearby grove of maple or beech, the sensation of nature's cycle will catch you up in its advenutre. The last bits of color are just as effective as the first.

Winter is a time for introspection. The gray days of rain and early darkness bring us closer to the fireside, and to contemplation of things left undecided in the months of sunshine. And there is snow. Sudden and surprising in most of the mountains, it comes often at night and leaves the world dressed in white. To wake to this beauty is like having Christmas without warning. There is usually just enough time to sense its magic and explore the new world it has created before it is gone. Only in the deep mountains does it linger to become, for a time, a way of living.

And so it goes. The seasons — the little flashes of beauty and insight that the mountains have to offer the attentive visitor — and the deep sense of permanence that is all around you.

In the end this is what calls most of us back to the hills. When all else fails, the hills still will be there to comfort us. Somewhere, in some bend of the road, or in some silent stand of pine trees we will feel full of peace and hope again. And to that we will always return.

John Kollock
*Artist, author, historian*
*Clarksville, Georgia*

# Preface

"I only went for a walk and finally concluded to stay out til sundown, for going out, I found, was really going in." Those are the words of John Muir, who in 1867 walked from central Kentucky to the tip of southern Florida, compiling a daily log of his activities. The log was later published as *John Muir's Longest Walk*.

In many ways, I can identify with John Muir and also with the poet Robert Frost, who wrote in "The Road Not Taken": "Two roads diverged in a wood, and — I took the one less traveled by, and that has made all the difference."

By venturing out and taking the less-traveled road, I discovered the real Blue Ridge Mountains. My purpose in this book is simple: to provide an accurate, up-to-date guide to the countless things to see and do in this beautiful region of our country. My task was monumental, the hours long, the work never ending for about four years of my life — but the result was a completed project that was enjoyable, interesting and rewarding. I hope you will find it equally enjoyable and that it will help you take full advantage of the pleasures that wait in the Blue Ridge Mountains.

# Introduction

Before you begin using the A to Z chapters that list the astounding array of things to see and do in the Blue Ridge region, you may find the following general information helpful: what area this guide covers; tips about traveling to the area; some state, regional and local information sources; and pointers for using this guide most effectively.

## The Area Covered in This Guide

The Blue Ridge Mountains stretch from Virginia to north Georgia. This book focuses on the southern part of the range, an area with Asheville, N.C., as its heart. The region begins at Grandfather Mountain in the north and takes in western North Carolina including Murphy, N.C., northwestern South Carolina along the North Carolina-South Carolina border, and northeast Georgia. These boundaries were chosen because they encompass the area most familiar to the author and because the vastness of the entire Blue Ridge area made it necessary to focus on just one part and to include in this book only the most unique, interesting, varied events and attractions in that part. Certain events and attractions are highlighted with an asterisk(*), which denotes that the location is outside the designated area. These events and attractions were included because of their special interest or because they were so close to the designated area.

## Traveling to the Blue Ridge Area

Depending on your purpose, pocketbook and time, you have any number of roads from which to choose to reach the area. Asheville, N.C., which is roughly at the center of the region, is accessible within 24 hours driving time to 50 percent of the cities of the northern, mid-western, and eastern United States. You can drive on sleek interstate highways or winding country roads.

If you are coming from the Northeast or Mid-West, there are three main routes: New Yorkers and New Englanders can travel south on I-95 to Petersburg, Va., then on I-85 to Winston-Salem, N.C., and then on I-40 to Asheville, N.C. Central New Yorkers and Pennsylvanians can travel I-81 south and join I-40 south to Asheville, N.C. Mid-Westerners can head for Knoxville, Tenn., and then take I-81 north to I-40.

Floridians have a choice of two routes. The first is I-95 to I-26, proceeding north to Asheville. The second includes the Sunshine Turnpike north to I-75; I-75 to I-85 (by-passing Atlanta on I-285); I-85 to I-26 at Spartanburg, S.C.; I-26 to Asheville, N.C.

The most picturesque and leisurely way to travel through the Blue Ridge area is the Blue Ridge Parkway, which meanders along the crests of mountains from Front Royal, Va., in the Shenandoah National Park Area, to near Cherokee, N.C. The parkway speed limit is 45 m.p.h., and the slow pace allows you to take in the splendid vistas and rustic roadside sights. Overlooks, stopovers, visitor centers, picnic areas and lodges are scattered along the parkway. The visitor facilities and lodges are usually open from May 1 through October. Beware — some stretches of the parkway are closed by ice and snow in the winter months.

Entrances to the parkway in the Asheville area are located at US-25 south near the Biltmore House: US-191 south (Brevard Road) Exit I-26; US-70 east; US-75 east (Lake Lure-Chimney Rock Road); and NC-695 (Mountain Road) off US-70.

See Appendix B for a list of map resources, including official state maps.

You can simplify matters by taking the bus, either Greyhound or Trailways, and forgetting about driving altogether. Bus depots are located all through the region.

There are plenty of flights into Asheville, and there you can rent a car. Airline routes are subject to frequent change, of course, but at the time of this writing, the following airports have flights that terminate in Asheville:

**Atlanta, Ga.** Hartsfield International. Many major airlines.

**Greenville, S.C.** Greenville-Spartanburg Jet Port. Eastern, Piedmont.

**Chattanooga, Tenn.** Lovell Field. Delta, Eastern, Republic, Sunbird, Tennessee Airways.

**Knoxville, Tenn.** Tenn-McGhee-Tyson. American, Delta, Piedmont, Republic, TWA, Tennessee Airways, United.

Small plane enthusiasts should consult flight information manuals for available municipal and private airports.

## State, Regional and Local Information Sources

Some of the best places to obtain information are the local chamber of commerce offices. You can write for information when you're planning your trip or drop by after you're in the area for information about climate, recreation, transportation, history, restaurants, churches, motels, camping, health care, businesses, schools, libraries, clubs, organizations, city offices, real estate offices, financial institutions, and more.

Most chambers have displays of current brochures and detailed maps, and information ranging from local attractions to purchasing a home or finding a job in the area.

See Appendix A for a list of state, regional and local information sources.

## Using This Guide Most Effectively

The following suggestions will help you use *Blue Ridge Mountain Pleasures* most efficiently:

• Use it as an itinerary planner for your daily, weekly or monthly activities while you are in the area.

• Call the phone number at the end of most listings or contact the area chamber of commerce for the latest information about an event or place you plan to visit — especially if you are traveling from out of town or state. Events, attractions, dates and locations do change, so call ahead to be safe.

Most listings contain the following information in this order: town and state; name of the attraction or event; address or directions; sponsor (if any); brief description; date held (for events) or days open (for attractions); phone number. However, not all this information was available for every listing, and only information that seems reasonably certain to remain unchanged was included. For example, many local events such as festivals are handled by volunteers, and the contact phone number changes each year; such phone numbers are not listed, for they would quickly become obsolete.

While every effort has been made to insure that the information in this guide is accurate and up to date, it is almost inevitable that some particulars will have changed by the time you use the book. The author welcomes suggestions for corrections and additions for future editions. These should be mailed to the publisher (see the address on the second page of the book).

*Blue Ridge Mountain Pleasures* includes hundreds of pleasurable activities and places to visit — most of them free. Enjoy as many of them — from A to Z — as you can when you are in this unique and beautiful region.

# Amusements and Attractions

If simply relaxing and breathing in pure mountain air start to bore you, take in one of the region's theme parks or the less commercial resort parks.

Mystery seekers will like Mystery House at Cherokee, N.C., or Mystery Hill between Boone and Blowing Rock, N.C. At both the law of gravity seems to be defied.

Fortune seekers might try their luck at winning the $100,000 jackpot at Bingo Night in Cherokee, N.C. Or you can find live entertainment, rides, arts and crafts, and the largest zoo in the area at Santa's Land, also in Cherokee.

The Wild West comes alive at Ghost Town in the Sky in Maggie Valley, N.C. Lawmen, shopkeepers, dancers, cowboys and musicians, all dressed in period costumes, help take visitors back in time. Ride the chair lift or incline railway up the face of a mountain to the site of the fun. A similar attraction, with plenty of rides, games and entertainment, is in Gold City in Franklin, N.C.

Cool off at Magic Waters, a wet, wild theme park at Cherokee, N.C., where skiers and high divers perform. Or test your own skill by zipping down "Ragin' Waters" or the "Super Loop Slide."

Cabbage Patch doll fans will want to visit the birthplace of their "babies" — Babyland General Hospital in Cleveland, Ga. That's where creator Xavier Roberts started the uproar.

Children will like Mt. Yonah Alpine Storyland in Sautee-Nacoochee, Ga., north of Cleveland. They can view miniature storyland scenes and pet animals, or let some stray energy loose on the playground.

**ASHEVILLE, N.C.   Sunday in the Park.** Every other Sunday afternoon in a different city park. Varied family entertainment: amateur dance, musicians, bands, drama and storytelling. Late May to early September. (704) 258-3858.

**ATLANTA, GA.   Six Flags Over Georgia,** 12 mi. west of Atlanta on I-20 at Six Flags Drive. More than 100 rides in a 331-acre family entertainment park: triple roller coaster, whitewater raft ride and a 225-foot parachute jump ride. Admission; children under 2, free. Admission covers all rides and shows. Open daily, mid May-Labor Day. Open certain days in March, April, May and in September and October. (404) 948-9290.

**BLOWING ROCK, N.C.** **Mystery Hill,** Rte. 1, Box 278, US-221/321. Mystifying house; educational attraction. Visit antique museum, mystery platform, scorpion's den, Old World candy shop and hall of mystery. Open all year except Thanksgiving and Christmas. Admission. (704) 264-2792.

**Tweetsie Railroad,** P. O. Box 388, US-321. Memorial Day-end of October, Mon.-Sat. Family park with railroad theme. Authentic western town. Admission. (704) 264-9061.

**BRYSON CITY, N.C.** **Perry's Water Gardens,** NC-28 south from Bryson City to Franklin; on Cowee Valley Road. 2-acre park with ponds, sunken gardens, small waterfall, picnic facilities and walking trails. (704) 488-3681.

**BUFORD, GA.** **Lake Lanier Islands.** A 1200-acre recreation resort built on land that was meant to be flooded by the overflow from Buford Dam. A mathematical miscalculation resulted in four green islands, the tops of foothills that were not completely submerged. Lake Lanier is one of the South's major lakes for sailing. The resort area has boat rentals, fishing, trout ponds, riding stables, beaches and bathhouses, 430-foot water slide, speed slide, amphitheatre, and camping and lodging facilities. The parking fee includes shuttle bus. Island Welcome Center: always open. (404) 945-6701.

**CHATSWORTH, GA.** **Fort Mountain Frontier Lands,** 2 mi. east of Chatsworth on US-76. A Western frontier town, complete with gunfights, saloon shows and an animal farm. Rides and picnic areas. Open Thurs.-Mon., Memorial Day-Labor Day. Open weekends in April, May, September, October.

**CHEROKEE, N.C.** **Bears Den,** on Big Cove Road, next to Saunooke's Trading Post. Home of "Victor, the Rasslin Bear," who starred in the movie *Paint Your Wagon* and appeared on the "Ed Sullivan Show." Ten other bears also featured. (704) 497-3001.

**Cherokee Amusement Park,** intersection of US-19 and US-23. Miniature golf, arcade, shooting gallery, go-cart track. Open May to October.

**Cherokee Bingo,** US-19E. Home of the Giant Jackpot. First and third Sat. each month. (704) 397-2770.

**Cherokee Chair Lift,** in the heart of Cherokee, covers nearly a mile (round trip) at moderate speed to show you spectacular views of the Cherokee Indian Reservation and the Great Smoky Mountains. Discount to groups and senior citizens. Open April-October. (704) 497-2330.

**Cherokee Fountain of Youth,** US-441 north. One of the largest water slides in the Southeast: 825 feet of curves and fun. Hot showers available for National Park campers. Cherokee's favorite hangout. Open summer months.

**Cherokee Recreation Park,** at the junction of US-19 and 441 in downtown Cherokee. Offers a variety of entertainment: mini-golf, go-cart track, arcade, educated animals and many other amusements. (704) 497-3351.

**Cherokee Water Slides:** 1) Cherokee River Valley, Big Cove Road, 4 mi. north of Cherokee; 2) Frontier Water Slide, Frontier Shopping Center, US 19. Open summer months.

**Cyclorama of the Cherokee Indian,** US-19, ¾ mi. east of Cherokee. Presents Cherokee history through dramatic tableau peopled with larger than life sized, authentically costumed figures. The dwindling empire of the Cherokee is shown on a large electronic map. Daily, April-October; nightly, July 1-Labor Day. Admission. (704) 497-4521.

**Dash 'N' Splash,** on US-19, 1 mi. north of Cherokee. Open mid-May-October. Bumper boats, arcade games and concession. (704) 497-7111.

**Mystery House,** on US-441 N, ½ mi. from **Unto These Hills.**Can the law of gravity be defied? A scientific phenomenon that defies description, it's perplexing, entertaining, and fun for kids and adults, too. Guided tours only. Open March-December. (704) 497-9542.

**Magic Waters,** on US-19, ½ mi. north of Cherokee. Water theme attraction featuring a world-class ski show, American high diving show and Magic Waters show. Two giant water flumes carry you down the side of a mountain through tunnels and waterfalls. Gift shops, restaurants and free picnic and parking areas. Open daily, Memorial Day-Labor Day. (704) 497-4311.

**Santa's Land,** on US-19, 3 mi. east of Cherokee. Home of Santa Claus and his helpers. See merry elves, Santa's reindeer and Old Saint Nick himself. Entertainment for the entire family. Discover the arts of pioneer America in the new Heritage section. Watch corn being ground at the 100-year-old grist mill; watch brooms being made on antique equipment. One-man sawmill, blacksmith, shingle splitter and more. Largest zoo in the area, featuring both exotic and domestic animals, displayed in beautiful floral gardens. Open daily, May-October. (704) 497-9191.

**CHIMNEY ROCK, N.C.** **Chimney Rock Park,** on US-74 and US-64. A 1,000-acre park with picnic and playground area, 75-mile view from granite Chimney Rock, Hickory Nut Falls (highest in eastern U.S.). Moonshiner's cave is constant temperature. Walk the Skyline nature trail and the Cliff trail. Open March 1-Nov. 30. (704) 625-9611

**CLEVELAND, GA.** **Babyland General Hospital,** on Underwood Street. Cabbage Patch Home and Clinic. "Little People," created by Xavier Roberts. Mon.-Sat. Open year-round. (404) 865-5164.

**DAHLONEGA, GA.** **Gold Mountain Park,** on G-60, ½ mi. south of the Town Square. Tour the mine, museum and blacksmith shop. Pan for gold. Collect rock and ore specimens. Open during summer and fall. (404) 864-3377.

**FRANKLIN, N.C.** **Gold City Amusement Park,** Rte. 7, Box 750; 7 mi. north on US-441-23. Chairlift, gunfights, incline railroad, Western town. Late May to late October. Admission. (704) 369-7591.

**HORSE SHOE, N.C.** **Forge Valley Fun Park,** Box 164-B; NC-280. Pet Park, Fun Park, baby animals, crafts, old mill. Admission. Open daily, May - October. (704) 891-3241.

**MAGGIE VALLEY, N.C.** **Ghost Town in the Sky,** P.O. Box 369, US-19. Amusement center on top of Ghost Mountain, via chair lift/incline railway; 20 rides, 15 specialty shops, 7 eateries, authentic Western town. Early May to early November. (704) 926-0256.

**Hotwheels 'n' Waterbugs,** next to Pancake House. Open May-August. (704) 926-3956.

**Soco Gardens Zoo and Amusement Park,** US-19, Rte. 1, Box 355. Open May-October. (Refer to zoo chapter for more information.) (704) 926-1746.

**SAUTEE-NACOOCHE, GA.** **Mt. Yonah Alpine Storyland Fantasy Theme Park,** G-75 between Helen and Cleveland, Rte. 1, Box 175A. This unique park features storybook displays in miniature scale, petting zoo (imported and domestic animals), picnic area, and pottery and coffee shop. Daily. May 1 to late October. (404) 865-3613.

# Antiques and Auctions

Sold to the lady in the flowered hat! That winning bidder could be you if you go to one of the many auctions held in the region. Auctions are the up-and-coming events these days in rural areas, and some sociologists are even calling them "the new religion of the mountains."

Even if you are not bidding, the suspense of seeing who will get the porcelain figure of a boy tending sheep, and for how much, makes an auction exciting and fun. But those brave enough to bid are the real winners. Perhaps an oak table will go for an unbelievable $100 or an unusual crystal bird for $300. Those who bid and buy won't have a case of the "I should haves" later.

Both old and new goods are waiting to be discovered. Some auction houses even specialize in such down-to-earth merchandise as goats, horses, mules, pigeons and geese.

Many auctions include enough junk to match the unglamorous surroundings in which they are held, such as an old schoolhouse. Others like the Scudder's Gallery in Highlands, N.C., sell museum quality furniture, paintings and other valuables.

Some people go to auctions not only to buy or trade, but also to watch the action, mingle with the crowds, see friends and neighbors and catch up on gossip. Others, of course, go in search of an antique they hope may one day be priceless. If that is your goal, visits to an antique dealer or antique shows may be worth your time. The Asheville Antique Fair held in August features many exhibitors and even includes antique cars.

Getting to know antiques is educational as well as entertaining. Terms like primitive, early American, Victorian and Chippendale will soon become familiar to those who spend time browsing in shops and attending auctions.

## Antique Shows

————April————

**ASHEVILLE, N.C. Antique Show,** the Great Smokies Hilton. Second week. (704) 258-5225.

————May————

**WESTMINSTER, S.C. Annual Antique & Classic Car Show.** Sidewalk show is downtown; car show is at Westminster High School. Second week. (803) 882-2097.

**ASHEVILLE, N.C.  Antique Car Show and Swap Meet,** Asheville Mall. Fourth week. (704) 258-5225.
**Annual Land of the Sky Auto Show,** Deerpark on Biltmore Estate. Fourth week. (704) 684-0537.

**GAINESVILLE, GA.  Lake Shore Mall's Antique Alley** (Show and Sell), 1285 W. Washington St. 30501. Fourth week. (404) 532-6206.

————June————

**ASHEVILLE, N.C.  Chapman's Antique Show,** Civic Center. Third week. (704) 625-9261.

**HELEN, GA.  Summer in Helen Antique Show,** at Helen Pavilion. Fourth week. (404) 878-2521.

————July————

**HENDERSONVILLE, N.C.  Antiques Show and Sale,** National Guard Armory by Hendersonville Woman's Club. NC-176. Since 1938. First week. (704) 692-1413.

**MAGGIE VALLEY, N.C.  Antique Car Show,** at Chamber of Commerce. First week. (704) 926-1686.

**ASHEVILLE, N.C.  Antique Car Show,** V.A. Medical Center. Fourth week. (704) 258-5225.

**CASHIERS, N.C.  Antiques Show and Sale,** Blue Ridge School, NC-107. Held by Cashiers Jaycees. Fourth week. (704) 743-5191.

**HELEN, GA.  Alpine Helen Antique Car Show.** Fourth week. (404) 878-2521.

————August————

**ASHEVILLE, N.C.  Asheville Antique Fair,** Civic Center. Since 1945, held by Vetust Study Club. First week. (704) 252-3182.
   **Antique Shows and Sales,** N.C. Civic Center. First week. (704) 258-5225.

**CASHIERS, N.C.  Antique Show and Sale,** Blue Ridge School Gym. First week. (704) 743-5191.

**FRANKLIN, N.C.  Franklin Antiques Show,** Macon County Community Bldg., US-441. Sponsored by Rotary Club. Admission. First Week. (704) 743-2619.
   **Antique Car Show,** Macon County Fairgrounds. Third week. (704) 524-5971.

**CLEVELAND, GA.  N.C. Georgia Antique Auto Show,** Truett-McConnell Campus. Fourth week. (404) 865-2039.

————September————

**ASHEVILLE, N.C.  Chapman's Antique Show,** Civic Center. Third week. (704) 625-9261.

**FRANKLIN, N.C.  Antique Car Show,** Macon County Recreation Park. Sponsored by the Lions Club. Fourth week. (704) 524-2222.

————October————

**ASHEVILLE, N.C.  Antique Cars,** Groveland Road near Macon Avenue, 2 mi. northeast of town. 34 antique and vintage autos. First week. (704) 253-7651.
   **Antique Shows and Sales,** Asheboro, Episcopal Church of the Good Shepherd. First week. (704) 258-5225.
   **Antique Show and Sales,** Civic Center. First week. (704) 258-5225.

**HENDERSONVILLE, N.C.** Chapman's Antiques Show, National Guard Armory. First week. (704) 625-9261.

**BREVARD, N.C.** Antiques Show and Sale, Elementary School, Greenville Highway. Admission. Sponsored by Transylvania Comm. Hospital Auxiliary. Third week. (704) 883-3700.

**FRANKLIN, N.C.** Jaycee's Antique Show, Community Facilities Bldg. Third week. (704) 524-6421.

**GAINESVILLE, GA.** Antique Show and Sale, Civic Center. Third week. (404) 532-6206.

**HELEN, GA.** Fall in Helen Antique Show, Helen Pavilion. Third week. (404) 878-2521.

**MARION, N.C.** The Wonderful Blue Ridge Mountain Auto Show. Includes 30 different classes of antique vehicles. Third week. (704) 652-4240.

————November————

**SENECA, S.C.** Antique Car Parade. Sponsored by Seneca Chamber of Commerce. County Christmas Festival. 4 P.M. Late November. (803) 882-2097.

## Auctions

**BLACK MOUNTAIN, N.C.** Cherry Street Antique Mall, 1 Cherry Lane. Open seven days. (704) 669-9945.

**BLAIRSVILLE, GA.** Brown's Auction, US-76, 4½ mi. from Blairsville. Every Friday night. (404) 379-3155.

**BRASSTOWN, N.C.** John C. Campbell Folk School Crafts, Auction, Keith House. Open to the public. Crafts made and donated by students for moneymaking projects at school. Second week.

**BUFORD, GA.** Lake Lanier Antique Auction, Main Street. First and third Saturdays.

**CLEVELAND, GA.** North Georgia Biggest Auction/Yard Sale, Truett-McConnell College. By Baptist Women's Missionary Unions. Auction (cars, furniture). Flea Market, refreshments. First week.

**CORNELIA, GA.** Woody's Trading Post, US-23 and 441. Saturday afternoons.

**DILLARD, GA.** House of Specials, US-441 N. Closed Sunday. (404) 746-5359.
  **Dillard House Tent,** South Rabun County Elementary Club. First week. (404) 782-3831
  **Vintage Emporium Auction, 23/441. Saturdays.**

**GAINESVILLE, GA.** Red Barn Antiques Auction, 1260 S. Bradford Street. Saturday.

**HELEN, GA.** Helen Antique Shows Sales and Auction, near Helen Pavilion. Friday and Saturday nights.

**HENDERSONVILLE, N.C.** Art and Auction Gallery, 532 N. Main Street. (704) 692-2554.
  **Village Green Antique Mall,** 1208 Greenville Highway, US-25 S. Largest in Western North Carolina. (704) 692-9057.

**HIGHLANDS, N.C.** Highlands Art Gallery, Main Street (704) 526-2155.
  **Scudders Galleries,** Main Street. Art, rugs, jewelry, furniture. June-October. (704) 526-5335.

**OTTO, N.C.** Otto Auction, US-441, 10 mi. south of Franklin. (404) 524-4707.

**TALMO, GA.** Pardue's Antique Auctions, US-129. (404) 693-2500.

**TOCCOA, GA.** Currahee Arts Council Auction, National Guard Armory. New and old items; after-Christmas parade. Second week. (404) 886-9446.

**WAYNESVILLE, N.C.** Ivy Hill Antique Mall, 2223 Pellwood Road. (704) 926-0135. Thad Woods Auction, exit 276, Russ Avenue. Friday and Saturday nights.

**YOUNG HARRIS, GA.** Cane Creek Auction. Auction Saturday night. (404) 379-3671.

# Art

While folk art has always been popular in the South, today everything from Renaissance to contemporary paintings and sculpture graces galleries and exhibit halls.

Although Atlanta dominates the art world in this part of the country, smaller cities such as Athens and Young Harris in Georgia, Greenville in South Carolina, and Asheville in North Carolina, to name a few, have offerings well worth seeing.

Tucked away in rural Ashe County, N.C., in two small Episcopal churches are four frescoes that have attracted a lot of attention — partly because the fresco, done by painting on wet plaster, is seldom seen these days. A Statesville, N.C., artist, Ben Long, and his students painted the frescoes in the churches in West Jefferson and Glendale Springs after larger churches rejected the idea. The works include *The Mystery of Faith,* depicting Christ's crucifixion, *The Last Supper, St. John the Baptist,* and *Mary Great with Child.* The stunning frescoes, the last of which was completed in 1980, earned Long the Leonardo da Vinci International Art Award.

Atlanta's High Museum of Art, one of the largest art institutions in the South, has a new contemporary building. With its gleaming porcelain-enameled steel exterior and glittering glass interior, it has created a stir in the art world. The museum's collection includes early Italian, Renaissance, baroque, rococo, 19th-century French and contemporary American art. Be sure to ask about traveling exhibits — some very fine ones come to the High Museum.

Art festivals are held at Toccoa and Lake Burton, Ga., as well as in other cities. Most feature art shows, sales and entertainment.

Greenville, S.C., has both the Bob Jones University Museum of Sacred Art and the Greenville County Museum of Art with its fine collection of Andrew Wyeth paintings. The 26 Wyeth paintings became a permanent exhibit through the donation of Greenville industrialist Arthur Magill in 1979. Numerous Wyeth sketches and pre-studies make up the finest collection of Wyeth works in the world. Bob Jones University's Sacred Art Museum features one of the world's finest and best known collections of religious paintings by old masters as well as the Bowen Collection of Religious Antiquities gathered from Israel, Egypt and other Mediterranean areas. Nearby Clemson, S.C., holds an art festival in April and also is the site of the Rudolph Lee Gallery at Clemson University.

North Carolina offers art lovers sidewalk shows in both Hendersonville and Brevard in August. A highlight is Asheville's famous Folk Art Center on the Blue Ridge Parkway.

# Art Events

------March------

**SPRUCE PINE, N.C.** Annual Art Auction, at Beam's Chinese Restaurant, US-19E, east of Spruce Pine. Fourth week. (704) 682-7215.

------April------

**ASHEVILLE, N.C.** Annual Art Museum Auction, Asheville Civic Center on Haywood Street. First week.

**CLEMSON, S.C.** Blue Ridge Invitational Art Festival, Clemson House grounds. 65 artists. Third week.

Arts Festival, Kalmia Gardens, Clemson House. Fourth week. (803) 882-2097.

**SWANNANOA, N.C.** Fine Arts Festival, Warren Wilson College, 28778. Late April. (704) 298-3325.

**WALHALA, S.C.** Spring Fine Arts Festival at the Family Life Center in Seneca. By the Oconee County School District. Fourth week. (803) 882-2097.

------May------

**TOCCOA, GA.** Cuarrahee Arts Festival, at Henderson Falls Park, on Henderson Falls Road. Over 100 craftsmen sell their crafts and compete for money at this juried show. First week. (404) 886-2132.

**ASHEVILLE, N.C.** Annual World Whimmy Diddle Contest, at Folk Art Center, near milepost 382 on the Blue Ridge Pkwy. just outside Asheville. Second week. (704) 298-7928.

**CULLOWHEE, N.C.** Western N.C. High School Art Exhibit, Western Carolina University. Second week. (704) 488-3681.

**MURPHY, N.C.** Cherokee Spring Sidewalk Art Festival. Second week. (704) 837-2242.

**DAHLONEGA, GA.** Annual Art Field Day. North Georgia College Fine Arts Dept. and Georgia for Arts and Humanities. Workshop to demonstrate skills; 12 area high schools represented. Third week. (404) 864-3711.

**BLUE RIDGE, GA.** Arts in the Park Festival, in Blue Ridge City Park on Main Street. Arts, crafts, entertainment. Fourth week. (404) 632-2144.

**FRANKLIN, N.C.** Sidewalk Art Show, Courthouse Plaza. Fourth week. (704) 524-3161.

**YOUNG HARRIS, GA.** Spring Arts Exhibit, Clegg Fine Arts, Young Harris College. Fourth week.

------June------

**FRANKLIN, N.C.** Old Jailhouse Gallery Art Exhibit. In conjunction with Spring Fling celebration. 9 A.M.-6 P.M. Third week.

**SENECA, S.C.** Starving Artist Show, Oconee Square. By Blue Ridge Art Assoc. Third week. (803) 638-5708.

------July------

**HIGHLANDS, N.C.** Sidewalk Art Show, Our Lady of the Mountains Catholic Church. First week. (704) 526-2112.

**HORSESHOE, N.C.** **Sunset Festival of the Arts,** Sunset Campground. Arts, crafts, bluegrass band, food. First week. (704) 891-9924.

**ASHEVILLE, N.C.** **Festival of the Arts Week.** Arts, demos, exhibits, crafts, concerts, etc. Second week. (704) 258-5225.

**BREVARD, N.C.** **Festival of the Arts Week,** Brevard Music Center, Brevard Elementary School. Demos, exhibits, crafts, concerts, sports events. Second week. (704) 883-3700.

————August————

**BLACK MOUNTAIN, N.C.** **Annual Swannanoa Valley Art Show.** By Swannanoa Art League. Black Mountain Public Library. First and second weeks. (704) 669-2652.

**BREVARD, N.C.** **Sidewalk Art Show,** Courthouse Lawn. First week. (704) 883-3700.

**HENDERSONVILLE, N.C.** **Mrs. John Forrest Memorial Art Show.** First week. (704) 692-1413.

**HIGHLANDS, N.C.** **Annual Oriental Arts Festival,** Stone Lantern, Inc., 309 Main Street, 28741. Highlands School Lectures and exhibits on flower arranging, Oriental porcelains and carpets, bonsai. First week. (704) 526-2769.

**BREVARD, N.C.** **Art Auction,** St. Philips Episcopal Church, Parish Hall. By Brevard Womans' Assoc. Admission. Second week. (704) 883-3700.
   **Sidewalk Art Show,** Courthouse, Transylvania Art Guild, P.O. Box 655, 28712. Second week.

**BLACK MOUNTAIN, N.C.** **Swannanoa Art League Show.** Second week. (704) 669-7224.

**LAKE BURTON, GA.** **Annual Lake Burton Art Show,** Moccasin Creek State Park Pavilion, near State Fish Hatchery, G-197. 40 artists. Third week.

————September————

**ASHEVILLE, N.C.** **Folk Toys and Other Folk Art Objects,** at the Folk Art Center, east of Asheville on Blue Ridge Pkwy. Exhibit of Folk toys by members of the Southern Highland Handicraft Guild. Month of September (704) 258-5225.

**EASLEY, S.C.** **Foothills Art Week,** Old Market Square. Different program each night: dancing, singing, etc. First week. (803) 859-2693.

**HIGHLANDS, N.C.** **Macon County Art Assoc. Sidewalk Art Sale.** By local artists. First week. (704) 526-2112.

————October————

**PLEASANT GARDEN, N.C.** **Pioneer Arts Festival,** Historic Carson House, McDowell County, NC-70. All-day celebration of pioneer heritage. First week.

**SENECA, S.C.** **Art Show and Sale,** South Cove Park. First week. (803) 882-2097.

**BURNSVILLE, N.C.** **Burnsville Fall Festival of the Arts.** Second week. (704) 682-7413.

**ASHEVILLE, N.C.** **October Show,** Asheville Art Museum. By University of North Carolina-Asheville Alumni Art Chapter, High County Crafters. Late October to mid-November. (704) 254-0070.

**BLUE RIDGE, GA.** **Art Exhibit,** E. Main Street. By Blue Ridge Mountain Art Assoc. First week. (404) 632-5680.

**YOUNG HARRIS, GA.** **Appalachian Art.** Appalachian Studio Gallery. Free. First week. (404) 379-3807.

## Art Displays

**ASHEVILLE, N.C.** **Asheville Art Museum,** Civic Center, 28801. Tues.-Sun. Changing exhibits of quality visual arts; permanent collection. (704) 253-3227.

**Folk Art Center,** P.O. Box 9545, Blue Ridge Pkwy., mile post 382, 28815. Open daily. Variety of crafts; demonstrations daily during summer. (704) 298-7928.

**Highwater Center, Inc.,** 75 Thompson Street, 28803. Open Sunday, May-November. Monthly exhibits of members' work. (704) 252-6618.

**Iris Photographic Printworks,** 15 W. Walnut Street, 28801. Mon.-Sat. Changing exhibits of photography. (704) 254-6103.

**New Morning Gallery,** 7 Boston Way. Open daily, May-December. Retail sales of quality handmade objects. (704) 274-2831.

**Owen Gallery,** University Heights, University of North Carolina at Asheville, 28804. Mon.-Fri. Senior students' exhibitions, faculty exhibitions. (704) 258-6559.

**Walker Arts Center,** Campus of Asheville School. Reservations necessary. Free.

**\*ATHENS, GA.** **Georgia Museum of Art,** University of Georgia campus. Traveling exhibits and the permanent Holbrook and Kress collections on display. Mon.-Fri. Closed on academic and legal holidays. Free. (404) 542-3254.

**\*ATLANTA, GA.** **The High Museum of Art,** Peachtree and Sixteenth streets in the Robert W. Woodruff Arts Center. The six levels of the complex total 46,000 square feet of exhibition space. The major collection of American decorative art, the Crawford exhibit, is on permanent display. The fourth level is dedicated to modern art and traveling exhibitions. Excellent children's hands-on exhibit in lower level. Open daily except Monday, 8:30 A.M. to 10:00 P.M. and on Sundays from 12:00 to 6:00 P.M. Admission. Hotline for art exhibits: (404) 893-4444. Museum's regular number: (404) 892-3600.

**BLUE RIDGE, GA.** **Blue Ridge Mountains Arts Assoc.,** Main Street. Mon.-Fri. (404) 632-2144.

**\*BOONE, N.C.** **Farthing Gallery,** Department of Art, Appalachian State University. Open Mon.-Fri. Changing exhibits of painting, sculpture and printmaking. (704) 262-2220.

**CLAYTON, GA.** **Hambridge Center.** Arts/crafts programs, visiting professionals. (404) 746-5718.

**CLEMSON, S.C.** **Rudolph E. Lee Gallery,** Clemson University College of Architecture, Lee Hall. Mon.-Fri., Sunday afternoons. (803) 656-3081.

**CORNELIA, GA.** **Pierian Studios,** 43 Wells Street. (404) 778-9221.

**CULLOWHEE, N.C.** **Chelsea Gallery,** Hinds University Center, Box 1989, Western Carolina University. Open daily. All media. (704) 227-7206.

**DILLSBORO, N.C.** **Misty Mountain Unicorn Gallery,** Church and Back Streets.

**GAINESVILLE, GA.** **Elachee Cottage,** downtown, US-129. Appalachian art and natural life exhibits. Mon.-Fri.

**Quinlan Art Center,** 514 Green Street NE. Features traveling exhibits by regional and national artists. Year-round. Mon.-Fri., Sunday afternoons. Free. (404) 536-2575.

**˙GREENVILLE, S.C.** **Bob Jones University Museum of Sacred Art,** Wade Hampton Blvd. (US-29 north). One of the most sacred art collections in the Southeast. Includes thirty rooms displaying art of Europe from 13th-19th centuries. Open Tues.-Sun. (2 P.M. to 5 P.M.). Free. (803) 242-5100 ext. 2701.

**Greenville County Museum of Art,** 420 College Street (two blocks off Main Street). Twenty-six works by Andrew Wyeth from the Holly and Arthur Magill Collection on permanent exhibit. Also displayed are American paintings, sculpture, graphics, and crafts. Open daily. Free. (803) 271-7570.

**LAKE RABUN, GA.** **The Boat House Studio,** Lake Rabun Road, Rt. 1, Lakemont, G-3. (404) 736-7973.

**PICKENS, S.C.** **Pickens County Art Museum.** Pendleton and Johnston streets. The permanent collection here consists primarily of works by county artists. Temporary exhibits are also offered. Tues. and Fri. mornings; Wed. and Thurs. afternoons. (803) 878-4965.

**SALUDA, N.C.** **Spring Park Studio,** Church Street. Showplace for the work of Jane Armstrong, sculptor. Hours are posted.

**TALLULAH FALLS, GA.** **Tallulah Gallery,** US-441. Original works by mountain artists: pottery, paintings, weavings. Daily.

**TRYON, N.C.** **Fine Arts Center,** Melrose Avenue. Home to theater, crafts, painting, sculpture, concerts and films. Free. (704) 859-6236.

**Trade Street Gallery,** 247 N. Trade Street., 28782. Focus on contemporary crafts and fine art. Mon.-Sat. (704) 859-5102.

**The Upstairs, Inc.,** 117 S. Trade Street. Variety of art; experimental artist space. Mon. and Wed. (704) 859-9673.

# B

# Battlefields

Grab your muskets! Round up your horses and man your cannons! Be prepared to face the enemy!

Those were the commands shouted to the brave men who fought in Revolutionary and Civil War battles all over the South. Today, visitors to those historical battlefields can, with some imagination, almost relive those tense and bloody moments.

The major Revolutionary War battle in the South was fought in Cowpens, S.C. There, backwoods American riflemen defeated British troops in January, 1781. The clash is considered by some to be the battle that broke the back of the British in the war. British losses amounted to 110 dead, more than 200 wounded and 500 captured. Colonial Commander Daniel Morgan lost only 12 of his men, with 60 wounded. Kings Mountain National Military Park, which spans the border of South Carolina and North Carolina, is another Revolutionary War site. It marks the spot where American frontiersmen defeated pro-British forces on October 7, 1780. Exhibits, complete with gunfire, infantry commands and booming cannon, interpret the battle. A foot trail leads around the battlefield.

Civil War afficionados will find much to interest them at Chickamauga Battlefield at Chickamauga and Chattanooga National Military Park, which straddles Georgia and Tennessee. On that soil 4,000 men lost their lives while farmers along Chickamauga Creek watched their land become a battlefield. It was the last major Confederate victory, despite more than 18,000 casualties to the Union's 16,000.

The battlefield has a seven-mile automobile tour with points of interest marked by arrows, cannonball monuments and iron plaques. Visitor center exhibits and programs explain the battle and its place in the Civil War. There is also a rare collection of 355 American military weapons.

The Chickamauga and Chattanooga National Military Parks depict both the seige and battle of Chattanooga. Visits to Ochs Museum and other areas in the park round out the story of the war in the locale. Civil War musket demonstrations are held at Fort Oglethorpe.

Kennesaw Mountain National Battlefield Park in Marietta, Ga., was the site of the major battle that led to the siege and fall of Atlanta. Exhibits there depict the Atlanta campaign.

Battlefields

*Note: Many of the battlefield sites listed in this section are outside the Blue Ridge area covered in this book. They are included because of their exceptional educational value and importance to Revolutionary and Civil War buffs. These battlefields are located along major travel routes to the Blue Ridge area.*

**CHICKAMAUGA, GA. Chickamauga-Chattanooga National Military Park.** Site of two decisive battles of Civil War, which opened the way for General Sherman to wage his fiery campaign through Georgia. Slide presentation and one of the largest military gun collections in the world at the Visitor Center. Automobile tour, 7 mi., of battlefield. Summertime cannon demonstrations every day except Wed. and Thurs. Open daily. I-75 to Fort Oglethorpe exit and follow signs. Free.

**CHESNEE, S.C. Cowpens National Battlefield,** junction of SC-11 and SC-110. At the Battle of Cowpens on Jan. 17, 1781, American patriots gave the British their defeat of the Southern campaign. A visitors center interprets the battle through visuals, memorabilia and art work. Tour road and walking trail. Daily. Free.

**\*KENNESAW, GA. Kennesaw Mountain National Battlefield Park,** off US-41. Site of the major Civil War battle that preceded the siege and fall of Atlanta. General Joseph E. Johnston's Confederate Army of about 50,000 held Kennesaw Mountain against two coordinated attacks by General Sherman's troops on June 27, 1864. The Visitors Center and exhibits along park routes through the battlefield depict the Atlanta campaign. Daily, year-round. Free. (404) 432-8011.

**\*KINGS MOUNTAIN, N.C. Kings Mountain National Military Park.** At this site American frontiersmen defeated pro-British forces on Oct. 7, 1780, at a critical point during the American Revolution. Exhibits in the Visitors Center interpret the battle; a foot trail from the center leads to the chief features of the battlefield. Daily, year-round. Free. (803) 936-7508.

# Bicycling

For a close look at the Blue Ridge countryside, nothing beats bicycling. Bikers breathe the fresh air and see the forests enjoyed by hikers, yet remain within reach of conveniences such as hotels and restaurants.

The state governments of Georgia, North Carolina, South Carolina and Tennessee have acknowledged the growing popularity of cheap, ecology-conscious bike travel. They provide free bike maps of routes chosen for low traffic flow, smooth road surfaces and access to interesting places, stores, hotels and, of course, bike shops. The Trans-Georgia Trail, for example, starts in the southwest corner of the state and meanders to Providence Canyon State Park, then heads northeast through Atlanta and Gainesville, ending near Clayton.

Perhaps the most comprehensive maps and information are provided by North Carolina's Department of Transportation. The established trails include Mountains to Sea (700 miles), Piedmont Spur (200 miles), Carolina Connection (200 miles) and other routes. Each guide contains a series of strip maps detailing the shorter sections. The Trail of Tears, a section of the Mountains to Sea route, covers 48 miles from Murphy, N.C., to a remote area near Wayah Crest. The grueling trip through mountainous terrain is recommended only for well-equipped, experienced cyclists, however. The King Cotton route, a 33-mile stretch of the Carolina Connection, offers an easier ride: it winds over flat land.

The Tennessee Department of Tourist Development uses the same excellent format that North Carolina does. Tennessee has a 983-mile system divided into four routes. Booklets include maps, facts about temperatures, events, terrain and other details.

Even those who left their bikes at home can have a fling at biking, since rentals are available. For example, Cades Cove Bicycle Rental, near Gatlinburg, Tenn., in the Great Smoky Mountains National Park, has one-speed bicycles. Avid bicyclists can whiz on into the nation's largest cycling event held in Linville, N.C., in May. America's Scenic Challenge Race is the highlight. Bicycle touring clubs are an excellent source of information.

## Bicycle Tours

**BICYCLE USA,** Suite 209, 6707 Whitestone Road, Baltimore, Md. 21207. (301) 944-3399.

**DOWNHILL SPOKERS BICYCLE TOURS, INC.,** 121 Madison Avenue, New York, N.Y. 10016. Carolina area, (212) 684-7847.

**EAGLE'S NEST CAMP,** 43 Hart Road, Pisgah Forest, N.C. 28768. North Carolina area, (704) 877-4349.

**CADES COVE BIKE RENTALS,** Great Smoky Mountains National Park, Gatlinburg, Tenn. 37738. (615) 448-9311 or 9316.

**NANTAHALA OUTDOOR CENTER,** US-19 West, Box 41AW, Bryson City, N.C. 28713. (704) 488-9221.

**NORTH CAROLINA BICYCLE TOURING SOCIETY,** P.O. Box 2436, Winston-Salem, N.C. 27102. (919) 785-0677.

**SOUTHERN BICYCLE LEAGUE,** Box 29474, Atlanta, Ga. 30359. (404) 325-1925.

# Bicycling Events

————May————

**\*ATHENS, GA.** **Pepsi Twilight Criterium.** Racers from the U.S. Cycling Federation compete, as well as racers from foreign countries. First week. (404) 353-VELO.

**ASHEVILLE, N.C.** **Biltmore Estate/McDonald's Bike Race.** By the U.S. Cycling Federation. 100 national and international racers. Second week. (704) 274-1776.
  **Bike A Thon.** March of Dimes Benefit. Third week. (704) 255-8491.

**\*LINVILLE, N.C.** **America's Scenic Challenge,** beginning at Grandfather Mountain. Largest bicycling event in the United States. Second week.

————August————

**WAYNESVILLE, N.C.** **Balsam Ridge Break Away** bicycle race along the Blue Ridge Parkway. Second week. (704) 456-5301.

# Bicycling Organizations

*National Resources:*
  For bike paths and accommodations, contact state tourist offices. Send stamped envelope to Bicycles USA, Dept. P, 6607 Whitestone, Baltimore, Md. 21207.
  The Sierra Club also offers bike trips. Information: Sierra Club Outing Dept., 530 Bush Street, San Francisco, Ca. 94108. (415) 981-8634.
  The Amateur Bicycle League of America, official governing body for bicycle racing in the United States. Floral Park, Long Island, N.Y.
*State Biking Resources:*
  Department of Industry and Trade, Box 1776, Atlanta, Ga. 30301.
  Southern Bicycle League, Box 29474, Atlanta, Ga. 30359. Lists biking events throughout the year in northwest, northeast and Atlanta areas.
  Gainesville Huff and Puff Bicycle Club, c/o Gainesville Park and Recreation Dept. Organized for women who are interested in health and fitness. Rides during early evening hours.
*N.C. State Biking Resources:*
  The Bicycle Program, North Carolina Dept. of Transportation, P.O. Box 25201, Raleigh, N.C. 27611. (919) 733-2804.
  North Carolina Bicycle Touring Society, P.O. Box 2436, Winston-Salem, N.C. 27102. Promotes organized bike tours throughout North Carolina.
*S.C. State Biking Resources:*
  S.C. Dept. of Highways and Public Transportation, P.O. Box 191, Columbia, S.C. 29202. State and county road maps. Send a self-addressed, stamped envelope, business size. (803) 758-3001.

## Bicycling

Carolina Cyclers, P.O. Box 11163, Columbia, S.C. 29211.

Clemson University Bicycling Club, Clemson University, Clemson, S.C. 29631. Plans long-distance tours and family events; some competitive rides.

Greenville Spinners, P.O. Box 2663, Greenville, S.C. 29602.

Spartanburg Freewheelers, P.O. Box 6171, Spartanburg, S.C. 29304.

# Bluegrass Music

Hands are clapping, toes are tapping. Ears are filled with the twangy, down-home sounds of country and bluegrass music ringing across the hills. Children frolic, then rest with their families on beach towels and blankets. Country cookin' is consumed as if it were going out of style.

That's the scene at country and bluegrass music festivals. From spring to fall, musicians pick and sing their cares away, while hill folks and their city cousins listen, laugh, dance, whistle, yell and stomp.

In the old days, mountain music broke the monotony of daily chores and brought isolated people together. They sang and socialized at square dances and midnight suppers. Their treasured instruments were the fiddle, the banjo, the dulcimer and, later, the guitar.

In the 1920's and 1930's, radio spread the sounds of the South to the rest of the nation. Country-western and the fast tempo bluegrass became known and loved.

Bill Monroe, a member of the Country Music Hall of Fame, brought bluegrass music to prominence in the late 1930's. His group became famous for its tight vocal harmonies, backed up by guitars, fiddles and mandolins. But plenty of less well known musicians are still around, tapping their feet on back porches. The best place to hear them is at one of the many festivals held throughout the South. The first was held in the summer of 1965 at Fincastle, Va., near Roanoke, Va. Since then, others, such as the Upperstate Bluegrass Festival in Easley, S.C., have become popular.

Bluegrass weekend in Blue Ridge, Ga., welcomes bluegrass bands and includes free camping with ticket purchase. Other events are the Georgia State Bluegrass Festival in July at Shoal Creek Park in Lavonia, Ga., and the Hamby Mountain Bluegrass Music Festival held in June just south of Cornelia, Ga.

The spring Country Music Festival in May near Hiawassee, Ga., fills the hills with the sounds of country and western bands. In the fall two festivals are held, one focusing on country and the other on bluegrass.

Even more fiddling can be heard at the Georgia State Fiddlin' Championship in September at Stone Mountain Park, near Atlanta. Banjo, mandolin, guitar, bluegrass band, old time fiddle band, and junior and senior fiddle categories are full of strumming competitors.

Shindig-on-the-Green, in Asheville, N.C., in July, offers traditional mountain string music, bluegrass, clogging and opportunities for audience participation, including street dancing. The Southwest North Carolina Spring Bluegrass Festival at Sunnypoint Music Park, near Murphy, attracts fans each June.

Maggie Valley, N.C., claims to be the clogging capital of the world. At the Stompin' Ground there, you can square dance every Saturday night and listen to country and bluegrass music.

For a glimpse at new talent, attend the Country Music Scholarship Show in Toccoa, Ga., in March.

## Bluegrass Events

———March———

**HELEN, GA.** **Spring Bluegrass Concert and Dance,** Unicoi Lodge, lower level, by Unicoi State Park. Admission. Third week. (404) 878-2201.

**TOCCOA, GA.** **Annual Country Music Scholarship Show.** Since 1963 in the Stephens County High School gym-auditorium. By the VICA Club. Third week.

**SATOLAH, GA.** **Bluegrass-Country Music Show,** G-28. Satolah Volunteer Fire Department Ladies Auxiliary. Fourth week.

———April———

**DAHLONEGA, GA.** **Spring Bluegrass Festival,** Mountain Music Park, G-60 South. Music and dancing. Third week. (404) 864-7203.

**BLUE RIDGE, GA.** **Sugar Creek Music Park.** Music and clogging. Third week. (404) 632-2560.
   **Bluegrass Festival,** Sugar Creek Music Park, G-5 North. Fourth week. (404) 632-2564.

———May———

**EASLEY, S.C.** **Upper State Bluegrass Festival,** Upper State Fairgrounds. First week.

**BLUE RIDGE, GA.** **Sugar Creek Bluegrass Festival,** Sugar Creek Music Park, 3 1/2 mi. north of Blue Ridge on 5. Second week. (404) 632-2560.
   **Country and western music show,** at Sugar Creek Music Park. Admission. Third week. (404) 632-2560.

**HIAWASSEE, GA.** **Spring Country Music Festival,** Georgia Mountain Fair music auditorium. By Towns County Lions Club. Fiddlin', pickin', clogging. Admission. Third week. (404) 896-2256.

———June———

**BLAIRSVILLE, GA.** **Georgia Mountain Country and Bluegrass Festival,** Nottley River Campground. First week. (404) 745-5789.

**CORNELIA, GA.** **Hamby Mountain Bluegrass Music Festival,** Hamby Mountain Music Park, 2 mi. south of Cornelia. First week. (404) 778-5829 or 532-4232.

**MURPHY, N.C.** **Southwest North Carolina Spring Bluegrass Festival,** Sunnypoint Music Park, US-64. Admission. First week. (704) 644-5109.

**BLUE RIDGE, GA.** **Sugar Creek Bluegrass,** Sugar Creek Music Park, G-5. Second week. (404) 632-2560.

**BLAIRSVILLE, GA.** **Mountain Jamboree.** Third week. (404) 745-5789.

**\*CLIFFSIDE, N.C.** **Annual Snuffy Jenkins Old-Time and Bluegrass Festival,** Snuffy Jenkins Music Park. This park claims to be the place "where the bluegrass banjo was born," and the annual festival promises to be a family event with bluegrass talent from the Eastern Seaboard. Mid-June. (704) 287-7751.

**DAHLONEGA, GA.** **Bluegrass Festival,** Mountain Music Park, G-60. Admission. Third week. (404) 864-7203.

**LINVILLE, N.C.** **Annual Grandfather Mountain Singing on the Mountain.** Since 1923. Day-long event featuring preaching and gospel singing by individuals and musical groups. Third week. (704) 387-9283.

**ASHEVILLE, N.C.** **Byard Ray Folk Festival,** Civic Center. Musical tradition of southern Appalachians: ballad singing, string bands, fiddle, banjo and dulcimer music. Fourth week. (704) 255-5736.

————July————

**ASHEVILLE, N.C.** **Shindig-on-the-Green,** City-County Plaza. Traditional mountain string music, bluegrass, clogging, audience participation, street dancing, ballads. Weekends. (704) 258-5225.

**BLAIRSVILLE, GA.** **Annual Randall Collins Georgia Mountain Bluegrass Festival.** Nottely River Campground. Barbecue and music. First week. (404) 745-5995.

**HELEN, GA.** **Annual Appalachian Music Festival.** Unicoi State Park. Many of the Southeast's finest musicians perform bluegrass, folk, traditional and old-time mountain music. Also some mountain round dancing. Second week. (404) 878-2201, ext. 282.

**PICKENS, S.C.** **Bluegrass music,** Table Rock State Park (Canteen area). Admission for adults and children. Second week.

**DAHLONEGA, GA.** **Annual Dahlonega Bluegrass Festival,** Mountain Music Park. Admission. Multiple-day tickets available. Third week. (404) 864-7203.

**BLUE RIDGE, GA.** **Country and Western Music Concert,** Sugar Creek Music Park, G-5, 3 mi. north of Blue Ridge. Local and regional bands perform. Admission. Children under 12, free. Third week. (404) 632-2560.

**Bluegrass Weekend,** Sugar Creek Music Park. All bluegrass bands welcome. Open stage. Kitchen open all weekend with good home cooking. Free camping with ticket. Admission. Fourth week. (404) 632-2560.

————August————

**ASHEVILLE, N.C.** **Shindig-on-the-Green,** City-County Plaza. Traditional mountain string music, bluegrass, clogging, audience participation, street dancing, ballads. Weekends. (704) 254-1981.

**Annual Mountain Dance and Folk Festival,** Asheville Civic Center, Haywood Street. Small admission. Nation's oldest and most colorful. Since 1926. Mountain pickers, fiddlers, ballad singers, dulcimer players, cloggers, square dancers. Family entertainment and lots of fun. First week. (704) 258-3858.

**\*BURLINGTON, N.C.** **Bluegrass Festival,** Bass Mountain Bluegrass Park. Second week.

**HIAWASSEE, GA.** **Georgia Mountain Fair Bluegrass Festival.** Bluegrass day at the fair. Early August. (404) 896-2256.

**LAKE LANIER, GA.** **Mountain Do,** Lake Lanier Islands. Georgia music, dance, arts, crafts. Third week. (404) 532-6206.

**BLAIRSVILLE, GA.** **Old Timers' Day at Vogel State Park.** Story-telling, fiddling and banjo playing and an old-fashioned hoedown. Third week. (404) 745-2628.

**Annual Nottely River "Old Time Music Festival,"** Nottely River Campground on US-19/129, 4 mi. south of Blairsville. Fourth week. (404) 745-5124.

————September————

**ASHEVILLE, N.C.** **Shindig-on-the-Green,** City-County Plaza. Traditional mountain string music, bluegrass, clogging, audience participation, street dancing, ballads. Weekends. (704) 254-1981.

**CROSSNORE, N.C.** **Fiddlers' Convention,** Jim and Jennie's High Country Music Park. Features bluegrass, gospel, country music and dancing. Camping facilities available. First week. (704) 733-2807.

**DAHLONEGA, GA.** **Bluegrass Festival,** Mountain Music Park, G-60 south. Admission. First and second weeks. (404) 864-7203.

**HIAWASSEE, GA.** **Labor Day Show,** Georgia Mountain Fair Music Hall. By Towns County Lions Club. First week. (404) 896-2256.

**PICKENS, S.C.** **Outdoor Concert,** Caesars Head State Park. US-276. Admission. First week. (803) 836-6115.

**'STONE MOUNTAIN, GA.** **Georgia State Fiddling Championship,** Coliseum at Stone Mountain Park. Admission. Second week. (404) 469-9831.

**ELLIJAY, GA.** **Annual Ellijay Fall Bluegrass Festival.** Third week. (404) 993-3997.

————October————

**CLARKESVILLE, GA.** **Homemade Musical Instruments,** Moccasin Creek State Park. A homemade musical instrument display and demonstration during the day. After supper, homemade music and an old-time hoedown. First week. (404) 947-3194.

**EASLEY, S.C.** **Annual Upper State Bluegrass Festival,** Upper State Fairgrounds. By Southern Music Festival. First week. (803) 859-2693.

**BLUE RIDGE, GA.** **Sugar Creek Bluegrass Festival,** Sugar Creek Music Park. Bluegrass groups, clogging and buck dancing. Admission, adults; children, free. Second week. (404) 632-2560.

**PICKENS, S.C.** **Concert at the Barn,** Table Rock State Park. Admission. Mid-October. (803) 758-3622.

**HELEN, GA.** **Unicoi State Park Fall Harvest Music and Dance.** Live traditional Appalachian music; folk and mountain round dancing. Third week. (404) 878-2201, ext. 282.

**HIAWASSEE, GA.** **Fall Bluegrass Festival,** at the Georgia Mountain Fairgrounds, 1 mi. west of Hiawassee on US-76. Over 100 bluegrass bands and musicians perform during this outdoor music festival. Admission, children under 12 free. Fri., 8 P.M.-midnight, Sat., 10 A.M.-4 P.M. and 8 P.M.-midnight. Third and fourth weeks. (404) 896-2256.

**GAINESVILLE, GA. Annual Mountain Clogging and Bluegrass Festival,** Georgia Mountains Center. Fourth week. (404) 532-6206.

————November————

**HELEN, GA. Mountain Music Dance,** Unicoi Lodge, G-356. "Old Time Music and Dancing." Admission. Second week. (404) 878-2201, ext. 232.

## Bluegrass Establishments

**CHEROKEE, N.C. Country Jamboree,** on Big Cove Road, across from the Best Western Motel. Country music nightly. (704) 497-7613.

**HARTWELL, GA. The Chicken House.** Country music spot for families.

**HELEN, GA. Alpine Valley Complex,** ½ mi. north of Helen. Outdoor music. Summer weekends. Free. (404) 878-2803.

**HIGHLANDS, N.C. Helen's Barn,** US-64. Fri. and Sat. nights.

**LAKE BURTON, GA. Laurel Lodge.** Clogging, buck dancing, picking. Every Sat. night from May till August. Adults, $3; children 6-12, $1.

**MAGGIE VALLEY, N.C. Stompin' Ground.** Country and bluegrass music. Open square dancing every Saturday night. Billed as "The Clogging Capital of the World." Daily.

**LAKEMONT, GA. Hall's Boat House,** Lake Rabun Road, Sat. nights during summer. (404) 782-4981.

*Note: See also Music section for a list of music parks.*

# Blue Ridge Parkway

Winding through the mountains of southern Appalachia is America's most scenic highway: the 469-mile-long Blue Ridge Parkway, offering an unparalled panorama of misty peaks and valleys.

In summer, the parkway route is dotted with purple, pink and white rhododendrons nestled beneath deep green forests of Carolina hemlocks, white pine, cedar, oak, locust, poplar, hickory and cherry. And from spring through early fall, the parkway takes on the added color of mountain laurel, flame azalea and dozens of wildflower species.

Mid-October is the peak of brilliant fall color. Mountainsides are painted with red, gold, green and yellow leaves that shimmer in the autumn breeze.

The tranquil road, free of commercial development and congestion, links the Shenandoah National Park in northern Virginia to the Great Smoky Mountains National Park in North Carolina and Tennessee. Several overlooks, campgrounds, picnic areas, trails, wayside exhibits, visitor centers and recreation areas along the way make the parkway a vacationer's dream.

The speed limit is 45 mph — slow enough so that travelers can enjoy views of rugged mountain cabins and small, isolated farms. Crafts made by the local hill people can be bought at stores along the route.

The parkway's architects tried to preserve as much of the forest as possible when planning the road. Squirrels, chipmunks and birds are always visible; and early morning or evening travelers may spot an elusive white-tailed deer or black bear. At night, striped skunks, bobcats, fox, opossums and racoons forage along the roadside.

A scenic highway through the Blue Ridge Mountains was envisioned as early as 1909 by Col. Joseph Hyde Pratt, head of the North Carolina Geological Survey. Pratt managed to have a short section of the road built before World War I, but it was not until 1933, when President Franklin D. Roosevelt authorized funds for the project, that it became more than a dream. Construction began in September, 1935, and in mid-1936 the parkway was placed under the jurisdiction of the National Park Service.

Today the beauty of the mountains can be enjoyed at every twist and turn of the road, at elevations from 649 to 6,053 feet.

The seasonal publication "Milepost," available at parkway concessions or by writing the superintendent's office (see address at end of this section), provides information about what to see and do along the parkway.

Following is a list of spots to stop and explore along the parkway, from the southern terminus at Cherokee, N.C., to the Linville Falls area.

# Blue Ridge Parkway Attractions

*Milepost*    *Location*

**308.3**   **Flat Rock.** Trail to a superb view of Grandfather Mountain and Linville Valley.

**316.3**   **Linville Falls.** Elevation: 3,250 feet. The 3,000-acre park has 20 trailer sites, 55 tent sites and a 100-site picnic area. Trails to spectacular views of the Linville waterfalls and Linville Gorge, a wilderness of the Pisgah National Forest. Campground, picnic area, trail to overlook of falls and a gorge. John D. Rockefeller, Jr., donated the land. Trout fishing in the Linville River.

**320.7**   **Chestoa.** Short walk to view from cliffs of Humpback Mountain.

**330**   **Museum of North Carolina Minerals.** Displays some of North Carolina's abundance of gems and minerals. May-October, daily. Free. (704) 765-2761.

**339.5**   **Crabtree Meadows.** Elevation: 3,850 feet. The 253-acre park has 22 trailer sites, 71 tent sites and an 82-site picnic area. A 40-minute hike away from the campground is Crabtree Falls.

**355.4**   **Mt. Mitchell State Park.** Contains virgin balsam forests, hiking and nature trails, picnicking and camping facilities. Highest point in North Carolina at 6,684 feet. Always open. Free. (704) 675-4611.

**363.4 to 369.6**   **Craggy Gardens.** About 10 mi. north of Asheville. More than 1,500 species of wildflowers bloom from late spring through fall. May-October, daily. (704) 258-2850. Visitors center, self-guide trail; spectacular purple rhododendron bloom mid- to late June.

**382**   **The Folk Art Center,** ½ mi. from intersection with US-70 and 5 mi. east of Asheville. Home of the Southern Highland Handicraft Guild. Exhibitions include folk dancing, folk music and film programs. Year-round, daily. Free. (704) 298-7928.

**408.6**   **Mt. Pisgah.** Elevation: 5,000 feet. The 690-acre park has 70 trailer sites, 70 tent sites and 50 picnic sites. Also a restaurant, campstore, gas station and lodge.

**412**   **Cradle of Forestry in America,** US-276, several miles from Asheville. Early April-October. Daily. Free. (704) 253-2352.

**422.4**   **Devil's Courthouse.** Rock summit with a 360-degree view across mountains of North Carolina, South Carolina, Georgia and Tennessee.

**431**   **Richard Balsam Mountain.** Highest point (6,053 feet) on the parkway; self-guided trail through spruce and fir forests.

**451.2**   **Waterrock Knob.** Loop trail to dramatic views in every direction from the Knob. Interpretative exhibits.

**461.9**   **Cherokee Exhibit.** Depicts legends.

**469**   **Terminus of Parkway,** near Cherokee, North Carolina.

## Parkway Concessions

| *Milepost* | *Facility* |
| --- | --- |

**339.5**     **Crabtree Meadows.** Restaurant, gift shop, gas station and camp store. (704) 675-4236.

**382.0**     **Folk Art Center.** Craft center. (704) 258-2850, ext. 277, (704) 298-7928.

**408.6**     **Pisgah Inn.** Restaurant, gift shop, gas station and camp store. (704) 235-8228.

## Self-Guiding Nature Trails

| *Milepost* | *Trail* |
| --- | --- |

**308.3**     **Flat Rock Trail:** traverses a high-elevation forest community shaped by harsh weather; includes views of Grandfather Mountain; 45 minutes.

**316.4**     **Duggers Loop Trail:** passes through virgin pine and hemlock forest along Duggers Creek; 30 minutes.

**364.6**     **Craggy Gardens Trail:** outstanding purple rhododendron bloom in this area, usually in mid-June; 20 minutes.

**431.0**     **Richland Balsam Trail:** here spruce fir forest crowns the highest point along the Parkway; 60 minutes.

*Parkway Information:* Superintendent, Blue Ridge Parkway, 700 Northwestern Bank Building, Asheville, N.C. 28801.

# C

## Christmas Cheer

Christmas in the South may be as hectic and commercialized as Christmas anywhere else, but the traveler in the region can easily find links to the simpler Christmases of the past.

The tradition of open house at Christmas still is carried on, with many historic homes decked out in holly for the holidays.

Live nativity scenes, such as those presented by the Oak Grove Baptist Church near Waynesville, N.C., and at Cove Park near Seneca, S.C., remind viewers of the true meaning of Christmas.

The whole town of Marion, N.C., celebrates the season with an "Ole Mountain Christmas," which includes house tours, crafts and a drama.

Crafts, art, singing and music are featured at the annual High Country Christmas Art and Craft Show held in the Civic Center of Asheville, N.C., in late November.

In Georgia, state historic sites reflect traditions through decorations and celebrations. A "Golden Christmas" is held at the Dahlonega Gold Museum, and a "Moravian Christmas" at Vann House in Chatsworth.

At Traveler's Rest Historic Site at Toccoa, Ga., the 19th-century stagecoach inn and plantation house is decorated with natural materials. A tree is trimmed with handmade items. Hot spiced cider, punch and home-baked cookies are enjoyed by those who gather to sing Christmas carols at the old-time celebration.

The band and choral groups at Western Carolina University in Cullowhee, N.C., delight listeners with a recital in early December. Another popular musical event is "The Many Moods of Christmas," held at the First Baptist Church of Asheville, N.C. The church's choir and the full Asheville Symphony Orchestra are known for their polished performances.

Indeed, a Blue Ridge Mountain Christmas is celebrated jubilantly — with parades and carols, cookies and crafts, and much more than store-bought gifts.

*(Contact local chambers of commerce for additional information.)*

**ANDREWS, N.C.** **Andrews Christmas Parade,** downtown. Floats, bands. First week of December.

**ASHEVILLE, N.C.** **Mountain Christmas Show,** Civic Center, Haywood Street. Christmas exhibits. Second week in November.

**Annual Christmas Parade,** downtown. Third week in November.

**Annual Christmas Show,** Civic Center, Haywood Street. A juried show. Third week in November.

**High Country Christmas,** Civic Center. Fourth week in November.

**Christmas at the Biltmore House.** Late 1800s period Christmas. Concerts on Saturdays and Sundays; candlelit tours on Saturdays. Month of December.

**Christmas with the Guild.** The Folk Art Center. Holiday celebration includes theme trees by local garden clubs. Month of December.

**Zebulon Vance Birthplace 1830 Period Christmas,** on Reems Creek Road. Decorations and dress of period. Free. Month of December.

**Christmas Open House,** Smith McDowell House, Victoria Road. First week in December.

**Holiday Concert,** University of North Carolina at Asheville. Chorus, band, university singers. Lipinsky Auditorium on campus. First week in December.

**Merry Christmas Greens Market,** Biltmore Country Market, US-25 south. Items for sale. First week in December.

**Christmas Candlelight Tour of Homes,** Asheville-Biltmore. Afterglow and Concert. Second week in December.

*A Christmas Carol,* performed at Lipinsky Auditorium by Montford Park Players. Third week in December.

**"The Many Moods Of Christmas,"** performed at the Church of Asheville. By the church choir and Asheville Symphony Orchestra. Third week in December.

**Thomas Wolfe Memorial House.** Decorated for the holiday season. Tue.-Sun. Admission. Third and fourth weeks in December.

**BLACK MOUNTAIN, N.C.** **Christmas Parade.** Bellringers, carolers, clowns, bands, and Santa Claus. First week in December.

**Annual Floating Christmas Tree,** Lake Tomahawk. Two lighted Christmas trees are floated on the lake. Mid-December to January.

**BLAIRSVILLE, GA.** **Annual Tree Lighting Service,** Courthouse Square. Choir, songs, tree lighting. Third week in December.

**BRASSTOWN, N.C.** **Christmas Dinner at John C. Campbell Folk School.** First week in December.

**Annual Fireside Sale,** John C. Campbell Folk School. About 20 craftsmen show their wares. First week in December.

**Christmas Madrigal Play,** John C. Campbell Folk School. Second week in December.

**BREVARD, N.C.** **Christmas Parade,** from Brevard High School through town to Brevard College. First week in December.

**Yulefest.** In tradition of Elizabeth I's Christmas feasts, with food and costume from late 1500s. First week in December.

**BURNSVILLE, N.C.** **Christmas Parade,** Burnsville Junior Woman's Club. First week in December.

**CANTON, N.C.** **Christmas Tour of Homes,** Central United Methodist Church. Second week in December.

**CASHIERS, N.C.** **Christmas Parade.** First week in December.

**CHATSWORTH, GA.** **Vann House Moravian Christmas,** Vann House Historic Site. Christmas candlelight tours, 6-10 P.M. Second week in December.

**CLARKESVILLE, GA.** **Hills of Habersham Holidays Christmas Parade,** Cornelia and Clarkesville. First week in December.

**CLAYTON, GA.** **Christmas Creations,** Rabun County Courthouse. Demonstrations of Christmas projects. First week in December.

**CLEMSON, S.C.** **St. Andrew's Holiday Bazaar,** St. Andrew's Hall, Edgewood and Sloan streets. Second week in November.

**Clemson Children's Christmas Parade.** By Senior Girl Scout Troop 39 and Chamber of Commerce. Prizes for floats. First week in December.

**Clemson University Choirs,** Tillman Auditorium. Christmas Cantata. Free. First week in December.

**Hanover House Tour by Candlelight.** Colonial Christmas decorations in a house built in 1716. First week in December.

**CLEVELAND, GA.** **Christmas Open House,** Bob Owens Pottery Studio, Rte. 4, Old Blue Creek Road. First week in December.

**An Old Fashioned Christmas Bazaar,** Cleveland United Methodist Church on Kytle Street. Second week in November.

**CORNELIA, GA.** **Annual Christmas Arts and Crafts Fair,** Cornelia Women's Club House. Third week in November.

**CULLOWHEE, N.C.** **Christmas Bazaar,** Western Carolina University Center. Student organizations, area craftsmen, local churches and clubs. Second week in December.

**Christmas Music Celebration.** By Western Carolina University Band and choral groups. Recital Hall in Music-English Building. First week in December.

**Madrigal Christmas Dinner,** grandroom of the Western Carolina University Center. First week in December.

**DAHLONEGA, GA.** **Victorian Christmas Open House.** Annual event in the restored Vickery House, listed on the National Register. First week in December.

**A Golden Christmas,** Dahlonega Gold Museum. Christmas tree lighting, old-fashioned decorations and stories about Georgia's Gold Rush Days. First week in December.

**DILLSBORO, N.C.** **Nancy Tut's Christmas Shop,** Haywood Street. Open year-round. Unique items.

**EASLEY, S.C.** **Christmas Bazaar.** By Pickens County Extension Homemakers Clubs. Hamilton House. Third week in November.

**\*ELBERTON, GA.** **Christmas at the Christmas Tree House.** Home of Georgia's First Christmas Tree, 305 Heard Street. Decorations featuring traditions of 1858 period. First week in December.

**FLAT ROCK, N.C.** **Carl Sandburg Home.** The house is decorated in the Sandburg holiday tradition. Free. Mid-December to early January.

**FRANKLIN, N.C.** **Franklin Christmas Parade.** Billed as the area's biggest parade. First week in December.

**GAINESVILLE, GA.** **Mountain Christmas Show,** Georgia Mountains Center. Festive holiday preview features sights, sounds and smells of Christmas. Second week in November.

**HAYESVILLE, N.C.** **Christmas Bazaar,** Old Jail Museum. By Clay County Historical Arts Council. Crafts, lunch, baked goods for sale. Second week in December.

**HELEN, GA.** **Christmas in the Country,** Unicoi State Park. Christmas ornaments from natural material, hot cider, music. Second week in December.

**Christmas in Helen.** Several village events and activities. December.

**Christmas Tree Lighting,** Unicoi Hill, overlooking Helen. Usually largest live tree in Georgia. Third week in November.

**HENDERSONVILLE, N.C.** **A Christmas House,** 1515 Haywood Road. Mon.-Sat.

**Merry Christmas Greens Market,** Clems Cabin, 1800 Hendersonville Road. First, second, third weeks in December.

**HIGHLANDS, N.C.** **A Christmas Show,** Arts Center. By the Instant Theatre Co. First and second weeks in December.

**LAKE JUNALUSKA, N.C.** **Christmas-in-August Program.** Free. Second week in August.

**MARION, N.C.** *A Christmas Carol.* Foothills Community Theatre presents an unusual rendition of Charles Dickens' classic Christmas story. McDowell Tech. Auditorium. Second week in December.

**Ole Mountain Christmas,** courthouse lawn. Home tours, antique show, music. First and second weeks in December.

**Ole Mountain Christmas Parade,** downtown. First week in December.

**MORGANTON, GA.** **Annual Christmas Open House,** The Baroque Unicorn Studio, US-76. Works by regional artists. First three weeks in December. (404) 632-2144.

**MARS HILL, N.C.** **Christmas Concert of Music and Art,** Mars Hill College, Moore Auditorium. First week in December.

**PENDLETON, S.C.** **Christmas Crafts Event,** at Hunter's Store. By Pendleton District and Recreation Commission. First weekend in December.

**Christmastime in Olde Pendleton.** Held every two years by Junior Assembly of Pendleton. Tour begins at Village Green.

**PLEASANT GARDEN, N.C.** **Candlelight Christmas Tea,** at Carson House. By the Carson House Restoration Corp. Second week in December.

**SALEM, S.C.** **Christmas Parade.** By Salem Iris Garden Club. Second week in December.

**SENECA, S.C.** **Country Christmas,** downtown parking lot. By Seneca Chamber of Commerce. Second week in November. (803) 882-2097 or 5620.

**Christmas Parade.** By Seneca Chamber of Commerce. Fourth week in November. (803) 882-2097.

**Outdoor Christmas Drama,** at South Cove Park. Performed by Full Gospel Temple of Seneca. Visitors are driven around the island in a hay wagon. Early December. (803) 882-3054.

**SYLVA, N.C. Christmas in July Bazaar,** First Methodist Church. By C.J. Harris Hospital Auxiliary. First week in July.

**Sylva Christmas Parade,** downtown. First week in December.

**TOCCOA, GA. Christmas in the Country Bazaar,** Camp Mikell Road, 1½ mi. off Prather Bridge Road. Third week in November.

**Christmas Concert,** First United Methodist Church. By Atlanta Boy Choir. Admission. First week in December.

**Annual Christmas Program,** Georgia Baptist Assembly. First week in December.

**Annual Christmas Parade.** By Toccoa-Stephens County Jaycees. Second week in December. (404) 886-1159.

**Calvary Nativity Scene,** Calvary Baptist Church, E. Tupelo Street. Live nativity. Mid-December.

**A Christmas for Travelers,** Travelers Rest High School. Handmade items, baked goods, hot cider, string music. Second week in December. (404) 886-2256.

**WALHALLA, S.C. Christmas Auction,** Oconee County Library. Second week in November.

**Christmas Parade.** By Walhalla Sertoma Club and Junior Woman's Club. First week in December. (803) 638-9356.

**The Holiday Showcase,** College Street Baptist Church. By Oconee County Council of Extension Homemakers Clubs. First week in December.

**WAYNESVILLE, N.C. Christmas Bazaar.** By Salvation Army Women's Home League. Second week in November.

**Christmas Arts/Crafts.** Students from Haywood Technical College display crafts. First week in December.

**Christmas at Shelton House,** Pigeon and Shelton streets. First week in December.

**Haywood County Christmas Concert.** Free. First week in December.

*Messiah.* By Haywood County Community Chorus and First Baptist Choir, with University of North Carolina at Asheville String Ensemble. Admission. First week in December.

**WESTMINSTER, S.C. Christmas Parade.** By Great Town Association. First week in December.

**WEAVERVILLE, N.C. Zebulon Vance Birthplace 1830 period Christmas,** Reems Creek Road. 1830s Christmas decorations. Free. First week in December.

**YOUNG HARRIS, GA. Christmas Star Program,** Rollins Planetarium. Star of Bethlehem. Every Friday in December.

**Appalachian Gallery,** Main Street. Christmas show and sale of crafts by member artists. First week in December.

**Christmas Show/Sale,** New Homestead School. First week in December.

# Covered Bridges

A few covered bridges still dot the roadways of the South. Sometimes called "tunnels of nostalgia," they remind the traveler of another era, when folks used the bridges for more than getting from one side of the river to the other.

Because the bridges were usually dark and vine-covered, they beckoned to lovers who were out for a horse-and-buggy ride, or to adventurous children who were in search of a hideaway. Farmers used them as gathering places, and families found them ideal for picnics and handy for refuge from rain or snow.

Folklore sent many a woman to covered bridges to weave a daisy chain across the entrance: the first person to break the daisy chain would be the lady's new beau. Children, it was said, would have their wishes come true if they could hold their breath while running the length of the tunnel.

Nostalgia and folklore, however, did little to save the covered bridges that are now so scarce. Most of the remaining ones in the region are in northeast Georgia, home to 12 of that state's 20 covered bridges. (At one time, the state had as many as 250.)

North Carolina has three surviving covered bridges. A 54-foot bridge two miles west of Pisgah over a branch of the Little River has short buttresses, stepping stone piers and three spans.

While North Carolina probably had more than 100 covered bridges, South Carolina had only about 20. Col. Samuel Knox, a landowner on the Georgia side of the Tugaloo River, profited from the bridge he built for $10,000. The bridge was built in 1853 and for 50 years an estimated $2,000 to $3,000 was collected annually in tolls. Some paid tolls by bartering chickens or farm products. The colonel's heir sold out in 1908 to the adjoining states and there were no more tolls. The bridge lasted until the 1950s.

Covered bridges still standing in the Blue Ridge region in South Carolina are Prather's, which joins Westminster, S.C., and Toccoa, Ga., and Chapman's Bridge over the Keowee River between Easatoe and Jocassee.

*CARNESVILLE, GA.  **Gromer's Mill covered bridge,** 8 mi. south via G-106; east on county road. J.M. Hunt built this bridge around 1906. One span wide, 132 feet long and town lattice design.

*CARTERSVILLE, GA.  **Lowry covered bridge,** 6 mi. west of Cartersville via G-113, 2 mi. north on county road to Euharlee. Constructed in 1886 by Horace King. Designed in town lattice style, it measures one span wide and 116 feet long. Numbers still legible on bridge timbers indicate that such structures often were assembled in a nearby field to assure perfect fit, then rebuilt over the stream.

**\*CLAREMONT, N.C.** **Bunker Hill covered bridge.** Built in 1895; over 80 feet long and stands over Lyles Creek. Lattice design by Herman Haupt. One of two bridges of this type left in the United States.

**CLEMSON, S.C.** **Chapman's bridge,** Keowee Toxaway State Park.

**CUMMING, GA.** **Pool's Mill bridge,** 7 miles west of city on G-20 to Ducktown, then 3 mi. north to Heardville and 1 mi. north on Pool's Mill Road. Spans Settendown Creek. Built in 1906. One span wide, 90 feet long. Being restored.

**GOWENSVILLE, S.C.** **Campbell's bridge.** Built 1909. Only covered bridge in state that still carries traffic. Picnic area. Located off SC-23-114, 4 mi. southwest of Gowensville. This county road is approximately ¼ mi. south of SC-414 and 2½ mi. east of SC-101. Follow signs from SC-101. Free.

**HIGHLANDS, N.C.** **Dillard Road covered bridge,** 4 mi. west on Dillard Road. Waldron's property. Part of Lick Log Mill Historic Area and store. Restored.

**LULA, GA.** **Lula Bridge,** Route 51.

**PICKENS, S.C.** **Lower Gassaway covered bridge.** Pickens County.

**PISGAH, N.C.** **Little River bridge,** 2 mi. west of Pisgah. Fifty-four feet long.

**SAUTEE, GA.** **Stovall covered bridge,** 3 mi. north of city on G-255. At 33 feet long, Georgia's smallest covered bridge. Built in 1895; Kingsport design. One span wide. Featured in the movie *I'd Climb the Highest Mountain*.

**SMYRNA, GA.** **Concord bridge,** 2½ mi. southwest of Smyrna. Queenpost design; 133 feet long. Built in 1848.

**TOCCOA, GA.** **Prather's covered bridge,** 6 mi. northeast from Toccoa on G-184. Spans the Tugaloo River and the Georgia-South Carolina line. This town lattice style bridge, listed in the U.S. National Register of Historic Places, measures two spans wide and 175 feet long. It was built around 1913 as a replacement for the original bridge, which was erected in the early 1800s.

# Crafts Events

Potters, weavers, quiltmakers and other craftspeople were once vital to survival in the mountains. Because the mountain people were poor and isolated, they made almost everything they needed. Today those one-time necessities are admired as folk art and displayed in the best art galleries.

The Blue Ridge Mountain area has a number of talented craftsmen who hope to preserve these traditions. And craft fairs are a great place to see their work. Two of the largest are the Blue Ridge Hearthside Crafts Association Festival, held in Boone, N.C., and the Southern Highland Handicraft Guild Fair in Asheville, N.C. The Southern Highland Handicraft Guild is one of the oldest and most influential craft associations in Appalachia. Among its founders were Miss Lucy Morgan, who also founded the Penland School, and the legendary craftsman Elmer Kear, a Tennessee broom maker. The guild has more than 600 members today. It holds fairs in the summer and fall at the Asheville, N.C., Civic Center. Another popular North Carolina show is Blowing Rock's "Art in the Park," in which artists display their works in an informal outdoor setting. Shows are held in August, September and October.

Clarkesville, Ga., has a clothesline arts and crafts show at Moccasin Creek State Park, featuring bluegrass music, clogging, watermelon cutting and other events.

At these and other fairs, you will see traditional and modern artists' work, glassblowing, painting, sculpting, photography, furniture and toys.

————February————

**HELEN, GA.** **Fireside Craft/Art Show,** Parks Lodge and Conference Center, Unicoi State Park. Exhibit and sales. Third week. (404) 878-2201.

**ASHEVILLE, N.C.** **Winterfest Arts/Crafts Festival,** S. Tunnel Road. By University of North Carolina at Asheville Alumni. Crafts exhibits. Mid-February. (704) 253-6893.

————March————

**ASHEVILLE, N.C.** **Annual Art Museum Auction,** Asheville Art Museum, Haywood Street. Fourth week.

————April————

**BLAIRSVILLE, GA.** **Easter Craft and Needlework Festival,** Recreation Center. County Extension Service. Easter week. (404) 745-4744.

**CUMMING, GA.** **Annual Spring Chicken House Arts and Crafts Show.** Old time craft exhibit. Fourth week. (404) 877-1702 or 887-9629.

**TOCCOA, GA.** **Currahee Arts and Crafts Festival.** By Chamber of Commerce. Fourth week. (404) 886-2132.

# Crafts Events
## ———May———

**ASHEVILLE, N.C.** **Annual High Country Design Show,** 29 Haywood Street. By High Country Crafters. First week. (704) 258-3858 or 254-0070.

**CLEMSON, S.C.** **Annual Arts and Crafts Festival,** Keowee-Toxaway Visitor Center, SC-130-183. Free. First Week. (803) 882-5620.

**GAINESVILLE, GA.** **Georgia Arts and Crafts Show.** First week. (404) 265-3320.
**Georgia Mountains Jubilee,** Downtown Square. 200 craftsmen. Second week. (404) 534-1100.

**SYLVA, N.C.** **Sunday in the Park.** By Jackson County Recreation and Parks and Arts Council. First week. (704) 488-3681.

**CHATSWORTH, GA.** **Crafts Fair,** Mountain Village. Third week. (404) 695-7208.

**HELEN, GA.** **Blacksmith Convention,** Unicoi State Park. Craftsmen forge and shape metals into tools and articles of beauty. Third week. (404) 878-2201.

**TALLULAH FALLS, GA.** **Arts and Crafts Exhibits,** US-441 between Clarkesville and Clayton. Third week. (404) 782-4812.

**BLUE RIDGE, GA.** **Arts in the Park.** Memorial Day weekend. By Blue Ridge Mountain Arts Assoc. (404) 632-2144.

**BREVARD, N.C.** **Western North Carolina Ceramic Assoc. Fair,** at the National Guard Armory on Brevard Road, NC-191 south. Fourth week. (704) 254-6069 or 252-3288.

**HELEN, GA.** **Unicoi Crafts Outdoor Show,** Unicoi State Park Lodge. Crafts, camping, workshops. Fourth week. (404) 878-2201.

**MURPHY, N.C.** **Sidewalk Arts and Crafts Show,** downtown. Fourth week. (704) 837-6822.

## ———June———

**ASHEVILLE, N.C.** **A Highland Heritage,** Asheville Mall. By High Country Crafters. First week. (704) 254-0070.
**High Country Craft Show,** Civic Center, Haywood Street. First week. (704) 254-0070.
**Western N.C. Cermic Show.** First week. (704) 252-3288.

**BRASSTOWN, N.C.** **Spring Crafts,** John C. Campbell Folk School. US-64 east. Extensive crafts workshops. First week. (704) 837-2775.

**HELEN, GA.** **Alpine Village Arts and Crafts Fair,** Helen Pavilion. Second week. (404) 878-2400.

**HENDERSONVILLE, N.C.** **Summer Craft Show and Sale,** Four Seasons Mall. Henderson County Crafters Assoc. Second week. (704) 693-0027.

**SALUDA, N.C.** **Celebrate Saluda Day.** By Saluda Assoc. of Artists and Craftsmen. An all-day celebration. Mid-June.

**CAESAR'S HEAD STATE PARK** **Caesar's Head Crafts Show,** at the shelter, US-276 south of Brevard, N.C. Traditional mountain crafts. Second week. (704) 758-3622.

**ASHEVILLE, N.C.** **Highland Heritage Arts and Craft Show,** Asheville Mall. 65 exhibitors. Third week. (704) 253-6893.

**FRANKLIN, N.C.** Maco Crafts Spring Fling, Community Building and Maco Crafts. Crafts, quilt contest. Third week. (704) 524-7878.

**LAVONIA, GA.** Good Ol' Summertime Crafts Show, Tugaloo State Park. Third week.

**CLAYTON, GA.** Mountaineer Arts and Crafts Festival, Rabun County High School, US-76 west. By Parks and Recreation Dept. Free. Fourth week. (404) 782-4600.

**HARTWELL, S.C.** Pre-Fourth Extravaganza, the town square, E. Howell Street at Franklin Street. Fourth week. (404) 376-3764.

**SAPPHIRE VALLEY, N.C.** Arts and Crafts Show. Fairfield, Sapphire Valley. Fourth week. (704) 254-0700.

————July————

**CASHIERS, N.C.** A High Country Art and Craft Show. First week. (704) 254-0070.

**HAYESVILLE, N.C.** Festival on the Square. First week. (704) 389-3259.

**HIGHLANDS, N.C.** High Country Art and Craft Show, Helen's Barn. By High Country Crafters. 100 artists. Free. First week. (704) 254-0070.

**MURPHY, N.C.** Arts & Crafts Show, Pied Piper Camp Resort, US-64 west. First week. (704) 632-2144.
  Smoky Mountain Arts and Crafts Show, Annual, held in Rock Gym over July 4th weekend. (704) 837-2141.

**PENDLETON, S.C.** 4th of July Arts and Crafts Show. (803) 646-3182.

**SCALY MOUNTAIN, N.C.** Mountain Hillbilly Crafts. By High Country Crafters. First week in July; first week in August. (704) 254-0700.

**SUNSET, N.C.** Sunset Festival of the Arts, Sunset Campground, S. Mills River Road. First week. (704) 891-9924, 9941.

**BREVARD, N.C.** Festival of the Arts Week. Exhibits, music, drama, dance. Second week. (704) 883-3700.

**MAGGIE VALLEY, N.C.** Arts and Crafts Show. Maggie Valley Chamber of Commerce, P.O. Box 87, 28751. Second week. (704) 926-1686.

**ASHEVILLE, N.C.** Fair of the Southern Highland Handicrafts Guild, Civic Center, Haywood Street. Since 1946. Third week. (704) 298-7928.

**BREVARD, N.C.** Festival of the Arts. Music, crafts, art, flowers. Third week. (704) 883-3700.

**ASHEVILLE, N.C.** Annual Guild Fair. Wilson Somerville Guild Fairs of Southern Highland Handicraft Guild, P.O. Box 9545, 28815. Late July and late October. (704) 298-2928.

**DAWSONVILLE, GA.** Crafts and Music Show, Amicalola State Park. Fourth week. (404) 265-2885.

**GAINESVILLE, GA.** Georgia Arts and Crafts. Fourth week. (404) 265-3324.

**HIGHLANDS, N.C.** Highlands-Cashiers Garden Club Arts and Crafts Show and Sale, Highlands School. Fourth week. (704) 526-2112.

————August————

**ASHEVILLE, N.C.** Annual Village Art and Craft Fair, Biltmore Village. 100 artists and craftspersons. First week. (704) 274-2831.

**Annual Village Art and Craft Fair,** All Souls Episcopal Church. 100 exhibitors. First week. (704) 274-2831.

**BURNSVILLE, N.C.** Mt. Mitchell Crafts Fair, Town Square. Barbecue, square dancing, crafts. Early August. (704) 683-0070.

**HIGHLANDS, N.C.** Annual High Country Art and Craft Show, Helen's Barn. First week. (704) 254-0070.

**SCALY MOUNTAIN, N.C.** Arts and Crafts. First week.

**BREVARD, N.C.** Annual Sidewalk Show and Sale, Courthouse lawn. Second week. (704) 883-3700.

**\*BOONE, N.C.** Blue Ridge Hearthside Craft Fair, Holiday Inn Conference Center. Second week.

**CLARKESVILLE, GA.** Clothesline Arts and Crafts Show, Moccasin Creek State Park. Annual juried show. By the Georgia Dept. of Natural Resources. Second week. (404) 947-3194.

**ASHEVILLE, N.C.** High Country Summerfest, Civic Center, Haywood Street. Third week. (704) 253-6893.

**BUFORD, GA.** Arts and Crafts Show, Lake Lanier Islands. Third week. (404) 993-8806.

**EASLEY, S.C.** Foothills Festival Arts and Crafts, Foothills Mall. Third week. (803) 859-2693.

**HENDERSONVILLE, N.C.** Opportunity House Arts and Crafts Fair, Fleming Street. Third week. (704) 692-1413.

**LAKE LANIER, GA.** Mountain-Do. Arts and Crafts festival plus country music and cloggers. Third week. (404) 945-6701.

**SAPPHIRE, N.C.** Arts and Crafts. Third week. (704) 743-5191.

**CASHIERS, N.C.** Craft Show. By High Country Crafters. Fourth week. (704) 254-0700.

**HARTWELL, GA.** Arts and Crafts Festival, Lake Hartwell. Fourth week. (404) 993-8806.

**HENDERSONVILLE, N.C.** Walking Folk Arts and Crafts Fair, downtown churches of Hendersonville. Fourth week. (704) 692-1413.

**WAYNESVILLE, N.C.** Arts and Crafts Fair, courthouse lawn. Free. Fourth week. (704) 456-3285.

————September————

**ASHEVILLE, N.C.** Mid Summer Arts and Crafts Show, Asheville Mall. First week. (704) 791-3918.

**CASHIERS, N.C.** Annual High Country Art and Craft Show, High Country Crafters. First week. (704) 254-0070.

**CUMMING, GA.** Autumn Days, Lanier Village Shopping Center, US-19. Show and sale by exhibitors. Second week. (404) 887-8040.

**ELBERTON, GA.** **Granite City Arts and Crafts Festival.** National Guard Armory on Calhoun Highway. Second week. (404) 283-7432.

**CHATSWORTH, GA.** **Fort Mountain Craft Fair,** near Cohutta Lodge, atop Fort Mountain. Third weekend. (404) 695-6060.

**HELEN, GA.** **Fabric Creations from the Mountains,** Conference Center, Unicoi State Park, G-356. Third week. (404) 878-2201.

**CANTON, GA.** **Village Arts and Crafts Show.** Fourth week. (404) 479-5309.

**•GATLINBURG, TENN.** **Gatlinburg Craftsmen's Fair,** W. L. Mills Auditorium, Civic Coliseum. Over 200 craftspeople demonstrate and sell items during the 24-day fair. Late September to late October. 1-800-251-9868.

   **Annual Fall Exhibition,** US-321 north, a few blocks from downtown. Late September through late October.

**GAINESVILLE, GA.** **Georgia Arts and Crafts Show.** Fourth week. (404) 265-3320.

————October————

**•PIGEON FORGE, TENN.** **National Crafts Festival,** at Silver Dollar City. Largest collection of wooden Indians in the United States. Month of October.

**ASHEVILLE, N.C.** **Indian Summer Arts and Crafts Show,** Asheville Shopping Mall. By University of North Carolina at Asheville Alumni Art Chapter, 35 mediums represented. First week. (704) 253-6893.

**BRASSTOWN, N.C.** **Folk School Fall Festival,** John C. Campbell Folk School. Arts, crafts. First week. (704) 837-2275.

**CASHIERS, N.C.** **High Country Art and Craft Show.** First week. (704) 743-5191.

**CLAYTON, GA.** **High Country Art and Craft Show.** Mountain City Playhouse on US-441, 3 mi. north of Clayton. First week. (704) 253-6893.

**•DUCKTOWN, TENN.** **First Tuesday,** Main Street at the Community Center, 2 mi. west of town on US-64. Arts and crafts show and sale. First week. (615) 496-3646.

**JASPER, GA.** **Sharptop Mountain Arts and Crafts Fall Show and Sale.** Jasper Elementary Gym. First week. (404) 692-6565.

**BLUE RIDGE, GA.** **Annual Mountain Harvest Sale of Arts and Crafts,** State Farmers Market. Second and third week. (404) 632-5223.

**CLEMSON, S.C.** **Y-Beach Arts and Crafts.** Second week. (803) 882-2097.

**DILLARD, GA.** **Harvest Sale,** at the Farmers Market on US-441. Mountain products and crafts for sale. Second and third week. (404) 782-5113.

**ELLIJAY, GA.** **Georgia Apple Festival and Crafts Fair.** Second week. (404) 635-7400.

**HELEN, GA.** **Creations from the Mountains,** Unicoi State Park. Second week. (404) 878-2201, ext. 283.

**HENDERSONVILLE, N.C.** **Autumn Craft Show,** Four Seasons Mall, US-64 east. Second week. (704) 693-0027.

**HIGHLANDS, N.C.** **Annual Art and Craft Outdoor Show,** at Helen's Barn. Second week. (704) 254-0070.

**MARION, N.C.** **Mountain Glory Crafts Festival.** Native art/craft items for sale and exhibit. Second weekend. (704) 652-4240.

**MAGGIE VALLEY, N.C.** **Arts and Crafts Show.** By Chamber of Commerce, P.O. Box 87, 28751. Second week. (704) 926-1680.

**ASHEVILLE, N.C.** **Asheville National Guard Ladies Auxiliary Arts and Crafts Show,** National Guard Armory. Third week. (704) 258-6900.

**Southern Highlands Handicraft Guild Fall Show,** Civic Center, Haywood Street. Third week. (704) 298-7928.

**BLUE RIDGE, GA.** **Mountain Harvest Sale,** State Farmers Market on US-76. Third and fourth weeks. (404) 632-5223.

**\*BOONE, N.C.** **Annual Autumn Boone Craft Festival,** Holiday Inn Center. Third week. (704) 297-2398.

**BREVARD, N.C.** **Craft Fair,** Masonic Temple. By Brevard's Christian Women's Club. Third week. (704) 883-3700.

**CUMMING, GA.** **Cumming Country Creations Bazaar.** Third week. (404) 887-6461.

**\*GREENVILLE, S.C.** **Annual "Hill Skills" Craft Show,** Greenville Memorial Auditorium. Third week. (803) 242-1050.

**HELEN, GA.** **Arts and Crafts Fair,** at Skylake. Fourth week. (404) 878-2292.

**MURPHY, N.C.** **Annual Mountain Leaves Sidewalk Arts and Crafts Festival.** Fourth week. (704) 837-6822.

————November————

**CUMMING, GA.** **Annual Great Chicken House Arts and Crafts Festival,** Shilo Road, off G-9. Held inside two large chicken houses. First week. (404) 887-1702 or 577-3549.

**SIX MILE, S.C.** **Village Arts and Crafts Fair,** Six Mile Elementary School. First week. (803) 868-9804.

**McCAYSVILLE, GA.** **Wonderful Wednesday Arts and Crafts Festival.** Second week. (615) 496-5405.

**BLUE RIDGE, GA.** **Holiday Extravaganza Exhibit.** By Blue Ridge Arts Assoc. Third week. (404) 632-2144.

**GAINESVILLE, GA.** **Georgia Arts and Crafts.** Third week. (404) 265-3324.

**SENECA, S.C.** **Arts and Crafts Show,** downtown. Third week.

**\*SPARTANBURG, S.C.** **Arts and Crafts Show,** Arts Center. Mid-November to mid-December.

**ASHEVILLE, N.C.** **High Country Christmas Art and Craft Show,** Civic Center, Haywood Street. Fourth week. (704) 253-6893.

**CLAYTON, GA.** **Mountain Holiday Arts and Crafts Festival,** Old Rabun County High Gym. Fourth week. (404) 782-4600.

————December————

**GAINESVILLE, GA.** **Annual Holiday Exhibit and Sale,** Gainesville Junior College Student Center, Exit 4, G-365. First week. (404) 532-6206.

**TALLULAH FALLS, GA.** **Handmade and Homemade Bazaar.** First week. (404) 754-3276.

# Craft Schools

The area's folk and craft schools teach improved farming techniques, how to throw pottery, how to cast silver jewelry.

While philosophies of the various folk and craft schools differ, all are aimed at improving people's lives. As shuttles click on weaving looms and blacksmith's anvils clang, the skills of yesteryear are being used and preserved.

The John C. Campbell Folk School in Brasstown, N.C., home of the famous Brasstown Carvers, was begun in 1925. Today it attracts both beginning hobbyists and serious craftspeople. Courses offer instruction in basketry, batik, chairmaking, blacksmithing, enameling, copper sculpturing, pottery, making things from stone, quilting, silversmithing, spinning and dyeing, stained glass, weaving, wood carving and woodworking. A nine-month course in the art and science of homesteading teaches the skills needed to build a house and to be self-sufficient.

The Penland School of Crafts in Penland, N.C., the oldest and largest crafts school in America, began classes in 1923. Miss Lucy Morgan taught women to spin and weave and placed looms in countless mountain homes. Today, craftspeople from all over the United States and from 60 foreign countries work in pottery, sculpture, wood, glass, metal, graphics and photography.

Eco-Village in Hendersonville, N.C., is a 622-acre national center for ecological research run by Mother Earth News. Self-reliance experts demonstrate beekeeping, hydropower, wind power, fuel production, food preservation, fish farming and other skills. Students can visit daily or camp on the grounds.

The Hambidge Center for Creative Arts and Sciences in Rabun Gap, Ga., provides craft workshops and retreats for working artists and scientists in a rustic 800-acre setting. The harmony between nature and man's creative process is stressed. Experimentation is encouraged in the study of such subjects as astronomy, botany, photography, pottery, painting, weaving and writing.

The Arrowmont School of Arts and Crafts in Gatlinburg, Tenn., has been supported since 1912 by Pi Beta Phi, a national collegiate sorority, and is affiliated with the University of Tennessee. Students don't mind tourists watching as they work in fiber arts, ceramics, photography, enameling, design, papermaking and woodworking.

At the Folks Art Center, in Asheville, N.C., home of the Southern Highland Handicraft Guild, visitors can see exhibits of crafts, folk dancing, story telling and music.

Visit the Cradle of Forestry Visitor Center in Brevard, N.C., to learn the story of the Biltmore Forest School, in operation from 1898-1913. Restored and reconstructed buildings are open for visitors.

**ASHEVILLE, N.C.** **Folk Art Center,** Blue Ridge Parkway, milepost 382. Home of Southern Highland Handicrafts Guild. Craftsmen from nine states. Exhibits, folk dancing, story telling, music. 9 A.M.-5 P.M. daily, except Christmas, Thanksgiving, New Year's.

**BRASSTOWN, N.C.** **John C. Campbell Folk School,** off US-64. Founded in 1925 in the tradition of the Danish folk schools. It serves as a folk dance and music center, crafts outlet, crafts school, and the home of the Brasstown carvers, a woodcarving cottage industry that supplements the income of many farm families. Students come to the school from every part of the country for one- or two-week courses in traditional highland crafts or for a nine-month course in homesteading. Permanent collections include early wood carvings and Doris Ulmann photographs. Craft wares are sold in gift shop. (704) 837-2775.

**Little Folk School** at John C. Campbell Folk School. Folk dancing, games, songs, pottery and crafts for ages 6-12. (704) 837-2775.

**BREVARD, N.C.** **Biltmore Forestry School** (1898), 3.3 mi. south of Blue Ridge Parkway on US-276. Originally part of the Biltmore estate, but now called the Cradle of Forestry Visitor Center.

**CROSSNORE, N.C.** **Crossnore Crafts School,** near Linville on US-221 south. Has taught traditional crafts since 1911.

**'GATLINBURG, TENN.** **Arrowmont School of Arts and Crafts,** Friday afternoon crafts school tour. Pi Beta Phi Arrowmont Crafts School, Box 567. Gatlinburg, Tenn. 37738. This 37-year-old crafts school is a joint venture of Pi Beta Phi national sorority and the University of Tennessee. The school offers courses and year-round workshops in fabrics, clay, metal, enamel, photography, stained glass, paper, wood, painting and graphic arts. The sorority provides the funding; the university provides the teachers and course credits. Students in the workshops will gladly describe their creations to tourists. A second-floor gallery displays faculty works. Outside the main building are large weaving and pottery workshops, with rows of looms and wheels. Adjoining the pottery workshop is a handmade kiln, built by the students and faculty. The Arrowcraft Shop, also run by Pi Beta Phi, is the oldest of all Gatlinburg craft shops (opened in 1926). It sells the work of 150 Appalachian craftsmen. Features weaving, pottery and wood carvings. (615) 436-5860.

**HENDERSONVILLE, N.C.** **Eco-Village,** 105 Stoney Mountain Road, 28791. 622-acre mountain research center; 12-acre lake. Operated by Mother Earth News. Open house demonstrates self-sufficiency: beekeeping, hydropower, gardening, wind power, wild gourmet foods, fuel production. Admission. (704) 693-0211.

**PENLAND, N.C.** **Penland School of Crafts,** off NC-226 west of Spruce Pine. Oldest and largest crafts school in America, now internationally known. Began in 1923 when Miss Lucy Morgan placed looms in mountain homes to encourage women to spin and weave. Craftsmen now work in pottery, sculpture, wood, glass, metal, graphics and photography. Frequent exhibits. (704) 765-2359.

**RABUN GAP, GA.** **Hambidge Center for Creative Arts and Sciences,** Betty's Creek Road. Offers a wide range of courses, from weaving and pottery to poetry and music, in a rustic 800-acre setting. Courses stress harmony between nature and man's creative process. P.O. Box 33, 30568. (404) 746-5718.

**YOUNG HARRIS, GA. New Homestead School: Alternative Lifestyle Learning Center,** Main Street, Box 7. Educational, scientific, humanitarian purposes. (404) 837-8873 or (404) 379-2231.

# Craft Shops

Deep in the Appalachian Mountains sits a weatherworn woman at an old wooden loom, weaving beautiful rugs that reflect the deep hues of the woods which surround her. Her nearest neighbor, a mile down the road, is a young woman who makes dolls using scraps of cloth and twigs.

Their skills are traditional, but the merchandising of such work is often quite modern. Many of these mountain craftsmen have organized craft co-operatives, joining together to sell their work on a large-scale basis. They are talented people with business savvy.

Hundreds of craft shops are scattered along the highways in the Blue Ridge area. Not all the wares you will find are true mountain crafts, however. The smart shopper should try to distinguish the handmade, traditional work from mass produced, factory-made items.

One way to find genuine crafts is to shop at display centers run by craft co-operatives. Among them are Georgia Craft Galleries in Gainesville, Ga., and Tallulah Falls Co-op in Tallulah Falls, Ga. Tallulah Falls Co-op has about 100 members. Their works are also sold at the Forge Mill Crossing Restaurant in Blue Ridge, Ga. Unicoi Crafts, a shop in the main lodge in Unicoi State Park near Helen, Ga., features a wide variety of high quality crafts.

Green River Gallery in Saluda, N.C., is a co-operative gallery that presents outstanding works by area craftsmen in both traditional and contemporary designs. Saluda Mountain Crafts, on the same street, represents more than 150 craftsmen. It offers rustic pine furniture, woodwork, pottery and toys.

Other North Carolina craft shops include Maco Crafts and Heritage Hollow, a village of shops and restaurants in Franklin, Riverwood Shops in Dillsboro, and Carolina Mountain Crafts in Murphy. The Old School House in Sylva is a group of crafts shops, resident craftsmen and antique dealers. Nearby Bryson City's Mountain Skill Craft Shop provides lots of handmade, traditional work.

The Biltmore Country Market in Asheville, N.C., features plenty of crafts sure to please someone on your Christmas list. In that same city, don't miss the Biltmore Handwoven Homespun shops on the grounds of the Grove Park Inn. The city's High Country Crafters, a regional center for western North Carolina, buys and sells crafts.

Mountain crafts are also exhibited and sold at many craft and country fairs and at flea markets and farmers' markets (see chapters on Fairs, Crafts, and Flea Markets and Farmers' Markets).

**ANDREWS, N.C.** **The Mountain Emporium**, Main Street. Works made by 200 crafts-people from afghans to Yule houses. (704) 321-3297.

**ARDEN, N.C.   Carolina Cabin,** US-25. Unique pottery, crafts, antiques, mineral specimens. (704) 684-5337.

**ASHEVILLE, N.C.   Allanstand Mountain Craft Shop,** 16 College Street. Mon.-Sat. (704) 253-2051.

**Appalachian Village,** Route 1, Box 191C. (704) 645-5847.

**Appalachian Craft Center,** 10 Spruce Street. Handmade rugs, folk pottery; rug weaving and braiding demonstrated. (704) 253-8499.

**Biltmore Country Market,** 1000 Hendersonville Road. Mon.-Sat. Crafts by women. (704) 274-1626.

**Biltmore Homespun Shops,** Grovewood Road, on grounds of Grove Park Inn. Handwoven homespun. Tours. Mon.-Fri. (704) 253-7651.

**Guild Shop,** 20 Tunnel Road. Stuart Nye jewelry. Mon.-Sat. (704) 298-7903.

**Heritage Decoys,** 4 mi. south on US-276. Handcarved and handpainted wildlife, folk art style. (704) 235-8607.

**High Country Crafters,** 29 Haywood Street. Traditional handcrafted works of the Carolina mountains. (704) 254-0070.

**High Country Crafters,** 34 Haywood Street. Regional Center for Western North Carolina. Buying, selling, exhibiting, demonstrations. Tues.-Sat. (704) 255-9355.

**New Morning Gallery,** 7 Boston Way, Biltmore Village. Open daily, May-December. Retail sales of quality handmade objects. 400 artists and craftsmen. (704) 274-2831.

**Out of the Woods,** 16 S. Pack Square. Open Tues.-Sat. (winter), Mon.-Sat. (summer). Handcrafted wooden furniture and other wood crafts. (704) 252-7860.

**Smoky Mountain Crafts,** 64 N. Lexington Avenue. Pottery, weavings, quilts, woodcrafts, jewelry. **(704)** 254-5168.

**The Country Touch,** 1000 Hendersonville Road, Biltmore. Handmade gifts, pine cone crafts, **antiques.** (704) 274-5410.

**The Spinning Wheel,** 1096 Hendersonville Road. Mon.-Sat.. (704) 274-0720.

**BLAIRSVILLE, GA.   Mountain Village Crafts,** Main Street. (404) 745-9546.

**Robyn's Nest (1880) Shoppe,** Town Creek Road. Handcrafted furniture, quilts, foods, soft goods. (404) 745-4786.

**Wellborn Mountain Gift Shop,** Rte. 129, Foster Building, Gainesville Highway. Handmade stuffed animals, dolls, pillow quilts. (404) 745-4759.

**BATESVILLE, GA.   Serendipity,** G-197. Stained-glass shop. (404) 947-3643.

**BLACK MOUNTAIN, N.C.   Gallery,** 206 Sutton Avenue. Windchimes, bells, mobiles, unique handmade objects. (704) 669-9331.

**Ole Depot Arts and Crafts Center,** Sutton Avenue. Retail sales of juried craft objects. Local mountain crafters. Daily. April 1-Dec. 24. (704) 669-6583.

**The Seven Sisters Gallery,** 117 Cherry Street. Quality arts and crafts; country primitive antiques. (704) 669-5107.

**BLUE RIDGE, GA.   Forge Mill Crossing Restaurant,** US-76, Forge Mill Road. Crafts from the Tallulah Falls Co-op. Daily.

**Mountain Do Shop,** US-76. Gifts and antiques, quilts, dolls, handcrafts, primitives. (404) 632-3822.

**BRASSTOWN, N.C.   The John C. Campbell Folk School,** US-64. Craft shop for area and resident craftsmen. Daily. (704) 837-2775.

**BREVARD, N.C.   Sherwood Forest Craft Shop,** US-276. Old Milking Barn. Supplied by area crafters. Closed Mondays.

**BRYSON CITY, N.C.** **Mountain Skill Craft Shop,** P.O. Box 771, on the square. Genuine mountain co-op, featuring handmade crafts. April-December, Mon.-Sat. (704) 488-6424.

**CANTON, N.C.** **Wood 'n' Things,** 129 Main. Primitive pine wood, accessories, handmade crafts and gifts. (704) 648-2412.

**CEDAR MOUNTAIN, N.C.** **Noah's Ark,** Dupont Road and Rte. 276, 28718. Crafts, gifts, craft supplies, free instruction. Tues.-Sat. (704) 885-2855.

**CHATSWORTH, GA.** **Fort Mountain Crafts Village,** US-76 east of Chatsworth, on top of Fort Mountain. Pottery, woodcrafts, quilts, macrame and other handmade items. (404) 695-9371.

**CHEROKEE, N.C.** **Saunooke Mill Shops and Village,** US-441 north. A variety of shops. Open daily. (704) 497-9879.

**CLARKESVILLE, GA.** **Mark of the Potter, Inc.,**Soque River, G-197, Rte. 3, 30523. Glen-John La Rowe, Pottery Studio: 30 to 40 craftsmen. Retail price set by craftsmen or joint agreement. Spring to late summer, daily. (404) 947-3440.

**The Market Place,** Beaver Dam Road. Daily. (404) 754-6226.

**The Station,** US-441 (second light). Arts, crafts, gifts; pine furniture featured. (404) 754-6533.

**CLAYTON, GA.** **Country Antiques,** Earl's Circle, P.O. Box 644, 30525. Country antiques. (404) 782-3579.

**Grandma's Country Store and Crafts,** between Appalachian Inn and Green Frog Rink. Consignment items.

**Granny's Hilltop Craft Store,** US-441, 2 mi. south of Clayton. Locally handmade mountain crafts, gifts and toys.

**Mountain Treasures,** US-441, 6 mi. south of Clayton. Crafts: wood, ceramic, crochet, dough art. (404) 782-3260.

**Sheffield's Arts/Crafts,** US-441 and 23. (404) 782-3565.

**The Fence Rail,** corner of Derrick and Church streets. Quilts. (404) 782-3579.

**Savannah Place Shoppes,** E. Savannah Street. A group of shops. The architecture is Williamsburg style with hundreds of flowers. Shops feature art, antiques, books, crafts, clocks and music boxes, custom jewelry, homemade candy, ice cream, cards, collectible dolls, video equipment. There's a delightful place to eat indoors or out on the upper deck.

**CLEVELAND, GA.** **The Chattahoochee Country Store,** public square. Custom-made quilts, meaders pottery.

**CORNELIA, GA.** **The Dandelion Craft Shop,** Yonah Village Shopping Center. (404) 778-1818.

**DAHLONEGA, GA.** **All In Stitches,** Chestatee Village, Shop #2. Quilts and handmade gifts.

**Forrest Hills Studio,** G-52 west. Forrest Hill Mountain Resort. 100-year-old homestead with craftspeople at work. (404) 864-6456.

**Hampton's Forge,** US-19, 2 mi. north of Dahlonega. Custom wrought-iron work, early American design. Mon.-Fri. (404) 864-7393.

**Mrs. Plum's Country Things,** on the Square. (404) 864-2253.

**DILLARD, GA.** **Crafts by Chance,** US-441, Farmer's Market. Quilts, original arts, crafts, wood toys, pottery, instruction. (404) 746-5754.

**Merry Christmas Shop.** Handcrafted items and quilts. (404) 746-5899.

**Mountain Hillbilly Crafts,** NC-106 between Dillard and Highlands. Mon.-Sat.
**Something Else,** US-441. (404) 746-5330.

**DILLSBORO, N.C.   The Old School,** US-441 and US-23, 4 mi. south of Dillsboro.
Shops include Granny Grunt's Antiques, T.B.S. Treasures, Times Past, This 'n' That,
Christmas Shop. Closed Monday. (704) 586-5049.

**Riverwood Shops,** downtown, off US-441. Nancy Tut's Christmas, Riverwood Craft,
Riverwood Pewter, Wellhouse Sandwich Emporium.

**ELLIJAY, GA.   Apple Valley Antiques, Gifts and Country Store,** 19 River Street,
30540. (404) 635-5178.

**The June Bug,** 21 River Street, 30540. Country antiques, American primitives, collectibles, glassware.

**FRANKLIN, N.C.   Blue Ridge Crafts,** NC-19, 3 mi. west of Ghost Town. Handmade
quilts, handmade "Adoption" dolls, large selection of china and ironstone dishes.

**Bulgin Forge,** 319 W. Main Street. Craft shop, blacksmith. Family-owned shop since
1908.

**Heritage Hollow,** 75 Porter Street, 28734. A village of shops. Each shop positioned in
a naturally wooded setting to create a friendly atmosphere. (704) 369-9400.

**Linda's Quilting Cabin,** 75 Porter Street, 28734. Patchwork and quilted items and
supplies. (704) 369-8221.

**Maco Crafts, Inc.,** US-441 south, 28734. See the world's largest quilt. (704)
524-7878.

**Ole Joe Clark's,** Rte. 7, Box 747, US-441 north. Handmade mountain crafts. (704)
369-9930.

**GAINESVILLE, GA.   Carol's Country Cupboard,** Exit 4 off G-365 in College Square
Shopping Center. Antiques, porcelain, pottery, dolls, gifts, pewter, quilts, handcrafted
pine furniture by Red Barn. (404) 352-1405.

**Georgia Craft Galleries, Inc.,** 311 Green Street S., Old City Fire Station. Traditional
and contemporary handcrafted works. (404) 534-4272.

**HELEN, GA.   Chimney Mountain Fiberarts,** G-356, 2 mi. north of Unicoi Park.
Teaching, supplying and promoting spinning and weaving. (404) 878-2851.

**Tekawitha,** Main Street. American Indian handmade works. P.O. Box 338. (404)
878-2938.

**Two Crafty Guys,** Main Street, Lower Mall. Handmade woodcrafts.

**Unicoi Craft Shop,** 1 mi. northwest of Helen via G-356. A well-stocked, high-quality
crafts co-operative in the Unicoi State Park main lodge. Features a wide variety of Appalachian handicrafts. Daily, except last Tues. each month.

**HENDERSONVILLE, N.C.   Martin's Handcrafted Gifts,** 1014 Greenville Highway,
US-25. (704) 692-3685.

**Long Cabin Crafts,** Eco-Village Grounds, US-64. May to October. 50 craftsmen.

**HIGHLANDS, N.C.   Lick Log Mill Store (1851),** 4 mi. west on Dillard Road. Cluster
of quaint, historic buildings at Lick Log Mill. Country-style antiques and reproductions,
baskets and quilts, grist mill, log chapel, covered bridge, cabin. Open daily.

**Mountain Makings,** Franklin Road. Open daily. (704) 526-5910.

**LITTLE SWITZERLAND, N.C.   The Chalet Shopping Plaza,** Blue Ridge Parkway,
milepost 334. (704) 765-2153.

**Toe River Crafts,** NC-80. Area crafts work displayed. Closed Mondays. (704)
675-5446.

**MAGGIE VALLEY, N.C.** Art, Etc., Maggie Valley Shopping Center. Arts and local crafts. (704) 926-0614.

Blue Ridge Crafts of Maggie, Inc., Soco Gap, Rte. 1, Box 557. (704) 926-0123.

Heritage Craft Center, next to Realty World on US-19. Scrimshaw, pottery, weaving, stained glass, painting, sculpture, woodcarving, woodworking.

Maggie Mountaineer Crafts, Box 427, 28751. Crafts, pottery, silk flowers, souvenirs. (704) 926-3129.

Mountain Home Crafts, P.O. Box 776, 28751. Stained glass, Raku, stoneware and porcelain, wood carvings, wooden toys, handwoven articles, scrimshaw, custom orders. (704) 926-0076.

Smoky Mountain Gift and Crafts, Inc., Soco Gap, P.O. Box 427. (704) 926-1138.

Soco Crafts, Soco Gap, US-19. (704) 926-1626.

The Cabin Door, Eagles Shopping Plaza. Handcrafted country furniture, gifts and crafts. (704) 926-3201.

**MARTIN, GA.** Cole's Collectibles, G-17. Antiques and collectibles. (404) 779-3712.

**MORGANTON, GA.** Georgia Mountain Crafts, US-76, P.O. Box 56, 30560. Formerly East Fannin School. (404) 374-5792.

Ann's Antiques 'n' Collectibles, US-76, Rte. 1, Box 247, 30560. Handmade oak rocking chairs, primitives. Open all year. (404) 374-5517.

**MURPHY, N.C.** Carolina Mountain Arts/Crafts, US-64 west, P.O. Box 573. Daily. (704) 644-5688.

**MOUNTAIN CITY, GA.** Log Cabin Crafts, US-441, across from Black Rock State Park Road. Handmade crafts, arts, quilts, wood items, dolls, collectibles. (404) 746-2991.

**PENDLETON, S.C.** The Foothills Arts and Crafts Shop, Hunter's Store. Special art and photo exhibits are displayed here throughout the year.

**RABUN GAP, GA.** Rabun Gap Crafts, US-441 North. 30568. Mountain crafts, weaving, pottery, woodcarvings. Owned by Rabun Gap Nacoochee School. (404) 746-5343.

**SALUDA, N.C.** Bear Creek Country Store, US-176 north.

Dukes' Pottery Workshop, 1 Church Street. Producing functional stoneware pottery. Retail sales. Tues.-Fri. (704) 749-9751.

Green River Gallery, Main Street. A co-operative gallery of area craftsmen presenting outstanding work in traditional and contemporary/original design. Tues.-Sun., May-December. Open weekends, January-April. (704) 749-9740.

Saluda Mountain Crafts, Main Street. More than 150 craftsmen offering a variety of quality items, including rustic pine furniture, woodwork, pottery, toys. Tues.-Sun., May-December. Open weekends, February-April. (704) 749-4341.

Snaggy Hollow Craftsmen, Main Street. Producer of a wide variety of handmade baskets, including planter cover, floral tubes, fern baskets, hand baskets and ovals. Also unique hardwood woven lampshades and swag lamps. Open daily.

The Whistle Stop, Main Street. A unique stop featuring natural sculpture, hand-crafted from native materials of Saluda Mountain, by Ruth Anderson. Roots, knots and burls, combined with mosses, lichens, cones and dried wild plants create dimensional compositions. Also presenting the work of other area craftsmen. Open Tues. - Sat.

**SAUTEE, GA.** Storyland Shop, G-75 (5 mi. north of Cleveland, next to Storyland Park), Rte. 1, Box 262. Imported German pottery, antiques, mountain furniture, woodcrafts. Open daily, May 1 - late October. (404) 865-3613.

**SYLVA, N.C.   The Old School House (1930s),** US-441, Sylva and Franklin. Series of craft shops with resident crafters and antique dealers. Open April-October. (704) 586-8097.

**TOCCOA, GA.   The Country Store,** Town Plaza. Tues.-Sat. (404) 886-9479.
   **The Dandelion Craft Shoppe,** 125 W. Doyle Street. Mon.-Sat. (404) 886-7011.

**TOPTON, N.C.   Country Cousins Crafts,** US-129. Mon.-Sat. (704) 479-8010.

**TRYON, N.C.   Blue Ridge Weavers,** 101 S. Trade Street. Unusual gifts and crafts. (704) 859-9550.
   **Ironhorse Guild,** 409 N. Trade Street. Art and craft supplies, full line of country furniture, American handcrafts, art gallery, quilts, gourmet foods. Open Mon.-Sat. (704) 859-6785.
   **Trade Street Gallery,** P.O. Box 596. Focus on contemporary crafts and fine art; wide variety. Mon.-Sat. (704) 859-5102.
   **Tryon Toy Makers,** S. Trade Street. Specialist in wooden toys and gifts. (704) 859-9550.
   **Valhalla Hand Weavers.** Handweaving and baskets. Open daily. (704) 859-6233.

**WAYNESVILLE, N.C.   Country Chairs and Colonial Crafts.** US-276 south, opposite Camp Hope. Mountain furniture, rockers, swings, hammocks, butcher blocks, solid oak, solid maple, Wilton "pewter," pottery, fine handcrafts. Open Mon.-Sat. (704) 235-8564.
   **The General Store,** 22 Howell Mill Road. An authentic 200-year-old log cabin store filled with antiques, crafts and nostalgia.
   **Harvest Collection,** 104 N. Main Street. Mon.-Sat.
   **Soco Crafts,** 401 Country Club Drive, 28786.
   **Tool Shed,** 1103 N. Main Street. Antiques, primitives, gifts, pottery. (704) 452-5720.
   **Wood 'n' Craft Shop,** 4 mi. south of Waynesville on US-276. Locally handmade woodcraft items, custom furniture, custom cabinets, furniture repair and refinishing. (704) 648-2820.

# Craft Co-ops

**'BOONE, N.C.    Blue Ridge Hearthside Crafts Assoc.**, P.O. Box 1388, 28607. Open daily, April-December; closed Sunday, January-March. (704) 264-9078.

**BRASSTOWN, N.C.    John C. Campbell Folk School**, US-64 east. Artists and craftsmen selected on a juried basis, from traditional to contemporary. (704) 837-2775.

**BRYSON CITY, N.C.    Mountain Skil-Craft**, on the Square. (704) 488-6424.

**BURNSVILLE, N.C.    Laurel Mountain Crafts and Toe River Craftsmen.** Exhibits and sale of local crafts. (704) 682-7527.

**CHEROKEE, N.C.    Qualla Arts and Crafts Mutual**, on NC-441 north, near entrance to *Unto These Hills*, Box 277, 28719. Sculpture, baskets, pottery by Cherokee artists. Open daily, March-December; closed Sundays, January and February. (704) 497-9193.

**CLAYTON, GA.    Rabun Gap Crafts**, Rabun Gap Nacoochee School, 6 mi. north of Clayton on US-441. An outlet for the creative works of students whose specialties are weaving, pottery and woodcarving. Mon.-Sat.

**FRANKLIN, N.C.    Maco Crafts, Inc.**, 3 mi. south of Franklin on US-441. A non-profit organization featuring authentic, locally made mountain crafts and Early American furniture and accessories in walnut and cherry. Quilts, pillows, soft toys, woven placemats and rugs, pine cone crafts, pottery, wall hangings, clocks, stained glass. Maco sponsors craft festivals the third Saturday in June and the second Saturday in October. Mon.-Sat.; open some evenings in the summer. (704) 524-7878.

**LITTLE SWITZERLAND, N.C.    Toe River Craftsmen**, NC-226A. Open summer only. (704) 975-4535.

**MARS HILL, N.C.    The Century Boutique**, log cabin on Mars Hill College campus. Exhibits and sells crafts. (704) 649-3231.

**MURPHY, N.C.    The Carolina Mountain Arts and Crafts Co-operative**, 8 mi. west of Murphy on US-64. A sales outlet for local artists and craftsmen. Demonstrations and workshops. Creations in many media. (704) 389-6661.

# Selected Wood Carvers

**BRASSTOWN, N.C.    Fred G. Smith.** Bowls and trays. Butternut, catalpa, linden, chestnut. (704) 837-2274.

**CLARKESVILLE, GA.    Benny Barrs**, Rte. 3, 30523. Toys, wood mosaics, cars from colored woods. (404) 754-9178.

**CLEVELAND, GA.    Kenneth G. McIntosh**, Rte. 3, Box 322, 30528. Models of tractors, cars; gun racks. Uses mostly fruitwoods. (404) 865-3861.

**DAHLONEGA, GA.    Dorothy Plum**, Box 2068, 30533, shop is on the town square. Apple-head dolls. (404) 864-2253.

**GAINESVILLE, GA. James C. Waldrop**, 5220 Trudy Circle, 30501. Animals, mountain-style people from basswood; also walnut, cherry and buckeye. (404) 536-3962.

**LAKEMONT, GA. Norwood Griffin**, Lake Rabun, Rte. 1, Box 101, 30552. Birds, ducks, quail, nightingales; white and yellow pine. All carvings mounted on wood. (404) 782-3015.

**WARNE, N.C. Ethel Hogsed**, Box 5, 28909. Swans; also ducks, squirrels, rabbits. Butternut, buckeye, wild cherry, basswood, black walnut. (704) 389-8858.

**Sue McClure.** Animals, especially turkeys. Apple, cherry, holly, walnut.

**YOUNG HARRIS, GA. Dexter Dockery**, Rte. 2, Box 66, 30582. Models of animals: owls, geese, wrens, horses, racoons. Butternut, black walnut, cherry, buckeye, linden-wood. (404) 745-6306.

**Jack Hall,** Rte. 2, Box 30, 30582. Carvings range from animals to birth of Christ. Fruitwoods, apple, cherry, walnut, holly, maple, basswood. (404) 379-3486.

# Dancing

Barn raisin's and corn shuckin's are rare these days, but the down home dancing that turned them into social occasions is alive and swinging.

Clogging's clicking rhythms resound in just about every village, hamlet and city in the southern Appalachian Mountains. Folk dancing brought by mountain settlers from England, Ireland, Scotland and Denmark has been revived. And plain old square dancing has been elevated to a complex mental and physical challenge.

Clogging can be found all over the region. The Franklin, N.C., Leaf-Lookers Clogging Competition in October is just one of the countless clogging events held annually. And there is even a Master's Invitational Clogging Hoedown and a State Clogging Festival, both held annually in Georgia.

There are three clogging methods: free style, precision dancing and smooth dancing. Free style and precision clogging feature eight couples dancing with tap shoes. Each dancer performs his or her own style in free-style clogging, while precision cloggers perform the same step throughout the routine. In smooth dancing, couples perform a square dance routine without clogging steps or taps. Clogging is said to be descended from buck dancing, in which dancers perform without partners or taps and hold their bodies erect.

Not to be overlooked, square dancers, too, have organized into dozens of clubs. Even some resorts are devoted to the pleasures of square dancing. Bumper stickers proclaim, "I'd rather be square dancing," in the Blue Ridge area.

Copecrest Square Dance Resort in Dillard, Ga., features top national square dance callers, a comfortable hall, hearty food, square dance workshops and a full dress dance each night. Fontana Village at Fontana Dam, N.C., sponsors ten dance vacations annually and holds a World Clog Dance Competition in October and a square dancing festival in May.

In summer, the Top of Georgia Jamboree enlivens Saturday nights in Dillard with country music, ballads, fast songs, comedy routines and clogging.

Shindig-on-the-Green, held in the summer in Asheville, N.C., is the place to see both square dancing and clogging, and to listen to southern Appalachian ballads. For more than 50 years Asheville has been home of the oldest festival of its kind in the country, the Annual

Mountain Dance and Folk Festival, with lots of smooth clog and buck dancing in August.

Street dances bring out the summer crowds at three North Carolina locales: Lake Lure, Hendersonville and Black Mountain. And Folkmoot USA, in Waynesville, N.C., is a paradise for folk dancing and music fans, who come from all over the world to the two week festival in late July.

The John C. Campbell Folk School in Brasstown, N.C., is also a center for folk dancing, and each year it draws dancers from all over the country for a week in June.

## Clogging

———April———

**TOCCOA, GA. Annual Georgia State Clogging Festival,** Stephens County High School. By S.C. Athletic Boosters Club. Free style, precision, smooth and hoedown. Third week. (404) 886-1228.

———May———

**HELEN, GA. Helen Clogging Convention,** at the Pavilion off G-75. Exhibitions each weekend. Admission. Sat., noon-5 P.M., Sun., noon-7 P.M. (404) 878-2521.

**WALHALLA, S.C. Spring Hoedown,** Oconee State Park. First week. (803) 758-3622.
**Spring Clogging Festival,** Oconee State Park. Second week. (803) 758-3622.
**Clogging Contest.** Walhalla Lions Club. Third week. (803) 638-2727.

———June———

**ASHEVILLE, N.C. Mountain Hoedown,** 20 S. Spruce Street, 28801 (Bill Stanley's Barbecue and Bluegrass). Clogging and dancing. June - August. (704) 253-4871.

**CORNELIA, GA. Dance,** Cornelia Community House. Every Friday night. June - August. (404) 778-4654.

**DILLARD, GA. Top of Georgia Jamboree,** Rabun Gap Community School. Country music and clogging. Weekends late June - early August. (404) 779-2263.

**HIGHLANDS, N.C. Square Dancing and Clogging,** Helen's Barn. Fri. and Sat. nights. June to August. (704) 526-3823.

———July———

**DILLARD, GA. Top of Georgia Jamboree,** Rabun Gap Community School. Country music and clogging. Admission. Weekends. (404) 779-2263.

**MOUNTAIN REST, S.C. Mountain Rest Hillbilly Day,** Mountain Rest Community Club. Clogging, barbecue, country music. First week. (803) 638-6450.

# Dancing

————August————

**ASHEVILLE, N.C.** Annual Mountain Dance and Folk Festival, Civic Center. Traditional mountain string music. First week. (704) 258-5200.

**GAINESVILLE, GA.** Blue Ridge Mountain Clogging Championship, Georgia Mountain Center. Second week. (404) 534-8420.

**CHEROKEE, N.C.** Clogging Festival, Magic Waters Park, US-19. Third week. (704) 497-4311.

————September————

**FONTANA, N.C.** Festival of Champions, Fontana Resort. Clog College. First week. (704) 498-2211.

**Semi-annual Accent on Rounds,** Fontana Resort. Square dancing. First week. Also: Semi-annual Rebel Roundup, second week. (704) 498-2211.

**HELEN, GA.** Oktoberfest. Clogging events throughout festival, with village cloggers. Weekends, September and October. (404) 878-2521.

**WESTMINSTER, S.C.** Apple Festival Cloggers Convention, Chan-Ram Park. First week. (803) 638-9586.

**CHIMNEY ROCK, N.C.** Dance Festival, at the Opry House, Hickory Nut Falls. Fourth week. (704) 625-9611.

————October————

**LAKE LANIER ISLANDS, GA.** Master's Invitational Clogging Hoedown. Early October. (404) 945-6701.

**FONTANA, N.C.** World Clog Dance Competition, Fontana Village Resort, 28733. Second week. (704) 779-1137.

**FRANKLIN, N.C.** Leaf-Lookers Clogging Competition. Second week. (704) 524-3161.

**FONTANA, N.C.** Grand Finals, Festival of Champions Clog Dancing, Fontana Resort, 28733. Third week. (704) 498-2211.

**HELEN, GA.** Mountain Music and Dance, Unicoi State Park. Fourth week. (404) 878-2201.

————November————

**WALHALLA, S.C.** Fall Clogging Festival, Oconee State Park. First week. (803) 758-3622.

*Dancing*
# "Dancin"

————May————

**TRYON, N.C.** N.C. Dance Theater Performance, Fine Arts Center. Second week. (704) 859-5428.

————June————

**LAKE LURE, N.C.** Monday Night Street Dance, Lake Lure Community Building. Street dances every Monday through August. Second week. (704) 625-4614.

**BRASSTOWN, N.C.** Folk Dance Week, John C. Campbell Folk School. Second week. (704) 837-2775.

**BLACK MOUNTAIN, N.C.** Mid-June Street Dance. (704) 669-2300.

————July————

**HENDERSONVILLE, N.C.** Street Dance, Main Street. By Greater Hendersonville Chamber of Commerce. First and second week. (704) 692-1413.

————August————

**ASHEVILLE, N.C.** Annual Mountain Dance and Folk Festival, Civic Center. Oldest in the United States (since 1926). First week. (704) 258-5200.

**WAYNESVILLE, N.C.** Folkmoot USA. Music and folk dancing. Largest international folk dance festival in the United States. First and second weeks. (704) 452-2997.

**BLACK MOUNTAIN, N.C.** Street Dance. Second week. (704) 669-2300.

————September————

**HENDERSONVILLE, N.C.** Carolina Mountain Folk Dance Festival. First week. (704) 692-1413.

## Square Dancing

**BREVARD, N.C.** Rainbow Lake Square Dance Center, E. Fork Road. 3 mi. from Brevard. Family vacation resort catering to Western-style square dancers. Public invited. Weekends throughout the year. (704) 862-4443.

**DILLARD, GA.** Copecrest Square Dance Resort, Betty's Creek Road. Western square dancing. April - October. (404) 746-2134.

Top of Georgia Jamboree, Rabun Gap Community School. Saturday evening dancing. Mid-June to early September. (404) 779-2263.

**MAGGIE VALLEY, N.C.** Maggie Valley Playhouse, US-19. June-August. (704) 926-1864.

## Dancing

——February——

**FONTANA, N.C.** **Fontana Funtime,** Fontana Dam Resort. Mid-February. (704) 498-2211.

——March——

**FONTANA, N.C.** **Fontana Escape,** Fontana Dam Resort. Second weekend. (704) 498-2211.

——April——

**FONTANA, N.C.** **Semi-annual Square Dance Festival,** Fontana Dam Resort. Oldest established western-style square dance. Fourth week. Also first week in May. (704) 498-2211.

**Annual Spring Fling,** Fontana Dam Resort. Square dance festival. Third week. (704) 498-2211.

——May——

**FONTANA, N.C.** **Semi-annual Rebel Roundup Square Dance Festival,** Fontana Resort. Second week. (704) 498-2211.

**WALHALLA, S.C.** **Spring Festival,** Oconee State Park. Second week. (803) 638-5353.

**TABLE ROCK STATE PARK, S.C.** **Spring into Summer.** Afternoon and evening dancing. By Piedmont Callers Assoc. of South Carolina. Second week. (803) 244-1697.

**FONTANA, N.C.** **Semi-annual Accent on Rounds with Squares,** Fontana Dam Resort. Dance festival. Third week. (704) 498-2211.

**MOUNTAIN CITY, GA.** **Wake Robin Western Dance Festival,** Mountain City Playhouse. Fourth week. (404) 746-2134.

**FONTANA, N.C.** **Semi-annual Fun Fest.** Square dance festival. Fourth week. (704) 498-2211.

——July and August——

**ASHEVILLE, N.C.** **Shindig-on-the-Green,** City County Plaza. Square and clog dancing. July and August. (704) 258-5222.

——September——

**FONTANA, N.C.** **Semi-annual Fun Fest.** Fontana Dam Resort. Square dance festival. First week. (704) 498-2211.

**Semi-annual Swap Shop Square Dance Festival.** Third week. (704) 498-2211.

**LAVONIA, GA.** **Square Dance Festival,** Tugaloo State Park. Third week. (404) 356-4362.

**WALHALLA, S.C.** **Fall Festival,** Oconee State Park. Third week. (803) 638-5353.

## Dancing
——October——

**MARS HILL, N.C.** Bascom Lamar Lunsford Mountain Music and Dance Festival, Mars Hill College. Old-time music and dancing. First week.

**ELLIJAY, GA.** Apple Festival Dance, Ellijay Elementary School. First week. (404) 635-7400.

**FONTANA, N.C.** Annual Fall Jubilee. Fontana Dam Resort. Square dance festival. First week. (704) 498-2211.

**TOCCOA, GA.** The Autumn Promenade, Nacoochee gym. Third week. (404) 886-2132.

——November——

**FONTANA, N.C.** Fontana Funtime, Fontana Dam Resort. First weekend. (704) 498-2211.

*For additional information, contact: National Square Dance Directory, P.O. Box 54055, Jackson, Mississippi, 39208. (601) 825-6831.*

# E

## Educational Places and Events

When you've had your fill of the lazy, vacation doldrums, you may want to spend a few hours improving your mind. Opportunities are all around you.

Duke Power Company's Keowee-Toxaway Visitor Center, near Clemson, S.C., takes visitors on an audio-visual walk through the history of energy and into such energy-oriented exhibits as a fission chamber. It is adjacent to the Oconee nuclear station.

Observe nature underground at Linville Caverns between Linville and Marion, N.C. The admission fee entitles you to a tour of the stalactite and stalagmite formations in this cave.

Or, visit a center where scientists work daily, such as Mountain Horticultural Crops Research Station in Fletcher, N.C., Cowetta Hydrologic Laboratory in Franklin, N.C., or Georgia Mountain Branch Experiment Station near Blairsville, Ga. All are studying ways to improve forestry or agriculture, testing plants and animals to see how they fare under a variety of conditions.

At the *Mother Earth News* Eco-Village, near Hendersonville, N.C., mind stretching how-to demonstrations are held on topics such as solar energy, low-cost construction, high-yield gardening, alternative energy systems, beekeeping and log construction.

Budding scientists, ages 6 to 18, will want to check out BIOS, an outdoor school near Robbinsville, N.C., where students stay for three to five days while studying the environment, nature, ecology, archaeology and creatures ranging from organisms to humans.

The Cradle of Forestry in America, operated by the U.S. Forest Service, is a national historic site. It commemorates the beginnings of scientific forestry in this country. Visit the restored and preserved buildings of the Biltmore School of Forestry in the Pisgah National Forest, 5 miles north of Brevard, N.C. See a movie, a logging locomotive and cars and demonstrations of forest management.

For a look at the latest in scientific developments, tour one of NASA's tracking stations at Rosman, N.C., a site selected for its bowl-shaped terrain, which limits radio signal interference.

In Asheville, N.C., learn about the weather from Alaska to Puerto Rico at the National Climatic Center where all U.S. weather records are kept.

————March————

**HELEN, GA.** **Gardening Workshop,** Unicoi State Park.

**SYLVA, N.C.** **Annual Blue Ridge Science Fair.** By Jackson County Schools, grades K-12. First week.

————April————

**HELEN, GA.** **School Days,** Unicoi State Park. Environment Education Center activities. Month of April.

**YOUNG HARRIS, GA.** **Annual Byron H. Reece Memorial Lecture,** Susan B. Harris Chapel, Young Harris College. First week.

————May————

**FRANKLIN, N.C.** **Bartram Day** (honors naturalist William Bartram). Slide lecture at Macon County Library; auto tour through country Bartram explored; hike Bartram Trail (Wayah Bald Mountain). Third week.

————June————

**FLAT ROCK, N.C.** **The World of Carl Sandburg,** Carl Sandburg Home National Historic Site. Mid-June to mid-August. (704) 693-4178.

**HELEN, GA.** **Mountain Living at Unicoi State Park Campground,** 3 mi. north of Helen, on G-356. Demonstrations of old time mountain crafts and chores.

————July————

**FLAT ROCK, N.C.** **Rootabaga Stories,** Carl Sandburg Home National Historic Site. Children's stories adapted to drama. Early July - early August. (704) 693-4178.

**BLAIRSVILLE, GA.** **Horticultural Field Day,** Georgia Mountain Branch Experiment Station. (404) 745-6197.

————October————

**CLEMSON, S.C.** **Clemson Chautauga Cultural Week.** By colleges of Architecture and Liberal Arts. Lectures, musical events, films, plays. Free. First week.

## Educational Places

**ASHEVILLE, N.C.** **National Climatic Center,** Page Street, 28802. (U.S. Dept. of Commerce.) Oversees weather from Alaska to Puerto Rico; custodian of all U.S. weather records, including National Oceanic and Atmospheric Admin., FAA, and the Armed Forces. (704) 254-6283, 259-0682.

**Western North Carolina Nature Center.** Gashes Creek Road. Includes 15 acres of native plants and animals, special natural history exhibits and educational programs. Open year-round. Tues.-Sun.

**BLAIRSVILLE, GA.  Blood Mountain Archeological Area,** US-19 and 129. Off Appalachian Trail. Site of Cherokee and Creek battle.

**Lantern Collection,** Jackson Service Station. Unique display of 124 lanterns, all types and shapes; the largest stands 2 feet, 1 inch tall, and the smallest is only 6 inches tall.

**Georgia Mountain Branch Experiment Station.** US-129. Experiments with mountain crops and vegetations.

**Track Rock Archeological Area,** County Road 95 (Town Creek Road). Preserved petroglyph of ancient Indian rock carvings in a 52-acre site.

**Wolfcreek Wilderness School.** Private, non-profit educational organization emphasizing humanistic approach to outdoor education. Sponsors monthly activities. (404) 745-5789.

**CHEROKEE, N.C.  Indian Museum.** Considered to be the most modern facility of its kind in America today. Open daily. Admission fee. (704) 497-3481.

**CLEMSON, S.C.  Keowee-Toxaway Visitors Center,** on SC-130 near Clemson. Audio-visual tour uses colorful animated displays and exhibits on a trip through history of energy. Daily. Free. (803) 882-5620.

**CULLOWHEE, N.C.  Western Carolina University Mountain Heritage Center.** Promotes mountain culture and history. Programs, activities, information.

**FLETCHER, N.C.  Mountain Horticultural Crops Research Station,** off NC-191. State-operated center (one of three) conducts research related to agricultural problems; develops new strains and techniques. Free tour.

**FRANKLIN, N.C.  Coweeta Hydrologic Laboratory.** A 5,400-acre forest experimental station maintained by the U.S. Forest Service since 1934. Provides valuable studies related to the natural forest soil and water system functions.

**HENDERSONVILLE, N.C.  Eco-Village.** The *Mother Earth News* center on US-64 west. 622 mountain acres. How-to demonstrations that can help you save money on energy, housing, food, transportation and recreation. (704) 693-0211.

**Holmes State Forest,** Crab Creek Road, NC-235. Environmental classroom demonstration. Forest, trails, exhibits, picnic tables. Free.

**HIGHLANDS, N.C.  Highlands Nature Center,** Highlands Biological Research Station, Horse Cove Road ½ mi. east of Highlands. Includes an outstanding collection of Indian artifacts and displays of geology, wildflowers and animals.

**LINVILLE, N.C.  Linville Caverns.** NC-221 between Linville and Marion. Year-round. Stalactite and stalagmite formations. Temperature is a constant 52 degrees. Fee.

**ROBBINSVILLE, N.C.  BIOS.** Outdoor school with courses and experiences in nature appreciation ecological and archaeological studies with emphasis on student involvement; outdoor classroom activities. Ages 6 to 18. April-May; Sept.-Oct. (704) 479-8884.

**ROSMAN, N.C.** **Rosman Tracking Station,** US-64 at Rosman. One of NASA's worldwide network of tracking stations. Group tours Mon.-Fri. (704) 883-8211.

**TALLULAH FALLS, GA.** **Terrora Visitors Center,** US-441. Contains exhibits on the production of electricity. (404) 754-3276.

**TOCCOA, GA.** **Camp Toccoa,** Hodgson Nature Center. 200-acre site with five wooded trails, a pond, three waterfalls and wildlife displays. Available to community groups and individuals. (404) 886-2457.

**WALHALLA, S.C.** **Oconee Nuclear Station,** SC-130. Three generating units; output reaches 2½ million kilowatts. (803) 882-5620.

**YOUNG HARRIS, GA.** **Mountain Regional Library,** US-76. Includes Appalachian archives: books, records, video tapes and periodicals on southern Appalachian way of life. (404) 379-3732.

**Rollins Planetarium,** Young Harris College. Creative star programs on Friday nights. Free. (404) 379-3990.

# F

## Fairs

Looking for something to do that will please the whole family? Try a fair. The Blue Ridge area has plenty of old-fashioned fairs with everything from cattle shows to arts and craft demonstrations and softball tournaments. Of course, modern inventions like the ferris wheel and roller coaster are in abundance, too. Most fairs are held in summer or fall and are sponsored by civic clubs or businesses.

Walk into a fair and your ears will be filled and your spirits lifted with the sounds of country, bluegrass or gospel music. You'll see lots of foot-stompin' and toe tappin', as squeaky clean cloggers swirl in their colorful costumes.

Your taste buds will be tempted with Southern delicacies such as barbecued beef, pork and chicken, hickory-smoked rainbow trout, homemade fudge, corn bread, vegetable soup or freshly churned ice cream. The smell of freshly baked pecan pies, pound cake or blueberry muffins is enough to make any dieter desert his diet for the day.

You may see beautiful woodcrafts, rows of home canned, garden fresh vegetables, stained glass, pottery, needlework, wildflower pictures, cornshuck dolls and more.

The Georgia Mountain Fair, held in early August in Hiawassee, is one of the biggest and most popular. The Pioneer Village includes a replica of an old general store complete with cracker barrels, checkerboard and spittoon; an old mountain home as it would have looked 100 years ago, and a farm museum.

Many fairs are a showcase of talent as craftsmen perform such forgotten arts as moonshine making, corn milling, board splitting, blacksmithing, soap and hominy making, quilting and leatherworking.

———January———

**GAINESVILLE, GA.**  N.C.-Georgia Energy Fair, Georgia Mountain Center. Second week. (404) 274-8560.

———February———

**HELEN, GA.**  Georgia Mountain Turkey Fair, Unicoi State Park. Second week. (404) 878-2201.

Fireside Fair, Unicoi State Park. Third week. (404) 878-2201.

———March———

**GAINESVILLE, GA.**  Gun Fair, Georgia Mountain Center. Second week. (404) 543-8420.

Sports Travel Fair, Georgia Mountain Center. Third week. (404) 534-8420.

# Fairs

## ———April———

**WAYNESVILLE, N.C. Ramp Convention,** American Legion Park. Honors wild mountain vegetable, "ramp." Ramp-eating contest, dancing, folk music. Fourth week. (704) 452-5801.

## ———May———

**LAKE LANIER ISLANDS, GA. Medieval Faire,** off G-347 in southern Hall County. Recreates medieval life; stages tournaments and mock battles. Sat. and Sun. First week. (404) 945-6701.

**BLAIRSVILLE, GA. Mountain Settlers Quilt Fair,** Civic Center. By Union County Historical Society. Third week. (404) 745-5472.

## ———July———

**SAPPHIRE/WHITEWATER, N.C. Country Fair,** Sapphire/Whitewater Community Center, US-64 east. Arts, crafts, flea market, food, plants, produce, games. First week.

**FRANKLIN, N.C. Mountaineer Book Fair,** Macon County Facilities Building. Second week. (704) 524-3600.

**WAYNESVILLE, N.C. Museum Guild's Family Fun Fair,** Museum of North Carolina Handicrafts. Second week. (704) 452-1551.

**ASHEVILLE, N.C. Fair of the Southern Highlands Handicraft Guild,** Civic Center. Over 100 Guild members demonstrate traditional crafts. Entertainment. Third week. (704) 298-7928.

**WAYNESVILLE, N.C. Smoky Mountain Folk Festival,** Waynesville Junior High. Old-time music, contests, crafts, antique fair, black powder shoot. Fourth week.

**'BOONE, N.C. High Country Mountain Fair.** More than 100 activities and events. Fourth week. (704) 264-5731.

**MURPHY, N.C. Annual Cherokee County Fair,** US-129 north. By Murphy Lions Club. Arts, crafts, science, agriculture, entertainment. Since 1917. Fourth week.

## ———August———

**ASHEVILLE, N.C. Antiques Fair,** since 1945, at the Civic Center. By Vetust Study Club, Inc.; 57 exhibitors. Admission. First week. (704) 252-3182 or 254-5400.

**Annual Village Art and Craft Fair,** All Souls Episcopal Church. Arts, crafts, food, music. First week. (704) 274-2831.

**BURNSVILLE, N.C. Mount Mitchell Crafts Fair,** US-19 east, Town Square. Since 1955. Mountain crafts, music, games, clogging, barbecue. Early August. (704) 682-7413.

**HENDERSONVILLE, N.C. Western N.C. Fair,** at the fairgrounds. Annual event. Mid-August.

**HIAWASSEE, GA. Georgia Mountain Fair,** at the fairgrounds on US-76, west of Hiawassee. Show and sale of crafts. Over 40 craftsmen demonstrate. Exhibition of primitive farm tools. Music nightly. Early August. (404) 896-2256.

**BLUE RIDGE, GA. Fannin County Fair.** By Blue Ridge Kiwanis Club. Third week.

**CLARKESVILLE, GA. Chattahoochee Mountain Fair,** at the fairgrounds on G-115, east of Clarkesville. Habersham Chamber of Commerce. More than 60 exhibitors show and sell their arts and crafts. Livestock show, entertainment. Third week. (404) 778-4654.

**MARION, N.C.** McDowell County Fair, at the fairgrounds, 3 mi. south of Marion on NC-226. Late August.

————September————

**BREVARD, N.C.** Transylvania County Fair, Straus Park. Agricultural and industrial exhibits, crafts, art, woodworking, music. First week. (704) 877-4450.

**CLEMSON, S.C.** Getting to Know You Clemson Fair. By Clemson area Newcomers Club. Second week. (803) 654-1200.

**EASLEY, S.C.** Upper South Carolina State Fair, State Fairgrounds. Second week. (803) 269-3061.

**ELLIJAY, GA.** Gilmer County Fair. Second week. (404) 635-7357.

**FRANKLIN, N.C.** Macon County Fair. Second week. (704) 524-2912.

**WESTMINSTER, S.C.** Apple Festival Craft Fair, at depot on Main Street. Barbecue, clogging, races, Apple Queen, dancing, kiddy parade, road races. Second week.

**ASHEVILLE, N.C.** Annual Hey Day Festival, country fair at Western North Carolina Nature Center. Crafts, displays. Third week. (704) 298-5600.

**HENDERSONVILLE, N.C.** Western North Carolina Fair, at the Western North Carolina Fairgrounds, US-176. By American Legion. Fourth week.

————October————

**HARTWELL, GA.** Hart County Fair, Hartwell Fairgrounds. First week. (404) 245-6116.

**ASHEVILLE, N.C.** Carolina Fall Fair, Box 1732, 28802. Second week. (704) 258-5200.

Guild Fair of the Southern Highlands, Civic Center. Crafts by members Southern Highlands Handicraft Guild. P.O. Box 9545, 28805. Second week. (704) 298-7928.

**BREVARD, N.C.** Transylvania County Fire Prevention Fair. By area fire departments. Exhibits, demos, films, classes. Second week.

**SENECA, S.C.** Oconee Country Festival. Second week. (803) 638-5985.

**SAUTEE, GA.** The Country Store Annual Arts and Crafts Fair, Skylake (resort). Third week. (404) 394-3522 or 878-2292.

————November————

**\*HARTWELL, GA.** Town and Country Fair, downtown Hartwell. Third week. (404) 376-3121.

*Although state fairs in the tri-state region are held far from the Blue Ridge Mountains, travelers to and from the mountains might want to visit the N.C. State Fair in Raleigh, (919) 821-7400; the S.C. State Fair in Columbia, (803) 799-3387; and the Georgia State Fair in Macon, (912) 746-7184. All are held the second week in October.*

# Festivals

For more down-home entertainment packed into one place than just about anywhere, head to a mountain festival. You'll find old-fashioned folk dancing, bagpipe playing, buck dancing, clogging, hang-gliding, fiddling, woodcrafting, white-water rafting and good country food.

At Mountain Heritage Day in September in Cullowhee, N.C., you can mingle with the mountain folks. Try your hand at chain sawing, log splitting and tobacco spitting, if you dare. At the Georgia Mountains Jubilee in Gainesville in May, mountaineers demonstrate their skills at making lye soap, hominy, lard candles and other necessities. Franklin, N.C., bills its Festival of Festivals as a showcase of entertainment depicting the heritage and ancestry of the Cherokees, Scots, Germans and Irish who settled in the southern Appalachian Mountains.

Sample plenty of biscuits dripping with syrup at Blairsville, Ga., at the Sorghum Festival in October. Local products are the focus at other festivals such as the Apple Festival in Ellijay, Ga., in October. Visitors can buy apples in any form — jelly, jam, sauce or in bulk. Experience a taste of Bavaria at the various Oktoberfests staged from Helen, Ga., to Maggie Valley, N.C. Celebrate to the oom-pah-pah of German bands, try some polka dancing, then restore your energy with sauerbraten or Wiener Schnitzel.

Scottish kilts are proudly sported at the Annual Grandfather Mountain Highland Games and Gathering of the Scottish Clans in North Carolina. Thousands gather at the spectacular two-day reunion. Scottish traditions — dancing the Highland Fling, bag piping, drumming, and tossing the Sheaf or the 100 pound Caber — alternate with such contemporary contests as the 100 yard dash.

Neighborhood festivals, such as the one held in Atlanta's restored Inman Park in April, focus on tours of historic houses. Entertainment includes a parade and crafts displays.

## Apple Festivals

**ELLIJAY, GA.** Annual Georgia Apple Festival and Crafts Fair, Civic Center on G-5. This festival is timed to coincide with the height of the apple harvest. Fun run, pet parade, antique auto show, bingo, rodeo and moonshine still exhibit. Early October. (404) 635-7400.

**LONG CREEK, S.C.** Annual South Carolina Apple Festival, Westminster and Long Creek. Early September. (803) 647-9709.

*Festivals*

**˙LINCOLNTON, N.C.** Lincoln County Apple Festival. September. (704) 732-3361.

**TALLULAH FALLS, GA.** Apple Festival. September. (704) 754-3276.

**HENDERSONVILLE, N.C.** North Carolina Apple Festival. Early September. (704) 692-1413.

## Country Festivals

**CULLOWHEE, N.C.** Mountain Heritage Day. Belk Building and Intramural Field, Western Carolina University. September. (704) 227-7234.

**GAINESVILLE, GA.** Mountain Jubilee, downtown Gainesville on the Square and in the Georgia Mountain Center. P.O. Box 1061, 30503. May. (404) 534-6080.

**˙BLACKSBURG, S.C.** Pioneer Days, Kings Mountain State Park. For information, contact Program Section, Div. of State Parks, 1205 Pendleton Street, Columbia, S.C., 29201. September. (803) 758-3622.

**LAKE LANIER ISLANDS, GA.** Mountain Do, at Laurel Pavilion. August. (404) 945-6701.

**BURNSVILLE, N.C.** Lumberjack Day, E. Yancey Middle School. Yancey County Chamber of Commerce, 2 Town Square, Rm. 3, 28714. October.

**CANTON, N.C.** Haywood County Farm Festival, Canton Recreation Park. September.

**MOUNTAIN REST, S.C.** Hillbilly Day, Mountain Rest Community Club. July. (803) 638-2038.

**GAINESVILLE, GA.** Georgia Mountain Jubilee, the Georgia Mountain Center. Jubilee, Box 1418, 30503. May. (404) 543-1100.

**BLAIRSVILLE, GA.** Sorghum Festival, downtown, US-76 and US-129. October. (404) 745-4488.

## Scottish Festivals

**˙STONE MOUNTAIN, GA.** Scottish Festival and Highland Games, Georgia's Stone Mountain Park. Mid-October.

**LINVILLE, N.C.** Annual Grandfather Mountain Highland Games and Gathering of the Scottish Clan. July. (704) 387-9283.

**CAESAR'S HEAD STATE PARK, S.C.** Scottish Fling. August. (803) 859-7625.

# Oktoberfests

**HELEN, GA.** **Oktoberfest,** at the Pavilion. Weekends during September and October. (404) 878-2181.

**MAGGIE VALLEY, N.C.** **Oktoberfest,** Ghost Town in the Sky. Weekends during October and November.

**'SPARTANBURG, S.C.** **Oktoberfest,** October. (803) 572-2927.

**WALHALLA, S.C.** **Oktoberfest,** Mid-October. (803) 638-2727.

## Festivals — Month by Month

————January————

**HELEN, GA.** **Fasching Karnival.** Community activities and events. Late January to early March, Fri. and Sat. nights. (404) 878-2181.

————February————

**BEECH MOUNTAIN, N.C.** **Winterfest,** Beech Mountain Resort. First week. (704) 387-2011.

**GAINESVILLE, GA.** **Car Festival,** Georgia Mountain Center. Third week. (404) 534-8420.

————March————

**ASHEVILLE, N.C.** **Mountain Youth Festival,** Civic Center, Haywood Street. By Asheville Jaycees. Fourth week. (704) 258-3858.

**CULLOWHEE, N.C.** **Western Carolina University's Annual Science Festival.** 800 juniors and seniors from 38 schools. Fourth week.

————April————

**CHEROKEE, N.C.** **Ramp Festival,** Cherokee Ceremonial Grounds. First week.

**MOUNTAIN REST, S.C.** **Spring Hoedown,** Oconee State Park. First week.

**PENDLETON, S.C.** **Historic Pendleton Spring Jubilee.** First week. (803) 646-3782.

**YOUNG HARRIS, GA.** **Young Harris Festival.** First week. (404) 379-2222.

**CHEROKEE, N.C.** **Cherokee Ramp Day,** Elementary school on US-441. Second week.

**DAWSONVILLE, GA.** **Mountain Lore and Legends Fair,** Amicalola Falls State Park. Second week. (404) 265-2885.

**WEAVERVILLE, N.C.** **Pioneer Living Day.** Second week. (704) 645-6706.

**HARTWELL, GA.** **Animal Crackers,** Hart State Park. Third week. (404) 376-8756.

**LAKE LANIER ISLANDS, GA.** **Medieval Faire.** Third week. (404) 945-6701.

**ASHEVILLE, N.C.   May Day-Montford Park.** Montford Park Players. Fourth week. (704) 254-4550.

**HELEN, GA.   South Appalachian Spring Rendezvous,** Unicoi State Park. Fourth week. (404) 878-2201, ext. 282.

**RABUN GAP, GA.   Western Day Festival,** Rabun Gap School. Fourth week.

————May————

**ASHEVILLE, N.C.   May Day Celebration,** Montford Park. First week. (704) 258-0710.

**BARNARDSVILLE, N.C.   Annual Ramp Festival,** Big Ivy Community Center, Madison County. First week. (704) 626-2814.

**CLEVELAND, GA.   Mountain Shadows.** Memorial Day Celebration. (404) 865-4742.

**GAINESVILLE, GA.   Georgia Mountain Jubilee,** Georgia Mountain Center. First week. (404) 534-6080 or 534-1160.

**HAYESVILLE, N.C.   Hayesville Folklife Festival,** Hayesville High School. First week. (704) 389-3313.

**HELEN, GA.   Southeastern Frontiersman Rendezvous,** Unicoi State Park. First week. (404) 878-2201.

**SYLVA, N.C.   Sunday in the Park,** Mark Watson Park. First week. (704) 586-6333.

**WAYNESVILLE, N.C.   Ramp Festival.** American Legion Grounds, US-19-23. First week. (704) 456-3021.

**CLARKESVILLE, GA.   Mountain Laurel Festival.** Second week. (404) 778-4654.

**MARION, N.C.   Summerfest,** McDowell Technical College. Second week.

**MURPHY, N.C.   Cherokee Spring Sidewalk Art Festival,** the square. Second week. (704) 837-6822.

**SALEM, S.C.   Salem's Spring Festival,** Tamassee-Salem High School. Second week. (803) 994-2525.

**˙WHITE LAKE, N.C.   White Lake Water Festival.** Second week.

**BLACK MOUNTAIN, N.C.   Black Mountain Spring Festival,** Rockmount Boys Camp. By Grey Eagle and Friends. Third week. (704) 669-2456.

**CLARKESVILLE, GA.   Mountain Laurel Festival.** Third week. (404) 754-2131.

**ELLIJAY, GA.   Coosawattee River Festival,** Lions Club Fairgrounds. Third week. (404) 635-5858.

**HELEN, GA.   Blacksmith Festival,** Unicoi State Park. Third week. (404) 878-2201.
   **Arrival of Spring Celebration,** Helen Pavilion. Weekends. (404) 878-2181.
   **Spring Mountain Festival,** Unicoi State Park. Fourth week. (404) 878-2201.

**LAKE LANIER, GA.   Lake Lanier Festival.** Fourth week. (404) 536-5209.

**ASHEVILLE, N.C.** **High Country Spring Show,** Civic Center. Haywood Street. First week. (704) 258-5200.

**GAINESVILLE, GA.** **Mexican Fiesta Weekend,** Lake Lanier Islands. Early June. (404) 945-6701.

**HELEN, GA.** **Alpine Balloon Festival.** First week. (404) 878-2521.

**WALHALLA, S.C.** **Annual Gateway Festival.** By Chamber of Commerce. First week. (803) 638-2313.

**WAYNESVILLE, N.C.** **Fireman's Day,** Waynesville Recreation Horse Show Grounds. First week. (704) 456-8611.

**BRASSTOWN, N.C.** **John C. Campbell Folk School Folk Festival.** Second and third weeks. (704) 837-2775.

**HELEN, GA.** **Smithcreek Folklife Festival,** Unicoi State Park Lodge. Second week. (404) 878-2201 ext. 283.

**NINETY-SIX, S.C.** **Historical Heritage Days.** Second week. (803) 543-2900.

**BAKERSVILLE, N.C.** **Annual N.C. Rhododendron Festival.** Since 1945. Roan Mountain. Third week.

**·COWPENS, S.C.** **Mighty Moo Festival,** Old Southern Railway Depot. Third week.

**FRANKLIN, N.C.** **Festival of Festivals,** County Recreation Park. Third week. (704) 524-3161.

**ANDREWS, N.C.** **Wagon Train Kick-Off Festival.** Since 1956. Fourth week. (704) 837-2242.

**ASHEVILLE, N.C.** **Ryard Ray Folk Festival,** Civic Center. Fourth week. (704) 258-3858.

**DILLARD, GA.** **Top of Georgia Jamboree,** Dillard Community School Auditorium. Third and fourth weeks. (404) 779-2263.

**HARTWELL, GA.** **Pre-Fourth Extravaganza,** town square. All-day festivities. Fourth week.

**ROBBINSVILLE, N.C.** **Great Smoky Mountain Heritage Festival.** Fourth week. (704) 479-3250.

——July——

**ASHEVILLE, N.C.** **Shindig-on-the-Green,** City-County Square. Month of July. (704) 258-5200.

**BLAIRSVILLE, GA.** **July Extravaganza** (Family Day Celebration), Fort Sorghum. By Chamber of Commerce. First week. (404) 745-5789.

**FRANKLIN, N.C.** **Lotus Blossom Festival.** First week. (704) 524-3161.

**HAYESVILLE, N.C.** Festival on the Square, Courthouse Square. First week. (704) 389-6814.

**MOUNTAIN REST, S.C.** Mountain Rest Hillbilly Day. First week. (803) 638-5251.

**BEECH MOUNTAIN, N.C.** Great Garbage Day. Second week. (704) 387-9283.

**CHATSWORTH, GA.** Appalachian Wagon Train. Ten days of activities. Second week. (404) 695-6060.

**LINVILLE, N.C.** Grandfather Mountain Highland Games and Gathering of Scottish Clans. Second week. (704) 898-4720 or 733-2013.

**SALUDA, N.C.** Coon Dog Day. Old-fashioned festival. Second week. (704) 749-2231.

**BEECH MOUNTAIN, N.C.** Appalachian Folklife Festival. Third week. (704) 387-9283.

**ASHEVILLE, N.C.** Bele Chere Festival, downtown. Fourth week. (704) 255-5264.

**CHEROKEE, N.C.** Cherokee Indian Jamboree, ceremonial grounds. Fourth week. (704) 497-3157.

**FRANKLIN, N.C.** Annual Macon County Gemboree, Macon County Fairgrounds. Fourth week. (704) 524-3161.

**GAINESVILLE, GA.** Mountain Food Festival, Georgia Mountain Center. Fourth week. (404) 534-8420.

**HIGHLANDS, N.C.** Highlands-Cashiers Hospital Bazaar, high school gym. By Hospital Auxiliary. Fourth week.

**NEWLAND, N.C.** On The Square Festival. Fourth week. (704) 733-2919.

**PICKENS, S.C.** Pickens Summer Celebration. By Pickens Jaycees. Fourth week. (803) 878-6625.

**WAYNESVILLE, N.C.** Smoky Mountain Folk Festival. Fourth week. (704) 456-6834.

## Festivals

**ASHEVILLE, N.C.**   Shindig-on-the-Green, City-County Plaza. (704) 258-5200.

**BEECH MOUNTAIN, N.C.**   July 4th Celebration. (704) 387-9283.

**BLAIRSVILLE, GA.**   July Extravaganza and Family Fun Day. (404) 745-5789.

**BRYSON CITY, N.C.**   Festival on the Square, Courthouse Lawn. (704) 488-3681.

**BUFORD, GA.**   Great American Escape, Lake Lanier Islands. (404) 945-6701.

**CASHIERS, N.C.**   July 4th Celebration, Fairfield Sapphire Valley. By Cashiers Community.

**CLAYTON, GA.**   July 4th, By Chamber of Commerce. (404) 782-4812.

**CLEVELAND, GA.**   White County Celebration, Nacoochee Gymnasium. By White County Parks and Recreation Dept. and Sautee-Nacoochee Community Assoc. (404) 865-5275 or 878-2491.

**CUMMING, GA.**   Festival in the Park. (404) 887-5655.

**DAHLONEGA, GA.**   Fourth of July Celebration, downtown square. (404) 864-3711.

**DAWSONVILLE, GA.**   Annual Independence Day Mountain Rendezvous, Amicalola Falls State Park. (404) 265-2885.

**FONTANA, N.C.**   4th of July Celebration. (704) 498-2211.

**FRANKLIN, N.C.**   Jaycees Fun Day, Macon County Recreation Park. (704) 524-5044.

**GAINESVILLE, GA.**   Music in the Park. (404) 534-2787.

**\*GREENVILLE, S.C.**   Freedom Weekend Aloft, Donald Center. By Chamber of Commerce. (803) 242-1050.

**HAZELWOOD, N.C.**   4th of July Celebration.

**HELEN, GA.**   Old Fashioned July 4th Celebration, Helen Pavilion, Main Street. (404) 878-2181.

**HENDERSONVILLE, N.C.**   Fabulous 4th Celebration, Jackson Park, Glover Street off US-176. By Rotary Club. (704) 693-4820.

**HIGHLANDS, N.C.**   Barbecue, Community Building. By Rotary Club. (704) 526-2112.

**LAKE LANIER ISLANDS, GA.**   Great American Escape. (404) 945-6701.

**MOUNTAIN REST, S.C.**   Hillbilly Day, Community Club. (803) 638-6450.

**MURPHY, N.C.**   Piper Art and Craft Show, Pied Piper Camp Resort on US-64, 12 mi. west of town. (704) 644-5771 or 632-2144.

**NEWLAND, N.C.**   On the Square Festival. (704) 733-2919.

**RABUN GAP, GA.**   Spirit of America Celebration, Hambidge Center. (404) 746-5718.

**ROBBINSVILLE, N.C.**   Great Smoky Mountains Heritage Festival. (704) 479-3790.

**TALLULAH FALLS, GA.** July 4th Terrora Park, US-441 and 23. (404) 754-6036.

**YOUNG HARRIS, GA.** July 4th Barbecue. By Volunteer Fire Dept.

————August————

**ASHEVILLE, N.C.** Annual Mountain Dance and Folk Festival. Oldest in the United States. Since 1926. First week. (704) 258-5200.

**BLACK MOUNTAIN, N.C.** Annual Sourwood Festival. First week. (704) 669-2300.

**CENTRAL, S.C.** Hillbilly Day. By Central Hillbilly Club. First week.

**DILLARD, GA.** Top of Georgia Jamboree, Rabun Gap Community School. Month of August. (404) 779-2263.

**MAGGIE VALLEY, N.C.** International Folk Festival. First week. (704) 456-7392.

**MOUNTAIN CITY, GA.** MountainLore and Legends, Black Rock Mountain State Park. First week. (404) 746-2141.

**SWANNANOA, N.C.** Swannanoa Valley Sourwood Festival. First week. (704) 669-2300.

**WAYNESVILLE, N.C.** Folkmoot Festival USA. First and second weeks. (704) 452-2997.

**ASHEVILLE, N.C.** Bele Chere Street Festival, Haywood, Church and Lexington Park. Second week. (704) 255-5264.

**CASHIERS, N.C.** Pioneer Day. Second week. (704) 743-5191.

**FRANKLIN, N.C.** Jaycee's Folk Festival, Franklin High School. Second week. (704) 524-6421.

**ASHEVILLE, N.C.** High Country Summerfest, Civic Center, Haywood Street. Third week. (704) 253-6893.

**BREVARD, N.C.** Byard Ray Folk Festival. Third week. (704) 884-3628.

**BUFORD, GA.** Mountain Do, Lake Lanier Islands. Third week. (404) 945-6701.

**HELEN, GA.** Georgia Mountain Eatin's and Squeezin's, Unicoi State Park. Third week. (404) 878-2201.

**HENDERSONVILLE, N.C.** Annual N.C. Apple Festival. Third and fourth weeks. (704) 693-6336.

————September————

**ASHEVILLE, N.C.** Shindig-on-the-Green, City-County Plaza, Patton Street. First week. (704) 258-5200.

**CANTON, N.C.** Labor Day Celebration. First week. (704) 648-3742.

**FRANKLIN, N.C.** Jaycee Folk Festival, Franklin Fine Arts Center. First week. (704) 524-0421.

**RABUN GAP, GA.** Folk Festival, Hambidge Center, Bettys Creek Road. First week. (404) 746-5718.

**CANTON, N.C.** Annual Farm Festival, Canton Armory. Second week. (704) 648-3742.

**HELEN, GA.** Alpine Helen Oktoberfest. Mid-September to mid-October. (404) 878-2521 or 878-2181.

**WAYNESVILLE, N.C.** Mountain Magic. Second week. (704) 456-3021.

**CUMMING, GA.** Falling Leaves Festival, Village Shopping Center, 1 mi. south of town on US-19. Third week. (404) 887-6925 or 887-6168.

**LAKE LANIER, GA.** Indian Summerfest. Third week. (404) 945-6701.

**MAGGIE VALLEY, N.C.** Octoberfest. Third and fourth weeks. (704) 926-1686.

**WEAVERVILLE, N.C.** Pioneer Day, Reems Creek Road at Zebulon Vance Home. Third week.

**ASHEVILLE, N.C.** Hey Day Festival, Western North Carolina Nature Center. Fourth week. (704) 667-6929.
  River Week Festival. By Land of Sky Regional Council, P.O. Box 2175, 28802. Fourth week. (704) 254-8131.

**BUFORD, GA.** Indian Summerfest, Lake Lanier Islands. Fourth week. (404) 945-6701.

**CLEMSON, S.C.** Fall Festival, Y Beach. By Helping Hands of Clemson. Fourth week. (803) 654-1200.

**CULLOWHEE, N.C.** Mountain Heritage Day, Western North Carolina University. Fourth week. (704) 227-7234.

**˙KINGS MOUNTAIN, N.C.** Pioneer Days, Kings Mountain State Park. Fourth week. (704) 758-3622.

**MURPHY, N.C.** Fall Fun Fair, Pied Piper Camp, US-64. Fourth week. (704) 644-5771.

**SUCHES, GA.** Indian Summer Festival, Woody Gap School. Fourth week.

**WAYNESVILLE, N.C.** Haywood County Farm Festival. Fourth week.
  Mountain Magic, Lake Junaluska Assembly Grounds. Fourth week.

**˙TURTLETOWN, TENN.** Turtletown-Farmer Fall Festival, TN-68. Fourth week.

––––October––––

**ASHEVILLE, N.C.** Hallelujah Asheville Festival, downtown. Month of October. (704) 254-1776.

**BEECH MOUNTAIN, N.C.** Oktoberfest. First week. (704) 387-2011.

**BLAIRSVILLE, GA.** Sorghum Festival, Fort Sorghum. First three weekends. (404) 745-5789.

**BRASSTOWN, N.C.** Folk School Fall Festival, John C. Campbell Folk School. First week. (704) 837-2775.

**CHEROKEE, N.C.** **Cherokee Fall Festival.** First week. (704) 497-3157.

**CLAYTON, GA.** **Fall Festival,** Clayton Elementary School. By Clayton PTO. First week.

**CLEMSON, S.C.** **Helping Hands Fall Festival,** Y Beach. By Helping Hands of Clemson, Inc. First week. (803) 654-2733.

**GAINESVILLE, GA.** **Harvest Festival.** First week. (404) 532-4313.

**HARTWELL, GA.** **Heart to Hart Festival,** Hart State Park. First week. (404) 376-8756.

**HAYESVILLE, N.C.** **Fall Festival,** Community Service Building. By Clay County Extension Homemakers. First week. (704) 389-8407 or 6301.

**JASPER, GA.** **Pickens County Marble Festival.** First week. (404) 692-5100 or 5600.

**MARION, N.C.** **Western North Carolina Pioneer Arts Festival,** Carson House at Pleasant Gardens, US-70. First week. (704) 652-7502.

**MARS HILL, N.C.** **Lunsford Festival,** Mars Hill College campus. First week. (704) 689-1217.

**PUMPKINTOWN, S.C.** **Annual Pumpkin Festival.** By Volunteer Fire Dept. First week. (803) 878-3258.

**SUCHES, GA.** **Indian Summer Festival,** Woody Gap School. First week. (404) 747-3852 or 3169.

**WAYNESVILLE, N.C.** **Mountain Magic,** Lake Junaluska. First week. (704) 456-3021.

**BURNSVILLE, N.C.** **Lumberjack Day,** E. Yancey Middle School. Second week. (704) 682-7413.

**CHEROKEE, N.C.** **Harvest Festival,** Santa's Land, US-19. Second week. (704) 497-9191.

**CLEVELAND, GA.** **Fall Leaf Festival,** Everhart Kiwanis Park. Last three weekends. (404) 865-2487.

**DILLARD, GA.** **Harvest Festival,** Old Farmer's Market. Second and third weeks. (404) 746-2537.

**DAHLONEGA, GA.** **Gold Rush Days,** Town Square. Second and third weeks. (404) 864-2531.

**GAINESVILLE, GA.** **Harvest Curb Market,** Washington and Green streets. Second week. (404) 532-4313.

**JASPER, GA.** **Georgia Marble Festival.** Second, third and fourth weeks. (404) 692-2531.

**BLUE RIDGE, GA.** **Mountain Harvest Sale,** US-76. Third and fourth weeks. (404) 632-5223.

**LAVONIA, GA.** **Harvest Festival,** Tugaloo State Park. Third week. (404) 356-4362.
  **Gum Log Cider Squeezin' and Dancin' Day,** Tugaloo State Park. Fourth week. (404) 356-4362.

**BLAIRSVILLE, GA.** **Appalachian Autumn Festival,** Vogel State Park. Fourth week. (404) 745-5789.

**TOCCOA, GA.** **Harvest Festival,** downtown Toccoa on the Mall. By Downtown Merchants Assoc. Fourth week. (404) 886-2132.

————November————

**CHEROKEE, N.C.** **Festival of Champions,** Qually Civic Center. First week. (704) 497-9195.

**CLAYTON, GA.** **Harvest Moon Festival,** Dillard Open Air Market. By Clayton Junior Woman's Club. First week. (404) 782-2510 or 2700.

**CUMMING, GA.** **Great Chicken House Festival.** First and second weeks. (404) 877-1702.

**TOCCOA, GA.** **Annual Harvest Festival.** See listing under October.

**HENDERSONVILLE, N.C.** **Holiday Festival.** By Garden Club of Hendersonville. Second week. (704) 692-1413.

**SENECA, S.C.** **Fall Bazaar,** Episcopal Church of the Ascension, Second and Townville streets. Second week. (803) 882-2097.

**BANNER ELK, N.C.** **Woolly Worm Festival.** Third week. From North Carolina, 1 (800) 222-7515; from the eastern United States, 1 (800) 438-7500.

**HARTWELL, GA.** **Town and Country Festival,** Downtown Hart County Farm Bureau. Third week. (404) 376-3121.

**TOCCOA, GA.** **Holiday Craft Festival,** By Student/Faculty Wives of David Owens Student Center, Toccoa Falls College. Third week.

**CORNELIA, CLARKESVILLE, DEMOREST, GA.** **Hills of Habersham Holidays Festivities,** Cornelia Railroad Depot; Clarkesville Courthouse Square; Demorest Square and Park. Last three days of November. (404) 778-4654.

**FONTANA, N.C.** **Annual Thanksgiving Weekend.** Fourth week. (404) 498-2211.

**GAINESVILLE, GA.** **Thanksgiving-Christmas Show,** Civic Center. By Parks and Recreation Dept. Fourth week. (404) 532-6122.

# Fishing

Whether you prefer wading among the boulders in an ice-cold mountain stream or casting your line from the shore of a stocked pool, bass, bream, crappie, trout and other tasty Southern fish are to be caught in the Blue Ridge area.

The best fishing for game fish is from March through May. The heat of summer slows it down, but fishing improves in September and October. Trout season begins in March or April and ends in September or October with special opening and closing dates in the Wildlife Management areas and Smoky Mountains National Park. All other species are fair game any season. Winter fishing may appeal to the hardy at spots such as Lake Blue Ridge in North Georgia.

For guaranteed fishing, try the various private fish ponds open to the public. Anglers pay only for what they catch. No license or stamps are needed. Catch all the fish you want and have them cleaned.

## Fishing Events

————March————

**BLAIRSVILLE, GA.** **Striper Tournament**, US-19/129 north. By Lynn's General Store. Mid-March through April 30.

**FONTANA, N.C.** **Annual Bass Tournament.** Cash prizes. Fourth week.

————April————

**'BLOWING ROCK, N.C.** **Trout Derby,** for largest trout caught. Any public stream or lake in northwest North Carolina. First week.

**HELEN, GA.** **Helen Fish Fry,** Helen Pavilion. Country music. Fourth week.

**MOCCASIN CREEK STATE PARK, GA.** **All About Mountain Trout.** 8:00 A.M., Fish contest. 10:00 A.M., Lake Burton Fish Hatchery Tour. 2:00 P.M., demonstrations. 7:30 P.M., trout movie. Fourth week.

**HELEN, GA.** **Chattahoochee Trout Festival.** Daily competition, prizes for longest catch. Helen Chamber of Commerce on Chattahoochee Street. Fourth week in April to first week in May.

**CHEROKEE, N.C.** **Cherokee Trout Rodeo,** ceremonial grounds. Cherokee Merchants Assoc., Box 465, 28719. First week.

————May————

**HIAWASSEE, GA.** **Carp Rodeo,** Lake Chatuge. Second week.

**BUFORD, GA.** **Chunkin' and Windin' Bass Tournament,** Lake Lanier Islands. Third week.

**HELEN, GA.** Trout Fishing Weekend, at Unicoi State Park. Third week.

**HIAWASSEE, GA.** Georgia Carp Rodeo, Lake Chatuge. By Georgia Mountain Fair, Towns County Lions, Clay County Lions. Third week.

**BLAIRSVILLE, GA.** Mountain Trout Festival. By American Legion Post 121, Fort Sorghum. Fourth week.

**TRYON, N.C.** Trout Fishing Weekend. Fourth week.

————June————

**LAKE LANIER ISLANDS, GA.** Fishing Derby, Lake Lanier Islands, Buford. First week.

**GAINESVILLE, GA.** Fishing Derby/Great Outdoor Show, Lake Lanier Islands. Second week.

**BUFORD, GA.** WPLO's Fishing Derby. Open for professionals and amateurs. Prizes include boats and cash. Third and fourth weeks.

————September————

**SENECA, S.C.** Apple Festival Bass Tournament, South Cove Park, Lake Keowee. Second week.

## Fish Hatcheries

**BALSAM, N.C.** State Trout Hatchery, US-19 and 23A, near Balsam Mountain. Open daily.

**BREVARD, N.C.** Pisgah National Forest Fish Hatchery, P.O. Box 153, Pisgah Forest, N.C. 28768; west of Brevard on the Davidson River, off US-276. Operated by the U.S. Fish and Wildlife Service. One of the largest trout hatcheries in the East. Visitors welcome. Daily, including Sundays and holidays. (704) 877-3121.

**'COHUTTA, GA.** Cohutta National Fish Hatchery, P.O. Box 48, 30710; in the Chattahoochee National Forest, about 15 mi. north of Dalton. Established 1936. (404) 694-3451.

**LAKE BURTON, GA.** Georgia State Fish Hatchery, on G-197 north, at Lake Burton.

**MARION, N.C.** McDowell County: Armstrong Fish Hatchery, off 226-A. Open to the public every day. **Marion Fish Hatchery,** off Hankins Road, is open October-May for group tours, by appt. only. (704) 746-4179 or (704) 652-4040.

**SUCHES, GA.** Chattahoochee Forest National Fish Hatchery, at nearby Frank Gross Campground. Raises approximately 850,000 rainbow trout for stocking into the tailwaters, streams and lakes of northern Georgia. (404) 838-4753.

**SYLVA, N.C.** **Fish Hatchery,** junction of Parkway and US-19A/23.

**WALHALLA, S.C.** **Walhalla National Fish Hatchery,** north of town on SC-28, then right on SC-107, approx. 11 mi.; follow signs. Raises more than a million rainbow, brook and brown trout. (803) 638-2866.

# Fish Ponds

*(See also Lakes section.)*

**ALMOND, N.C.** **Panther Creek Campground and Trout Farm,** Panther Creek Road, Box 52, 28702. Reservations. (704) 479-6109.

**BALSAM GROVE, N.C.** **McCall's Trout Pond,** near Wood Church. Rainbow trout by the pound.
   **North Fork Trout Farm,** near post office. Campground nearby.
   **Zeigler Trout Farm,** at Cathy's Creek.

**BLAIRSVILLE, GA.** **Goose Creek,** Rte. US-129 and 19, north of Vogel State Park. Rainbow trout pond. (404) 745-5111.

**BUFORD, GA.** **Double B Trout Ranch,** G-347, Lake Lanier Islands. March 1-Oct. 15. (404) 945-3840.
   **Rainbow Ranch,** G-20, 5 mi. east of G-400. Claims to be the biggest Georgia public trout fishing pond. Open daily. (404) 887-4797.

**BREVARD, N.C.** **Silver Creek Trout Farm,** Asheville Highway (Little Mountain). No limit catch.

**CASHIERS, N.C.** **Scotsman Creek Trout Farm,** Bull Pen Road, NC-63, Box 106B, 28717. (704) 743-3398.

**CHEROKEE, N.C.** **Cherokee Trout Farm,** 10 mi. north of Cherokee. On Big Cove Road; follow signs. No license, no limit, open daily, daylight to dark. (704) 497-9227.
   **Trout Fishing,** Cherokee Indian reservation. Fish and Game Management. Enterprise, Box 302, 28719. (704) 497-5201.

**DILLARD, GA.** **Copecrest Trout Farm and Square Dance Resort,** Betty's Creek Road, 5 mi. west of US-441. (404) 746-2134.

**ELLIJAY, GA.** **Logan's Trout Pond,** off US-76 (Boardtown Road). March to mid-November. (404) 635-2828.

**FRANKLIN, N.C.** **Holland Trout Farm,** 6 mi. east of US-64 (Highlands Road). Turn at Old Corundum Campground. No catch, no pay. Closed Sunday. (704) 524-4224.

**HELEN, GA.** **Alpine Valley Fish Pond,** G-17, 2½ mi. north of Helen. Only pay when you catch.

**HIAWASSEE, GA.** Bradley's Trout Pond. US-76 and G-17 and 75. Ten ponds. April-October (404) 896-2778.

   **Dyer's Trout Farm,** off G-17 and 75. (404) 896-2345.

   **Eagle Mountain Trout Farm,** off G-75. (404) 896-2823.

**MARION, N.C.** Elliots Fish Pond, north of Marion, NC-221.

**LAKE BURTON, GA.** La Prade's Fish Camp, on G-197. Built in 1916; 21 rustic cabins. April-Dec. 1. Serves Southern food, family style.

**LAKEMONT, GA.** Dad's Creek Trout Pond, south of Lake Burton Dam. Daylight to darkness, weekends only, November-March. (404) 782-4935.

**LINVILLE, N.C.** Grandfather Trout Ponds, NC-105, Watauga River. May-October.

**RABUN GAP, GA.** Moon Valley Trout Pond, Betty's Creek Road, Box 680, Rte. 1. (404) 746-2466.

**SUCHES, GA.** Gooch's Trout Pond, G-60, 15 mi. north of Suches. All year from sunup to sundown. (404) 838-4734.

**WAYNESVILLE, N.C.** Rainbow Park, 4 mi. west of Waynesville, NC-19A-23. Mon.-Sat., all day; Sunday afternoon. (704) 452-5249.

**TOPTON, N.C.** Fish Pond in Nantahala Gorge, US-19/129.

## Resources:

*Georgia Department of Natural Resources*
*270 Washington Street SW*
*Atlanta, Georgia 30334*

*N.C. Wildlife Resources Commission*
*512 N. Salisbury Street*
*Raleigh, N.C. 27611*

*S.C. Wildlife and Marine Resources Dept.*
*Box 167*
*Columbia, S.C. 29202*

# Flea Markets and Farmer's Markets

There is no better way to soak in some true local color than to spend a few hours at a farmer's market or flea market. Both are plentiful as apple pies in the Carolinas and Georgia.

What you won't find in farmer's markets are plastic-covered vegetables or "no-squeezing" signs. Farmers, who are making higher profits than if they sold to a wholesaler and generally enjoying their role as merchants, are usually bursting with goodwill. They take pride in those pole beans.

The Biltmore Country Market in Asheville, N.C., about a mile and a half south of the Biltmore Estate, is something out of the ordinary. Four gardens — vegetable, herb, perennial and wildflower — are open for touring, free of charge. The market, begun in 1927 so mountain people would have a place to sell vegetables, crafts and baked goods, has a crafts shop and a knit shop. Mountain people still sell produce on summer market days and evergreen boughs at Christmas.

Another sort of colorful, crazy gathering is the flea market. You never know what you might discover while rummaging through acres of boxes, tables and booths where sellers wait to unload their wares. It's a holdover from the days when all purchases were made at the town market with lots of haggling, bargaining and visiting.

## Farmer's Markets

**ANDERSON, S.C.** **Anderson Jockey Lot and Farmer's Market,** SC-29, 8 mi. northeast of Anderson. Biggest in the South: 2,000 dealers. Weekly. (803) 224-2027.

**ASHEVILLE, N.C.** **Farmer's Market,** easy access from I-40 and I-26. One of the most modern, best-planned markets in the country. Open year round. (704) 253-1691.

**Tailgate Market,** Northland Shopping Center, Merrimon Avenue. Sat. and Wed. mornings.

**Western N.C. Farmer's Market,** 570 Brevard Road. One of the busiest in the Southeast. Fruits, vegetables, crafts.

**BALDWIN, GA.** **Jaemor Farm Market,** G-365. Large peach orchard.

**BLAIRSVILLE, GA.** **Pappy's Market Place,** US-19/129, south of Blairsville. Open every weekend.

**Town and Country Farmer's Market,** US-129 south. Open daily. (404) 745-4230.

**BLUE RIDGE, GA.** **Georgia Farmer's Market,** US-76. (404) 632-5273.

**BREVARD, N.C.** **Transylvania County Fresh Fruit and Vegetable Market,** Citizens Telephone Co. parking lot at Jordan and Johnson streets. Open early July to mid-August. Tues., Thurs. and Sat. mornings. (704) 884-2112.

**CLAYTON, GA.** **Rabun Farmer's Market,** County Courthouse Square. Beginning mid-July. (404) 782-3113.

**CULLOWHEE, N.C.** Jackson County Farmer's Market, NC-107 and Long Branch Road. Opens in late June. Sat. morning; Tues. evening. (704) 293-3423.

**HENDERSONVILLE, N.C.** Henderson County Farmer's Mutual Curb Market, 221 N. Church Street. Home grown vegetables and mountain crafts. Market has been held for more than 50 years. Tues., Thurs. and Sat. mornings. April-December.

**MARION, N.C.** Farmer's Market.Fresh produce grown and sold by farmers. Sat. morning.

**MURPHY, N.C.** Murphy Farmer's Market, US-64 west. Selling produce and livestock; auctions.

**SENECA, S.C.** Farmer's Market. Tues. and Sat.

**WALHALLA, S.C.** Sunken Springs Apple and Berry Farm, SC-11, Box 368, Route 2. (803) 944-1048.

**WESTMINSTER, S.C.** Farmer's Market.Thurs.

## Flea Markets

**˙ANDERSON, S.C.** Anderson Jockey Lot and Farmer's Market, SC-29. Largest in the Southeast. (803) 224-2027.

**ASHEVILLE, N.C.** Dreamland Drive-In, Swannanoa River Road. Western North Carolina's largest. Fri., Sat. and Sun. (704) 255-7777.

**BLAIRSVILLE, GA.** Pappy's Flea Market, US-19/129 south. Fri., Sat., Sun. afternoons. Sell, buy, trade. (404) 745-9129.

Town Creek Market Place, Old Town Creek School Building. Auction, Fridays. (404) 745-9434.

**BREVARD, N.C.** Flea Market, Top of the Falls Restaurant parking lot, 6 mi. south of Brevard, US-276. By Connestee Falls Volunteer Fire Dept. End of April.

**BREVARD, N.C.** Rosman Highway Flea Market, Antique Auction., 1½ mi. west of Brevard, US-64. (704) 883-2899.

**CHEROKEE, N.C.** Cherokee Flea Market, US-441. Auction every Saturday at 2 P.M. (704) 586-8188.

**CLEMSON, S.C.** Auction-Flea Market, YMCA Barn. End of October. (803) 654-4942 or 654-5961.

**CLEVELAND, GA.** Cleveland Valley Flea Market and Auction, 4 mi. east of Cleveland on G-115. Dawn till dark; later on auction nights. (404) 865-2709.

**DILLARD, GA.** Mountain Made, US-441, Box 99, 30537. Jewelry, gemstones, quilts, treasures, collectibles. (404) 746-5754.

**FRANKLIN, N.C.** Franklin Flea, Craft and Farmer's Market. Eleven stores; booths. Open Fri., Sat., Sun. April-November (704) 524-6671.

**GAINESVILLE, GA.** Flea Market, Mule Camp Trade Days, Gainesville Fairgrounds, 6 mi. south of Gainesville, G-135. Every third weekend. (404) 536-8068.

**HELEN, GA.** Alpine Valley Complex, ½ mi. north of Helen, G-75. 200 stalls. Open daily. (404) 878-2803.

**HIAWASSEE, GA.** **Giant Flea Market,** at Bald Mountain Park. Labor Day weekend. (404) 896-2274.

**HIGHLANDS, N.C.** **Highlands Lions Flea Market,** Community Building. Third week in August.

**HOLLYWOOD, GA.** **North 441 Flea Market/Produce,** north of G-17 and US-441 intersection. All day, every day.

**LAKE RABUN, GA.** **Lake Rabun Flea Market,** Hall's Boat House. By Lake Rabun Assoc. and Lakemont-Wiley Volunteer Fire Dept. (404) 782-3684 or 782-4050.

**MARION, N.C.** **Johnny's Trade Lot,** north of town. **Marion's Trade Lot,** south of town. NC-221.

**MURPHY, N.C.** **Murphy Flea Market,** US-64, first traffic light entering town, or last light going west. Tues. and Sat.

**ROSMAN, N.C.** **Rosman Highway Flea Market,** NC-64. Thurs. thru Sun. 9 - 5. Auction Sat. nights. (704) 883-2899.

**SENECA, S.C.** **Oconee County Humane Society Yard Sale,** Keowee Village Shopping Center. Third week in November (803) 882-7689.

**SUCHES, GA.** **Tailgate Market.** Fresh produce; arts and crafts. Summer. (404) 747-3172.

**SYLVA, N.C.** **Gateway Flea Market,** US-19A and 441. Mon.-Fri.; dancing, Sat. nights. (704) 497-9664.
   **441 Flea Market,** US-441. Fresh produce. Daily.

**TOCCOA, GA.** **Flea Market and Chickenque,** Martin Community Center. By Martin's Women's Club and Lions Club. First week in October.
   **Falls Road Flea Market,** Falls Road, G-17 north next to Golden Pantry. Every Fri. and Sat. (404) 886-4651.

**WALHALLA, S.C.** **Walhalla Flea Market/Auction.** Tues.-Sat., all day; Sun. afternoon. (803) 638-2052.

**WAYNESVILLE, N.C.** **Rag Mill Mall,** 108 Allens Creek Ext. Open daily. Reported to be the largest indoor flea market. (704) 456-8627.
   **Waynesville Drive-In. Weekends.**

**YOUNG HARRIS, GA.** **Flea Market,** Country Rhoades Music Park. Every Thursday (summer).

# Flowers

The beauty of the Blue Ridge area is sometimes found in the simplest things, such as a tiny wildflower, as well as in spectacular clusters of rhododendron and mountain laurel in bloom. In addition to the profusion of natural blooming plants in the area, there are botanical gardens and an array of flower festivals.

As early as February, purple-brown skunk cabbage, a relative of jack-in-the-pulpit, emerges from the bogs and swamps. Tiny yellow coltsfoot flowers are often found along the roadsides in early March. Other early arrivals include pinkish white hepatica flowers, snowy white bloodroot blossoms, purple violets and white-flowered serviceberries. In April they are joined by the troutlilly, with small yellow flowers, the dwarf iris and trailing arbutus, with its pink tubular flowers. As late as summer and fall, hikers may still see the ox-eye daisy, black-eyed Susan, sunflowers, goldenrod, ironwood, joe-pye weed and many others.

The Horticultural Gardens of Clemson University in South Carolina cover about 70 acres and include 2,200 varieties of plants. Trails wind through camellia, rhododendron and azalea gardens, with stops at a tea house by a lake, a picnic area with a fountain, pagodas and other shelters. The Pioneer complex includes a continuous Braille trail. The annual flower day held in August attracts thousands.

The University of Georgia's Botanical Garden of 293 acres has more than five miles of walking trails and collections of camellias, azaleas, roses, dogwoods, magnolias, redbuds, laurels, perennials and annuals. Visitors may view characteristic plants of the flood-plain, upland slope, ravine and streams.

At the University of North Carolina Botanical Gardens near the center of Asheville, the beauty of ferns, wildflowers, plants, trees and mosses native to the Southern Highlands may be seen.

## Botanical Attractions

**ASHEVILLE, N.C.   Craggy Gardens,** 37 mi. north of town at mile post 363.4 Blue Ridge Parkway. The gardens reach their peak in mid-to late June when the rhododendrons bloom. Self-guided trail. (704) 258-5222.

**Asheville Botanical Gardens,** at the University of North Carolina. Hundreds of species native to the Southern Highlands. Free. Sunrise to sunset. (704) 258-6600.

**ATHENS, GA.   University of Georgia Botanical Garden,** 2450 S. Milledge Avenue, 1 mi. south of Athens Bypass. A broad cross section of the Georgia Piedmont; 5 mi. of trails, 293 acres. Open daily. (404) 542-1244.

**Founders Memorial Garden,** S. Lumpkin Street and Bocock Drive, on University of Georgia Campus (north end). Commemorates the founding in 1891 of the Ladies Club of Athens, the first garden club in the world. Open daily. (404) 542-1244.

**BAKERSVILLE, N.C. Roan Mountain Gardens,** 13 mi. north of Bakersville on NC-261. Open all year, anytime during the day. From May to mid-June your stay will be limited to one hour, unless you plan to hike the trails. Free. Contact: District Ranger, U.S. Forest Service, Burnsville. (704) 682-2567.

**CHEROKEE, N.C. Cherokee Nature Trail and Botanical Gardens,** adjacent to and part of Oconaluftee Indian Village. Identified native plants.

**CLEMSON, S.C. Clemson University, Horticulture Greenhouses and Gardens,** US-76 east. Some 2,200 varities of plants grown in the 70-acre garden which features a pioneer garden labeled in Braille. Largest shrub collection in the eastern United States. Includes arboretum, hortitherapy, mini-zoo, Garden of Meditation, Bog Gardens and Mini-garden. Daily.

**HIAWASSEE, GA. Hamilton Rhododendron Garden,** Georgia Mountain Fairgrounds. More than 400 varieties, 1,600 assorted flowers. Free.

## Flower Festivals and Events

———March———

**GAINESVILLE, GA. Violets Among the Shamrocks,** Civic Building. By Georgia State African Violet Council. First week.

**RABUN COUNTY/CLAYTON, GA. Annual Botanical Society Trip,** paper plant along Wolf Creek. By Rabun County Botanical Society. Wiley Post Office. First week.

**'ATHENS, GA. Wildflower Walk,** S. Milledge Avenue. By University of Georgia Botanical Garden. Free. Fourth week.

**HELEN, GA. Spring Wild Flowers,** Unicoi State Park. Fourth week.

———April———

**CLAYTON, GA. Wildflower Walk.** Georgia Extension Service. Second week.

**GAINESVILLE, GA. African Violet Show,** Gainesville Civic Center. Free. Sat. and Sun. Second week.

**LAVONIA, GA. Spring Wildflower Day,** Tugaloo State Park. Second week.

**RABUN GAP, GA. Wildflower Walks,** Hambidge Center. Walks, tours, workshops. Second week.

**HELEN, GA. Spring Wildflower Weekend,** Unicoi State Park. Third week.

**ASHEVILLE, N.C. French Broad River Garden Club Plant Sale,** held at the Market on Hendersonville Road, NC-25 south. Fourth week.

*Flowers*

**Biltmore House and Gardens Azalea Festival,** on the grounds of the Biltmore estate, NC-25 south. Seventeen acres of gardens. Late April.

**Garden Club of North Carolina, Inc.,** annual show, Great Smokies Hilton Hotel. Since 1925. Fourth week.

**Spring Wildflower Pilgrimage,** University of North Carolina. Illustrated lectures, hikes, birdwatching on Parkway, botanical motorcades. Last week. (704) 258-6623.

**BLAIRSVILLE, GA.  Along the Wildflower Trail,** Vogel State Park. Fourth week.

**CHATSWORTH, GA.  Fort Mountain State Park.** Walks, slides, programs. Fourth week.

**HELEN, GA.  Spring Wildflowers,** Unicoi State Park. Mountain wildflower programs, walks, slide shows. Fourth week. (404) 878-2201.

**MOUNTAIN CITY, GA.  Wildflowers Weekend,** Black Rock Mountain State Park. Wildflower discovery through lectures, hikes. Fourth week. (404) 746-2141.

**RABUN GAP, GA.  Nature Rambles — Wildflowers.** Fourth week. (404) 746-5718.

————May————

**ASHEVILLE, N.C.  Biltmore Country Market Plant Sale,** Biltmore Market, NC-25 south. By French Broad Garden Club. Early May. (704) 274-1744.

**Biltmore House and Gardens Azalea Festival.** 17 acres of gardens and plants. Early May.

**Day in the Gardens,** botanical gardens at University of North Carolina. 1st week. (704) 254-2272.

**Spring Wildflower Pilgrimage.** Guided field trips along Blue Ridge Parkway. Admission. Early May. (704) 258-6444.

**\*BOONE, N.C.  Daniel Boone Native Gardens,** *Horn in the West* theatre grounds. First week.

**MOUNTAIN CITY, GA.  Bloomin' Wild Flower Fair,** Black Rock Mountain State Park. First week.

**ASHEVILLE, N.C.  Spring Wildflower Pilgrimage,** University of North Carolina. Second week.

**Rhododendron and Azalea Show,** Asheville Mall. By Southeastern Chapter, American Rhododendron Society. Sat. and Sun. Second week.

**BREVARD, N.C.  Annual Rhododendron and Azalea Exhibit Show,** at Brevard Chamber of Commerce. 150 varieties. Second week.

**HOLMES STATE FOREST, N.C.  Wildflower Slide Show,** Holmes State Forest. Second week.

**CLARKESVILLE, GA.  Mountain Laurel Festival.** Clarkesville Lions Club. Mid-May.

## Flowers
### ————June————

**ASHEVILLE, N.C.   Purple rhododendron display,** at Craggy Gardens. Early June.

**RABUN GAP, GA.   Nature Rambles: Special Wild Edibles,** Hambidge Center. Second week.

 **Nature Rambles: Family of Flowers,** Hambidge Center. Third week.

 **Nature Rambles: Folklore of Flowers,** Hambidge Center. Fourth week.

**BAKERSVILLE, N.C.   North Carolina Rhododendron Festival.** Also arts and crafts festival. Mid-June.

**˙ROAN MOUNTAIN, TN.   Annual Rhododendron Festival,** held on Roan Mountain. Since 1948. Mid-June.


### ————July————

**˙ATHENS, GA.   University of Georgia Summer Workshops,** Ga. Botanical Gardens, Callaway Building. Basketry, pruning, ferns, nature photography, silk flowers, herbs, walks, tour. Fee.

 **Annual Perennial Garden Walk,** at University of Georgia Botanical Garden. Third week. (404) 542-1244.

**FRANKLIN, N.C.   Lotus Blossom Festival,** Perry's Water Gardens, Route 4, Box 437, 28734. First week.

**CLEMSON, S.C.   Flower Day,** Horticulture Dept., Clemson University. Blooming annuals on display; lectures. Mid-July.

**RABUN GAP, GA.   Ramble Fern Green,** Hambidge Center. Third week. (404) 746-5718.


### ————August————

**CLEMSON, S.C.   Flower Show and Display.** By Clemson Dept. of Horticulture and the Garden Club of South Carolina. First week.

**HIGHLANDS, N.C.   Flower Show,** Cashiers Community Center. By Cashiers Garden Club. First week.

 **Highlands-Cashiers Garden Club Flower Show,** Highlands Community Center. Since 1965. Third week.


### ————September————

**CHATSWORTH, GA.   Wonderful Wildflowers,** Fort Mountain State Park. Third week.


### ————October————

**HENDERSONVILLE, N.C.   Chrysanthemum Show,** Flat Rock Junior High School. By N.C. Chrysanthemum Society. Second and third weeks.

**CASHIERS, N.C.   Fall Color Woodland Harvest,** High Hampton Inn and Country Club. Informal walks, talks and demonstrations. Third week.

**MOUNTAIN REST, S.C.  Color Walk,** Oconee State Park. To Long Mountain Fire Tower, 4 mi. Fee. Division of State Parks, Columbia, 29201. Third week.

———November———

**HENDERSONVILLE, N.C.  Annual Chrysanthemum Show,** Flat Rock Junior High School, 1030 Indian Hill Road, 28739. Fourth week.

# Flowering Seasons of Some Common Plants

Remember, Plants bloom earliest at lowest elevations.

| *Plant* | *Peak of Bloom* |
| --- | --- |
| Catalpa Tree | May |
| Crab Apple | May |
| Dogwood | April-May |
| Flame Azalea | May-June |
| Japanese Magnolia | June-July |
| Japonica | April-May |
| Mountain Laurel (Kalmia) | Mid-May-June |
| Magnolia | June-July |
| Mimosa | June |
| Royal Paulownia | Late April-May |
| Primrose | June-Sept. |
| Queen Anne's Lace | June-early Sept. |
| Rhododendron (many varieties) | Late April-July |
| Sweet Shrub | May-early July |
| Trailing Arbutus | March-early May |
| Trillium | April-June |
| Violets | March-early May |
| Wild Rose | June-July |
| Wisteria | May |

# Golf

Emerald green carpets of grass surrounded by hills and mountains combine with crisp, cool air to make the Blue Ridge area a golfer's paradise. The tees and greens, sand traps and fairways offer a variety of shots and courses to challenge even the touring professional.

With more than 340 golf courses, North Carolina claims the distinction of having more golf courses per square mile than anywhere else in the world. Legend has it that golf was introduced to the state in 1728 at Fayetteville by a resident swatting at a feather ball in a field. Black Mountain Golf Club boasts the longest hole in the world: Hole 17 rambles for 745 yards and is the world's only par 6 hole. Wolf Laurel, west of Asheville near Mars Hill, is said to be the highest course east of the Mississippi at 4,785 feet. This year-round resort is surrounded by half a million acres of National Forest. The private Grandfather Golf and Country Club in Linville, also in a wilderness setting, is known for its beauty and quality. Although High Hampton's course in Cashiers is at the base of the mammoth granite Whiteside Mountain and the eighth hole is in the middle of a lake, the 18-hole course is known as one of the easier courses.

Georgia's fine golf resorts include the Chattahoochee Golf Club north of Gainesville, where golfers enjoy views of Lake Lanier as they play the 18-hole, 6,700-yard course. Skitt Mountain Golf Course, 6 miles south of Cleveland near Alpine Helen, features three ponds, sand traps, cart paths and a pro shop. Other Georgia favorites are Sky Valley Country Club, par 72 resort course in Dillard, the nine-hole Rabun Country Club in Clayton, and the Heritage Golf Course in Clarkesville.

South Carolina holds more than 200 golf courses scattered from the Sea Islands to the mountains. While the coastal courses at Hilton Head and Myrtle Beach are best known to vacationers, there are many fine public courses in the Blue Ridge area, including Woodhaven South in Pendleton and Lan Yair Country Club, Peach Valley Golf Club, and Reidville Par Three in Spartanburg.

### Golf Events

————April————

\*AUGUSTA, GA.  **Masters Golf Tournament.** The best in the United States. Gallery admission. Early April. (404) 738-7761.

**CULLOWHEE, N.C.** Mill Creek Golf Club's Spring Four Ball Golf Tournament. First week.

**HIGHLANDS/CASHIERS, N.C.** Walter Hagen Tournament, High Hampton Country Club. By Jackson County Chapter of American Cancer Society. First week.

**TOCCOA, GA.** Walter Hagen Benefit Golf Tournament. All proceeds go to the American Cancer Society. First week.

**BLAIRSVILLE, GA.** Annual Invitational Golf Tournament, Butternut Creek Golf Course. Second week.

————May————

**BLAIRSVILLE, GA.** Spring Invitational Golf Tournament, Butternut Creek Golf Course. First week.

**CLAYTON, GA.** Annual Spring Team Golf Tournament, Kingwood Country Club, by Clayton Rotary Club. First week.

**CONNESTEE FALLS, N.C.** Pro-Am Tournament, Connestee Falls Country Club. First week.

**·RUTHERFORDTON, N.C.** Cleghorn Country Club Pro-Am. First week.

**BLACK MOUNTAIN, N.C.** Annual Memorial Day Four Ball Golf Tournament, Black Mountain Golf Course. Fourth week.

**BLAIRSVILLE, GA.** Tom Reece Memorial Golf Tournament, Butternut Creek Golf Course. Fourth week.

**ETOWAH, N.C.** Ingles Pro Am, Etowah Golf Course. Fourth week.

**SKY VALLEY, GA.** Rabun County Cancer Society's Annual 18 hole Golf Tournament. Fourth week.

————June————

**ASHEVILLE, N.C.** Over 50 Four Ball, Great Smokies Hilton Country Club. First week.

**HIAWASSEE, GA.** Golf Tournament, North Georgia Annual Conference at Chatuge Shores Golf Course, P.O. Box 77, 30546. Second week.

**MAGGIE VALLEY, N.C.** June Four Ball Tournament, Maggie Valley Golf and Country Club. Mid-June.

**·RUTHERFORDTON, N.C.** Cleghorn Open. Second week.

**ASHEVILLE, N.C.** Father-Son Tournament, Asheville Golf Club. Third week.
Asheville Country Club Pro Lady. Third week.

**MAGGIE VALLEY, N.C.** Pro Lady Tournament, Maggie Valley County Club. Third week.

**ARDEN, N.C.** **Miller High Life Mountain Amateur,** High Vista Country Club. Fourth week.

**TOCCOA, GA.** **Ladies Golf Invitational Tournament,** Toccoa Golf Club. Fourth week.

————July————

**BLAIRSVILLE, GA.** **Summer Open Golf Tournament,** Butternut Creek Golf Course. First week.

**BREVARD, N.C.** **Junior Open,** Connestee Falls Country Club. By Brevard Federal Savings and Loan. Ages 12-17. Second week.

**ASHEVILLE, N.C.** **Sky View Open,** Asheville Golf Course. Third week.

**BEECH MOUNTAIN, N.C.** **Beech Mountain Annual Golf Tournament.** By Volunteer Fire Dept. Third week.

————August————

**BLACK MOUNTAIN, N.C.** **Golf Tournament,** Black Mountain Golf Club. Early August.

**BLAIRSVILLE, GA.** **Howard O. Thomas Golf Tournament,** Butternut Creek Golf Course. By Recreation Department. First week.

**FRANKLIN, N.C.** **Four Ball Golf Tournament,** Mill Creek Country Club. By Franklin Jaycees. First week.

**BLAIRSVILLE, GA.** **Thomas Insurance Open Golf Tournament and Barbecue,** Butternut Creek Golf Course. Second week.

**LAKE LURE, N.C.** **Pro Am Tournament,** Fairfield Mountain Country Club. Second week.

**BLAIRSVILLE, GA.** **Womens Invitational Golf Tournament.** By the Union County Bank. Fourth week.

**HENDERSONVILLE, N.C.** **Apple Jill Golf Tournament,** Etowah Valley Golf Course. Fourth week.
**Apple Jack Tournament,** Crooked Creek Golf Course. Fourth week.

————September————

**ASHEVILLE, N.C.** **Pro-Am Tournament,** Grove Park Inn Country Club. First week.

**BLACK MOUNTAIN, N.C.** **Annual Labor Day Golf Tournament,** Black Mountain Golf Course. By Recreation and Parks, 225 W. State Street., 28711. First week.

**BLAIRSVILLE, GA.** **Ladies Tournament,** Butternut Creek Golf Course. First week.

**BREVARD, N.C.** **Four Ball Tournament,** Connestee Falls Country Club. Second week.

**BLAIRSVILLE, GA.**  Sadie Hawkins Golf Tournament, Butternut Creek Golf Course. Third week.

**FRANKLIN, N.C.**  Four Ball Golf Tournament, Mill Creek Golf Club. By Franklin Jaycees. US-64. Third week.

**HIGHLANDS, N.C.**  Pro-Am Golf Tournament, Highlands Country Club. Third week.

**·ROYSTON, GA.**  Golf Tournaments and Clinics, Victoria Bryant State Park. Third week.

**BLACK MOUNTAIN, GA.**  Golf Tournament. Black Mountain Golf Course. Late September.

————October————

**ARDEN, N.C.**  Western North Carolina Tournament of Champions, High Vista Country Club. First week.

**ASHEVILLE, N.C.**  Four Ball Tournament, Great Smokies Hilton Country Club. First week.

**MAGGIE VALLEY, N.C.**  Four Ball Tournament, Maggie Valley Country Club. Second week.

**TRYON, N.C.**  Western North Carolina Classic, Red Fox Country Club. Second week.

**BLAIRSVILLE, GA.**  Shotgun Golf Tournament, Butternut Creek Golf Course. Third week.

**TOCCOA, GA.**  C.S. Open Golf Tournament, Toccoa Golf Club, Toccoa Ladies Golf Assoc. Third week.

# Golf Courses

PU = Public   PR = Private   R = Resort

| Location | Course | Holes/Par; Type; Phone |
|---|---|---|
| Asheville, N.C. | Beaver Lake Golf Course | 18/72; R; (704) 254-6391 |
| | Biltmore Forest Country Club | 18/71; PR; (704) 274-1261 |
| | Country Club at Asheville | 18/71; PR; (704) 258-9183 |
| | Great Smokies Golf Club | 18/72; R; (704) 254-3211 |
| | Grove Park Inn Country Club | 18/71; R; (704) 252-2711 |
| | Municipal Golf Course | 18/72; PU; (704) 298-1867 |
| Banner Elk, N.C. | Beach Mountain Golf Club | 18/72; R;(704) 387-2372 |
| | Seven Devils Golf Club | 18/71; R; (704) 963-5665 |
| | Sugar Hollow Golf Club | 18/64; R; (704) 898-4521. |
| Black Mountain, N.C. | Black Mountain Golf Club | 18/71; PU; (704) 669-2710 |
| Blairsville, Ga. | Butternut Creek Golf Course | 9/32; PU; (404) 745-4744 |
| 'Blowing Rock, N.C. | Blowing Rock Country Club | 18/71; R; (704) 295-7311 |
| | Hound Ears Golf Club | 18/72; R; (704) 963-4321 |
| 'Boone, N.C. | Boone Golf Club | 18/71; PU; (704) 264-8760 |
| Brevard, N.C. | Glen Cannon Country Club | 18/72; PR; (704) 883-8155 |
| | Connestee Falls Country Club | 18/72; PR; (704) 885-2410 |
| Buford, Ga. | Pine Isle Golf Course | 18/72; R; (404) 945-8921, ext. 531 |
| Burnsville, N.C. | Mt. Mitchell Golf Club | 18/72; PU; (704) 675-5454 675-4923 |
| Canton, N.C. | Springdale Country Club | 18/72; R; (704) 648-2971 |
| | Mountain View Golf Course | 9/35; PU; (704) 648-1311 |
| Clarkesville, Ga. | Heritage Golf Course | 9/36; PU; (404) 754-9422 |
| Cashiers, N.C. | High Hampton Inn | 18/71; R; (704) 743-2411 |
| Cedar Mountain, N.C. | Sherwood Forest Golf Course | 18/54; PU; (704) 885-2300 885-2091 |
| Clayton, Ga. | Rabun County Country Club | 9/36; PU; (404) 782-5500 |
| Cleveland, Ga. | Skitt Mountain Golf Course | 18/72; PU; (404) 865-2277 |
| Cullowhee, N.C. | Forest Hills Golf Course | 9/36; PU; (704) 293-5442 |
| Dillard, Ga. | Sky Valley Country Club | 18/72; R; (404) 746-5301 |
| Demorest, Ga. | Piedmont College Golf Course | 9/36; PU; (404) 778-2774 |
| Easley, S.C. | Rolling Green Golf Course | 18/72; PR; (803) 859-7716 |
| Flat Rock, N.C. | Lost Diamond Valley Country Club | 18/72; PU; (704) 692-0143 |

| | | |
|---|---|---|
| **Fontana, N.C.** | Fontana Village Resort | 9/3; R; (704) 498-2211 |
| **Franklin, N.C.** | Franklin Golf Course | 9/36; PU; (704) 524-2288 |
| | Franklin Lodge and Golf Course | 9/36; PR; (704) 524-2287 |
| | Holly Springs Golf Course | 18/72; R; (704) 524-7792 |
| | Mill Creek Country Club | 18/72; PU; (704) 524-4653 |
| **Gainesville, Ga.** | Chattahoochee Golf Club | 18/72; PU; (404) 532-0066 |
| **Hartwell, Ga.** | Hartwell Golf Course | 18/72; PU; (404) 376-8161 |
| **Hayesville, N.C.** | Chatuge Shores Golf Course | 18/72; PU; (704) 389-8940 |
| **Hendersonville, N.C.** | Crooked Creek Golf Course | 18/71; PU; (704) 692-2011 |
| | Etowah Valley Golf Course | 18/71; PU; (704) 891-7022 |
| | Hendersonville Country Club | 18/71; PR; (704) 693-6507 |
| **High Shoals, N.C.** | Gallagher Trails Golf Course | 18/72; PU; (704) 922-4208 |
| **Highlands, N.C.** | Highlands Falls Country Club | 18/72; PR; (704) 526-3651 |
| | Highlands Country Club | 18/70; PR; (704) 526-2181 |
| | Sky Lake Golf Course | 9/35; PR; |
| | Wildcat Cliffs Country Club | 18/72; PR; (704) 526-2165 |
| **Jasper, Ga.** | Bent Tree Country Club | 18/72; PR; (404) 893-2627 |
| | Arrowhead Golf Course | 9/36; PU; (404) 692-5634 |
| **Lake Lure, N.C.** | Country Club of the Mountains | 18/72; R; (704) 625-9111 |
| | Lake Lure Municipal Golf Course | 9/34; PU; (704) 625-4472 |
| **Lake Toxaway, N.C.** | Lake Toxaway Country Club | 18/72; PR; (704) 966-4260 |
| **Linville, N.C.** | Linville Golf Club | 18/72; R; (704) 733-4363 |
| | Grandfather Golf and Country Club | 18/72; PR; (704) 898-4531 |
| **Lula, Ga.** | Pine Hills Golf Course | 9/36; PU; (404) 677-3245 |
| **Maggie Valley, N.C.** | Maggie Valley Country Club | 18/71; R; (704) 926-1616 |
| **Marion, N.C.** | Marion Lake Club | 18/72; PR; (704) 652-6232 |
| **Mars Hill, N.C.** | Wolf Laurel Golf Club | 18/72; R; (704) 689-4111 |
| **Murphy, N.C.** | Cherokee Hills Golf Club | 18/72; PU; (704) 837-5853 |
| **Newland, N.C.** | Mountain Glen Golf Course | 18/72; PR; (704) 733-5804 |
| **Norwood, N.C.** | Piney Point Golf Club | 18/72; PR; (704) 474-3985 |
| **Pendleton, S.C.** | Boscobel Country Club | 18/71; PR; (803) 646-3404 |
| | Woodhaven Golf Club | 9/29; PU; (803) 646-9511 |
| **Pickens, S.C.** | Gauley Falls Golf Course | 9/36; PU; (803) 878-2030 |
| | Pickens Country Club | 18/72; PR; (803) 878-6083 |

## Golf Courses

| | | |
|---|---|---|
| *Royston, Ga. | Victoria Bryant State Park | 9/36; PU; (404) 245-5092 |
| Sapphire Valley, N.C. | Country Club of Sapphire Valley | 18/72; R; (704) 743-3441 |
| Salem, S.C. | Keowee Key Country Club | 18/72; R; (803) 944-2222 |
| Seneca, S.C. | Oconee County Country Club | 18/71; PR; (803) 882-8037 |
| Spruce Pine, N.C. | Grassy Creek Golf Course | 18/72; PU; (704) 765-2950 |
| Toccoa, Ga. | Toccoa Golf Club | 9/36;      (404) 886-6545 |
| Tryon, N.C. | Red Fox Country Club | 18/72; PR; (704) 894-8251 |
| | Tryon Country Club | 9/36; PR; (704) 859-9561 |
| Waynesville, N.C. | Lake Junaluska Golf Club | 9/36; PU; (704) 456-5777 |
| | Mountain Valley Golf Club | 18/54; PR; (704) 456-5644 |
| | Waynesville Country Club | 18/71; PR; (704) 456-3551 |

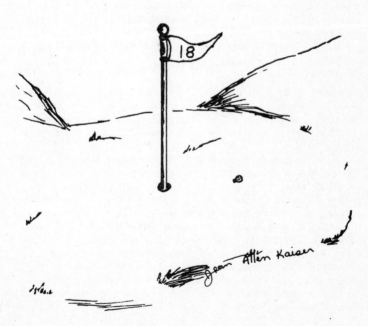

# Grist Mills

You can experience the unique process of grinding meal at a grist mill, whether the meal be corn, rye, oats, whole wheat or buckwheat. Once these grist mills were both a necessity and a social center. Today many of them are picture perfect: the old, weathered clapboard mill with its huge wood water wheel splashing creek water as it turns slowly.

Where do you find these grist mills? Some are along highways, but most are hidden down country roads. A surprising number of them still operate on waterpower. When you visit, be sure to notice the interior workings: shafts, gears, wheels and pulleys. Today's technology has made the grist mill obsolete. Yet they are a testament to craftsmanship, to conservation of natural resources and to a process that produced nutritious, wholesome grains without preservatives, additives or coloring.

**BRASSTOWN, N.C.** **Small Water Wheel,** grounds of John C. Campbell Folk School, US-64 east.

**BREVARD, N.C.** **Morgan Mill** (1850), Kahdalea Camp Road, 5 mi. southwest of Brevard off US-64. Mill wheel is two stories high, 30 feet in diameter. Open Mon.-Sat.

**CASHIERS, N.C.** **Grist Mill,** Oakmont Lodge Area. (704) 743-2297.

**CLARKESVILLE, GA.** **Grandpa Walts Water Ground Meal Mill,** G-197. Built in 1930 to replace original mills on Sogue River. Now "Mark of the Potter" pottery shop. Inner mill may be viewed. (404) 947-3440.
    **Hazel Creek Mill,** G-197 between Clarkesville and intersection with G-123. Medium-sized mill.
    **Short's Mill.** Overshot waterwheel.

**CHEROKEE, N.C.** **Little Mill,** US-441 north, across from the Cherokee Mini-Mart. One of the few remaining mills of the early 1880s, with two stones that run vertically grinding the grain as you watch. The mill is powered by a one-cylinder kerosene engine built around 1917; it also is water powered. Cornmeal, flour and grits are ground fresh daily.
    **Magic Waters Park,** small water wheel, US-19. Open late May-early September.
    **Mingus Mill,** in the Great Smoky Mountains National Park, ½ mi. north of the Oconaluftee Visitor Center. An original, water-powered, turbine mill, built in 1886. Open April-October. Operated by the Great Smoky Mountains Natural History Assoc. in cooperation with the National Park Service.
    **Newfound Lodge Watermill,** US-441 north. Grist mill.
    **Old Hayes Mill,** US-441, 1 mi. south. Yellow and white cornmeal. Daily, May-August. Weekends, March-April, September-November. (704) 497-2726.
    **Santa's Land Theme Park.** Operating water wheel and grist mill.
    **Saunooke's Mill and Shop,** on US-441 north, at the entrance to the National Park. Old-fashioned water-ground cornmeal made fresh daily. Mountain jams and jellies. Pleasant atmosphere. Gifts and hand-crafted Indian items. (704) 497-9879.

**GREER, S.C.   Gilreath Mill.** The whitewashed mill appears at a sharp curve in SC-101 north of Greer on the banks of Shoal Creek. Built in 1812, the mill building and the towering water wheel and two 250-pound millstones still stand. Free.

**HELEN, GA.    Nora Mill,** G-175, north of G-17. John Martin built the mill with overshot wheel around 1876 to mill corn, wheat and rice. It was later converted into a turbine operation and still later, used in the 1950 movie *I'd Climb the Highest Mountain.*

**HIAWASSEE, GA. Georgia Mountain Fair Waterwheel,** Georgia Mountain Fairgrounds. Working waterwheel and mill that grinds cornmeal. Early August.

**HIGHLANDS, N.C.   Lick Log Mill Store Property,** 4 mi. west of Highlands (Dillard Road). One-man grist mill, dated 1874.

**HORSE SHOE, N.C.   Forge Valley Mill,** on grounds of Forge Valley Fun Park. 16-foot, 65-year-old Fitz water wheel; inner parts gathered from old N.C. mills. Ground corn and wheat. Parking fee. (704) 891-3022.

**RABUN GAP, GA.   Sylvan Falls Mill,** Wolf Fork Road, 2 mi. west of US-441, 4½ mi. north of Clayton. Grist mill since 1840; 27-foot water wheel and 100-foot waterfall. Cornmeal, whole-wheat flour. April-October. (404) 746-2762.

  **Hambidge Center for Creative Arts/Sciences,** Betty's Creek Road. Working grist mill.

# Hiking

From leisurely afternoon strolls on loop nature trails in state parks to rugged mountainous climbs in wilderness areas, there is something for every hiker in the Blue Ridge Mountains.

The trails will offer the most enjoyment if all hikers remember the motto: "Leave nothing but footprints, take nothing but memories." Prepare before you hike by collecting hiking maps or details about the terrain. Hiker's guides to trails in the national forests are free from forest service rangers. Guide books, available in most bookstores and outdoor stores in the area, describe hiking trails in north Georgia, South Carolina and North Carolina in detail (see Resources, end of this chapter, for more information).

While it is not possible to include all the hiking trails in the Blue Ridge Mountain area in this book, some of the most popular and interesting trails are listed.

The granddaddy of hiking trails, the Appalachian Trail, begins in Georgia's Amicalola Falls State Park and stretches 2,100 miles through 14 states to Mt. Katahdin, Maine. Completed in 1937, the Appalachian is the longest continuous marked trail in the world. The famous path attracts millions each year.

"Now I see the secret of the making of the best persons; it is to grow in the open air and to eat and sleep with the earth."

Walt Whitman
*Song of the Open Road*

## Hiking Trails

**APPALACHIAN TRAIL.** Covers 2,100 miles from Maine to Springer Mountain, Ga. Trail touches 14 states; protected by the National Trails System Act of 1968 and maintained by various trail clubs and volunteers under the leadership of the U.S. Forest Service, National Park Service and the Appalachian Trail Conference. Trail was first a dream of Benton Mackaye of Shirley Center, Maine, followed by the leadership in 1926 of Arthur Parkins of Hartford, Conn., and Myron H. Avery, of Labec, Maine. There are 293 mi. of the trail in North Carolina and 79.54 mi. in Georgia. Refer to "Resource Information" for sources of more information.

**BARTRAM TRAIL SYSTEM.** In honor of the famous naturalist William Bartram. Section I: 10½ mi., Scaly Mountain, N.C.; Section II: 17½ mi., Topton, N.C. (Wayah Bald); Section III: 11½ mi., Tulula Gap (Robbinsville); Section IV: 10½ mi., Tatham Gap. Bartram Trail covers 80 mi. Clayton, Ga., near Warwoman Road is half-way point.

**BLUE RIDGE PARKWAY TRAIL SYSTEM.** The Parkway's 241 mi. through North Carolina provide for more than 90 trails or 120-plus mi. of hiking. Parkway trails are clearly marked including trail distance. Visitor centers provide excellent resource information. See also Blue Ridge Parkway section for more information.

**JOYCE KILMER-SLICKROCK WILDERNESS AREA TRAILS.** Includes 15 trails in the 14,000-acre area: 60 mi. of hiking trails following mountain streams and ridge tops. Some trails in the wilderness area are rugged and steep.

**SMOKY MOUNTAIN NATIONAL PARK TRAIL SYSTEM.** More than 8.5 million people visit the park annually. The highest point is Clingmans Dome, 6,643 feet. The park was authorized by Congress in 1926 and dedicated by President Roosevelt in 1940. The park includes 600 mi. of trails and over 600 mi. of streams. A ''naturalist's wonder'' with more than 1,400 varieties of flowering plants, 150 tree species, 200 bird species and 80 kinds of freshwater fish. The Smokies are about 125 million years older than the Rockies.

**STATE PARK TRAIL SYSTEMS.** Many state parks in the Blue Ridge area have well-planned trail systems clearly marked for leisure hiking. The short loop trails are very popular with weekend hikers. Refer to the chapter on Parks and the ''Resource Information'' section of this chapter for more information.

## Hiking Activities

————January————

**CHATSWORTH, GA.** **Winter Hiking,** at Fort Mountain State Park. Third and fourth week. (404) 695-2621.

————February————

**ASHEVILLE, N.C.** **Mountain Living Show,** Asheville Civic Center, Haywood Street. Exhibits of outdoor living. Third week.

————April————

**BLAIRSVILLE, GA.** **Backcountry Weekend,** Vogel State Park. Second week.

**FONTANA, N.C.** **Spring Flower Hiking Week,** Fontana Dam. Third week.

————October————

**LINVILLE, N.C.** **Annual High Country Hiker's Holiday Weekend.** Day hikes in Linville Gorge, Roan Mountain, portions of Appalachian Trail and Grandfather Mountain. First week. 1 (800) 438-7575 from North Carolina or 1 (800) 438-7500 outside North Carolina.

**MOUNTAIN REST, S.C.** **Backpacking Trek,** 25-mi. hiking tour from Walhalla Fish Hatchery to Oconee State Park. By American Lung Assoc. First week.

**ASHEVILLE, N.C.** **University of North Carolina at Asheville Autumn Walk.** Non-competitive, walk-at-your-own-pace 10-K and 20-K walks. Second week.

**CHATSWORTH, GA.** **Fort Mountain State Park Backcountry Weekend Adventure.** Overnight backpacking trip led by park naturalists. Participants provide their own equipment, food and transportation. Limited to 15 participants. Third week.

**FONTANA, N.C.** **Fall Colors Hiking Week,** Fontana Dam. Third week.

**WESTMINSTER, S.C.** **Oconee State Park Foothills Trek,** Oconee to Chattooga River and back. Third week.

—— November ——

**BRYSON CITY, N.C.** **Shelter Institute Course,** Nantahala Outdoor Center. Third week. (704) 488-2175.

—— December ——

**AMICALOLA FALLS, GA.** **Hike at Amicalola Falls State Park,** 16 mi. northwest of Dawsonville via G-183. Helping wildlife through the winter. Second week. (404) 265-2885.

**BREVARD, N.C.** **AARP Hiking,** meets at Fast Fare store, Main Street. Strollers: less than 4 mi. Venture hikes: longer hikes.

—— May through October ——

**ASHEVILLE, N.C.** **Mountain Hikes,** 151 Haywood Street. Join the Carolina Mountain Club for weekly hikes. It meets at the downtown post office on Sundays at 8 A.M. and 2 P.M.

# Outdoor Centers

**ALMOND, N.C.** **Rolling Thunder River Co.,** Box 88. Outfitters; wilderness clinics and weekend canoe and kayak clinics available. April-October. (704) 488-2030.

**ANDERSON, S.C.** **Grady's Wholesale Sports,** Belvedere Plaza, 29621.

**ASHEVILLE, N.C.** **Climb East, Inc.,** Box 475, Hot Springs, 28743. Snake's Den area; rockclimb discovery: half day. (704) 622-3535.

**BLAIRSVILLE, GA.** **Wolfcreek Wilderness,** Box 596, 30512. Outdoor trips. (404) 745-6460.

**BRYSON CITY, N.C.** **Nantahala Outdoor Center,** Star Route, Box 68, 28713. A combination inn, restaurant, outdoor sporting goods shop and guide outdoor adventure center. (704) 488-2175.

**CHEROKEE, N.C.** **The Hiking Post,** Rte. 1, Box 86D, 28719. Adventure trips.

**CLEMSON, S.C.** **Appalachian Trail Outfitters,** 612A Greenville Highway, 29631. **Ole Norm, Inc.,** P.O. Box 966, SC-93 and 123, 29631.

**CULLOWHEE, N.C.** **Cullowhee Outfitters,** Old Highway 107. (704) 293-9741.

**DAHLONEGA, GA.** **Appalachian Adventures,** Box 2057, 16 Public Square, 30533. (404) 864-3562.

**GAINESVILLE, GA.** **Buckhorn Mountain Shop,** 2341 Thompson Bridge Road, 37501. (404) 536-0081.

**HELEN, GA.** **The Wildewood Shop,** River Street. Outdoor supplies. (404) 878-2541.

**HIGHLANDS, N.C.** **The Happy Hiker,** Chestnut Street. Hiking boutique. (704) 526-5298.

**NAPLES, N.C.** **Diamond Brand Camping Center,** US-25, I-26, Mountain Home Exit. Outdoor equipment. (704) 684-6262.

**TRAVELERS REST, S.C.** **Sunrift Adventures,** 426 N. Poinsett Highway, 29690.

## *Resource Information:*

# NATIONAL

American Camping Assoc., Inc.
Bradford Woods
Martinsville, In. 46151

American Hiking Society
1701 18th Street, N.W.
Washington, D.C. 20009  (202)234-4610

Appalachian Trail Conference, Inc.
P.O. Box 236
Harpers Ferry, W.Va. 25428  (304) 535-6331

Department of the Interior
National Park Regional Director
75 Spring Street, S.W.
Atlanta, Ga. 30303  (404) 221-5185

Department of the Interior
National Park Service
Interior Building
Washington, D.C. 20240  (202) 343-4747

Department of the Interior
U.S. Fish and Wildlife Service
Washington, D.C. 20240

National Campers and Hikers Assoc.
7172 Transit Road
Buffalo, N.Y. 14221  (716) 634-5433

National Parks and Recreation Assoc.
1601 N. Kent Street
Arlington, Va. 22209  (202) 265-2717

National Wildlife Federation
1412 16th Street N.W.
Washington, D.C. 20036  (202) 796-6800

Sierra Club
530 Bush Street
San Francisco, Cal. 94108  (415) 981-8634

Wilderness Society
1901 Pennsylvania Avenue N.W.
Washington, D.C. 20006  (202) 828-6600

# GEORGIA

Bartram Trail Society
6688 Marsh Avenue
Lithia Springs, Ga. 30057  (404) 948-3871

"Hikers Guide to the
Chattahoochee National Forest"
Free at District Ranger Station

Georgia Dept. of Natural Resources
Office of Information and Education
270 Washington Street, S.W.
Atlanta, Ga. 30334  (404) 656-3530

The Georgia Appalachian Trail
Club, Inc.
P.O. Box 654
Atlanta, Ga. 30301

*The Hiking Trails of North Georgia*,
by Tim Homan.
Peachtree Publishers

# NORTH CAROLINA

Haywood County Trails
Waynesville Chamber of Commerce
(Trail map includes foot, water, bike
and motorcycle trails.)

Carolina Hiking Club
Hendersonville, N.C.
(Schedules hiking events in western
North Carolina.)
(704) 254-4953 or 693-4631

*North Carolina Hiking Trails*, by
Allen de Hart
Appalachian Mountain Club
5 Joy Street
Boston, Mass. 02108

*Day Hikes of the Highland,
Cashiers, and Walhalla Area*, by
Jan and Steve Ianniellos

Carolina Mountain Club
P.O. Box 68
Asheville, N.C. 28802
(704) 254-4953 or 693-4631

"100 Favorite Trails of the Great
Smokies and Carolina Blue Ridge,"
by Carolina Mountain Club.
P.O. Box 68
Asheville, N.C. 28802

"North Carolina Camping and Outdoors Directory" (FREE)
North Carolina Travel and Tourism Division
Raleigh, N.C.

Western Carolina Walking Club
P.O. Box 1383
Asheville, N.C. 28802
(704) 667-5633, evening.

Supervisor, National Forests in North Carolina
P.O. Box 2750
Asheville, N.C. 28802
(704) 258-2850, ext. 601

North Carolina Bartram Trail Society
Rte. 3, Box 406
Sylva, N.C. 28723    (704) 293-9661

Smoky Mountain Hiking Club
Asheville, N.C.    (704) 254-4953

Nantahala Hiking Club
Rte. 1
Franklin, N.C. 28734

Nantahala Appalachian Trail Club
Rte. 1
Franklin, N.C. 28734

## SOUTH CAROLINA

Foothills Trail Conference
P.O. Box 3041
Greenville, S.C. 29602

"Hiking Trails"
Program Section, Division of State Parks
1205 Pendleton Street
Columbia, S.C. 29201

*South Carolina Hiking Trails,* by
Allen de Hart
The East Woods Press

South Carolina Wildlife Federation
Box 4186
Columbia, S.C. 29204
(803) 786-6419

Wildlife Society of South Carolina
P.O. Box 167
Columbia, S.C. 29202
(803) 758-0007

## MISCELLANEOUS

"Ambling and Scrambling on the Appalachian Trail"
Appalachian Trail Conference
P.O. Box 236
Harpers Ferry, W.Va. 25425

*Backpacking, One Step at a Time,*
by Harvey Manning
Vintage Books

*Hikers Guide to the Smokies,* by
Dick Murless and Constance Stallings
Sierra Club Books

*Walks and Hikes*
Great Smoky Mountains National Park
Gatlinburg, Tenn. 37738

*Walks in the Great Smokies,* by
Rod and Priscilla Albright
The East Woods Press

# History

Whether your interest is history, architecture, antiques or simply things of beauty, you'll enjoy touring historic homes and sites in the Blue Ridge area.

South Carolina's tri-county Pendleton District is one of the largest national historic districts in the nation. The Indian territory was settled in the late 1700s by hardy Scotch-Irish farmers. Wealthy coastal planters, politicians and businessmen were attracted to the burgeoning center of society and trade and built summer retreats there. Today, more than 40 historic sites include Fort Hill, the 1893 home of South Carolina statesman John C. Calhoun, and restored homes such as Ashtabula (c. 1830) or Woodburn, an antebellum plantation house.

Walking tours are an ideal way to get a close, leisurely look at styles of architecture such as Georgian (1720), Federal (1780-1820), or Greek Revival (1820-1860). Many towns and cities in the Blue Ridge area offer such tours.

Don't miss the fabulous Biltmore House and Gardens in Asheville, N.C. The 255-room mansion, which has been called "America's finest castle," was completed in 1895. George W. Vanderbilt wanted his estate to be America's finest country home. The French Renaissance house is a showcase for treasures and art objects he collected in his travels. The three-mile entrance drive winds through the gorgeously landscaped 12,000-acre grounds with forests, a deer park, gardens with 5,000 roses and flowers and shrubs from all over the world, wildlife, pools, a dairy herd and statuary.

A more humble historic house in Asheville is the boardinghouse where Thomas Wolfe, author of *Look Homeward, Angel*, grew up. Poet Carl Sandburg's home, "Connemara," is a national historic site in Flat Rock, N.C., five miles south of Hendersonville. Sandburg lived there for 22 years until he died in 1967.

Cherokee Indian and Moravian traditions complement each other in the Chief Vann House near Chatsworth, Ga. James Vann, a Cherokee leader and wealthy plantation owner, helped the Moravian settlers establish a mission school for Cherokee children in 1801. In 1805 Moravian craftsmen helped build his three-story brick house.

The Old Sautee Store, east of Helen, Ga., contains an unusual collection of merchandise from the 19th and 20th centuries in a 107-year-old country store. The Mast General Store in Valle Crucis, N.C., near Boone, has oak counters and display cabinets, an old potbelly stove and the original advertising posters. Today, the store built in 1883 and listed in the National Register of Historic Places, sells items such as old-time hardware and housewares and shoes and clothing appropriate for the mountains.

*Note: Although Athens, Ga., is south of the region covered in this book, it is included in this section because its historic places are rich and extensive.*

**ANDREWS, N.C.** **Franklin Pierce Cover House,** a Queen Anne brick dwelling built in 1900. In National Register of Historic Places.

**Walker Inn** (1840), Junaluska Road. Land owned by Chief Junaluska. By appointment. April-October (704) 321-4439.

**ASHEVILLE, N.C.** **Downtown Asheville Historic District,** bounded by SR-1240, Valley Street, Hilliard Avenue and Broad Avenue. Located on a series of hills and ridges between the French Broad River in the west and Beaucatcher Mountain in the east. Nineteenth and twentieth century architecture.

**Biltmore House and Gardens,** on US-25, off I-40 in south Asheville. Daily. (704) 274-1776.

**Buncombe County Courthouse** (1927-28), 60 Court Plaza, and **City Hall** (1926-28), 70 Court Plaza. A masterwork of Art Deco.

**First Baptist Church** (1925-27), Oak and Woodfin streets. Early Italian Renaissance with Art Deco detail. The **Catholic Church of St. Lawrence** (1909), 97 Haywood Street was designed in Spanish Baroque style.

**Montford Historic District,** late 19th and 20th century. More than 600 buildings in the district.

**Ravenscroft School** (1840s). A brick Greek Revival structure.

**St. Matthias Episcopal Church** (1896), Valley Street, between Grail and East Beaumont. A Gothic Revival building in the town's "East End."

**Smith-McDowell House** (1840), 283 Victoria Road. The oldest surviving house in town. Flemish Bond. Headquarters of the Western North Carolina Heritage Center, under development as a museum.

**Thomas Wolfe Memorial** (1883), 48 Spruce Street. National Historic Site. Boyhood home of the author.

**˙ATHENS, GA.** **Athens-Clarke Heritage Foundation.** Showcases more than 50 of the city's historic sites. (404) 546-1805 or 546-1818. Free.

**Garden Club of Georgia Museum** (1857), Lumpkin Street on the University of Georgia campus. Reservations. (404) 542-3631.

**Joseph Henry Lumpkin House,** 248 Prince Avenue. Home of Georgia's first state Supreme Court chief justice. By appointment.

**Church-Waddel Brumby House,** 280 E. Dougherty Street. Named for two former presidents of the University of Georgia. The town's Welcome Center. (404) 546-1805.

**Taylor-Grady House,** 634 Prince Avenue. (1839.) Greek Revival. Owned by Gen. Robert Taylor. In National Register of Historic Places. (404) 549-8688.

**Double-Barreled Cannon** (1863), City Hall lawn at College and Hannock Avenues. Only double-barreled cannon in the world.

**Tree That Owns Itself**, Dearing and Finley streets. White oak; descendant of the original tree; stands on plot deeded to it.

**BAKERSVILLE, N.C.** **Mitchell County Courthouse** (1907). Neo-Classical Revival.

**BLAIRSVILLE, GA.** **Union County Courthouse** (1899), Courthouse Square. Romanesque. Being restored.

**BREVARD, N.C.** **Silvermont** (1917), E. Main Street. A Colonial Revival mansion, now the county's main public recreation center.

**Transylvania Courthouse** (1873), Broadway and E. Main Street. Distinguished by a square central Italianate-style tower.

**BRYSON CITY, N.C.** **Swain County Courthouse** (1908), Main and Fry streets. An early Neo-Classical Revival building crowned with an octagonal cupola and clock.

**BURNSVILLE, N.C.** **The (Old) Yancey County Courthouse** (1908), W. Main and Town Streets. Now the police department. Has unusual projecting end bays and a blocky cupola.

**CHATSWORTH, GA.** **Vann House** (1820), US-76 and G-225 west of town. Noted for its elaborate hand carvings in the Cherokee Rose motif and brightly painted woodwork. (404) 695-2598.

**COLUMBUS, N.C.** **Polk County Courthouse** (1859), Courthouse Street. A dignified Greek Revival structure.

**CLARKESVILLE, GA.** **Grace-Calvary Church**, G-23 and US-441, Green Wilson Street. Built in 1840s. National Register. Episcopal church.

**CLEMSON, S.C.** **Fort Hill** (1803). The antebellum homeplace of John C. Calhoun, Vice President of the United States. (803) 656-2475.

**Hanover House** (1716). A classic example of Huguenot architecture. It served as a residence and frontier fort against the danger of Indian attack. (803) 656-2241.

**Old Stone Church** (1802), on US-76. The burial place for Gen. Andrew Pickens and other Revolutionary heroes.

**CLEVELAND, GA.** **The Old White County Courthouse** (1857-59). Houses the White County Historical Society. (404) 865-3225.

**'CONNESTEE, S.C.** **McBee Chapel** (1841), 1 mi. south of SC-291 on US-25. Turn east on Fork Shoals Road. Designed by mill-wright John Adams. One of the few remaining octagonal churches in America.

**DAHLONEGA, GA.** **Lumpkin County Courthouse** (1836), US-19, on the Square. National Register. Now the gold museum.

**Vickery House,** (1860), across from North Georgia College's Price Memorial Field. On the National Register.

**DEMOREST, GA.** **Historic Home District.** Includes Demorest Baptist Church, J. W. Ritchie home (Dutch Colonial Style; early 1900s), The Federated Church (1906), John Bridges home, Demorest Depot (1903) and Edward Flor Saddle Tree Co.

**FLAT ROCK, N.C.** **Historic District.** Large private estates in Federal, Greek and Gothic Revival, Second Empire and Neoclassical Revival styles. St. John in the Wilderness, a Gothic Revival Episcopal church of yellow brick, was built in 1834-36 by these early summer residents. National Register.

**Connemara.** Home of Carl Sandburg. Built 1839. Daily. U.S. Park Service. (704) 693-4178.

**HAYESVILLE, N.C.** **Clay County Courthouse** (1889), Main Street. An example of vernacular Italianate architecture.

**Clay County Art and Historical Museum.** In a restored jail of 1912.

**HELEN-SAUTEE, GA.** **Sautee-Nacoochee Mound.** This was the center of an ancient Cherokee town called Guaxale. A picturesque gazebo now tops the mound.

**HENDERSONVILLE, N.C.** **Henderson County Courthouse** (1904), Main Street. Neo-Classical Revival.

**Hendersonville Railroad Depot** (1879), Railroad Street and E. 7th Street. Now occupied by the Council on Aging.

**HIGHLANDS, N.C.** On Lick Log Mill Store Property, west of Highlands (Scaly Mountain): Chapel (served Turtle Pond Area) dates back to 1851; one-room cabin, dated 1812-1818, with stick and mud chimney; one-man grist mill (1875).

**JASPER, GA.** **Bargain Barn,** US-5 Alt. and G-53. Authentic General Mountain store. (404) 735-3340

**LINVILLE, N.C.** **Linville Historic District** (1888-1920), NC-181, 105 and US-221. Summer resort community with rustic cottages and neo-Tudor homes. All Saints Episcopal Church and Esseola Lodge are of particular interest.

**MARION, N.C.** **Carson House** (1780), US-70 west of town. Built by Col. John Carson. Between 1843 and 1845, served as courthouse, offices and jail. (704) 724-4640.

**McDowell County Courthouse** (1922-23), Main and E. Court streets, US-221 and 70. A late Neo-Classical Revival building.

**MOUNTAIN CITY, GA.** **York House,** US-441 and G-23. One of north Georgia's oldest and most famous mountain resort homes. Operated since 1896. (404) 746-2068.

**MURPHY, N.C.** **Cherokee Courthouse** (1926). A grandiose, marble-clad Neo-Classical Revival structure with a polygonal cupola. Contains marble tables inscribed with the Ten Commandments.

**Episcopal Church of the Messiah.** Murphy's Little Church Around the Corner. (1855.) Cornerstone laid in 1896. Herringbone pattern heart pine paneling, handmade altar (1897). Stained-glass windows executed by Tiffany's of New York.

**NEWLAND, N.C.** **Avery County Courthouse** (1912), Montezuma Street and Courthouse Drive. Neo-Classical Revival style and Beaux-Arts manner. The highest county seat in eastern America.

**Avery County Historical Museum,** in the Old Jail, Avery Square. Open April-October. Sunday afternoons.

**PENDLETON, S.C.** Pendleton Historical and Recreational District Commission, 125 E. Queen Street. Coordinates events and makes arrangements for tours in Oconee, Pickens and Anderson Counties. Start at the visitor's center in Pendleton, with cassette tape tours of Pendleton and information about the entire district.

**Ashtabula** (1830), SC-88, east of town. Home is restored and has furnishings of the early-to mid-19th century.

**Farmer's Hall.** The oldest farmer's hall in continuous use in the United States. Built in 1826.

**Pendleton Presbyterian Church** (1890). S. Mechanic Street. Roman and Gothic design.

**Willow Oak Farm** (1890). A colonial estate that includes leaded-glass windows and English stained-glass windows.

**Woodburn House** (1810). Built by C.C. Pinckney, Jr., one of the signers of the Constitution.

**PICKENS, S.C.** Pickens County Gaol, at the corner of Johnson and Pendleton streets. Turn of the century, resembles a Gothic castle with its crenelated turret. The restored jail now houses the Pickens County Museum for History and Art.

**Pickens Presbyterian Church.** Predates the American Revolution. Oldest active Presbyterian Church in South Carolina.

**PLEASANT GARDENS, N.C.** The Carson House (1893). By John Carson. Hosted Andrew Jackson and Davy Crockett.

**RABUN GAP, GA.** Hambidge Center, Betty's Creek area. On the National Historic Register.

**SAUTEE, GA.** Crescent Hill Church, off G-75 on G-17. Built early 1870s. Carpenter constructed "Gothic" form. Built by Captain Nichols.

**The Old Sautee Store,** G-17 and G-255. Houses a museum collection of general store merchandise from the 19th and 20th centuries in a 107-year-old country store. (404) 878-2281.

**SKY LAKE, GA.** Country Store, G-255. 1890-type store. (404) 878-2295.

**SYLVA, N.C.** The Jackson County Courthouse (1914), Main Street. White-painted Neo-Classical Revival building with a Corinthian portico, large cupola and a ribbed dome.

**TAMASSEE, S.C.** Oconee Station (1760). Oldest in Oconee County. Used as an outpost from Indian attacks and later as a trading post.

**TOCCOA, GA.** Traveler's Rest, on US-123. (1815.) One of the oldest buildings in Georgia. Authentically furnished. (404) 886-2256.

**TRYON, N.C.** Old Blockhouse (1756). The western terminus of the 1772 border between North Carolina and South Carolina and the beginning of the border's extension to the west. An Indian trading post.

**Sidney Lanier Home,** NC-108. Residence of the poet laureate of the South. Private residence.

**VALLE CRUCIS, N.C.** **The Mast General Store,** NC-194. (1883.) On the National Register. (704) 963-6511.

**WAYNESVILLE, N.C.** **The General Store,** 22 Howell Mill Road. An authentic 200-year-old log cabin store filled with antiques, crafts and nostalgia.

**WEAVERVILLE, N.C.** Vance Homestead, off US-19/23 and 5 mi. east on Reems Creek Road. Birthplace of Zebulon Baird Vance, Governor of North Carolina during the Civil War. Built in 1786. A Historic Site. (704) 645-6706.

# Home Tours

————April————

**TRYON, N.C.** **Tour of Homes and Gardens,** Box 149, 28782. First week.

**˚ATHENS, GA.** **Candlelight Tour.** Clarke-Heritage Foundation. A tour of Athens homes. Second week. (404) 353-1801.
 **Historic Home Tours.** Heritage Foundation. Second week. (404) 546-1818.

**WEAVERVILLE, N.C.** **Pioneer Living Day.** Living history exhibits of pioneer life. Second week. (704) 645-6706.

**˚ATHENS, GA.** **Historic Home Tours.** By Candlelight. Third week. (404) 546-1818.

————May————

**DEMOREST, GA.** **Annual Demorest Tour of Historic Homes and Places.** Third week. (404) 778-5008.

————June————

**DEMOREST, GA.** **Tour of Homes and Historic Places.** First week. (404) 778-5008.

————July————

**HIGHLANDS, N.C.** **Hudson Library's Tour of Homes.** Second week through first week in August. (704) 526-3031.

————August————

**FLAT ROCK, N.C.** **Tour of Homes,** Historic Flat Rock, Box 295, 28731. First week. (704) 693-1638.

**DAHLONEGA, GA.** **The Courthouse Story,** Gold Museum. Fourth week. (404) 864-2257.

————September————

**CLEVELAND, GA.** **Open House** at the 132-year-old Courthouse, on the Square. First week.

**WEAVERVILLE, N.C.** **Pioneer Living Day.** Third week. (704) 645-6706.

————October————

\*BOONE, N.C.   High Country Bus Tour of Mountain Churches. History of churches in eight parishes. (800) 222-7515, (800) 438-7500.

————December————

\*ATHENS, GA.   American Cancer Society Tour of Homes. Cancer Society office. First week. (404) 548-4893.

CLAYTON, GA.   Tour of Homes. By Pilot's Club. First week.

DAHLONEGA, GA.   Vickery Open House. First week. (404) 864-3365

# Horseback Riding

Saddle up! Those words may be familiar in a western movie, but in real life, most people don't hear them too often. Vacation may be the ideal time to tackle something new. Horses are the focus of leisure activities from trail rides to rodeos, horse shows and races.

The Blue Ridge area has plentry of places to experience the pleasures of riding. Most resort areas have rental stables and guided trail rides.

For adventure try riding a horse to the top of Mount Le Conte, which soars to 6,600 feet near Gatlinburg, Tenn., in the Great Smoky Mountains National Park. The rustic Le Conte Lodge rests at 5,400 feet. Many prefer to ride up the steep mountain, then hike down. Mounts may be rented at the base of the mountain. Stay at the lodge, open from March 30 to November 4, or go on a short one- or two-hour ride.

The Cohutta Wilderness, 34,102 acres in northwest Georgia, has more than 40 miles of riding trails. Watch out for wild boars and black bears and be prepared to cross rivers.

Mount Mitchell in North Carolina's Pisgah National Forest has 15 miles of trials winding around the peak. The mountain is the highest in the eastern United States at 6,684 feet. Mount Mitchell's trails include the Buncombe Horse Range, which ushers riders through spruce-fir forests on old logging roads. Maple Camp Bald Trail climbs the ridge line to the peak of the mountain. View the paths of natural landslides, the South Toe River Valley and surrounding peaks of western North Carolina.

The Annual Block House Steeplechase races at North Carolina's Tryon Riding and Hunt Club is a spectacular race traditionally held the first week in April. While in Tryon, don't forget to see the Tryon Wooden Horse on Howard Street. It is a symbol for horse country.

## Rodeos and Steeplechases

————April————

**CUMMING, GA.** Atlanta Steeplechase, Seven Branches Farm. Five races plus Atlanta Cup. First week.

**SHOOTING CREEK, N.C.** Horseshow-Rodeo, Shooting Creek Arena, US-64. By Clay County Lions. Fourth week.

**TRYON, N.C.** Block House Races, Tryon Riding and Hunt Club, Inc., Box 1096, 28782. Country steeplechasing, run in two states and three counties. Since 1945. First week.

————May————

**CHEROKEE, N.C.** **Memorial Day Rodeo,** Magic Waters. Six events. Treadway Rodeo Co. Fourth week.

————June————

**MURPHY, N.C.** **Rodeo,** Farmer's Market, US-64. Admission. Second week.

————July————

**CHEROKEE, N.C.** **Cherokee Rodeo,** Rodeo Complex, US-19. Admission. First week.

————August————

**CHATSWORTH, GA.** **MCSC Professional Rodeo.** Third week.

**MURPHY, N.C.** **PRCA Rodeo.** Farmer's Market, US-64 west. Fourth week.

————September————

**CLARKESVILLE, GA.** **Trail Ride Poker Run.** By Sogne Saddle Club. First week.

**MURPHY, N.C.** **Fall Round-up Rodeo,** Farmer's Market, US-64 west. Fourth week.

## Horse Shows

————April————

**TRYON, N.C.** **Junior Horse Show.** Tryon Riding and Hunt Club. Second week.

**ASHEVILLE, N.C.** **Carolina Mountains Arabian Horse Festival,** Western N.C. Horse Arena near Asheville. Third week.
  **Western North Carolina Arabian Horse Show,** Western N.C. Horse Arena near Asheville. Fourth week.

————May————

**'FAIRBURN, GA.** **Arlington Horse Show,** Arlington Schools, 4500 Ridge Road. First week.

**McCAYSVILLE, GA.** **Family Fun Show.** Fannin County Saddle Club. Races and pleasure class events. Second week.

**WAYNESVILLE, N.C.** **Western North Carolina 4H Youth Horse Show,** Waynesville Showgrounds. Second week.

**MURPHY, N.C.** **Western Horse Show,** State Farmer's Market, US-64 west. 400 entries. By Mountain Horseman's Assoc., Inc. Admission. Third week.

**ASHEVILLE, N.C.** **National Walking Horse Trainers Show,** Western N.C. Horse Arena near Asheville. 1,000 to 1,200 head. Fourth week.

**TRYON, N.C.** **Annual Spring Horse Show,** Harmon Field. Tryon Riding and Hunt Club. Since 1927. Fourth week.

————June————

**ASHEVILLE, N.C.** **Western N.C. Horse Trials,** Biltmore Estate. First week.

**BLACK MOUNTAIN, N.C.** **Western N.C. Appaloosa Club Horse Show,** at show grounds. First week.

**McCAYSVILLE, GA.  All Western Horse Show.** By Fannin County Saddle Club at Horseshoe Bend. 25 different classes of competition. Admission. Second week.

**TRYON, N.C.  Tryon Hounds Horse Show,** Harmon Field. Fourth week.

———July———

**CHATSWORTH, GA.  Georgia State Championship Racking Horse Show.** July 4th.

**ETOWAH, N.C.  Hunter-Jumper Horse Show.** By Etowah Riding Club. 20 classes. Noon. Third week.

**WAYNESVILLE, N.C.  Lions Horse Show,** Waynesville Recreation Dept., 217 W. Marshall Street. Third week.

**BLAIRSVILLE, GA.  Kiwanis Horse Show.** By Blairsville Kiwanis. 50 classes-events. US-129-19 north. Free. Since 1966. Fourth week.

———August———

**'BLOWING ROCK, N.C.  Blowing Rock Charity Horse Show.** Hunters, jumpers and gaited saddle horse competition. First week.

**LAVONIA, GA.  N.E. Georgia Saddle Club Show.** First week.

**CUMMING, GA.  Hunter Hill Jumper Horse Show,** Hunter Hill Farm. Second week.

**McCAYSVILLE, GA.  Family Fun Show,** Horseshoe Bend. Second week.

**MARION, N.C.  McDowell Saddle & Bridle Club's Annual Horse Show,** held at the fair grounds, south of Marion on NC-226. Second week.

**WAYNESVILLE, N.C.  Haywood County Trail Riders Horse Show,** Waynesville Recreation Dept. Second week.

**McCAYSVILLE, GA.  Guaranteed Money Horse Show,** Horseshoe Bend. Third week.

**TRYON, N.C.  Piedmont Paso Fino Horse Show,** Harmon Field, Tryon Riding and Hunt Club. Fourth week.

———September———

**TRYON, N.C.  Annual Tryon Hounds Horse Show,** Harmon Field. First week.

**WAYNESVILLE, N.C.  Fall Horse Show and Pulling Contest,** Waynesville Recreation Dept., 217 W. Marshall Street. First week.

**CLARKESVILLE, GA.  Soque Saddle Club Horse Show,** at Habersham County fairgrounds on G-115. Fourth week.

**McCAYSVILLE, GA.  Family Fun Horse Show,** Horseshoe Bend. Fourth week.

**SENECA, S.C.  Open horse show.** By the Blue Ridge Riding Club, at the Blue Ridge Riding Club Arena, off SC-188. Fourth week.

**TRYON, N.C.  Spartanburg Junior League Charity Horse Show.** Fourth week.

———October———

**CHATSWORTH, GA.  Georgia State Mule Pulling Show.** Includes a parade and draft horse show. First week.

**PENDLETON, S.C.  Horse Show by Pendleton Rescue Squad,** Hickory Hills Farm on Cherry Street. Also barbecue plates. Third week.

**TRYON, N.C.** **Annual Tryon Horse Trials,** Harmon Field, Tryon Riding and Hunt Club. Third week.

**BLAIRSVILLE, GA.** **Halloween Family Fun Show,** Fannin County Saddle Club. Fourth week.

## Stables and Riding Trails

**BLAIRSVILLE, GA.** **Trackrock Riding Academy, Inc.,** US-129, south of Blairsville at Track Rock Campground, G-180. Trail rides, boarding, training. (404) 745-5252 or 2420.

**BREVARD, N.C.** **Harmony Farm Riding School.** Instructional program. (704) 885-2350.
  **Keystone Camp.** Riding instruction for children and adults (704) 884-9125.

**BURNSVILLE, N.C.** **Mt. Mitchell,** in Pisgah National Forest. Two trails: Buncombe Horse Range takes riders through spruce-fir forests on old logging roads; Maple Camp Bald Trail climbs to the peak of this 5,782-foot mountain on steep switchbacks. Complete trail map with roads and elevation is available from Toecane Ranger District Office, Box 128, Burnsville, 28714. (704) 682-6146.

**CANDLER, N.C.** **Pisgah View Ranch,** Route 1, 28715. Horseback riding. (704) 667-9100.

**CASHIERS, N.C.** **High Hampton School of Equitation,** High Hampton Inn. Riding instruction, ages 10 years and up. (704) 743-2411.

**CHATSWORTH, GA.** **Cohutta Wilderness.** More than 40 miles of trails for horseback riding. Detailed topographical trail maps are available for $1.25 from Cohutta Ranger District Office, U.S. Forest Service, Chatsworth, Ga. 30605. (404) 695-6736.

**CHEROKEE, N.C.** **Smokemont Riding Stables,** in the Great Smoky Mountains National Park, adjacent to Smokemont Campground, 6 mi. north of Cherokee on Newfound Gap Road (US-441). Well-maintained trails, gentle horses, licensed guides, trail and waterfalls, rides. Open April 1-Nov. 1. (704) 497-2373.

**CLAYTON, GA.** **Mountain Horses.** From the stables behind the Dillard House restaurant, they take eight to ten riders on mountain trails that lead to rapids, waterfalls and caves on the river. Trips last for two, three or five days. Year-round. Mountain Horses, Box 619, 30525. (404) 782-4397.

**ELLIJAY, GA.** **Circle L-J Ranch.** Adult dude ranch, riding stables. (404) 635-7717.

**FONTANA DAM, N.C.** **Fontana Stables.** Horseback riding. (704) 498-2211.

**FRANKLIN, N.C.** **Rose Creek Stables,** Rte. 8, Box 370. April 15-Oct. 31. (704) 524-5726.

**·GATLINBURG, TENN.** **Le Conte Lodge.** Visitors must reach this unique lodge on foot or by horse (stable space is not available for visitors' horses). Mounts may be rented from two stables at the base of the mountain. Many people prefer to ride up and walk down. One-way rides leave the stables around 9 A.M. Fee. Guests and their horses climb 5,400 feet on one of the five steep mountain trails to the lodge. For those who don't want to stay at the lodge, the stables also offer one- and two-hour rides. Hourly fee. Contact: McCarter Stables, (615) 436-5354, or Smoky Mountain Stable, (615) 436-5634, to arrange horse rental. Le Conte Lodge, Box 350, Gatlinburg, Tenn. 37738. (615) 436-4473.

**HELEN, GA.** **Mountain Shadows Stable,** G-75 at Jellystone Park. April 1-Oct. 31. (404) 865-4742.

**INMAN, S.C.** **Earls Court Riding School,** Asheville Highway. Jumping, training, instruction, boarding. (803) 472-6352.

**LAKE LANIER ISLANDS, GA.** **Trail Rides.** Hour-long guided trail rides on a 5-mile horse trail. March-October. Horses may be rented for longer periods with advance reservations. Stables are just inside Lake Lanier Islands' main gate. Lake Lanier Islands Stables, 3001 Pebblebrook Drive, 30518. (404) 945-6164.

**LAKE TOXAWAY, N.C.** **Double J Stables, Inc.,** Knob Creek. Total program. (704) 883-2310.

**MURPHY, N.C.** **Boots and Saddles Riding Stables,** Ranger Community, US-64W on Dickey Road. Open Thurs.-Mon.; Tues. and Wed. by appointment. (704) 644-5917.

**SAUTEE, GA.** **Nacoochee Riding Stables,** G-17 before Old Sautee Store.

**SAUTEE-NACOOCHEE, GA.** **Sunburst Riding Stable,** On 255, across from Covered Bridge Restaurant, near Skylake. Open Tues.-Sun. (404) 878-2095.

**TOCCOA, GA.** **Annual Jaycee Trailride.** By Toccoa-Stephens County Jaycees. 54-mi., 2-day trek (Toccoa-Lake Russell). Fourth week in May.

**TRYON, N.C.** **Bay Horse Farm.** Horse rentals. (704) 862-4896.

**Riding Stables,** Skyfield, Rte. 1, Box 66, 28782. Horse farm and hotel. (704) 863-2395.

# I

# Indians

The word Indian conjures images of feathered headdresses, war-painted faces and teepees — an image that is totally inaccurate for the once-powerful Cherokees.

Instead, Spain's Hernando DeSoto in 1540 and other Europeans found the Cherokees living in a complex society with an organized government. The Cherokee empire included what is now parts of Georgia, South Carolina, Alabama, Tennessee, North Carolina, Kentucky, West Virginia and Virginia.

The Cherokees lived in harmony with nature, taking what they needed, but never destroying the environment. Their homes had wood posts and basketlike walls covered with a grass-and-clay plaster. Long before the white man arrived, they knew how to spin thread from animal hairs and bark fibers and weave cloth for clothing. They were farmers, planting and tending crops.

The Cherokees hunted game with blowguns and poison-tipped darts, used herbs to treat illness and bring good luck in love or hunting, and played competitive ball games. They believed in "The Great Spirit," one supreme being, and an afterlife.

Using a network of footpaths, they traded with other Indians. Each village met in council houses in Cherokee towns governed by two chiefs. The White Chief oversaw agriculture, community and religious events, while the Red Chief led them to war against the Creeks. A council of elders made decisions which had to be unanimous. Their lives were organized and orderly.

An influx of settlers brought wars over the fur trade and land possession. From 1684 to 1835 treaties with the Cherokees were made and broken. By 1776 the Cherokees had been driven into the Smokies and their towns, homes, crops and livestock had been destroyed.

The Cherokees adapted to a different way of life. From 1825 to 1838, New Echota, Ga., was the bustling capital of the Cherokee nation, with stores, homes, a print shop and government buildings. In 1821 the alphabet created by Sequoyah, who was known to the whites as George Guess or Gist, was approved by the Cherokee chiefs. Sequoyah spent years developing the symbols representing syllables which enabled Cherokees to read and write in their own language. In 1827 the Cherokees adopted a national constitution under the leadership of Chief John Ross, discarding the traditional Indian clan system for a republican form of government. From 1828 to 1834 the Cherokee newspaper, *The Phoenix*, thrived.

But the white settlers wanted the Cherokees off the valuable land. In 1835 a treaty for their removal to Oklahoma was signed. After the Cherokees refused to leave their homes, the U.S. military rounded them up and drove them, like cattle, to Oklahoma in 1838-39. On this "Trail of Tears" about 4,000 people died of starvation, exposure, grief and disease.

Approximately 1,000 Cherokees who had hidden in the mountains remained fugitives until 1866 when they were granted permission to remain in North Carolina. Eventually, land was purchased for the Cherokees, and in 1924 the federal govenment took the land into trust.

Today Qualla Boundary, commonly known as the Cherokee Indian Reservation in western North Carolina, is home to about 5,000 of the 8,500 Cherokees on the rolls of the Eastern Band of Cherokees. About 50,000 Cherokees live in the West.

Each summer the outdoor drama *Unto These Hills* tells the story of the Cherokees from 1540 until their tragic removal to the West. Cherokees play important roles in the drama in the Mountainside Theater in Cherokee, N.C.

Visible signs of the once great nation are Indian mounds like Nacoochee near Helen, Ga., and Etowah near Cartersville. The Indians' legacy is heard in the rich Indian words naming rivers, mountains, places and lakes in the area — Chattahoochee, Toccoa, Sautee. Yonah Mountain gets its name from the Cherokee word for bear; Hiawassee is derived from the word for savanna. Their language lives on in the things they valued, and our debt to them is great.

## Indian Events

———February———

*CARTERSVILLE, GA.   Indian History Lecture, Etowah Indian Mounds Historic Site. First week.

*CALHOUN, GA.   Phoenix Day, New Echota Historic Site. Third week.

———March———

*CARTERSVILLE, GA.   Artifacts Identification Day, Etowah Indian Mounds Historic Site. Third week.
   Indian Weaponry Day, Etowah Indian Mounds. Fourth week. (404) 382-2704.

———May———

CHEROKEE, N.C.   Annual Spring Indian Art Exhibit, at the Holiday Inn. By Earth Song American Indian Art. First and second weeks.

*CARTERSVILLE, GA.   Artifacts Identification Day, at Etowah Indian Mounds on Etowah Drive. Second week.

**\*CALHOUN, GA.** Cherokee Indian Spring Festival, New Echota Historic Site. Fourth week.

**\*CARTERSVILLE, GA.** Indian Skills Day, Etowah Indian Mounds. Fourth week.

————June————

**CHEROKEE, N.C.** *Unto These Hills.* America's most popular outdoor drama. For information or reservations write P.O. Box 398, Cherokee, N.C. 28719. Presented each night except Sundays in the beautiful Mountainside Theater. Mid-June-late August. (704) 497-2111.

**HELEN, GA.** Indian Day. Pays tribute to the Cherokee Indians. Includes Cherokee dancers, basket weavers, a turtle race for children, and an Indian costume contest. Second week. (404) 878-2938.

**\*CARTERSVILLE, GA.** Indian Fish Trap Exploration. A ride down the Etowah River to view fish traps built by Indians prior to 1838. Preregistration is required. Third week.

————July————

**CHEROKEE, N.C.** Indian Pow Wow, Ceremonial Grounds, US-441. First week.

**\*CARTERSVILLE, GA.** Indian Awareness Day, Etowah Mounds. For children 7-12 years. Activities teach the Indian way of life. Second week.

**\*LAVONIA, GA.** Cherokees of Tugaloo River Valley, Tugaloo State Park. Third week.

————August————

**\*CALHOUN, GA.** New Echota Town Life, New Echota State Historic Site. Residents will "return" to describe what it was like to live there during the early 1800s. Second week. (404) 629-8151.

**\*CARTERSVILLE, GA.** Indian Fish Trap Exploration, Etowah Indian Mounds. A canoe ride down the Etowah River to view fish traps that were built by Indians prior to 1838. Preregistration is required. Second week.

**Viewing the Heavens,** at Etowah Indian Mounds. Short course on how prehistoric Indians incorporated astronomy into their religious beliefs. Fourth week.

————September————

**\*CARTERSVILLE, GA.** Archery Skills Day, at Etowah Mounds Historic Site. Admission. First week.

————October————

**\*CARTERSVILLE, GA.** Indian Skills Day, at Etowah Indian Mounds. Demonstrations of the use of Indian weapons such as the blowgun, spear, throwing stick and bow and arrow. Admission. First week.

**CHEROKEE, N.C.** Cherokee Fall Festival, Ceremonial Grounds. Indian food, archery and blowgun competition, other events. First week.

**\*CARTERSVILLE, GA.** Artifacts Identification Day, Etowah Indian Mounds. Fourth week. (404) 382-2704.

————November————

**\*CARTERSVILLE, GA.** Indian Skills Day, Etowah Indian Mounds. First week.
**Artifacts Identification Day,** Etowah Indian Mounds. First week.

**BLAIRSVILLE, GA. Blood Mountain Archeological Area,** 15 mi. south on US-19/129, via Appalachian Trail. Site of Indian battle between Cherokees and Creeks.
**Track Rock Archeological Area,** 8 mi. south on County Road 95 (Town Creek Road). Ancient Indian carvings on rocks.

**\*CARTERSVILLE, GA. Etowah Indian Mounds,** 3 mi. south from Cartersville on marked route. The largest and most important Indian settlement in the Etowah Valley. Occupied between 1000 and 1500. The museum contains artifacts and displays. (404) 382-2704.

**CALHOUN, GA. New Echota State Historic Site,** exit 131 off I-75 near Calhoun, 1 mi. east. Capital of the Cherokee Indian Nation, 1825-1838, and home of Sequoyah during the time he invented the Cherokee ''alphabet.'' (404) 629-8151.

**CHATSWORTH, GA. Vann House,** 3 mi. west on US-76. Outstanding example of Cherokee wealth and culture. Open Tues.-Sun. Closed Christmas and Thanksgiving.

**CHEROKEE, N.C. Cherokee Ceremonial Grounds,** US-441 north. Site of the annual Cherokee Indian Fall Festival, usually the first week of October. Also the site of special entertainment beginning in early spring and lasting throughout the summer and fall.
**Cyclorama Cherokee Indian Wax Museum,** US-19, ½ mi. east of Cherokee. See the once vast empire of the Cherokee Nation fade away on large electronic maps. Open nightly, June to Labor Day. (704) 497-4521.
**Nununyi Mound,** across the river from the visitor center. In the National Registry; the only historic site retained by the Cherokees.
**Oconaluftee Indian Village,** US-441. Cherokee Historical Assoc. A full-size replica of an 18th-century Cherokee community. Guided tours and demonstrations. Open daily from mid-May through late October. (704) 497-2315 or 497-2111.
**The Museum of the Cherokee Indian,** P.O. Box 770-A, 28719. One of the most modern facilities of its kind in the United States. Shows the story of Cherokee culture and history through the use of multi-media theaters. (704) 497-3481.

**FRANKLIN, N.C. Cowee Mound and Village Site,** northwest of Franklin on NC-28, not visible from road. Inhabited from prehistoric time until the 18th century, this town was once the location of the Council House of the chief town of the Middle Cherokees.
**Judaculla Rock,** on NC-281 near East LaPorte. Rock covered with well-preserved Indian pictures of unknown origin. Whiteside Mountain contains Spanish inscriptions carved into the granite which are believed to date from DeSoto's expedition of 1540.
A mound in the center of Franklin marks the site of the old Cherokee town, Nikwasi.

**HARTWELL, GA. Indian Granite Monument,** G-29. The Cherokees called this spot ''the center of the world.'' Here they held councils and bartered with traders.

**HELEN, GA. Nacoochee Mound,** off G-75, south of town. A gazebo sits on top of this Indian burial mound.

**\*ROSSVILLE, GA. John Ross House,** off US-27. The two-story log cabin was the home of John Ross, principal chief of the Cherokee Indian Nation from 1828 to 1866. Ross was the leader of the forces opposed to the Treaty of New Echota, which led to the dismal ''Trail of Tears'' during the Cherokee Removal. A secret room upstairs originally had no door, and no one knows how it was entered or used. Daily, June-Labor Day.

**SENECA, S.C. Cherokee Indian Artifacts,** at Keowee-Toxaway State Park, 3 mi. west of town on SC-11. Once the center of Indian civilization in South Carolina. (803) 868-2605.

**TUGALOO, GA.** **Tugaloo Indian Mound,** G-123, north of Toccoa, Ga.

*Information:*

Department of Archives and History
330 Capitol Avenue, S.E.
Atlanta, Georgia 30334
(404) 656-2358, 656-2393
Office of Indian Heritage: (404) 656-4700

Department of Natural Resources
Parks and Historic Sites Division
Etowah Indian Mounds
Route 1
Cartersville, Georgia 30120
(404) 382-2704

Some books recommended by the Georgia Department of Archives and History:

*The Southern Frontier,* by Vernor Crane

*Old Frontiers,* by John P. Brown

*Cherokee Frontier: Conflict and Survival,* by David H. Corkran

*The Southeastern Indians,* by Charles Hudson

*The Cherokees,* by Grace Woodward

*The Cherokees of the Old South,* by Henry T. Malone

*John Stuart and the Southern Colonial Frontier,* by John Alden

*The Indian Boundary in the Southern Colonies, 1763-1775,* by Louis De Vorsey

# Inns and Lodges

Comfy and rustic. Warm, homey and more likely to be furnished with rough-hewn rockers than plastic-covered chairs. An American classic that's making a big comeback — the country inn.

Most of these places are owned by the people who run them and they offer breakfast spreads large and tempting enough to ruin any dieting resolutions. Typically you'll find homemade biscuits with fresh preserves, country sausage and bacon, grits, eggs and stewed apples.

While most of the inns are naturally inviting, it's the people who run them who make visitors want to come back: waitresses who remember you from meal to meal, owners who chat with you and are committed to making their guests comfortable. Each inn has its own special character.

Take the Fryemont Inn in Bryson City, N.C. (listed in the National Register of Historic Places). It opened in 1923 as the woodsy retreat of Capt. Amos Frye, a lumber baron and member of Bryson City's "first family." Travelers today can feel just as wealthy as they relax in a rocker on the Fryemont's porch and drink in the mountain view.

Across from the Fryemont sits the charming Randolph House, so full of antiques and bric-a-brac that children under 12 and pets are not accepted. It has just six rooms.

At the Blue Boar Lodge near Robbinsville, N.C., your room will be brightened with a vase of fresh mountain wildflowers. A bell calls guests to meals served family style around an eight-foot lazy Susan table. The fare is a little fancier than plain Southern and may include Chinese beef tips and peppers, zucchini, tomato-onion casserole, stir-fried cabbage and celery.

The Pines Country Inn, near Pisgah Forest, N.C., is on the slope of Hart Mountain. Guests may sleep in old iron bedsteads in rooms at the main lodge (built in 1883), or stay in a cottage. Either way, they are far from the madding crowd at this inn surrounded by 12 acres of woods and farmlands.

To revel in elaborate furnishings including Victorian antiques, stay at the Woodfield Inn in Flat Rock, N.C. It is within walking distance of the restored home of the late American poet, Carl Sandburg, with its well-manicured lawns and hemlock trees on the 25 graceful acres.

Down in Mountain City, Ga., York House — the oldest inn in north Georgia — offers 13 rooms at astonishingly low rates. Built in 1896, it was recently renovated.

The Lake Rabun Hotel in Lakemont, Ga., is on a large man-made lake and surrounded by tall hemlock trees, dogwoods and winding stone pathways. Guests are served a continental breakfast in the living room.

Visit one of these country inns and you'll wonder why you ever stayed anywhere else.

**ANDREWS, N.C.   Walker Inn,** 1 mi. from Andrews on US-129. Was an old inn and trading post; built in 1840. Opened for tours in 1970. Open April-October, by appointment only. (704) 321-4439.

**ASHEVILLE, N.C.   Albemarle Inn,** 86 Edgemont Road. Turn-of-the-century inn. National Historic Site. (704) 255-0027.

   **Flint Street Inn,** 116 Flint Street. (1915) Rooms in turn-of-the-century style. Year-round. Breakfast. (704) 253-6723.

   **Grove Park Inn and Country Club,** 290 Macon Avenue, 28804. 261 units. (704) 252-2711.

**BALSAM, N.C.   Balsam Mountain Inn,** P.O. Box 40, 28707, off US-19 and 23. (1906.) National Register of Historic Places. (704) 456-9498.

**BAT CAVE, N.C.   Stonehearth Inn,** Box 9, 28710-009; US-64 and 74. Four units. Riverfront, restaurant. Open Easter-Thanksgiving. (704) 625-9990.

**BLACK MOUNTAIN, N.C.   Red Rocker Inn,** 136 N. Dougherty Street, 28711. Old-fashioned inn serving country food family style; 18 units. Open June-October. (704) 689-5991.

**BLAIRSVILLE, GA.   Dogwood Haven,** US-19/129 south, Dogwood Drive. (404) 745-4256.

   **Stonehenge,** Rte. 3, Box 3084; US-19/129. Chattahoochee National Forest. Bed and breakfast inn. (404) 745-4675.

**\*BLOWING ROCK, N.C.   Green Park Inn,** Box 7, 28605. (1882.) 674 rooms; Victorian surroundings. (704) 295-3141.

**BREVARD, N.C.   Colonial Inn,** 410 E. Main Street, 28712. 12 units, restaurant. Open all year. (704) 884-2105.

   **The Womble Inn,** 301 W. Main Street., P.O. Box 1441, 28712. Six guest rooms, 18th- and 19th-century antiques. Breakfast and dinner: Southern traditional and French. (704) 884-4770.

**BRYSON CITY, N.C.   Folkestone Lodge,** Rte. 1, Box 310, 28713. (1926.) Five rooms. Open June 1-Oct. 31. (704) 488-2730.

   **Fryemont Inn,** P.O. Box 459, 28713. (1923.) Off US-19A. 36 units; facilities for conventions, meetings; tennis privileges; lounge; pool; restaurant. Open May-November. Foreign currency exchanged. (704) 488-2459.

   **Hemlock Inn,** P.O. Drawer EE, 28713. 25 units, kitchenettes, restaurant. No TV or phones. Open May-October. Rates include two meals. (704) 488-2885.

   **Randolph House** (1895), Fryemont Road, P.O. Box 816, 28713. Six units, color TV, restaurant, convention or private meeting facilities. Open all year. (704) 488-3472.

**BURNSVILLE, N.C.   Assembly Inn.** (1920's.) Built of mica rock; 100 guest rooms; The Porch, The Terrace, The Garden; mountain views; 11 meeting rooms.

   **Nu-Wray Inn,** P.O. Box 156; off US-19. (1833.) 35 units. Family-style food; Victorian antiques. Open May-December. (704) 682-2329.

   **The Rocking Chair Inn,** 600 W. Main Street, 28714. 14 units. Open April 1-Dec. 31. (704) 682-2112.

**CANDLER, N.C.** **Pisgah View Ranch Lodge,** Rte. 1, 28715. Fifty units, babysitting, meeting facilities, TV, tennis, horseback riding, pool, restaurant. Open May-December. (704) 667-9100.

**CANTON, N.C.** **Pisgah Inn,** Rte. 2, 28716; off NC-276. May 1-Oct. 31. (704) 648-5661.

**CASHIERS, N.C.** **Fairfield Inn** (1896-98), US-64 east. Queen Anne style; 100 rooms. National Register of Historic Places. (704) 743-3441.

**High Hampton Inn and Country Club,** 130 Hampton Road, Box 338, 28717. Large facilities for meetings, 120 units. American plan includes three meals daily. Famous dahlia gardens. (704) 743-2411.

**Oakmont Lodge.** Grist mill, covered bridge and pond on property. (704) 743-2298.

**CHATSWORTH, GA.** **Cohutta Lodge and Restaurant,** 5000 Cochise Trail, 30705, atop Fort Mountain, US-76. Scenic mountain views, 60 rooms, inside swimming, tennis, horseback riding, nature trails, arts and crafts shops. (404) 695-9601.

**CHIMNEY ROCK, N.C.** **Esmerelda Inn, Inc.,** P.O. Box 57, 28720, US-74. Late 1800s. Restaurant, 15 units. Open March-October. Foreign currency exchanged in vicinity. Clark Gable, Mary Pickford, William S. Hart, Douglas Fairbanks, Lew Wallace stayed here. (704) 625-9889.

**CLARKESVILLE, GA.** **Laurel Lodge,** G-197 north. Rustic lodge. Open April 1-Nov. 30. (404) 947-3241.

**The Charm House,** US-441. Turn-of-the-century Southern mansion. (404) 754-9347.

**DAHLONEGA, GA.** **The Smith House** (early 1900s), off US-19, 202 S. Chestatee Street. Neo-classic architectural style. Excellent food, country buffet style. (404) 864-3566.

**Worley Homestead,** W. Main Street. Seven rooms; 1845 atmosphere. (404) 864-7002.

**DILLSBORO, N.C.** **Altamonte Inn,** US-441. (Built 1884.) European-style lodging with Victorian influence. (704) 586-9303.

**The Jarrett House** (1884), P.O. Box 219, 28725; intersection of US-23, US-19A and US-441. Country cooking. Open April to October. (704) 586-9964.

**FLAT ROCK, N.C.** **Woodfield Inn** (mid 1800s), US-25; Box 98, 28731. One of the oldest inns in North Carolina; 22 guest rooms. Furnished with Victorian antiques. (704) 693-6016.

**FRANKLIN, N.C.** **Poor Richard's Summit Inn** (1890), Box 511, 28734. Fifteen guest rooms. Open year-round. (704) 524-2006.

**·GATLINBURG, TENN.** **Le Conte Lodge.** Remote mountain retreat: hike or ride horses to reach destination, 5½ mi. Two lodges, eight cabins available. March-Nov. 1. (615) 436-4473.

**HARTWELL, GA.** **Hartwell Inn.** Colonial style, 19th-century furniture.

**HELEN, GA.** **Helendorf Inn,** G-75; Box 305, 30545. Thirty rooms. Open year-round. (404) 878-2271.

**HENDERSONVILLE, N.C.** **Bonnie Haven Inn,** 1314 Hyman Avenue, 28793. Twenty rooms. Open all year. (704) 697-6151.

**Echo Mountain Inn** (1896), 2849 Laural Park Highway. Overlooks Hendersonville and Blue Ridge Parkway. April to November. (704) 693-9626.

**Havenshire Inn,** 64 West, Rte. 4, Box 455, 28739; Cummings Road. Redwood/cedar English country manor. (704) 692-4097.

**Hotel McCurry,** 755 N. Main Street, 28739. 22 units. June-October. (704) 693-9368.

**The Waverly,** 783 N. Main Street, 28739. 22 units, open all year. (704) 693-9193.

**HIGHLANDS, N.C.** **Colonial Pines Inn,** Hickory Street; P.O. Box 1145, 28741. Six units with private baths. Open year-round. (704) 526-2060.

**Highlands Inn** (1880), Box 1030, 28741. 30 rooms, restaurant. Open April-January. (704) 526-9380.

**Lee's Inn.** 50 units, babysitting. Open May-October. Rate includes three meals for two people. (704) 526-2171.

**Phelps House** (1900s), Main Street, 28741. Open most of the year. (704) 526-2590.

**The Old Edward's Inn,** Main Street, 28741. 21 units. Open May-October. (704) 526-5036.

**JASPER, GA.** **The Woodbridge Inn** (1848). 12 rooms; excellent food. Open year-round. (404) 692-6293.

**LAKE LURE, N.C.** **Pine Gable Inn,** Lake Lure and Chimney Rock Camp Road. Two centuries old. Includes three U.S. presidents on its register.

**Fairfield Mountains, Inc.,** 28746. 100 units. Open all year. (704) 625-9111.

**LAKEMONT, GA.** **Lake Rabun Hotel** (1922), Rte. 1, Box 101A, Lake Rabun Road. 16 rooms; buffet breakfast. April 15-Oct. 30. (404) 782-4946.

**LAKE TOXAWAY, N.C.** **Lake Toxaway Country Club Lodge** (1912), US-64. Victorian lodge, seven guest rooms. Open mid-May-late October. (704) 966-4488.

**LINVILLE, N.C.** **Eseeola Lodge,** P.O. Box 98, 28646. (1930.) 28 units, babysitting. Open June 1-Sept. 8. (704) 733-4311.

**LITTLE SWITZERLAND, N.C.** **Big Lynn Lodge.** NC-226A near milepost 334. Historic country inn; 34 units. (704) 765-4257.

**The Chalet Lodge and Restaurant.** Old world atmosphere. (704) 765-4089.

**MARS HILL, N.C.** **Baird House,** 121 S. Main Street, Box 490, 28754. A bed and breakfast guesthouse; 6 units. Open all year. (704) 689-5722 or 689-4542.

**MOUNTAIN CITY, GA.** **The York House** (1896), off US-441 and G-23, York House Road, north of Mountain City. Oldest inn in north Georgia. 22-room historic inn, meals not served. All year round. (404) 746-2068.

**PISGAH FOREST, N.C.** **The Pines Country Inn** (1883), Rte. 2, P.O. Box 7, 28768. 25 units; dining room. Open May 10-Oct. 31. Dinner and breakfast. (704) 877-3131.

**ROBBINSVILLE, N.C.** **Blue Boar Lodge,** Rte. 1, 28771. Seven units. Open May-Nov. 1. (704) 479-8126.

**Snowbird Mountain Lodge** (1941), Joyce Kilmer Forest Road, 28771. 18 units. Open mid-May-November. Rate includes three meals for two people. (704) 479-3433.

**SALUDA, N.C.** **Saluda Inn** at Greenville and Chestnut streets. Family-style dining, June-October. Open year-round for lodging. (704) 749-5036.

**The Orchard Inn** (early 1900s), US-176, Box 725, 28773. Ten units, restaurant. Open all year. (704) 749-5471.

**The Woods House** (1881), P.O. Box E, 28773. A country inn for city folks. Open May-October. (704) 749-9562.

**SAPPHIRE, N.C.** **Fairfield Inn** (1896), Fairfield Sapphire Valley, 28774. 20 units. (704) 743-3441.

**SAUTEE, GA.** Stovall House Country Inn and Restaurant (1837), G-255, Lake Burton Road. (404) 878-3355.

**SYLVA, N.C.** **Court Hill Inn,** Ridgeway Street, 28779. (704) 586-4484.

**TOCCOA, GA.** Travelers Rest, 6 mi. east of Toccoa on US-123. Built between 1815 and 1840; now a National Historic Landmark and a State Historic Site. Tues.-Sun.

**TRYON, N.C.** **Melrose Lodge,** 211 Melrose Avenue, 28782. Ten units, restaurant, open all year, facilities for handicapped. (704) 859-9419.

**Mill Farm Inn** (1939), NC-108, P.O. Box 1251, 28782. Eight rooms, country setting. (704) 859-6992.

**Pine Crest Inn** (1914), off NC-176, 200 Pine Crest Lane, Box 1030, 28782. 34 units; restaurant. Open all year, except January and February. (704) 859-9135.

**Stone Hedge Inn** (1935), Howard Gap Road. Three guest rooms; dining and lodging. (704) 859-9114.

**WAYNESVILLE, N.C.** **Hallcrest Inn** (1880), 299 Halltop Road, 28786. Twelve units, country inn atmosphere and Southern-style meals. Open June 1-October. (704) 456-6457.

**Heath Lodge,** 900 Dolan Road, 28786. Rustic lodge: 23 units, restaurant. Open mid-May-November. (704) 456-3333.

**The Piedmont Inn** (1880), 630 Eagles Nest Road, P.O. Box 419, 28786. Turn-of-the-century inn; 15 rooms. (704) 456-8636.

**Pisgah Inn,** P.O. Drawer 749, 28786. Fifty units. Open May 1-Nov. 1. (704) 235-8228.

**The Lodge,** 118 Ninevah Road. Dining and lodging. (704) 456-9073.

**The Swag,** Rte. 2, Box 280-A, 28786. Off US-276 near US-19A. Hand-hewn log lodge, elevation 5,000 feet; 12 units. Open end of May-Oct. 31. (704) 926-0430.

# J

# Jogging

The sport that can be undertaken just about anywhere — jogging — is perfect for the cool mountains. A mile or two uphill is sure to get your circulation going. And the scenery is never better than when seen at a jogger's pace.

Jogging events large and small are everywhere. For instance, you can test your toughness in the summertime by running the Island relay based in Dillard, Ga. Or experience a night run and beat the August heat in races such as the Liberty, S.C., Roadrunners Twilight Twosome Road Race and the Brooks Maggie Valley (N.C.) Moonlight Race.

For a real workout, experience a triathlon, such as the one held in Unicoi State Park in Helen, Ga., on Labor Day. Try your endurance as you swim, paddle and run. Bryson City, N.C., has a fall triathlon for swimming, running and canoeing, and a spring triathlon that features biking, running and canoeing. Similar events are held throughout the Blue Ridge area.

Waynesville, N.C., is headquarters for the Haywood Oil Golden Age Olympica, 55 and over, held in the fall. Ladies only compete in the Schlitz Lite Ladies Road Race in Asheville, N.C., in June. Asheville is also the scene of the Parkway Pant, featuring eight-mile and four-mile races.

Fall Apple Festivals in Ellijay, Ga., Westminster, S.C., and Hendersonville, N.C., include road races for the fit. Many other jogging events are associated with annual festivals.

————January————

**TOCCOA, GA.** **Burger King Half Marathon.** By Road Runners Club. Fourth week.

————March————

**LAKE LANIER ISLANDS, GA.** **Lake Lanier Islands,** Buford 500 Meter and 10,000 Meter Runs. Second week.

**CORNELIA, GA.** **Power of Tower Road Race.** By Habersham Recreation Dept. Three- and nine-mile races. Fourth week.

————April————

**ASHEVILLE, N.C.** **Thomas Wolfe 5 and 10 Kilometers.** By Asheville Track Club. First week.

**CHEROKEE, N.C.** **Moccasin Run,** Ceremonial Grounds, US-441. First week.

**PENDLETON, S.C.** **Historic Pendleton Jubilee Runs,** at Pendleton Junior High. First week.

**CULLOWHEE, N.C.** **Cat-A-Thou Race,** at Western Carolina University Track. By WCA Big Cat Club. Third week. (803) 227-7377.

**WAYNESVILLE, N.C.** **Union Ramp Race.** A 6.2-mile road race. By Haywood County Road Runners. Fourth week.

**WESSER, N.C.** **Spring Triathlon,** Nantahala Outdoor Center. 22-mile biking, 4-mile foot race, 8-mile canoe race. Fourth week.

———May———

**ASHEVILLE, N.C.** **Clean Air Road Race.** By Asheville Track Club. First week. (704) 298-5685.

**BRYSON CITY, N.C.** **Annual Spring Triathlon,** Nantahala Outdoor Center. Biking, running, canoeing. First week.

**CULLOWHEE, N.C.** **Jackson County Run for Fun,** Western Carolina University Track. County-wide field day for area school, grades 5-8. First week.

**\*HARTWELL LAKE, GA.** **Annual Hartwell Dam Race.** Hart County Jaycees with cooperation from U.S. Army Corps of Engineers. First week.

**CHEROKEE, N.C.** **Cherokee Fun Run.** By Shades of the Past Car Club. Games, contests, dancing, exhibits. Second week.

**SALEM, S.C.** **Salem Spring Road Run.** By Tamassee-Salem High School. Second week.

**ASHEVILLE, N.C.** **Volksmarch/Walk.** Western Carolina Hiking Club. 6- and 12-mile walks. Fourth week.

**BLAIRSVILLE, GA.** **Mountain Challenge 10K Race.** Young Harris College to Georgia Mountain Fair: 10,000 meters. Fourth week.

**BURNSVILLE, N.C.** **Toe River Valley Road Race.** Yancey County Chamber of Commerce. Fourth week.

———June———

**ASHEVILLE, N.C.** **Schlitz Lite Ladies Road Race,** Biltmore Town Hall. First week. (704) 298-5685.

———July———

**RABUN GAP, GA.** **Rabun Gap to Tybee Island Relay.** First week. (404) 754-3276.

**CHATSWORTH, GA.** **Appalachian Chase.** At U.S. Forest Service Office. 6.2 miles. Second week.

**DAHLONEGA, GA.** **Georgia Conservancy Biathlon.** Canoe and running race. Third week.

**ASHEVILLE, N.C.** **Bele Chere Foot Race.** Fourth week.

———August———

**MAGGIE VALLEY, N.C.** **Moon Light Race,** Waynesville Country Club. National certified runners race. First week.

**CLARKESVILLE, GA.** **Chattahoochee Mountain Fair 10K.** Also 1-mile run by Habersham County Recreation Dept. Second week.

**LIBERTY, S.C.** **Twilight Twosome Road Race.** Liberty Roadrunners. Mid-August.

**HENDERSONVILLE, N.C.** **Apple Festival Road Race,** gazebo on Main Street. Fourth week.

——September——

**ANDREWS, N.C.** **Hillbilly Hilltop Run.** Labor Day.

**HELEN, GA.** **Labor Day Triathlon,** at Unicoi State Park. Events include a swim, paddle and run. Labor Day.

**CANTON, N.C.** **Canton Labor Day Race,** Canton Town Hall. 10K.

**MAGGIE VALLEY, N.C.** **Smoky Mountain Sky High Roundup and Fun Run,** US-19, Ghost Town Amusement Park. First week.

**WESTMINSTER, S.C.** **Apple Festival Road Race,** Westminster High School. By Oconee Road Runners Club. 5,000 and 10,000 meters. First week.

**WAYNESVILLE, N.C.** **Haywood Oil Golden Age Olympics.** For those aged 55 and over. Greater Haywood Chamber of Commerce. Second week.

**ASHEVILLE, N.C.** **Volksmarch,** Biltmore Dairy, US-25. Ages 6-65. 6.2 miles or 12.4 miles. Western Carolina Walking Club. Third week.

**\*BLOWING ROCK, N.C.** **Autumn Road Race,** downtown and Blue Ridge Parkway. 10K foot race, half-mile marathon and mile fun run. By Blowing Rock Chamber of Commerce. Third week.

**CULLOWHEE, N.C.** **Mountain Heritage Day 5 Miler,** Reid Gym, Western Carolina University. By Ruckasegee Running Club. Third week.

**BRYSON CITY, N.C.** **Annual Fall Triathlon.** Swim, run and canoe. Fourth week.

**SUCHES, GA.** **Run Above the Clouds,** Winfield Scott Lake to Woody Gap School. 10K: highest run in Georgia. Fourth week.

——October——

**LAKE JUNALUSKA, N.C.** **Lake Junaluska Run.** 6.2-mile road race around lake. By Haywood County Road Runners. Second week.

**SYLVA, N.C.** **Fall Color Festival Road Race,** Mark Watson Park. By Jackson County Jaycees. Second week.

**CLYDE, N.C.** **Lake Junaluska Race,** Methodist Assembly Grounds. 10K. Second week.

**ELLIJAY, GA.** **Apple Festival Road Race.** Second week.

**WAYNESVILLE, N.C.** **Lake Junaluska Road Race.** 10,000-meter race. By Road Runner Club of America. Second week.

**JASPER, GA.** **Marble Festival Run.** 3.1 miles. Third week.

**WALHALLA, S.C.** **Cross Country Race.** By Oconee Road runners. 4-mile race. Third week.

**BLAIRSVILLE, GA.** **Sorghum Run,** at Civic Center by Kiwanis Club. Fourth week. (704) 745-6935.

## Jogging

**ASHEVILLE, N.C.   Blue Ridge Parkway Annual Parkway Pant.** Eight- and 4-mile races. By Asheville Track Club. Starts at NC-191 exit bridge off the Parkway. First week.

**Shut In Trail Run.** 19-mile race on a trail from Bent Creek to Pisgah Mountain. First week. (704) 298-5685.

**'BOONE, N.C.   Big Apple,** 5-mile run. Second week.

**BLUE RIDGE, GA.   Turkey Trot Run,** Aska Road. 10K. Thanksgiving morning.

**WALHALLA, S.C.   Mountain to the Sea Run.** Oconee Road Runners Club for Diabetes Assoc. Walhalla to Myrtle Beach. Runner obtains pledges and runs turns. Thanksgiving weekend.

# Lakes

The biggest recreational lakes in the Blue Ridge area did not exist when the Indians were in charge. The popular Tennessee Valley Authority Fontana Lake in North Carolina and the U.S. Army Corps of Engineers' projects, Lake Sidney Lanier and Carters Lake in Georgia, and Hartwell Lake bordering Georgia and South Carolina, were created by man.

Lake Sidney Lanier and its islands are the most visited of the 430 Army Corps lake recreation areas in the nation. The lake has a resort hotel, but is free of billboards, fast food stands and souvenir shops. The 60-square-mile lake is public property with miles and miles of tall Georgia pines — which developers cannot touch. Stay in one of the cottages or campsites or rent a houseboat. Fish, swim in the pool or lake, play tennis, indoors or out, hike on nature trails, canoe, boat or play golf. Snorkelers can see the underwater farm houses, churches and other structures covered about ten years ago when the Chattahoochee River was dammed.

The 480-foot-tall Fontana Dam in the Great Smoky Mountains is the highest dam in the eastern United States. The lake has 248 miles of shoreline and is pefect for canoeing and fishing. The Appalachian Trail cuts across its dam. Other major TVA dams and lakes in the area include Appalachia, Hiwassee, Chatuge, Blue Ridge and Nottely.

Protected from development, but open to the public, Lake Jocassee is a place to get away from it all. The lake and its sister, Lake Keowee in northwestern South Carolina, are Duke Power Company reservoirs.

Hartwell Lake borders Georgia and South Carolina on the Savannah, Tugaloo and Seneca rivers. The recreation season on its 962-mile shoreline is basically from April through October. Named after Nancy Hart, a Revolutionary War herione, Hartwell Lake is popular with largemouth bass fishermen, boaters and campers.

### Lake Events

——April——

**LAKE LANIER ISLANDS, GA. Dogwood Regatta.** By Pine Isle/Lanier Sailing Academy. Third week.

——June——

**SKYLAND, N.C. Smoky Mountain Spring Fling.** Water skiing competition at Lake Julian. Sanctioned by the American Ski Assoc. Third week.

——July——

**CHEROKEE, N.C.** **Water Ski Tournament,** Magic Waters Theme Park. Late July.

——September——

**SKYLAND, N.C.** **Smoky Mountain Fall Fling.** Water skiing competition at Lake Julian. Sanctioned by the American Ski Assoc. First week.

# Lakes

**ANDREWS, N.C.** **Nantahala Lake,** off US-19/129, east of Andrews. Remote lake centrally located in Nantahala National Forest.

**ASHEVILLE, N.C.** **Lake Powhatan.** From Asheville take Route 191 south for 4 mi., then Forest Service Road 3484 southwest for 3½ mi. Lakeside camping, picnicking, swimming, drinking water, flush toilets, hiking, fishing. Camping fee.

**BLAIRSVILLE, GA.** **Lake Nottely,** 2 mi. west of US-19 and 129, 10 mi. north of city. A 4,180-acre lake: boat docks, fishing camps. Highway crosses 184-foot dam on G-325.

**Lake Winfield Scott.** Take US-19 and 129 south from town for 10 mi., turn west on G-180 for 7 mi. Clear, 18-acre lake, high in the mountains. Picnicking, camping, swimming, boating and hiking.

**BLUE RIDGE, GA.** **Lake Blue Ridge,** 4 mi. east of Blue Ridge via US-76. A 3,290-acre body of water formed by the Blue Ridge Dam. Camping, fishing, swimming, picnicking and boating.

**BUFORD, GA.** **Lake Sidney Lanier,** north of Buford on G-347. Established in 1957 by Corps of Engineers. Covers 38,000 acres; 40 mi. long; 540 mi. of shoreline, seven marinas. Approximately 14 million visitors annually.

**CASHIERS, N.C.** **Cashiers Lake,** Jackson County off US-64. Boating, swimming, fishing.

**CHATSWORTH, GA.** **Carter's Lake,** G-136, 21 mi. east of I-75, Resaca Exit 133. The deepest Corp of Engineers lake in Georgia. In the Blue Ridge Mountains, south of Chatsworth and Ellijay. Eight public use areas. Highest earth-filled dam east of the Mississippi. Camping, boating, fishing, swimming, picnicking, foot trails.

**CLARKESVILLE, GA.** **Lake Burton,** in Rabun County off G-197. This 13,000-acre lake offers fishing, boating, swimming and other water sports; five public recreation facilities; marinas, and ramps. A public beach is located south of US-76 on the Charlie Mountain Road.

**Nancytown Lake.** Small lake 1½ mi. beyond Lake Russell. Picnicking and campgrounds. (404) 754-6221.

**CLAYTON, GA.** **Lake Rabun,** in Rabun County off G-197 and Old US-23 and 441. Lake offers fishing, boating, swimming and other water sports. Three public recreation facilities including concessions, marina, launching ramp and camping.

**Lake Seed,** in Rabun County off G-197 and old US-23 and 441. No public recreation facilities on this lake.

**Lake Tallulah,** in Rabun County off US-23 and 441.

**Lake Tugaloo,** in Rabun County off US-23 and 441.

**CORNELIA, GA.** **Lake Russell,** 1½ mi. northeast of city on US-123; take a right on Forest Service Road 52 for 2 mi. Tent and trailer camping, boat ramp, swimming, fishing, nature trails; 30-acres.

## Lakes

**FONTANA, N.C.** **Fontana Lake Dam and Power Plant,** on SR-1245 about 2 mi. from Fontana Village on the Little Tennessee River. Largest dam in TVA system and highest in eastern U.S. Dam is 480 feet high and 376 feet wide at its base. The Appalachian Trail runs across the dam; glass-walled power house six stories high is at the base. A cable car carries 40 passengers from the visitor center at the top of the dam down to the powerhouse.

**GLENVILLE, N.C.** **Lake Glenville** (Thorpe Reservoir), located 4 mi. north of Cashiers on NC-107. A 1,462-acre lake with 26 mi. of shoreline. Boating, boat ramps, water skiing, canoeing, fishing, sail boating. Open to the public.

**HARTWELL, GA.** **Lake Hartwell.** Easy access through the city or Hart State Park, 3 mi. north of Hartwell off US-29, or Tugaloo State Park, 6 mi. north of Lavonia, off G-328. A Corps of Engineers recreation lake with 962 miles of shoreline, impounding 56,000 acres. Four marinas and 68 public use areas. Water sports; no rental boats available. Daily.

**Lake Hartwell.** Borders three counties. One of the largest manmade lakes east of the Mississippi; a U.S. Army Corps of Engineers project. Over 56,000 acres with a shoreline of nearly 1,000 mi. Numerous boat ramps (31 in S.C.), camping, picnic facilities dotted about the lake. Two marinas on the S.C. side; several places provide docks for those wanting to dine at restaurants at the lake.

**HIAWASSEE, GA.** **Lake Chatuge,** 2½ mi. west of city, US-76, then ¾ mi. south, G-288. A TVA lake winding around and north of Hiawassee. Fishing, boating, water sports, campground, boat docks.

**HIGHLANDS, N.C.** **Cliffside Lake.** From Highlands take US-64 northwest for 4 mi., then Forest Service Road 57 north for 2 mi. Camping (14 units), picnicking (13 units), drinking water, vault toilets, shelter, swimming, hiking, fishing. Camping fee.

**Harris Lake,** Jackson County. Boating, swimming, fishing.

**Lake Sequoyah.** Named for Sequoyah, a crippled Cherokee hunter whose 85-character syllabary enabled his tribe to record its language for the first time. Lake is popular for boating, fishing and ice skating.

**Mirror Lake.** An impoundment of the Cullasaja River: US-64 to Franklin follows the gorge cut by the river.

**LAKE LURE, N.C.** **Lake Lure,** an impoundment of the Rocky Broad River just north of US-64 and 74 near Chimney Rock. Rimmed by mountains. Developed vacation facilities include an amusement park; lake is 1,500 acres.

**LAKE TOXAWAY, N.C.** **Lake Toxaway,** off US-64, in Jackson County. Fishing, boating, swimming, skiing.

**MARION, N.C.** **Lake James,** 4 mi. east of town. Wooded shoreline stretches 150 mi.; swimming beaches, fishing, picnicking, boating.

**MILL SPRING, N.C.** **Lake Adger,** NC-9 between Mill Spring and Lake Lune.

**MURPHY, N.C.** **Cherokee Lake,** 11 mi. west of Murphy, via US-64 and NC-294. Picnicking (21 units) and fishing.

**Lake Hiwassee.** TVA lake, 6,000 acres, 189 mi. of shoreline.

**PICKENS, S.C.** **Lake Jocassee.** The upper lake in the nuclear and hydro generating complex. A 7,500-acre lake with a 75-mi. shoreline and water depth up to 350 feet. One of the premier trout lakes in the South. Excellent boat ramps provided.

**Lake Keowee,** SC-183 west of Pickens. Eight public access areas, paved boat launching ramps; 18,750 acres with a 225-mi. shoreline. Permits required.

**ROBBINSVILLE, N.C.   Lake Santeelah,** north of Robbinsville off US-129. In Nantahala Forest, near Joyce Kilmer Memorial Forest.

**SAPPHIRE, N.C.   Lake Sapphire,** south of US-64, Jackson County. Boating, swimming, fishing, skiing.

**SUCHES, GA.   Dockery Lake,** off G-60 south, on Forest Service Road 654. A 6-acre trout lake.

**Lake Woody.** Take US-19 and 129 south from Blairsville 10 mi., turn west on G-180 for 12 mi. to Suches intersection off G-60.

**TOCCOA, GA.   Lake Yonay,** 8 mi. north of city, G-184. Remote, uncrowded.

**TRYON, N.C.   Lake Lanier,** on US-176 south. This unusual lake with its surrounding mountains has been compared with Switzerland for its natural beauty; 147 acres.

**WAYNESVILLE, N.C.   Lake Junaluska.** The summer recreational and education center of the World Methodist Council. A 250-acre lake with complete recreational facilities as well as the John Wesley Museum. Nominal charge to public.

# M

## Media

There is "good news" in the mountains if you like to keep abreast of the latest local, state and world happenings — news, sports, weather, music, local events, and public service. The Blue Ridge area has a variety of radio stations, both AM and FM, with programming ranging from classical to country and western music.

A variety of television stations broadcast major network and public television programming.

The printed word is available in many daily, bi-weekly, and weekly newspapers. The weekly newspaper is usually out by Wednesday or Thursday. The larger newspapers include the Asheville *Citizen*, the Atlanta *Constitution*, the Gainesville *Times*, the Greenville *News* and the Charlotte *Observer*.

Many local publications offer a wealth of information about the Blue Ridge area. *Discover Upcounty Carolina* is a quarterly magazine full of information about interesting events, area restaurants, and special outdoor features. *Mountain Vista* is a tabloid that highlights special mountain area attractions, people and events. Many of the local newspapers provide "summer attractions" monthly inserts. The *Mountain Visitor* also provides a wealth of information about mountain events and happenings. (Refer to Tourist Guides at the end of this chapter.)

## Radio Stations

| *Georgia:* | FM | | AM | |
|---|---|---|---|---|
| *Athens | WVOG | - 90.5 FM | WRFC - | 960 AM |
| | WHGC | - 95.5 FM | WCCD - | 1470 AM |
| | WAGQ | - 104.7 FM | WGAU - | 1340 AM |
| | WFOX | - 97.1 FM | | |
| | | | | |
| *Atlanta | WRAS | - 88.5 FM | WPLO - | 590 AM |
| | WRFG | - 89.3 FM | WSB - | 750 AM |
| | WABE | - 90.1 FM | WQXI - | 790 AM |
| | WREK | - 91.1 FM | WGKA - | 1190 AM |
| | WZGC | - 92.9 FM | WAOK - | 1380 AM |
| | WQXI | - 94.1 FM | WCNN - | 68 AM |
| | WPCH | - 94.9 FM | | |
| | WKLS | - 96.1 FM | | |
| | WSB | - 98.5 FM | | |
| | WLTA | - 99.7 FM | | |
| | WBIE | - 101.5 FM | | |
| | WVEE | - 102.2 FM | | |
| | | | | |
| Blue Ridge | WPPL | - 103.9 FM | | |
| Buford | WGCO | - 102.3 FM | WDYZ - | 1460 AM |
| Clarkesville | | | WIAF - | 1500 AM |
| Clayton | | | WGHC - | 1570 AM |
| Cleveland | | | WRWA - | 1350 AM |
| Commerce | | | WJJC - | 1270 AM |
| Cornelia | | | WCON - | 1450 AM |
| Cumming | WWEV | - 91.5 FM | | |
| Dahlonega | | | WDGR - | 1210 AM |
| Ellijay | | | WLEJ - | 1560 AM |
| Gainesville | WBCX | - 89.1 FM | WDUN - | 1240 AM |
| | WFOX | - 97.1 FM | WLBA - | 1130 AM |
| | WWID | - 106.1 FM | WGGA - | 550 AM |
| *Hartwell | | | WKLY - | 980 AM |
| Jasper | | | WYYZ - | 1490 AM |
| Toccoa Falls | WRAF | - 90.9 FM | WLET - | 1420 AM |
| | WLET | - 106.1 FM | WNEG - | 630 AM |
| Young Harris | | | WZEL - | 1380 AM |
| | | | | |
| *North Carolina:* | | | | |
| Asheville | WUNF | - 88.1 FM | WWNC | 570 AM |
| | WBMU | - 91.3 FM | WSKY | 1230 AM |
| | WLOS | - 99.9 FM | WISE | 1310 AM |
| | | | WRAQ | 1380 AM |
| | | | | |
| Black Mountain | WMIT | - 106.9 FM | WFGW | 1010 AM |
| | | | WPMS | 1320 AM |

| | | | | |
|---|---|---|---|---|
| *Boone | | | WATA | - 1450 AM |
| Brevard | | | WPNF | - 1240 AM |
| Bryson City | | | WBHN | - 1590 AM |
| Burnsville | | | WKYK | - 1540 AM |
| Canton | WPTL | - 92 FM | WPTL | - 920 AM |
| | WWIT | | WWIT | - 970 AM |
| Franklin | WRFR | - 97 FM | WFSC | - 1050 AM |
| | | | WLTM | - 1480 AM |
| Hendersonville | WKIT | - 102.5 FM | WHVL | - 1600 AM |
| | WXNC | - 92.5 FM | WHKP | - 1450 AM |
| Marion | | | WBRM | - 1250 AM |
| Mars Hill | WVMH | - 90.5 FM | | |
| Mooresville | | | WHIP | - 1350 AM |
| Murphy | WKRK | - 107.1 FM | WCVP | - 600 AM |
| | | | WKRK | - 1320 AM |
| Newland | | | WJTP | - 1130 AM |
| Spruce Pine | | | WTOE | - 1470 AM |
| Swannanoa | WMIT | - 108.9 FM | WFGW | - 1010 AM |
| | | | WBMS | - 1350 AM |
| Sylva | | | WRGC | - 680 AM |
| Tryon | | | WTYN | - 1550 AM |
| Waynesville | | | WPLT | - 920 AM |
| | | | WWIT | - 970 AM |
| | | | WHCC | - 1400 AM |

## South Carolina

| | | | | |
|---|---|---|---|---|
| *Anderson | WCKN | - 101.1 FM | WANS | - 1280 AM |
| | WANS | - 107.3 FM | WAIM | - 1230 AM |
| Clemson | WSBF | - 88.1 FM | WSNW | - 1150 AM |
| | WEPR | - 90 FM | WCCP | - 1560 AM |
| | WBFM | - 98.1 FM | | |
| Easley | | | WELP | - 1360 AM |
| | | | WPKZ | |
| *Gaffney | WAGI | - 105.3 FM | WEAC | - 1500 AM |
| | | | WFGN | - 1570 AM |
| *Greenville | WESC | - 92.5 FM | WHYZ | - 1070 AM |
| | WFBC | - 93.7 FM | WESC | - 660 AM |
| | WEPR | - 90 FM | WMRB | - 1490 AM |
| | WDRD | - 91 FM | WGLV | - 1440 AM |
| | WSPA | - 99 FM | WFBC | - 1330 AM |
| | WLJV | - 89.3 FM | WMUU | - 1260 AM |
| *Greer | | | WCKI | - 1300 AM |
| | | | WEAB | - 800 AM |
| Pickens | | | WPKZ | - 1540 AM |
| Seneca | WBFM | - 98.1 FM | WSNW | - 1150 AM |
| *Spartanburg | WSPA | - 98.9 FM | WASC | - 1530 AM |
| | | | WKDY | - 1400 AM |
| | | | WORD | - 910 AM |
| | | | WSPA | - 950 AM |
| Travelers Rest | | | WBBR | - 1580 AM |
| Walhalla | | | WGOG | - 1000 AM |

## National Public Radio Stations:

| | |
|---|---|
| *Atlanta, Ga. | WABE - 90.1 FM |
| *Greenville, S.C. | WEPR - 90.1 FM |
| *Columbia, S.C. | WLTR - 91.3 FM |

## Weather Information:

Common frequencies: (162.40, 162.475, 162.55 MHz)

| | |
|---|---|
| *Atlanta, Ga. | 162.55 MHz |
| *Atlanta, Ga. | (404) 871-1212 |
| *Raleigh, N.C. | (919) 829-1111 |
| *Columbia, S.C. | (803) 355-1212 |

# Television Stations

| | | |
|---|---|---|
| Asheville, N.C. | WLOS | - 13 |
| | | |
| *Atlanta, Ga. | WSB | - 2 |
| | WAGA | - 5 |
| | WGTV | - 8 |
| | WXIA | - 11 |
| | WIGG | - 17 |
| | WHAE | - 47 |
| | | |
| *Greenville, S.C. | WFBC | - 4 |
| | WGGS | - 16 |
| | WNTV | - 29 |
| | | |
| *Spartanburg, S.C. | WSPA | - 7 |

## Public Television

| | | |
|---|---|---|
| *Athens, Ga. | WGTV | - 8 |
| Chatsworth, Ga. | WCLP | - 18 |
| *Chapel Hill, N.C. | WUNC | - 33 |
| *Greenville, S.C. | WNTV | - 29 |
| *Sneedsville, Tenn. | WSJK | - 2 |

*Georgia Weeklies. Area Codes 404.*

*Athens. *Observer.* Thurs. Clark. 548-6346.
Blairsville. *North Georgia News.* Thurs. Union. 745-6343.
Blue Ridge. *Summit Post.* Thurs. Fannin. 623-2019.
Chatsworth. *Times.* Thurs. Murray. 695-4646.
Clarkesville. *Tri-County Advertiser.* Thurs. Habersham. 754-4139.
Clayton. *Tribune.* Thurs. Rabun. 782-3312.
Cleveland. *Telegraph.* Wed. 17 Counties. 865-5019.
Cleveland. *White County News.* Thurs. White. 865-4718.
Commerce. *News.* Wed. Jackson. 335-5121.
Cornelia. *Northeast Georgian.* Thurs. Habersham. 778-4215.
Dahlonega. *Nugget.* Thurs. Lumpkin. 864-3613.
Dahlonega. *Lumpkin Legend.* Thurs. Lumpkin. 864-7856.
Dawsonville. *Dawson County Advertiser and News.* Thurs. Dawson. 265-2345.
Ellijay. *Times Courier.* Thurs. Gilmer. 635-4313.
Gainesville. *Tribune.* Wed. Hall. 536-2331.
Hartwell. *Sun.* Thurs. Hart. 376-8025.
Hiawassee. *Towns County Herald.* Fri. Towns. 745-6343.
Hiawassee. *Mountain News.* Thurs. Towns. 896-4244.
Toccoa. *Record.* Thurs. Stephens. 886-7476.

*Georgia Dailies. Area Codes 404.*

*Athens. *Daily News* (A.M.), *Banner-Herald* (P.M.). 459-0123.
*Atlanta, *Constitution* (A.M.), *Journal* (P.M.). 572-5151
*Daily World* (Tues., Thurs., Fri., Sat.). 659-1110.
Gainesville. *Times.* 532-1234.

*North Carolina Weeklies. Area Codes 704.*

Andrews. *Journal.* Thurs. Cherokee. 321-4271.
*Bakersville. *Mitchell Ledger.* Thurs. Mitchell. 688-3613.
Black Mountain. *News.* Thurs. Buncombe. 669-8727.
Brevard. *Transylvania Times.* Mon./Thurs. Transylvania. 883-8156.
Burnsville. *Yancey Journal.* Thurs. Yancey. 682-2120.
Canton. *Enterprise.* Thurs. Haywood. 648-2381.
Cashiers. *Chronicle.* Thurs. Macon. 743-2246.
Franklin. *Press.* Mon./Thurs. Macon. 524-5122.
Highlands. *Highlander.* Thurs. Macon. 526-2962.
Marion. *McDowell News.* Mon./Wed./Fri. McDowell. 652-3313.
Sylva. *Herald and Ruralite.* Thurs. Jackson. 586-2611.
Waynesville. *Mountaineer.* Mon./Wed./Fri. 456-5301.

*North Carolina Dailies. Area Codes 704.*

Asheville. *Citizen* (A.M.), *Times* (P.M.). 252-5611.
*Charlotte. *Observer* (A.M.), *News* (P.M.). 379-6300.
Hendersonville. *Times News.* 692-0505.
Tryon. *Bulletin.* 859-9151.

### South Carolina Weeklies. Area Codes 803.

Clemson. *Messenger.* Wed. Pickens. 882-2375.
Easley. *Progress.* Wed. Pickens. 855-0355.
*Gaffney. *Ledger.* Mon./Wed./Fri. Cherokee. 489-1131.
*Mauldin. *Tribune.* Wed. Greenville. 963-8934.
Pickens. *Sentinel.* Wed. Pickens. 878-2453.
Seneca. *Journal Tribune.* Mon./Wed. Oconee. 882-2375.
Walhalla. *Keowee Courier.* Wed. Oconee. 638-5856.
Westminster. *News.* Oconee. 638-5856.

### South Carolina Dailies. Area Codes 803.

*Anderson. *Independent-Mail* (A.M.). 224-4321.
*Greenville. *News* (A.M.), *Piedmont* (P.M.). 298-4100.
*Spartanburg. *Herald* and *Journal* (A.M.). 582-4511.

## Tourist Guides

*Beech Mountain Tribune.* Winter guide to Beech Mountain. (Free.)

*Discover Upcountry Carolina.* Four seasons guide to northwestern South Carolina. (Free.)

*Four Seasons Weekly.* Weekly guide to what's happening in the Hendersonville, N.C., area. (Free.)

*Georgia Journal.* Every-other-month magazine covering Georgia. (Subscription.)

*Guide To Great Smoky Mountains National Park.* Listings of activities and events. (Free.)

*Look at Western North Carolina.* Activities and events on an every-other-month basis. (Free.)

*Milepost.* Complimentary magazine guide to the Blue Ridge Parkway.

*Mountain Trails.* Monthly, subscription paper covering the Smoky Mountain area.

*Mountain Vista.* Monthly paper printed from May to October covering western North Carolina and High Country. (Free.)

*Recreational Opportunity Guide to Pisgah National Forest.* Resource catalog to fun times at Ranger Stations.

*Smokies Guide.* Official newspaper of the Smokies Park, published quarterly.

*Summertime 19 ...* Annual summer supplement to the *Transylvania Times* (Brevard, N.C.).

*The Highlander Vacation Magazine.* Covers western North Carolina area.

*The Mountain Visitor.* Smoky Mountain area weekly. (Free.)

*This Week of Western North Carolina.* One of the oldest publications of its type in the U.S. (Free.)

*Tourist News.* Weekly guide printed from May to October covering western North Carolina (Bryson City). (Free.)

*Variety Vacationland.* Monthly insert in the Asheville *Citizen Times.*

# Mountain and Rock Climbing

The Blue Ridge area is blessed with a wide variety of mountain tops. Some, such as Brasstown Bald, Ga., and Mt. Mitchell, N.C., are very accessible by vehicles, while others such as Wayah Bald, Whitside Mountain, Table Rock and Hawkshill must be reached by foot trails.

For the more serious climber, the rugged, wild terrain of high country will satisfy even the most avid. Linville Gorge offers several climbs with varying degrees of difficulty. Just outside the gorge area are Table Rock, a 400-foot vertical wall with bolted and unbolted routes, and Shortoff Mountain, another 400-foot wall offering face and crack climbing. If friction and face climbing are your favorties, check out Looking Glass Rock near US-276, north of Brevard.

In northeast Georgia two popular climbing areas are Yonah Mountain near Helen, where both civilians and U.S. Army Rangers practice their skills, and Tallulah Gorge near Clayton on US-441.

*Note: See also Hiking section for a list of outdoor centers and resource information.*

## Mountains and Mountain Climbing

*Highest Mountains:*

| STATE | MOUNTAIN | ELEVATION |
| --- | --- | --- |
| GA | Brasstown Bald | 4,784 |
| NC | Mt. Mitchell | 6,684 |
| SC | Sassafras Mountain | 3,548 |
| TENN | Clingmans Dome | 6,643 |

**BAKERSVILLE, N.C.   Roan Mountain,** 13 mi. north of Bakersville via forest road off NC-261 at Carvers Gap. A unique 600-acre botanical area containing the world's largest natural garden of crimson-purple rhododendron. Elevation: 6,286 feet.

**BARNARDSVILLE, N.C.   Craggy Mountain Scenic Area.** Take County Route 2173 (Dillingham Road) southeast for 5 mi., then Forest Service Road 74 for 8 mi. to parking area. Near Craggy Gardens recreation area. Hiking, fishing. Free.

**BLAIRSVILLE, GA.   Brasstown Bald Mountain,** G-75 and G-66 or US-19/129, G-180, G-66. The visitor center provides information on recreation opportunities.

**BLOWING ROCK, N.C.   Blowing Rock,** US-221-321. A unique mountain peak 4,090 feet above Johns River Gorge. Observation tower.

**BREVARD, N.C.   Looking Glass Rock Scenic Area,** on US-276, 11 mi. north of Brevard. Has a sheer drop of some 400 feet on its north side. Acquired its name from the water that seeps down its face and glistens in the light.

**Fire Lookout Towers** on Frying Pan, Rich, Sassafras and Toxaway mountains provide panoramic perspectives. (704) 883-3700.

**BURNSVILLE, N.C. Mt. Mitchell,** highest peak in the eastern United States (6,684 feet). Named in honor of Dr. Elisha Mitchell of the University of North Carolina. Covered with spruce and fraser fir. (704) 675-4611.

**Black Mountain,** on the South Toe River near the foot of Mt. Mitchell. From Burnsville, take US-19 east for 5 mi., Route 80 south for 12 mi., then Forest Service Road 472 south for 3 mi. Camping, hiking, fishing. Mt. Mitchell Trail begins at campground. (704) 675-4611.

**CASHIERS, N.C. Whiteside Mountain,** off US-64. Rises more than 2,100 feet from the valley floor to an elevation of 4,930 feet; sheer granite cliffs from 400 to 750 feet high. A 2-mi. foot trail climbs to the top and circles the crest.

**CHEROKEE, N.C. Clingmans Dome,** Great Smoky Mountains National Park. Named in honor of Thomas Lanier Clingman. 6,643 feet. Includes spiral walk to observation platform.

**CLAYTON, GA. Rabun Bald Mountain,** from city via Rabun Bald Trail. Elevation: 4,663 feet. View of Chattahoochee National Forest.

**COWPENS, S.C. Glassy Mountain,** can be seen to the north between the Middle Tyger River and SC-101. Its 1,000-foot cliff and sheer rock face are part of the 2,542-foot mountain.

**FRANKLIN, N.C. Wayah Bald,** US-69 southwest for 5 mi.; Route 1310 (Wayah Bald Road) west for 10 mi.; Forest Service Road 69 north for 6 mi. A stone observation tower on the Appalachian Trail offers spectacular panoramas of the area mountains.

**HENDERSONVILLE, N.C. Jump-Off Rock,** West-Laurel Park. Rock hangs over valley. Panoramic view.

**Mt. Pisgah,** off the Blue Ridge Parkway. Rises to 5,749 feet. Hike the 1 mi. trail.

**JACKSON COUNTY, N.C. Whiteside Mountain.** 4,390 feet. See four states.

**LINVILLE, N.C. Hawksbill Mountains.** Rock formation resembles a hawk's bill. Elevation: over 3,000 feet.

**Grandfather Mountain,** Blue Ridge Parkway and US-221. Private scenic attraction: natural animal area, hang gliding and mile-high swinging bridge. April to mid-November (704) 733-4337.

**Table Rock,** NC-181 and County Road 210. Overlooks Linville Gorge. Elevation: 3,000 feet. Includes lookout tower.

**PICKENS, S.C. Table Rock Mountain.** Elevation: 3,124 feet. Where the Indians say a giant chieftain sat to dine. A nearby mountain called the Stool was said to be where he sat. (803) 878-9065.

**Caesar's Head Mountain,** north on US-276. Provides a place to view the Blue Ridge Mountain ranges. Facilities include an overlook, gift shop and a snack bar. Elevation: 3,028 feet.

**ROCKY BOTTOM, S.C. Sassafras Mountain.** A narrow, paved road winds off US-78 to the U.S. Forestry Lookout Tower; near Rocky Bottom off SC-11. From its summit you can see into North Carolina, Tennessee and Georgia.

**TOCCOA, GA. Currahee Mountain.** Its name is a Cherokee word meaning "standing alone." Rises 1,740 feet.

# Rock Climbing

**ASHEVILLE, N.C.** **Devil's Courthouse,** about 40 mi. south of Asheville on the Blue Ridge Parkway or 1 mi. north of NC-215. Routes: 1. Tourist route; 2. Direct route; 3. The Groove; 4. Zig Zag.

**BREVARD, N.C.** **Looking Glass Rock,** US-276 north from Brevard into Pisgah. Ranger Station provides maps and information. Routes: 1. South side, 12 routes; 2. Northwest face (the nose), 9 routes; 3. North face, 5 routes.

**CLEVELAND, GA.** **Yonah Mountain,** between Cleveland and Helen, Ga., on G-75 north to Helen for 3.8 mi. Routes: 1. The Boulder (teaching area) 3 routes; 2. The main face, 12 routes; 3. The Lowers, 11 routes. Note: Army rangers have used Mt. Yonah as a training ground.

**DAHLONEGA, GA.** **Camp Frank D. Merrill,** U.S. Army Ranger Camp. Rappelling, orienteeing, rock climbing, rope bridge building.

**\*GASTONIA, N.C.** **Crowders Mountain State Park,** 6 mi. west of Gastonia. Climbing available on many exposed rock faces.

**HIGHLANDS, N.C.** **Whiteside Mountain.** One of the sheerest cliffs in the eastern United States.

**MARION, N.C.** **Linville Gorge Wilderness Area,** located west of Marion. The gorge offers several climbs with varying degrees of difficulty. Permit required; obtain from the National Forest Services office in Marion.

**Shortoff Mountain,** south of Table Rock, outside the Linville Gorge Wilderness Area. The 400-foot wall presents classic face and crack climbs on the Carolina and Gold Coast walls.

**Table Rock,** just outside the Linville Gorge Wilderness Area. A 400-foot vertical wall has both bolted and unbolted routes on conventional face and crack climbing. Permit not required; it is suggested that you notify park officials when climbing.

**ROARING GAP, N.C.** **Stone Mountain.** 13 ascent routes. Elevation: 2,035 feet.

**TALLULAH FALLS, GA.** **Tallulah Gorge,** Clayton area, US-441. Digital Delight (a multi-pitch route rated at 5.7 or 5.8.).

**\*WINSTON-SALEM, N.C.** **Hanging Rock State Park,** 32 mi. north of Winston-Salem. Climbs are available on Moore's Knob and Cook's Wall.

**Pilot Mountain State Park,** 24 mi. north of Winston-Salem off US-52. Face climbing on Little Pinnacle.

*Climbing Resources:*

**DECATUR, GA.** **Bob Ordner,** 3792 Citation Drive, 30034. Instruction.

**HOT SPRINGS, N.C.** **Climb-East, Inc.,** Box 488, 28743. Climbing in Pisgah National Forest from June 1 to Sept. 5. Experienced instructors. (704) 622-3535.

**MORGANTON, N.C.** **N.C. Outward Bound School,** 28655.

**PISGAH, N.C.** **Eagle's Nest Camp,** Pisgah Forest, N.C.

Book: *Southern Rock — A Climber's Guide,* by Chris Hall, The East Woods Press.

# Museums

Museums in the Blue Ridge area offer enough excitement to dispel the myth that museums are boring places smelling like mothballs.

At the Museum of the Cherokee Indian in Cherokee, N.C., a priceless collection of artifacts is housed in a modern, million-dollar building. Visitors may hear English texts translated into Cherokee language and view 1,000-year-old fluted spearheads, 2,000-year-old pottery and unique visual displays.

The Folk Art Center on the Blue Ridge Highway near Asheville, N.C., is the home of the Southern Highland Handicraft Guild. The highly selective guild draws craftsmen from a nine-state area. The highest quality handmade baskets, dolls, dulcimers and other items are on display, and many are for sale.

Other museums such as those in Burnsville, N.C., and the Old Sautee Store near Helen, Ga., have a country flavor: antiques, pottery, soaps, candles, books and hundreds of other things, some of which are for sale.

One of the most important art collections in the Southeast is found at Bob Jones University's Gallery of Sacred Art and Bible Lands in Greenville, S.C. Great works of art such as Rembrandt's "Head of Christ" and "Christ on the Cross" by Peter Paul Rubens may be seen.

The N.C. Mining Museum at Little Switzerland, the Franklin Gem/Mineral Museum in Franklin, N.C., and the Coburn Mineral Museum in Asheville, N.C., focus on gems, minerals and mining.

Gold started a rush to Dahlonega, Ga., in 1828 — long before the forty-niners went to California. Today, the Dahlonega Courthouse Gold Museum tells the story of that first American gold rush.

Toy lovers will enjoy seeing the thousands of old and antique toys at the S.C. Antique Toy Museum in Pendleton. Cars, trucks, dolls, trains, boats, planes, games and toy soliders from the 1800s to 1940s may be seen. Western Carolina University's Mountain Heritage Center is a great place to learn about the history and culture of the mountains. Visit the C.W. Long Museum in Jefferson, Ga., the birthplace of anesthesia, to learn about early medicine.

*(Note: See also Art Displays.)*

**ASHEVILLE, N.C.   Coburn Mineral Museum,** Civic Center, Haywood Street. Has a collection of gems and minerals of North Carolina plus others from around the world. Year-round, Tues.-Fri., 10 A.M. to 5 P.M.; Sat.-Sun., 1 to 5 P.M. Free. (704) 254-7162.

**Estes-Winn Antique Car Museum,** Weavers Building, Biltmore Industries. Mon.-Sat.

**Western N.C. Museum and Heritage Center,** AB Tech Campus, 283 Victoria Road. Restoration of Smith-McDowell House, built in 1840. June-October. Closed Mondays. (704) 253-9231.

**BLAIRSVILLE, GA.   Choestoe Village Schoolhouse Museum,** intersection of G-180 and US-126. One-room country school with old-fashioned educational exhibits. Where Georgia poet Byron Herbert Reece went to school. Open year-round. Free. (404) 745-5472.

**BLOWING ROCK, N.C.   Mystery Hill and Blue Ridge Mountain Antique Museum.** On US-321, just off US-221, north of Blowing Rock, N.C. A well done series of optical illusions. Picnic area, well stocked antique museum. June-August, 8 A.M.-9 P.M.; April, May, September, October, 9 A.M.-5 P.M. (704) 264-2792.

**\*BRASELTON, GA.   Car Museum,** Road Atlanta, southeast of Gainesville on G-53. Home of the Sports Car Club of America National Championship Race as well as a racing and sports car museum. Year-round, Mon.-Fri. Museum: free. Races: admission. (404) 967-6143.

**BREVARD, N.C.   Brevard College,** Chelf Mineral and Gem Collection, Science building foyer. Open to the public.

**CHEROKEE, N.C.   Cyclorama Wax Museum,** located ¾ mi. from Cherokee on US-19 north. See the vast empire of the early Cherokee Nation fade away on large-scaled electronic maps. Over 75 life-sized figures authentically costumed and displayed in scenes. Hear 300 years of Cherokee history presented in an unusual and exciting manner. Open daily. April-October; open evenings June-Labor Day. Facilities for the handicapped. MasterCard and Visa accepted. (704) 497-4521.

**Museum of the American Indian,** on Main Street in downtown. Artifacts and modern handicrafts of the American Indian. Interesting, educational, varied and colorful. Exhibits range from ancient Yuma and Folsom Points of 10,000 to 15,000 years ago to modern wood carvings. Open April-October. Free. Donations accepted. (704) 497-2330.

**Museum of the Cherokee Indian,** on US-441 north at Drama Road. Presents the entire Cherokee story from the time of the first Americans to the present, using multimedia theaters and innovative exhibits. Prehistoric and historic artifacts on display. Open daily and evenings except Sunday, mid-June-August. Open daily, September-mid-June. Admission. Group rates available. (704) 497-3481.

**CLEMSON, S.C.   Indian History Museum,** Keowee-Toxaway State Park. Outdoor exhibit. Enclosed display of Cherokee history (past and present). Tues.-Sun.

**CHESNEE, S.C.   Cowpens Museum,** Cowpens National Battlefield, off US-11 (Scenic Highway). (803) 463-3201.

**CULLOWHEE, N.C.   Geology Museum at Western Carolina University,** Stillwell Building. Rock and mineral exhibits. Mon.-Fri. Free. (704) 227-7268.

**Mountain Heritage Center,** Western Carolina University, NC-107, administration building. Celebrates mountain life with a portrayal of the region's natural heritage, Indian heritage and pioneer heritage. The center encourages scholarship in the history of the region and makes available loan exhibits, lectures and media presentations. Mon.-Fri. Closed Dec. 15-Jan. 2.

**DAHLONEGA, GA.   The Dahlonega Courthouse Gold Museum,** town square. Commemorates the nation's first major gold rush in 1828 and recounts the operation of a branch of the U.S. Mint here from 1837 to 1861. Year-round. Tues.-Sun. Admission; under 12 free. (404) 864-2257.

**DAWSONVILLE, GA.   Moonshine Museum,** US-19 and G-53. Capital of moonshine whiskey belt. Four model stills in operation.

**DILLARD, GA.** **Vintage Auto Museum,** US-441. Private collection of over 250 cars. Elvis Presley's 1960 Mark V Lincoln; 1936 Lincoln Limo (Roosevelt, Truman and Eisenhower). (404) 746-2626.

**FRANKLIN, N.C.** **Franklin Gem and Mineral Museum,** Phillips Street off Main Street. Mineral specimens, fossils, gems, Indian artifacts. Mon.-Sat.

**GAINESVILLE, GA.** **Elachee Creative Museum and Nature Science Center,** Brenan Avenue and Sycamore Street. (404) 534-ARTS.

**GILLESPIE GAP, N.C.** **Museum of N.C. Minerals,** Blue Ridge Parkway Milepost 331. Show-and-tell museum about how N.C. minerals are utilized. By National Park Service. Free.

**HAYESVILLE, N.C.** **The Clay County Historical and Arts Center.** Houses a permanent exhibition of historical artifacts in the restored Old Clay County Jail. (704) 896-2244.

**HELEN, GA.** **Doll and Toy Museum,** downstairs, Gesellschaft Mall, Main Street. Unique collection of more than 2,000 antique dolls, 1835-1975. Open daily, June 1-Nov. 30. Open weekends, weather permitting, in April, May and December. Admission. (404) 878-3493.

**Museum of the Hills,** in the Castle Inn, Main Street. Features waxworks, artifacts and collected arts and crafts. Chronicles the history of the north Georgia mountains, socially, recreationally and historically. Educational for the entire family. Admission. Open daily. (404) 878-3140.

**HIGHLANDS, N.C.** **Highlands Biological Station, Inc. Museum of Natural History,** P.O. Box 404, 28741. Regional station for basic biological research. Exhibits and displays. Nature study classes for children. Lectures for adults. (704) 526-2112.

**'JEFFERSON, GA.** **The Crawford W. Long Museum,** College Street. Located at the site of the office where, on March 30, 1842, Dr. Long performed the first operation using ether. Displays include the doctor's personal possessions, photographs, and a story of the development of anesthesia. Year-round. Closed Mon. Free. (404) 367-5307.

**MARION, N.C.** **The Carson House,** US-70 west of Marion. Museum of local history built in 1780 by Col. John Carson.

**MARS HILL, N.C.** **The Southern Appalachian Center,** Mars Hill College library. Promotes activities and exhibits that preserve the cultural and social heritage in the Blue Ridge Mountains.

**MONTREAT, N.C.** **The Marion Boggs Museum,** Montreat-Anderson College. Contains items relating to church history, a children's museum, costumes, paintings, sculpture, graphics, music, coins, photographs. Open Mon.-Sat.

**MURPHY, N.C.** **Cherokee County Museum,** Valley River Avenue, near courthouse. Houses a collection of early American tools, housewares, gems, Indian artifacts.

**NEWLAND, N.C.** **Avery County Historical Museum,** to the left of the courthouse. Saturdays and Sundays. Special tours available by advance notice. (704) 733-5872, 733-5173, or 733-5407.

**OLD FORT, N.C.** **Mountain Gateway Museum,** Catawba Avenue and Water Street. Describes the culture of the region and includes the interior of a log building that was once the First Presbyterian Church. Tues.-Sat.

**PENDLETON, S.C.   Pendleton District Agriculture Museum,** off US-76. Pre-1925 farm machinery and implements. Administered by the Pendleton District Historical and Recreation Commission. Open by appointment.

**South Carolina Antique Toy Museum,** 106 W. Queen Street. Antique toys of every description. The historic house which contains the museum is interesting in itself. Open daily, March-September. (803) 646-3333.

**SALUDA, N.C.   Mineral Museum.** Open to the public. Free.

**SAUTEE-NACOOCHEE, GA.   Old Sautee Store Museum.** G-17, 4 mi. from Helen. National Register of Historic Places. Largest collection of old store memorabilia in Georgia. Built more than a century ago. Open daily. (404) 878-2281.

**SENECA, S.C.   The Lunney Museum,** 211 S. First Street. Historic home and furnishings of Dr. William J. Lunney. Open Thurs.-Sat. (803) 882-9656.

**SPRUCE PINE, N.C.   The North Carolina Minerals Museum,** 5 mi. south of Spruce Pine on the Blue Ridge Parkway at Gillespie Gap, milepost 330.9. Contains specimens of most of the more than 300 minerals indigenous to North Carolina. Open daily. April 15-Oct. 15. Free.

**SWANNANOA, N.C.   Warren Wilson Museum,** Warren Wilson College, Williams Building. Log structure contains Pisgah culture and artifacts during the 1000-1450 era.

**TRYON, N.C.   Polk County Historical Museum,** in a community center in the old Tryon Depot, at 1 Depot Street. The museum is in the baggage room. Tues.-Thurs.

**Tryon Antique Car Museum,** NC-108.

**WAYNESVILLE, N.C.   Museum of North Carolina Handicrafts** (Shelton House), 307 Shelton Street. Circa 1875. Heritage crafts by master workers from Manteo to Murphy are gathered, an outgrowth of the 1951 state fair "Village of Yesteryear." They include 19th-century handmade furniture, rugs, bed coverings, pottery, carvings, Letts portrait dolls, western Indian and Cherokee crafts. April 15-Nov. 15. Closed Mon. and Tues. Winter, by appointment. (704) 456-3664.

**YOUNG HARRIS, GA.   Appalachian Archives of Georgia,** Mountain Regional Library. Books, records, video tapes, cassettes and periodicals of mountain life; 8,000 songs. (404) 656-5030.

**Rollins Planetarium,** Young Harris College. Ask for printed schedule of events. (404) 379-3990.

# Music

The best in musical performances may be heard year-round in the Blue Ridge Mountains, but summer is special. That's when audiences venture outdoors to hear jazz artists lakeside or lunchtime concerts on downtown streets.

North Carolina's nationally acclaimed Brevard Music Center offers a summer season including chamber music, operas, pops concerts and symphony orchestras. Concerts are also held at Clemson University in Clemson, S.C., University of Georgia at Gainesville, and at Western Carolina University in Cullowhee, N.C.

Grandfather Mountain's annual "Singing on the Mountain" has drawn thousands of people for more than 60 years. The gospel festival and open air sing-along in Linville, N.C., has attracted evangelists Billy Graham and Oral Roberts.

Even small towns like Rabun Gap, Ga., have their share of culture. The town has a summer concert series offering talent such as the Southern Brass Quintet. Bryson City, N.C., shows off its local talent during summer concerts in the Swain County Recreational Park Amphitheater. Hiawassee, Ga., packs in the people when country singing stars appear in summer and early fall at the Georgia Mountain Fairgrounds.

Chamber music rings through Burnsville, N.C., when the Presbyterian Church holds its Music in the Mountains concert in August. Highlands, N.C., is the place to hear chamber music in July on Sunday afternoons at the Episcopal church.

Clarkesville, Ga., celebrates fall with a festival focusing on homemade musical instruments such as the fiddle, banjo and dulcimer. The October day ends with an after-dinner hoedown.

Winter events include Young Harris College's Madrigal Dinner Concert in November. At this Georgia college an English dinner is served while spectators enjoy music from the 15th, 16th and 17th centuries.

*Note: See also Bluegrass Music section.*

### Music Parks

**BLUE RIDGE, GA.** Sugar Creek Music Park, G-5 north. (404) 632-2560.

**CHEROKEE, N.C.** Smoky Mountain Jamboree, US-441 north. Outdoor music theater. Weekends. (704) 497-9195.

**CLAYTON, GA.** Appalachian Music Park. Open-air auditorium. (704) 369-3769.

**CROSSNORE, N.C.** Jim and Jennie's High Country Music Park. (704) 733-2807.

**CUMMING, GA.** **Lanierland Country Music Park,** 12 mi. from city off G-306; follow signs. Every other Sat. night, May-October. (404) 681-1596.

**YOUNG HARRIS, GA.** **New Country Rhoades Music Park,** Rte. 66 north. Sat., 2:30 P.M. and 7 P.M. (bluegrass). Sun., 2-6 P.M. (gospel). (404) 896-4191.

**The New Homestead Coffeehouse,** US-76. Blues, ballads, gospel, folk, country, historical tales, lullabyes. Every other Fri. night. (404) 379-2231 or (705) 837-9538.

**MURPHY, N.C.** **Sunnypoint Music Park,** US-64. (704) 644-5109.

# Musical Events

## ———February———

**GAINESVILLE, GA.** **Lanier Symphony Orchestra,** Brenau College. Since January, 1982. First week.

**CLEMSON, S.C.** **Chamber Music Concert,** Clemson University's Daniel Hall Auditorium. Since 1982. Second week.

**GAINESVILLE, GA.** **Gainesville Pro-Musica Concert Series,** Quinlan Art Center and Georgia Mountain Center. Third week.

**Lanier Symphony Series,** Gym of '36, Brenau College. February and May concerts.

## ———March———

**ASHEVILLE, N.C.** **Yo Yo Ma,** N.C. Symphony, Asheville Civic Center. Since 1980. Third week.

## ———April———

**BRASSTOWN, N.C.** **Brasstown Concert Assoc.,** John C. Campbell Folk School. Six concerts including spring concert on Sundays. (704) 837-2775.

**BLUE RIDGE, GA.** **Gospel Sing Celebration,** Sugar Creek Music Park. Since March 1982. First week. (404) 632-2560.

**ASHEVILLE, N.C.** **North Carolina Symphony,** Thomas Wolfe Auditorium. Since 1980. Second week. (919) 733-2750.

**GAINESVILLE, GA.** **Concert Series,** Pearce Auditorium, Brenau College. Second week.

**Performing Arts Showcase Festival,** Quinlan Art Center, Green Street. By Gainesville Music Club. Performing and listening to classical music. Second week.

**CULLOWHEE, N.C.** **Western Carolina University Recital,** at the Music/English building. Third week.

## ———May———

**LAKE LANIER ISLANDS, GA.** **Sunkist Sunset Concerts,** lakeside amphitheater. Weekend concerts for the entire family. Co-sponsored by Sunkist and WZGC Radio. May-August.

**WAYNESVILLE, N.C.** **Sunday Afternoon Concert Series,** public library. Free. Last Sun. of the month, May-September.

**ASHEVILLE, N.C.** **Asheville Symphony Orchestra with the North Carolina Dance Theater,** Thomas Wolfe Auditorium. Sun. First week.

**North Carolina Symphony,** Thomas Wolfe Auditorium. A night at the Pops. First week.

**FRANKLIN, N.C. Annual Mother's Day Concert.** By Macon County Arts Council. Atlanta Chamber Players. First week.

**ASHEVILLE, N.C.** "Song O' Sky" **Chapter of Sweet Adelines Annual Show,** at Thomas Wolfe Auditorium. Third week.

**GAINESVILLE, GA. Spring Choir Concert,** Pearce Auditorium at Brenau College. Third week.

**HAYESVILLE, N.C. Chamber Orchestra Omega,** N.C. Symphony, Hayesville High School. Third week.

**MARION, N.C. Musical.** East McDowell Junior High School. Fourth week.

**RABUN GAP, GA. Annual Concert Series.** Since 1973. Rabun Gap Hambidge Center. Third week.

**YOUNG HARRIS, GA. Annual Spring Concert,** Young Harris College Music Dept., Susan B. Harris Chapel. Third week.

————June————

**BRYSON CITY, N.C. Musical Concerts,** Swain County Recreational Park Amphitheater. Local talents. Summer months.

**ASHEVILLE, N.C. Hallelujah Asheville,** Sunday in the Park, city park. Family entertainment. June-early September.

**HELEN, GA. The River Palace,** P.O. Box 664, 30545; Main Street on the Chattahoochee River. A plush turn-of-the-century music hall featuring family entertainment and audience participation. Performances: June-October. Every night except Wed. Admission. Special group performances and rates available. (404) 878-3150.

**CANDLER, N.C. Annual Singing in Hominy Valley,** Hominy Valley singing grounds on NC-151 near Asheville. Top gospel quartets of the nation. Second week.

**CULLOWHEE, N.C. Cullowhee Music Festival,** at Western Carolina University. Features opera, pop concerts, musical theater and chamber music. Staged by the music department. Third week.

**'BOONE, N.C. Gospel Festival,** 17 mi. south of town on NC-105, then 2 mi. north on US-221. Fourth week.

**LINVILLE, N.C. Annual Singing on the Mountain.** Professional and amateur performers gather on Grandfather Mountain for a day-long program of traditional and gospel music. Since 1923. Fourth week. (704) 898-4720.

————July————

**HENDERSONVILLE, N.C. Chamber Music Concert.,** Blue Ridge Technical College Auditorium. Swannanoa Chamber Players. By Hendersonville Friends of Chamber Music. Admission. Weekends.

**HIGHLANDS, N.C. Highlands Chamber Music Festival,** Parish Hall of Episcopal Church. Sunday afternoons. Month of July.

**SWANNANOA, N.C. Annual Swannanoa Chamber Festival.** Hendersonville Friends of Chamber Music Concert Series; Warren Wilson College Concert Series, and Music in the Mountains Concert Series. Since 1968. Early July.

*Music*

**BREVARD, N.C.   Brevard Music Center.** Six stage productions highlight the Brevard Music Center's season which includes chamber music, orchestral and symphonic bands, individual recitals and ballet. Music camp offers an intense educational program for 330 music students. July 1-Mid Aug. (704) 884-2019

**HELEN, GA.   Musical Production.** Annual award-winning musical production performed on the banks of the Chattahoochee River in the new pavilion. Admission. Mid-July-first week of August. (404) 878-2521.

**CULLOWHEE, N.C.   Summer Music Camp,** Western Carolina University. First week. (704) 227-7242.

**RABUN GAP, GA.   Annual Concert Series,** Hambidge Center. Southern Brass Quintet. Second week. (404) 746-5718.

**SPRUCE PINE, N.C.   Music in the Mountains Chamber Music Series,** Methodist Church. Fourth week.

————August————

**ASHEVILLE, N.C.   "Hallelujah Asheville!" Festival,** downtown. Outdoor concerts every Friday afternoon. Quality Forward, P.O. Box 22, 28802. Month of August.

**HELEN, GA.   Good Old Days,** basement of Castle Inn. Afternoon or evening musical performances. Closed Wed. August-end of October.

**BURNSVILLE, N.C.   Music in the Mountains,** Presbyterian Church. Chamber Music series. First week.

**SWANNANOA, N.C.   Annual Swannanoa Chamber Festival.** Hendersonville Friends of Chamber Music Concert Series; Warren Wilson College Concert series; Music in the Mountains Concert Series. (704) 298-3325.

**BLAIRSVILLE, GA.   Old-Time Music Festival,** since 1980, Nottley River Campground, US-19/129. Third week.

**ASHEVILLE, N.C.   Sunday in the Park,** University of North Carolina Lipinski Auditorium. Includes Golden Rod Puppets, Maggie Ree, blues and jazz music. Free. Third week.

**HENDERSONVILLE, N.C.   Hendersonville Symphony Concert,** Hendersonville High School auditorium. Fourth week.

**TOCCOA, GA.   Citizens Band Jamboree** (since 1976), National Guard Armory. By Stephens County React. Fourth week.

————September————

**CLEMSON, S.C.   Clemson University Concert Series** (since 1938), Littlejohn Coliseum. September, October, February and March.

**LAKE LANIER, GA.   Labor Day Gospel Sing.**

**CENTRAL, S.C.   Central Wesleyan College Music Concert,** Folger Fine Arts Building. Free. Guest artist series. Third week.

**ENKA, N.C.   Land of the Sky Marching Band Festival,** Enka High School. Fourth week.

————October————

**GAINESVILLE, GA.   Gainesville/Brenau Pro Musica Concert Series,** Brenau/Pearce Auditorium. October, December, February, April.

*Music*

**DILLARD, GA.** **Music in the Mountains,** Hambidge Center. Free. Early October.

**MARS HILL, N.C.** **The Lamar Lunsford Music Festival,** Mars Hill College. First week.

**CULLOWHEE, N.C.** **Mountain Classic Marching Band Festival,** Music Dept., Western Carolina University. High school bands from North Carolina, South Carolina, Georgia, Tennessee. Second week.

**BRASSTOWN, N.C.** **Brasstown Concert Season,** John C. Campbell Folk School. Six concerts a year. Second week.

————November————

**ASHEVILLE, N.C.** **Asheville Symphony Concert,** Thomas Wolfe Auditorium. First week.

**YOUNG HARRIS, GA.** **Madrigal Dinner Concert,** Willis Dobbs Dining Hall, by Music Dept. College choir, vocal ensemble, Christmas carols. English dinner included. Admission. Second week.

**BLUE RIDGE, GA.** **Ensemble Musica Du Camera,** Fannin County High School. By Blue Ridge Mountain Arts Assoc. Chamber music. Third week.

**GAINESVILLE, GA.** **Atlanta Symphony Concert.** By Arts Council. Georgia Mountain Center. Admission. Fourth week.

————December————

**GAINESVILLE, GA.** **Chamber Music at Pearce Auditorium,** Brenau College. First week.

**TOCCOA, GA.** **Toccoa Symphony Orchestra.** Christmas concert. Georgia Baptist Assembly. Since 1975. First week.

**GAINESVILLE, GA.** **Gainesville Chorale,** Pearce Auditorium at Brenau College. The Gainesville Chorale performs Handel's Messiah. Performances Sun. and Mon. Admission. Second week.

# N

# National Forests, Recreation Areas and Wilderness Areas

The South's most valuable vacation paradise has no luxury hotels, no casinos, no gourmet restaurants. This paradise is 15 billion dollars worth of clean, usable water, recreational areas, timber, wildlife, and livestock grazing range — the national forests. But the worth of these forests can't be measured in dollars. Priceless assets include tranquility broken only by a foot stepping on a twig, rushing brooks that invite hikers to cool their feet and majestic trees that provide shade and shelter.

The Blue Ridge area includes Sumter National Forest's General Andrew Pickens section in South Carolina, home of the Walhalla Trout Hatchery. Chattahoochee National Forest in Georgia holds spectacular Tallulah Gorge and the southern end of the Appalachian Trail, as well as Brasstown Bald, at 4,784 feet, Georgia's highest point. Nantahala National Forest in North Carolina is known for gorgeous azalea and rhododendron displays. The Joyce Kilmer Memorial Forest is dedicated to the poet who wrote "Trees," published in 1914. Maintained in its natural state, this forest has yellow poplar, hemlock, sycamore, basswood, dogwood and white pine. North Carolina's Pisgah National Forest includes Mt. Mitchell, at 6,684 feet, the highest point east of the Mississippi; Linville Falls Gorge; Craggy Gardens, and Roan Mountain where purple rhododendrons bloom.

Within the national forests are special wilderness areas where no motorized conveyances are permitted and there are no amenities such as piped water, prepared shelters, toilets, tables or grills. Pisgah's Shining Rock Wilderness contains interesting vegetation, waterfalls and unique outcroppings of white quartz. Nantahala's Joyce Kilmer Slickrock Wilderness has 60 miles of hiking trails. The Chattahoochee National Forest contains archaeological sites: Blood Mountain, scene of a Cherokee Battle, and Track Rock Gap with ancient Indian carvings called petroglyphs. The primitive and undeveloped Chattooga River, also in the Chattahoochee, is classified as a wild and scenic river to protect its unique features. The Chattahoochee's wilderness areas are the Cohutta with its wild trout streams and the Ellicott Rock Wilderness.

Scientific forestry began in the Asheville area when George Vanderbilt brought Dr. Carl Schenck from Germany to serve as chief forester on his 125,000-acre estate. Schenck founded the first school of forestry in 1898. The site is marked today by the Cradle of Forestry in America in Pisgah National Forest.

## National Forests

**CHATTAHOOCHEE NATIONAL FOREST, GA.**  Located in the northern and northeastern part of Georgia, it is one of the largest national forests in the South (720,000 acres). Stretching from Lafayette in the northwest to Clayton in the northeast, Chattahoochee is noted for its many scenic and historical areas, delighting botanists, photographers and sightseers. The recreational areas include camping sites, picnicking areas, and points of interest and of special beauty. The areas are usually open from late spring to early fall.

**NANTAHALA NATIONAL FOREST, N.C.**  The Cherokees named the forest "The Land of the Noonday Sun." Located in the southwest section of North Carolina, covering the land area from Asheville to the Tennessee border (515,000 acres), it includes the rugged wilderness areas of Slickrock and Shining Rock. The Joyce Kilmer Memorial Forest, one of the few virgin forests in the region, is especially beautiful.

**PISGAH NATIONAL FOREST, N.C.**  The 493,000-acre forest is wild, yet accessible. It consists of two principal sections of the North Carolina Blue Ridge, one northeast and one south of Asheville, and includes in addition to the main Blue Ridge range, several of the cross ranges between the Blue Ridge and the Unakas, which are often more rugged than the main Appalachian ridges themselves. One of these west-east ranges in the Pisgah Forest, the Black Mountains northeast of Asheville, has 13 summits of more than 6,000 feet in its short span of 15 mi. The entire range rises about 4,000 feet above the surrounding country, and one of the Black Mountain peaks, Mount Mitchell, is the highest mountain elevation, 6,684 feet, in eastern North America. The Blue Ridge Parkway reaches its highest point as it crosses the longest of these cross ranges, the Balsam Mountains, at Richland Balsam, 6,410 feet, southwest of Asheville in the National Forest.

**SUMTER NATIONAL FOREST, S.C.**  Sumter National Forest comprises three divisions: Enoree, in the S.C. midlands, 157,140 acres with headquarters in Newberry; Long Cane, in the western portion, 111,909 acres with headquarters in Greenwood; and General Andrew Pickens, in the northwestern part, 72,593 acres with headquarters in Walhalla. Recreation areas, picnicking, camping and primitive camping areas are in the forests. Year-round, daily. Free.

## National Forest Wilderness Areas

**CHATTOOGA NATIONAL WILD AND SCENIC RIVER, GA., N.C.**  The Chattooga is familiar to thousands as the location for the filming of the movie *Deliverance*. Beginning on the crest of the Blue Ridge mountains in North Carolina, this sparkling mountain river divides South Carolina and Georgia for more than 40 mi. In this rush of water, the river drops an average of 49.3 feet per mile, sometimes following a narrow and treacherous route over rapids, around boulders and through rock flumes with intermittent quiet deep pools and calm stretches where paddlers can relax and enjoy the magnificent National Forest which flanks the river.

**COHUTTA WILDERNESS AREA, GA.**   Cohutta Wilderness is a large section (34,100 acres) of the Chattahoochee National Forest that includes the southern end of the Applachian Mountain chain and two of the best wild trout streams in Georgia (Conasauga and Jack rivers). Accessible by footpath only. Ideal for backpackers. Year-round, except coldest part of winter. US-411 north, Chatsworth, Ga.

**ELLICOTT ROCK WILDERNESS AREA, N.C., S.C., GA.**   It has changed little since the Cherokees lived and hunted in the area. The region is popular with campers, backpackers, anglers, photographers, hunters and nature lovers. A 4½-mi. trail leads you to Ellicott's Rock, a boundary marker for three states: South Carolina, North Carolina and Georgia.

**JOYCE KILMER-SLICKROCK WILDERNESS, N.C.**   A 15,000-acre wilderness in the Unicoi Mountains about 2 mi. southwest of the Great Smoky Mountains National Park. From Robbinsville, take US-129 north 1.1 mi., turn left onto Route 1116 and proceed 3.5 mi.; turn right onto Route 1127 and proceed 7.2 mi., then turn left onto Forest Service Road 416 and go 0.5 mi. In 1975 the 3,840-acre forest was combined with the watershed of Slickrock Creek on the Tennessee-North Carolina border to form this large wilderness area in one of the most primitive, remote, and botanically interesting regions of the southern Appalachians. The Joyce Kilmer Memorial Forest, named in honor of the author of "Trees," is one of the last remaining stands of virgin woodland in the United States. In this heavy rain forest, adjoining Big and Little Santeetlah creeks, stands of virgin poplar, hemlock, sycamore and oak have grown to rare proportions. Tulip poplars 20 feet around tower 125 feet above the forest floor. Within the Memorial Forest, Little Santeetlah Creek, together with its tributaries, offers miles of trout fishing on one of the most beautiful of all North Carolina streams.

**LINVILLE GORGE WILDERNESS AREA, N.C.**   From Marion, take US-221 north for 16 mi.; at Linville Falls, take Route 183 east for .8 mi. to Route 105. Some of the most rugged terrain and spectacular scenery in eastern America are in the 7,575 acres through which the swift-running Linville River has cut a 20-mile chasm, falling 2,000 feet through the gorge before slowing in the Catawba Valley. The gorge, which runs north-south, is deep and narrow, walled in by high bluffs and rock cliffs rising more than 1,000 feet on either side. This area was inaccessible to the loggers who timbered in the North Carolina mountains early in the 20th century, and virgin forest remains, along with a number of rare species of flora. Mountain laurel, sand myrtle and four native rhododendron species bloom in the gorge. The gorge is popular among trout fishermen. In the southeast, where trout streams are found only at high elevations and are generally of modest size, the Linville River is a rare pleasure because of its breadth, its swift currents, its wilderness setting and the quality of its habitat.

**SHINING ROCK WILDERNESS AREA, N.C.**   Southwest of Asheville is a 13,650-acre preserve named for its distinctive outcroppings of white quartz. The most massive and visible of these, Shining Rock Mountain itself, is near its center. Elevations vary from 3,500 feet to more than 6,000 feet at the summit of Cold Mountain, an unusual conical peak near the northern boundary of the Wilderness. The Pigeon River, a major tributary of the Tennessee River, arises in the Wilderness, and its headwaters provide rewarding and relatively accessible trout fishing. The Wilderness is maintained as a primitive area. Access to the interior is by foot trail only. There are no camping facilities, but primitive camping is permitted. The unique vegetation makes fires particularly hazardous, and the Forest Service requests caution. Access is off the Blue Ridge Parkway at milepost 420.2 southwest.

## National Forest Recreational Areas

*Chattahoochee Recreation Areas:*

**ANDREWS COVE.**  G-75 north from Cleveland for 14 mi.

**ANNA RUBY FALLS.**  G-75 north from Helen for 1 mi. to Robertstown. Turn right on G-356 to entrance of Unicoi State Park. Follow signs through park for 3⅓ mi. to parking area.

**BARNES CREEK.**  US-441 north from Chatsworth for 4 mi. Turn right at traffic light in Eton and follow Forest Service Road 18 east for 10 mi. Turn left on Forest Service Road 68 for 4 mi.

**BRASSTOWN BALD VISITOR CENTER.**  US-19/129 south from Blairsville for 8 mi. Turn left (east) on G-180 for 9 mi.; then turn left (north) on G-66 for 3 mi.

**COOPER CREEK.**  G-60 north from Dahlonega for 24 mi. Turn right on Forest Service Road 236 for 3 mi.

**DEEP HOLE.**  G-60 north from Dahlonega for 27 mi.

**DeSOTO FALLS.**  US-129 north from Cleveland for 15 mi.

**DOCKERY LAKE.**  G-60 north from Dahlonega for 12 mi. Turn right on Forest Service Road 654 for 1 mi.

**FERN SPRINGS.**  US-123 north from Cornelia for 6 mi.

**FRANK GROSS.**  G-60 north from Dahlonega for 27 mi. Turn left on Forest Service Road 69 for 5 mi.

**LAKE BLUE RIDGE.**  US-76 east from Blue Ridge for 2 mi. Turn south on Forest Service Road 605 for 2 mi.

**LAKE CHATUGE.**  US-76 west from Hiawassee for 2 mi. Turn left on G-288 for 1 mi.

**LAKE CONASAUGA.**  US-411 north from Chatsworth for 7 mi. Turn right at the traffic light in Eton and follow Forest Service Road 18 east for 10 mi. Turn left on Forest Service Road 78 for 10 mi.

**LAKE RUSSELL.**  US-123 north from Cornelia for 1½ mi. Turn right on Forest Service Road 59 and go 2 mi. to the entrance.

**LAKE WINFIELD SCOTT.**  US-19 south from Blairsville for 10 mi.; turn west on G-180 for 7 mi.

**MORGAN POINT.**  US-76 east from Blue Ridge for 6 mi. Turn right on paved County Road 616 for 1 mi.

**MULKY.**  G-60 north from Dahlonega for 26 mi. Turn right on Forest Service Road 4 for 5 mi.

**PANTHER CREEK.**  US-441/23 south from Tallulah Falls for 3 mi.

**RABUN BEACH.**  US-441/23 south from Clayton for 7 mi. Turn west on County Road 10 for 5 mi.

**TALLULAH RIVER.**  US-76 west from Clayton for 8 mi. Turn right on unnumbered, paved road for 4 mi. Turn left on Forest Service Road 70 for 1 mi.

**TATE BRANCH.** US-76 west from Clayton for 8 mi. Turn right on unnumbered paved road for 7 mi. Turn left on Forest Service Road 70 for 4 mi.

**WARWOMAN DELL.** County Road 5 east from Clayton for 3 mi.

**WATERS CREEK.** US-19 north from Dahlonega for 12 mi. Turn left on Forest Service Road 34 for 1 mi.

**WOODY GAP.** G-60 north from Dahlonega for 14 mi.

*Nantahala Recreation Areas:*

**APPLE TREE GROUP CAMP.** US-19/129 east from Andrews for 1 mi. to Junaluska Road (NC-1505); turn right (south) on Junaluska Road for about 10 mi.

**ARROWOOD GLADE.** US-64 west from Franklin for 5 mi.; turn right (west) on NC-1310 (Wayah Bald Road) for 3 mi.

**BOB ALLISON.** US-19 east from Andrews for 1 mi. Turn southeast on NC-1505 (Junaluska Road) for 5 mi. Turn south on Forest Service Road 440 and go 6 mi.

**CABLE COVE.** NC-28 east from Fontana Village for 4.7 mi.; turn left on Forest Service Road 520 for 1.4 mi.

**CHEOAH POINT.** US-129 north from Robbinsville for 7 mi.; turn left on NC-129, go .8 mi.

**CLIFFSIDE LAKE.** US-64 northwest from Highlands for 4 mi. Turn right (north) on Forest Service Road 57 for 2 mi.

**DRY FALLS.** US-64 northwest from Highlands for 3 mi.

**FEREBEE MEMORIAL.** From Bryson City go west on US-19 for 16 mi.

**FIRES CREEK.** From Hayesville take NC-1307 northeast 3 mi. to NC-1300. Go west 5.7 mi. to Forest Service Road 1344. Go north 1.6 mi.

**HANGING DOG.** NC-1326 (Joe Brown Highway) northwest from Murphy for 5 mi.

**HORSE COVE.** From Robbinsville go northwest on US-129 for 8 mi.; turn left on NC-1134 and go 2.5 mi.; turn left on Forest Road 416 and go 3.7 mi.

**JACKRABBIT MOUNTAIN.** US-64 east from Hayesville for 6.2 mi.; turn right (south) on NC-175 for 2.5 mi., then right (west) on NC-1155 for ¼ mi.

**JOYCE KILMER.** From Robbinsville, go northwest on US-129 for 8 mi. Turn left on NC-1134 and go 2.5 mi. Turn left on Forest Road 416 and go 3.7 mi. Turn right on Forest Road 305 and go to the end of the road.

**LAKE CHEROKEE.** US-64 southwest from Murphy for 8 mi.; turn right (northwest) on NC-294 for 3 mi.

**LLEWELLYN COVE TRAIL.** From Fontana Village, take NC-28 east for .5 mi.

**MAPLE SPRINGS OBSERVATION POINT.** From Robbinsville, go northwest on US-129 for 8 mi. Turn left on NC-1134 and go 2.5 mi. Turn left on Forest Road 416 and go 4 mi. Turn right on NC-1127 and go to end of road.

**NANTAHALA GORGE.** From Bryson City go west on US-19 for 16 mi.

**RATTLER FORD.** From Robbinsville go northwest on US-128 for 8 mi. Turn left on NC-1134 and go 2.5 mi. Turn left on Forest Road 416 and go 4 mi.

**SHOWBIRD.** From Robbinsville take US-129 north 1.1 mi. Turn left on NC-1116; go 3.5 mi. to NC-1127; turn right; go 1.3 mi.

**STANDING INDIAN** From Franklin go west on US-64 for 12 mi.; exit on old US-64 and go east 2 mi. Turn right (south) on Forest Road 67 and go 2 mi.

**TSALI.** US-19 south from Bryson City for 9 mi. Turn right (west) on NC-28 for 5.5 mi. Turn right (north) on Forest Service Road 521 (gravelled) for 1.5 mi.

**VAN HOOK GLADE.** US-64 northwest from Highlands for 5 mi.

**WAYAH BALD.** US-64 southwest from Franklin for 5 mi. Turn right (east) on Wayah Bald Road, NC-1310, for 10 mi.; right (north) on Forest Service Road 69 for 6 mi.

**WAYAH CREST.** US-64 southwest from Franklin for 5 mi. Turn right (west on NC-1310) and go 10 mi.

**WHITESIDE MOUNTAIN.** From Highlands go east on US-64 for 6 mi.

**WHITEWATER FALLS.** At Sapphire (on US-64, about midway between Rosman and Highland) turn south on NC-1149 for 9 mi. Or, approaching from the south, take SC-171 (paved) north from Salem for 16 mi.

*Pisgah Recreation Areas:*

**BALD MOUNTAIN.** US-19E west from Burnsville for 6 mi. to US-19W. Turn right (north) for 17 mi.

**BARKHOUSE.** Go north on US-221 from Marion for 16 mi. to Linville Falls; then take NC-183 east for 4 mi. Take NC-181 southeast for 5.5 mi.

**BLACK MOUNTAIN** From Burnsville, go east 5 mi. on US-19; then turn right on NC-80 south for 12 mi. Turn right (south) on Forest Service Road 472 for 3 mi.

**BOONE FORK.** From Lenoir take NC-90 northwest for 7 mi.; then north on Forest Service Road 101 for 3 mi.

**BRIAR BOTTOM GROUP CAMP.** From Burnsville, go east 5 mi. on US-19; then turn right on NC-80, south for 12 mi.; turn right (south) on Forest Service Road 472 for 3 mi.

**BROWN MOUNTAIN OVERLOOK.** From Linville Falls go east on NC-183 for 4 mi. Turn right (south) on NC-181 and go 7 mi. to overlook.

**CAROLINA HEMLOCK.** From Burnsville go east for 5 mi. on US-19. Turn right on NC-80 south for 9 mi.

**COONTREE CREEK.** US-276 north from Brevard for 9 mi.

**CORNER ROCK.** From Asheville go north 10 mi. on US-19-123. Exit on NC-197 and go east 5 mi. to Barnardsville. Turn right on Forest Road 231 and go 4 mi.

**COVE CREEK GROUP CAMP.** From Brevard take US-276 north for 8.4 mi.; go to Forest Service Road 475, turn west, and go 3.4 mi.

**CRADLE OF FORESTRY IN AMERICA.** On US-276, 15 mi. north of Brevard; 4 mi. south of intersection with Blue Ridge Parkway.

**CURTIS CREEK AUTO TOUR.** Take US-70 east from Old Fort for 1.7 mi. Turn north on Forest Road 482.

**DAVIDSON RIVER.** From Brevard take US-276 north for 5 mi.

**KUYKENDALL GROUP CAMP.** From Brevard, take US-64 west 3.5 mi. Turn north on Forest Service Road 471 for 1 mi. Turn northeast on Forest Service Road 2058, go 1 mi.

**LAKE POWHATAN.** Take NC-191 south from Asheville for 4 mi. Turn right (southwest) on Forest Service Road 3484 for 3.5 mi.

**LOOKING GLASS FALLS.** Go north from Brevard on US-276 for 9.4 mi. A short trail leads from the parking lot to the base of the falls.

**LOST COVE.** From Burnsville, go east 5 mi. on US-191. Turn right on NC-80 and go south for 12 mi. Turn right on Forest Road 472 and go 1 mi.

**MORTIMER.** NC-90 (Wilson Creek Road) northwest from Lenoir for 25 mi.

**MULBERRY.** From Lenoir take NC-90 northwest for 7 mi. to Forest Service Road 101 and go 5 mi. northwest.

**MURRAY BRANCH.** From Hot Springs go .5 mi. west on US-25-70. Turn left on NC-1304 and go 4 mi.

**NORTH MILLS RIVER.** NC-191 south from Asheville for 13.5 mi. Turn right (west) on Forest Service Road 478 for 5 mi.

**OLD FORT.** US-70 west from Old Fort for 2.5 mi.

**PINK BEDS.** On US-276, 15 mi. north of Brevard (4 mi. south of intersection with Blue Ridge Parkway).

**PISGAH ECOLOGY TRAIL.** Located behind Pisgah Ranger Station on US-276.

**ROAN MOUNTAIN.** NC-261 north from Bakersville for 10 mi. Turn left (west) on Forest Service Road 130 for about 2 mi. Approaching from the north, take Tenn-143 south from the city of Roan Mountain, for 12.5 mi.

**ROCKY BLUFF.** NC-209 south from Hot Springs for 3 mi.

**SLIDING ROCK.** On US-276, 12 mi. north of Brevard.

**STONY FORK.** From Asheville, go west on I-40 20 mi. to Candler; then go 7.5 mi. south on NC-151.

**SUNBURST.** US-276 east from Waynesville for 7 mi. Turn right (south) on NC-215 for 8 mi.

**SYCAMORE FLATS.** On US-276, 4 mi. north of Brevard.

**TABLEROCK.** From Linville Falls go east on NC-183 for 4 mi. to NC-181. Go south for 2 mi. and turn right on Forest Road 210. Go 4.9 mi. to Forest Road 210B; turn right; and go 1.6 mi.

**WHITE PINES.** From Brevard go north on US-276 for 6 mi.

**WISEMAN'S VIEW.** From Linville Falls go east on NC-183 for .5 mi. Turn right (south) on NC-1560 and go 4 mi.

# National Forest and Wilderness Resources:

## CHATTAHOOCHEE NATIONAL FOREST:

Brasstown Ranger District
Highway 76 West
Blairsville, Ga. 30512
(404) 745-6259

Chattooga Ranger District
Burton Road
Clarkesville, Ga. 30523
(404) 754-6221

Chestatee Ranger District
Warwick and N. Derrick Streets
Dahlonega, Ga. 30533
(404) 864-2541

Cohutta Ranger District
401 Old Ellijay Road
Chatsworth, Ga. 30705
(404) 695-6736

Tallulah Ranger District
N. Main Street
Clayton, Ga. 30525
(404) 782-3320

Toccoa Ranger District
Star Route
Blue Ridge, Ga. 30513
(404) 632-2031

## NANTAHALA NATIONAL FOREST:

District Ranger   (Cheaoah District)
U.S. Forest Service
Route 1, Box 16A
Robbinsville, N.C. 28771
(704) 479-6431

Tusquittee Ranger District:
District Ranger
U.S. Forest Service
201 Woodland Drive
Murphy, N.C. 28906
(704) 837-5152

Highlands Ranger District:
District Ranger
U.S. Forest Service
P.O. Box 749
Highlands, N.C. 28741
(704) 526-3765

Wayah Ranger District:
District Ranger
U.S. Forest Service
P.O. Box 469
Franklin, N.C. 28734
(704) 524-6441

## PISGAH NATIONAL FOREST:

Pisgah Ranger District:
District Ranger
U.S. Forest Service
P.O. Box 8
Pisgah Forest, N.C. 28768
(704) 877-3265

Toecane Ranger District:
District Ranger
U.S. Forest Service
P.O. Box 128
Burnsville, N.C. 28714
(704) 682-6146

Grandfather Ranger District:
District Ranger
U.S. Forest Service
P.O. Box 519
Marion, N.C. 28752
(704) 652-4841

French Broad Ranger District:
District Ranger
U.S. Forest Service
P.O. Box 128
Hot Springs, N.C. 28743
(704) 622-3202

Forest Supervisor
U.S. Forest Service
P.O. Box 1437
Gainesville, Ga. 30501
(404) 536-0541

National Forests in North Carolina
P.O. Box 2750
Asheville, N.C. 28802
(704) 258-2850, ext 601

## NATIONAL WILDERNESS RESOURCES:

Sumter National Forest
1801 Assembly Street
Columbia, S.C. 29202
(803) 765-5222

U.S. Fish and Wildlife Service
Southeast Regional Office
Box 95067
Atlanta, Ga. 30347

United States Forest Service
S.E. Regional Office
Suite 800
1720 Peachtree Road N.W.
Atlanta, Ga. 30309

## GOLDEN AGE PASSPORTS:

Golden Age and Golden Access Passports are now available from the Chattahoochee
and Oconee national forests. These passports allow citizens 62 years of age or older,
blind persons or permanently disabled persons to get a 50 percent discount on fees at all
National Forest Recreation Areas. Passports free. Available from any of the nine Forest
Service offices in Georgia. Identification or information that verifies age, disability or
blindness is needed to receive a Passport.

## FOR THE KIDS:

Ranger Rick magazine, published monthly by the National Wildlife Federation, is interesting and informative. Join Ranger Rick's Nature Club:

Ranger Rick
8925 Leesburg Pike
Vienna, Va. 22180

# O

# Outlets

Save money on your vacation — by spending! Spend some days and dollars shopping in the abundant factory outlets in Georgia and the Carolinas. Just about anything is sold for less in these stores, whether it's baked goods, textiles, carpets, clocks, or pots and pans.

The outlets are so plentiful it would take months to visit them all. But even a few hours is enough time to make lots of headway on your Christmas shopping. If you are pressed for time, try going to one of the outlet shopping centers such as Outlet Square in northeast Atlanta. The mall stores, while not necessarily connected to a factory, offer name brand merchandise at 20 to 70 percent discounts. You'll find books, luggage, clothing for the whole family, greeting cards, wall coverings, window treatments, health foods, jewelry and more.

Greenville, S.C., is the home of Mills Centre Factory Outlet Mall, originally a mill built in 1894. Stores specialize in baby care items, kitchen products, handbags, luggage, shirts, shoes, jewelry, designer loungewear, oriental rugs and sportswear.

The South's first enclosed factory outlet shopping mall was Westgate Outlet World in Macon, Ga. Stores there offer everything from linens and draperies at Bibb Outlet, to records and tapes at Dreamboat Annie's. There are plenty of clothing and textile products and even a maternity outlet.

If carpet is on your shopping list, Dalton, Ga., is a must. That's where 65 percent of the world's carpet is manufactured — more than 500 million yards per year. There are more than 80 carpet outlets that sell directly to the public.

Greenville, S.C., is the place to head for towels, bedspreads and more. Look for upholstery fabrics at J & J Upholstery, or try Home Maker Home Fashions for beautiful home furnishings.

Don't forget to search the smaller towns for bargains, too. Remember that the finds won't always be a great saving. Don't judge an outlet by its exterior. Carry sizes and measurements with you, and don't buy anything you aren't sure you want to keep. Be knowledgeable about prices, so you recognize the real bargains.

Outlets in the Atlanta metro area, in Anderson, S.C., in Spartanburg, S.C., and Greenville, S.C., have been included in the listings because of the tremendous variety and quality of outlet products and their proximity to the Blue Ridge area and to the popular tourist routes to the area.

**'ALPHARETTA, GA.** **Alpharetta Bargain Store,** 131 US-19. Designer wear.

**'ANDERSON, S.C.** **ABC Jeans,** Belvedere Plaza.
**Ashley's Outlet Store,** Lakeside Shopping Center, SC-28. Bypass.
**Home Maker Home Fashions,** Watson Village Shopping Center. Room fashions. (803) 225-6303.
**Kollege In,** Lakeside Shopping Center, SC-28 Bypass.
**Lady Outlet,** 1403 N. Main Street. Junior sportswear. (803) 226-3428.
**Piedmont Factory Outlet,** Belvedere Plaza. Men's, women's and boys' sportswear. (803) 226-6842.
**Ruth Fashions, Inc.,** 104 Concord Road. Women's dresses and sportswear. (803) 225-1375.
**S-Mart Store,** 3302 N. Main Street. Family clothing. (803) 224-2784.
**Tomorrow Mac Mfg. and Outlet,** Middleton Road. Sportswear.

**ASHEVILLE, N.C.** **Andrex Factory Outlet,** 180 Deareview Road. Fabrics. (704) 253-4534.
**Ann Michele Originals,** Innsbruck Mall. Sportswear.
**Arby's Shoe Store,** 1076 Patton Avenue. Factory defects. (704) 258-9154.
**Asheville Baggage Co.,** 68 Lexington Avenue. Luggage. (704) 252-8020.
**Banner House Factory Store,** 56 Haywood Street (downtown). Shoes, luggage, handbags. (704) 253-2040.
**Bazaar,** Leicester Highway. Collection of outlets under one roof.
**Brand Name Fashion Outlet,** 1380 Tunnel Road. Manhattan and Lanvin wear.
**Carolina Gift Factory,** outlet store, 40 Coxe Avenue. Decorative accessories. (704) 254-5660.
**Chipman's Factory Outlet,** 40 Coxe Avenue. Famous name clothing. (704) 258-3878. Also: US-176, E. Flat Rock. (704) 693-4231.
**Clothesworks,** 1380 Tunnel Road.
**Connie Fashions Mfg.** Three area locations: 325 Weaverville Highway; US-19/23 West (across from Holiday Inn at I-40); 156 Tunnel Road behind the Ramada Inn. Ladies wear.
**Fain's,** 15 Biltmore Avenue. (704) 258-2524.
**Foam and Fabric Outlet,** Mill Agents, 175 Biltmore Avenue. (704) 254-4585.
**Gerber Outlet,** 1838 Hendersonville Road. Infant and toddler clothing. (704) 274-7187.
**Hadley Factory Store,** 40 Coxe Avenue. Famous sportswear. (704) 258-1516.
**Jane Haber, Ltd.,** Asheville Mall, 40 Coxe Avenue. Jewelry. (704) 258-1536.
**Londontown-Factory Outlet Store,** Westgate Shopping Center. Sportswear (704) 258-8123.
**Rolane Factory Outlet,** Innsbruck Mall, 85 Tunnel Road. Sportswear. (704) 254-4981.
**The Hadley Corp. Factory Outlet,** 40 Coxe Avenue. Women's clothing. (704) 258-1516.
**The Knit Mill Store,** 180 Beaverview Road. Fabrics. (704) 253-4354.
**The Money Tree,** 40 Coxe Avenue. Linens. (704) 258-9100.
**The Outlet House, Inc.**4 Rocky Ridge Road. Gifts and home accessories. (704) 665-1616.
**Three Mountaineers, Inc.,** 40 Simpson Street. Solid pine household accessories. (704) 252-6046.
**Wood and Wicker Factory Outlet,** Biltmore Village, 30 Bryson Street. (704) 253-7526.
**Vanderbilt Factory Outlet,** Bingham Road (at the plant); Lodge Street; Lake Lure; Johnson City. Junior fashions.

**'ATLANTA, GA. ChickiBea,** Clairmont at N. Decatur Road, Decatur, Ga. Designer fashions. (404) 634-6995.

**China Chasers, Inc.,** 1811 Mt. Vernon Road, Dunwoody, Ga. Replacement specialists for discontinued china.

**Creative Outlet,** The Mall-West End, 872 Oak Street, southwest Atlanta.

**Joseph A. Bank Clothiers, Inc.,** 3384 Peachtree Road N.E. Men's clothing. (404) 262-7100.

**Lady Arrow Outlet 24,** 2022 Murphy Avenue. Clothing.

**Loehmann's,** 3299 Buford Highway. Women's clothing. (404) 633-4156.

**Maternity Wearhouse Outlet,** 3204 Northlake Parkway, Northlake II. (404) 934-5491. Also Akers Mill Square, 2953 Cobb Parkway. (404) 952-1440.

**Outlets Limited Mall,** Pleasantburg Road Exit, I-85 N.E.

**S & H Shoes,** Northeast Plaza Shopping Center, 3307 Buford Highway. Women's shoes.

**Sample Boutique,** 37 W. Paces Ferry Road. Women's sample apparel. (404) 233-1897.

**Skyland Factory Outlet,** 4485 Fulton Industrial Blvd. (inside the Fulton Merchandise Mart). Children's clothing.

**Slightly Imperfect,** 290 Hilderbrand Avenue (in the Balconies Shopping Cloister). Clothing. (404) 255-3030.

**Smart Money Children's Shop,** 2953 N. Druid Hills Road (Toco Hills Shopping Center). (404) 321-6035.

**Southern Linen Outlet,** I-85 North, Exit 37.

**Stephens Fashions,** 445 Commerce Drive, southwest Atlanta. Sportswear.

**The Shoe Inn,** 3184 Peachtree Road, N.E. (404) 231-0977.

**The Wear House,** 1280 Chattahoochee Avenue. Junior and misses sportswear. (404) 351-1785.

**The Week-Ender,** 2422 Cheshire Bridge Road. Women's apparel. (404) 321-6988.

**West Fashions, Inc.,** 3800 Wendell Drive. Junior and misses sportswear. (404) 691-4617.

**Wharton Factory Outlet,** 4445-B 11 Commerce Drive, S.W. Young men's and junior sportswear. (404) 691-9410.

**World Fashions, Inc.,** 4445-A-5 Commerce Drive, S.W. Atlanta Trade Center. Junior and misses sportswear. (404) 691-4336; 1 (800) 241-6910.

**BLACK MOUNTAIN, N.C. Mitchell Fabric Outlet,** 128 Montreat Road.

**Sobol House of Furnishings,** Richardson Boulevard, P.O. Box 757. (704) 669-8031.

**The Knits Factory Outlet Store,** off rte. 70, 2½ mi. west of town.

**BLAIRSVILLE, GA. Children's Wear Outlet,** Westgate Shopping Center. (404) 745-9333.

**Ella's Orbit Casual Sportswear Outlet,** Main Street. (404) 745-9313.

**Owenby Mfg. Outlet Store,** Ivy Log (G-129 N.). Adult and kid's wear.

**'BLOWING ROCK, N.C. The Way Station,** US-321 Bypass, P.O. Box 1208.

**BLUE RIDGE, GA. Goody's Discount,** US-76, Valley Village Shopping Center. Clothing, blankets.

**Blue Ridge Farmer's Market,** US-76.

**Cluett Factory Outlet,** US-76 S. Sportswear for all ages.

**'BREMEN, GA. Bremen Clothing Outlet,** 206 Atlantic Avenue. Men's and women's apparel.

**Cosco Outlet,** 837 Pacific Avenue. Men's, women's and children's apparel.

**Direct Clothing, Inc.,** 206 Hamilton Street. Men's and women's apparel.

**Sewell's Warehouse Outlet,** 115 Atlantic Avenue. Men's suits and sportscoats.

**T & E Factory Outlet,** 828 Pacific Avenue. Men's apparel.

**BREVARD, N.C.** **Gil's Factory Outlet,** 102 N. Broad. Jeans, tops, shoes and boots. (704) 884-4014.

  **Ruth Originals,** Dogwood Plaza. Women's clothing. (704) 884-9167.

**BRYSON CITY, N.C.** **Bryson Mfg. Corp.,** US-19 (½ mi. west). Jeans outlet.

**\*CANTON, GA.** **Canton Factory Outlet,** 1024 Marietta Road. Boys', girls' clothing.

**CANTON, N.C.** **Lamp Factory Outlet,** rte. 19-23. (704) 648-7876.

**\*CHAMBLEE, GA.** **Bags 'N' Things,** 5504 Peachtree Industrial Boulevard. Designer handbags.

  **Linen Tree,** I-285, Exit 27.

  **Menswear Factory Outlet,** 4974 Buford Highway.

  **Showroom,** 5480 Peachtree Industrial Boulevard. Women's wear.

  **Zeeman's,** 5700 Peachtree Industrial Boulevard. Clothing.

**CHEROKEE, N.C.** **Factory Direct Towel Outlet,** Main Street.

  **Homestead Crafts,** US-441 N., next to Dairy Queen. Factory outlet moccasins.

**CLARKESVILLE, GA.** **Mountain Outlet,** Washington Street. Draperies, linens, towels.

**CLAYTON, GA.** **Brenda's Home Fashions,** bedspread/drapery outlet. W. Savannah Street, Clayton, (404) 782-2532 or N. Washington Street, Clarkesville, (404) 754-3460.

  **Claybourne Mfg. Outlet,** US-441 N. Children's clothing.

  **Head to Toe,** US-441 N. Family clothing.

**CLEMSON, S.C.** **Swirl Factory Outlet,** Clemson Shopping Center. Women's sportswear. (803) 654-3571.

**\*COLLEGE PARK, GA.** **College Park Shoe Store,** 3787 Main Street.

  **Hit or Miss,** 5151 Old National Highway. Women's sportswear.

  **Linen Shop,** 5445 Riverdale Road.

  **Something Special,** 5195 Old National Highway. Women's apparel.

  **The Shoe Place,** 5421 Riverdale Road.

**\*COMMERCE, GA.** **Champion Mills Store,** 12 Central Avenue. Family clothing.

**\*CONYERS, GA.** **Conyers Outlet,** 1930 Iris Drive S.W. Jeans.

  **Southern Textile Outlet,** 1079 Railroad Street.

  **Sweetheart Plastics, Inc.,** 1149 West Avenue S.W. Plastic dinnerware.

**\*COVINGTON, GA.** **Oxford Sportswear Outlet,** 5120 Old Brown Bridge Road. Sportswear.

**CUMMING, GA.** **The Company Clothing Store,** G-9 S. Ladies' sportswear.

**DILLSBORO, N.C.** **Goodson Garments, Inc.,** Landfill Road (behind Western Builders). Infants', toddlers' and kids' clothing.

**\*DORAVILLE, GA.** **Elf Mode Children's Outlet,** 5093A Buford Highway. Sizes up to toddler 4.

**\*DUNWOODY, GA.** **Georgia Girl,** 8811 Roswell Road. Women's wear.

**EASLEY, S.C.** **Ruth Fashions, Inc.,** US-123. Women's wear, fabrics.

  **Swirl Factory Outlet,** US-123 Bypass, Heritage Center. Women's wear. (803) 859-9755.

**FLETCHER, N.C.** **Bazaar,** collection of outlets under one roof. US-25.

**Mountain Rug Mills,** factory store, US-25. Hand-hooked area rugs. (704) 684-2929.

**Foam and Fabrics Outlet,** US-25 north of Fletcher. Complete fabric center. (704) 684-0801.

**FLOWERY BRANCH, GA.** **Baxter Shoe Outlet,** G-13. Family shoes.

**\*FOREST PARK, GA.** J. C. **Penney Outlet Store,** 5500 S. Expressway. Off I-75.

**\*FOUNTAIN INN, S.C.** **The Bargain Cloth Store,** 125 N. Main Street. Quality fabrics. (803) 862-2211.

**FRANKLIN, N.C.** **Cosco F. Outlet Store,** 214 Palmer Street Shopping Center. First quality items, irregulars and samples. (704) 524-4891.

**David's,** Palmer Street Shopping Center. Levi's, Lee, Calvin Klein. Men, women, children. (704) 369-9222.

**Gil's Factory Outlet and Gift Shop,** 233 E. Main Street. Work clothes, footwear. Family. (704) 524-5180.

**The Way Station,** Div. of Tanner of N.C., Heritage Hollow, 75 Porter Street. Women's wear. (704) 524-8683.

**GAINESVILLE, GA.** **Berry Mfg. Co.,** G-369. Men's clothing.

**Warren Featherbone Co., Inc.,** 999 Chestnut Street S.E. Infant's/children's wear. Open second and fourth Sat. of each month.

**\*GREENVILLE, S.C.** **All American Fabrics,** Upholstery Fabric Outlet, 1401 Poinsett Highway. (803) 235-5222. Also: I-85 at Exit 76, Spartanburg, S.C.

**Allied Textile Cloth Shop,** US-124 and White Horse Road. (803) 268-9196.

**Athletic Footwear Outlet,** Mills Centre, 400 Mills Avenue. Men, women and children.

**Black and Decker, Inc.,** 407 Pendleton Street. Power tools. (803) 232-3038.

**Burlington Bag and Baggage,** Mills Centre, 400 Mills Avenue (off I-85 on I-185). (803) 232-4867.

**Cancellation Shoe Mart,** 207 S. Main. Ladies' shoes. (803) 232-6641.

**Carolina Baby,** Westgate Mall. Infant wear. (803) 574-1981.

**Carolina Blouse,** 2836 Laurens Road. Men's and women's clothing. (803) 288-3651.

**Carolyn Warehouses, Inc.,** Pelham Road, Pleasantburg Industrial Park. Cloth and notions. (803) 297-0566.

**Children's Factory Outlet,** SC-176. Children's clothing. (803) 578-8789.

**Children's World,** 1413 W. O. Ezell Boulevard. Clothing. (803) 576-5075.

**Colette's Originals Fashion Center,** Poinsett Highway, Hillandale Plaza. Women's apparel. (803) 235-8051.

**Discount Kurtain Korner,** US-276. Bedspreads, draperies. (803) 578-0278.

**Embroidery Emporium,** US-25 (17 mi. north of town), Travelers Rest, S.C. Retail outlet of Emb-Tex Corp. (803) 834-4128.

**Factory Bedspread and Drapery Outlet,** 1305 Asheville Highway. (803) 585-4786.

**Factory Close-Out, Inc.,** 121 W. Broad Street. Women's pantsuits and tops. (803) 271-3500. Also: Hillendale Shopping Center, 2101 Poinsett Highway. (803) 271-3490.

**Fairforest Remnant Shop,** SC-29 west, 7 mi. from Spartanburg. Name-brand rainwear.

**Fashions from Chris,** 7228 Asheville Highway. Men's and ladies' clothing. (803) 578-4600.

**Gantts Uniform Outlet, Inc.,** 2242 Augusta Street. Brand-name uniforms. (803) 232-0516.

**Hamricks of Greenville,** Westgate Plaza, Whitehorse Road. Ladies' clothing. (803) 246-0822.

## Outlets

**Heritage Quilts Factory Outlet,** 520 Mills Avenue. (803) 235-5441.

**Hold It! Things That Hold Things,** Mills Centre. 400 Mills Avenue, second floor. Plastic designer items. (803) 235-3431.

**Home Maker Home Fashions.** US-25 N., at the factory, Travelers Rest, S.C. Fashions for every room. (803) 834-4913.

**House of Eyes,** Mills Centre, 400 Mills Avenue. Sunglasses outlet.

**J. P. Stevens Store,** 2712 Laurens Road. Linens, fabrics, carpeting. (803) 288-7752.

**Kiddie Korner,** 173 E. Main Street. Infants' and children's wear. (803) 582-5146.

**Kollege Inn,** Road 57, also Mills Centre, 400 Mills Avenue. Junior sportswear. (803) 579-2956 or 242-9325.

**Ladies Factory Outlet,** Morgan Manor, 730 S. Pleasantburg Drive. Also: Mills Centre, 400 Mills Avenue. Women's sportswear. (803) 232-8441.

**Lady Outlet,** Poppy Square, (803) 585-6128.

**Lotties Name Brand Discount Shoes,** N. Hills Shopping Center (803) 244-8740.

**Lydia Fabrics,** I-85 at Exit 76. Quality fabrics. (803) 578-2020.

**Manufacturers Sample Shop,** 7144 Asheville Highway. Sample clothing for men and women.

**Marlowe Kids,** Mills Centre, 400 Mills Avenue. Kid's wear.

**Maternity Wearhouse Outlet,** Greenville Mall. (803) 288-5899.

**Menswear Factory Outlet,** 1272 Asheville Highway. (803) 583-5341.

**Mills Centre Factory Outlet Mall and Pottery Warehouse,** 400 Mills Avenue. Designated an Historic Landmark in 1983. (803) 271-0215.

**Mill End Carpets,** Wade Hampton Boulevard. (803) 877-1214. Also: 1506 Augusta Road. (803) 242-1761.

**Mr. Shirt, Inc.,** Lake Forest Shopping Center, N. Pleasantburg Drive. Men's shirts. (803) 244-6366.

**Patches and Sashes,** Country Corner, Reidville Road. (803) 574-6650.

**Piedmont Factory Store,** McKoy Street. Men's, women's, boys' sportswear. (803) 232-6545.

**Pinewood Ladies Factory Outlet,** Pinewood Shopping Center. Ladies' sportswear. (803) 585-9905.

**Ruth Fashions, Inc.,** 121 W. Broad Street. Women's dresses, sportswear, sewing accessories, fabrics. (803) 271-3500. Also: Hillandale Plaza, US-25, Poinsett Highway. (803) 271-3490.

**S-Mart Stores,** 2644 Laurens Road. (803) 288-5235. Apparel for the family. Also: 150 Poinsett Highway. (803) 232-7652. 1300 Asheville Highway. (803) 582-0610.

**Sanford Cancellation Shoes,** Lake Forest Shopping Center, 1382 N. Pleasantburg Drive, 291 Bypass. Girls' and ladies' shoes. (803) 244-2814.

**Shea's,** 856 Pine Street. (803) 582-5644. Women's apparel. Also: 993 Asheville Highway. (803) 585-5777.

**Southern Textile Sales, Inc.,** 520 Mills Avenue. (803) 242-0093. Linens. Also: 5623 Rivers Avenue, Charleston, S.C.

**Swirl Factory Outlet,** Mills Centre, 400 Mills Avenue. (803) 271-8299. Lounge and sleepwear. Also: Lake Forest Shopping Center, 1392 N. Pleasantburg Drive. (803) 268-3718.

**The Clothes Rack,** 2504 Laurens Road. Women's fashions. (803) 288-3969.

**The Crystal Shop,** 499 S. Pleasantburg Drive. Glassware and gifts. (803) 242-9147.

**The Enro Shirt Factory Outlet,** Greenville Mall, I-85 at Exit 385. (803) 297-4524.

**The Factory Connection,** 200 N. Pleasantburg Drive. (803) 235-5535.

**The Pottery Warehouse,** 400 Mills Avenue. First quality, outlet prices. (803) 232-0631.

**The Shoe Center,** 1420 Laurens Road. (803) 233-8711.

**The Shoe Inn,** 2109 Augusta Street. (803) 233-1596.

**The Value Outlet,** Sigsbee Road. Fabrics, clothing for men and women. (803) 576-3105.

**Tobin's Warehouse,** 518 E. Main Street. Sportswear for juniors and misses. (803) 583-8919.

**West Upholstery Fabric Outlet,** 1808 Augusta Street, 1 mi. north of I-85 on Bus. 25. (803) 271-1985.

**Window Fashions and Fabrics,** 1303 Laurens Road. (803) 233-4971.

**\*GREER, S.C. Dairy Sue,** County Plaza, Rte. 6. Women's clothing. (803) 877-1600.

**Fashion First, Inc.,** 109 Wade Hampton Boulevard. Women's wear. (803) 877-7414.

**Swirl Factory Outlet,** A & P Shopping Center. Women's sportswear. (803) 879-2238.

**Vaughns Fashions,** 103 N. Buncome Road. Women's and children's clothing. (803) 879-3209.

**HAZELWOOD, N.C. White Shield Factory Outlet,** 104 W. Main Street. Bedding and linens. (704) 456-3756.

**HELEN, GA. Orbit Factory Outlet,** Main Street. Knit sportswear.

**HENDERSONVILLE, N.C. Ashley's Outlet Store,** 1218 Spartanburg Highway. Family apparel and home fashions. (704) 692-2518.

**Chipman Factory Outlet,** 300 W. Walker, off US-176. Family clothing. (704) 693-4231.

**Colony Casuals,** Haywood Road. Ski and sportswear. (704) 692-4336.

**Connie Fashions,** Sky City Shopping Center. Women's sportswear.

**House of Towels,** 1971 Asheville Highway, US-25. Towels by the pound. (704) 692-9489.

**John Holley's Bootery,** I-26 at US-64 West Exit (across from McDonald's), 1900 Four Seasons Boulevard. Men's and women's shoes. (704) 692-2879.

**Ruth Originals Retail Store,** I-26 and US-64 east. Girl's wear. (704) 692-3689.

**Tee Cee's Bargain Wear House,** I-26 at US-64 East Exit (at the entrance to the Holiday Inn). (704) 697-6209

**The World of Clothing,** I-26 at US-64 East Exit. Apparel for men, women and children. (704) 693-4131.

**Young Generations Factory Outlet,** I-26 at US-64 East Exit (across from Ramada Inn). Sportswear and dresses for girls 7-14 and young junior teens.

**INMAN, S.C. Ann's Discount Shoes,** exit US-176 from I-85 or I-26 to Inman, located just north of Bi-Lo Plaza on right. Ladies' quality wide width shoes and boots. (803) 472-6210.

**Mill End Fabrics,** US-176. By the Bi-Lo Store.

**\*JONESBORO, GA. The Shoe Place,** 846 Southway Center.

**\*KENNESAW, GA. Genmark,** 3210 Wimbleton Street N.W. Women's apparel.

**\*LaFAYETTE, GA. LaFayette Outlet Store,** 313 Patton Avenue. Family clothing.

**\*LILBURN GA. Something Special,** 6429 US-29. Women's apparel.

**\*LITHONIA, GA. Zeeman's,** 6400 Hillandale Road. Men's clothing.

**\*LYMAN, S.C. Jeans Plus Factory Outlet,** US-29 (I-85 to Exit 66, 3 mi. south on US-29). Designer jeans. (803) 439-7689.

**Wamsutta Outlet Store,** 36 Groce Road, off I-85 at Exit 66, US-29 to Lyman; left at light, third block on left. Famous Wamsutta products. (803) 433-4330.

**Lyman Remnant Shop,** Lyman Print/Finishing Co., Groce Road. Linens and fabrics.
**Steppin Out Shoe Outlet,** 42A Groce Road. First-quality ladies' shoes.

•**MABLETON, GA.** **Million Dollar Fashions,** 1141 Bankhead Highway (in the White Columns Shopping Center). Junior and misses sportswear.

**MAGGIE VALLEY, N.C.** **Woodcrafters Novelty Co., Inc.** Early American wood. (704) 456-3550.

•**MARIETTA, GA.** **Arrowhead Sales Co., Inc.,** 793 Roswell Street N.E. Family casual wear.
**Bankers Note,** 3358 Canton Road N.E. Women's wear.
**Bed and Bath Fair,** 1859 Roswell Road. Linens.
**Big Smith, Inc.,** 423 Woodstone West Drive. Men's clothing.
**Burlington Coat Factory Warehouse,** 1255 Roswell Road N.E. Men's and women's coats.
**Kayser Roth Hosiery,** 531 Rose Lane Street. Men's, women's, children's.
**Linens, Inc.,** 2179 Roswell Road.
**McLaurin Factory Outlet,** 470 Sessions Street. Hosiery, shoes, handbags, lingerie.
**Michelle's,** 1311 Johnson Ferry Road. N.E. Women's apparel.
**Pockets,** 1935 Delk Industrial Drive. Brand-name jeans.
**Shoes Unlimited,** 781 Whitlock Avenue.
**Showroom,** 222 Johnson Ferry Road N.E. Women's apparel.
**Something Special,** 1225 Johnson Ferry Road N.E. and 783 Whitlock Avenue S.W. Women's apparel.
**The Shoe Factory,** 148 Radium Street, N.W.
**Vida Shoes International,** 3261 Turtle Lake Drive N.E.

**MARION, N.C.** **Ramble Rack, Inc.,** 207 E. Court Street. Children's wear. (704) 652-4950.

•**MAULDIN, S.C.** **ABC Jeans,** US-276 (Mauldin Plaza). Jeans.
**Home Maker Home Fashions,** 729 N. Main Street. Room fashions. (803) 297-1394.
**J & J Upholstery,** Golden Strip Shopping Center. US-276. Decorator fabrics. (803) 288-4000.
**Just Kids Outlet Store,** SC-417 off US-276. Children's clothes. (803) 288-2642.
**Southern Craftsmen Shop, Ltd,** US-276. Solid wood furniture. (803) 288-3425.
**Swirl Factory Outlet,** Golden Strip Shopping Center. Women's apparel. (803) 288-8962.

•**NORCROSS, GA.** **Between the Sheets, Inc.,** 5265 Jimmy Carter Boulevard. Linens.
**L & M Shoe Outlet,** 5050 Jimmy Carter Boulevard.

**PICKENS, S.C.** **Brunswick Yarns,** City View Circle, off SC-178, P.O. Box 276. (803) 878-6375.

•**PIEDMONT, S.C.** **Dairy Sue Fashions,** Frontage Road off I-85 at Exit 35. Women's sportswear. (803) 845-6917.

•**RINGGOLD, GA.** **Towel Shop of Ringgold,** 310 Highway (G-151 at I-75). Linens, towels.

•**ROSWELL, GA.** **Bargain Bin,** 14 Elizabeth Way. Jeans, etc.
**C. Edgar,** US-19, Roswell Square. Women's designer shoes.

**SALUDA, N.C.** **Saluda Factory Outlet,** 115 E. Church Street. Women's sportswear. (803) 445-3377.

•**SANDY SPRINGS, GA.** **Textile Mill Store,** 200 Johnson Ferry Road N.E.

**SMYRNA, GA.   Pant-O-Mine,** 2200 Cobb Drive S.E. Men's clothing.

**Papilio, Inc.,** 1175 Fleming Street S.E. Men's clothing.

**Riverboat Fashions,** 2965 Cobb Parkway S.E. Women's apparel.

**Showroom,** 2949 Cobb Parkway N.W. Women's apparel.

**Loehmann's Plaza:** Ten outlet stores, 1 mi. north of I-285 at Cobb Parkway Exit. Women's wear.

**T & E Factory Outlet,** 2620 Cobb Parkway S.E. Menswear.

**Tipco Sportswear, Inc.,** 1678 Atlanta Road S.E. Sportswear.

**Walton Clothes,** 2670 Cobb Parkway. Menswear.

**\*SPARTANBURG, S.C.   Accent Fabrics,** I-26 and I-85, Road 41 at Exit 69 at Jed's Farm. First-quality comforters, pillow shams, etc. (803) 576-8411.

**All American Fabrics,** upholstery fabric outlet, I-85 at Bryant Road, Exit 76. (803) 578-8513. Also: 1401 Poinsett Highway, Greenville, S.C.

**B.K. Factory Outlet** (formerly Butte Knit), I-85 at Sigsbee Road, Exit 71. Suits, dresses and sportswear. (803) 576-8066.

**Benborne's Inc.,** Sigsbee Road, I-85 at Exit 71. Family clothing. (803) 576-3029.

**Bottom Dollar Clothing Store,** SC-9, 2 ½ mi. north of I-85. Clothing for the family. (803) 578-3855.

**Butte Knit Fabric Outlet,** I-85. Material and clothing. (803) 576-6600.

**Calvert's Linen Closet,** Road 57, Exit 79, I-85.

**Caro Tex,** Sigsbee Road. Fabrics and cloth. (803) 576-3105.

**Carolina Casual Sportswear,** 8011 Greenville Highway. (803) 576-3214. Junior and misses designer sportswear. Also: Main Street, Jonesville, S.C.; 1111 B Avenue, W. Columbia, S.C.

**Children's Factory Outlet,** Ingles Shopping Center, US-176 west. Clothing for boys. (803) 578-8789.

**Factory Bedspread and Drapery Outlet,** 1305 Asheville Highway, Exit 72C (SC-56) toward Spartanburg. (803) 585-4786.

**Fairforest Outlet and Remnant Store,** US-29 (7 mi. south). Rainwear.

**Family Sock Outlet,** Old Furnace Road, 2 mi. off SC-9. Socks.

**Fashions from Chris,** 7228 Asheville Highway (SC-56). Men's and ladies' clothing. (803) 578-4600.

**Fashions Unlimited,** 1280 Asheville Highway. Women's casual apparel. (803) 583-5341.

**Favorite Fashions of Spartanburg,** 586 S. Pine Street (from I-85 take US-176, Exit 73A). Junior, misses wear.

**Fringe Mart,** 500 Farley Road. Fabric and fringe.

**Home Maker Home Fashions,** Pinewood Shopping Center. (803) 583-8316.

**Knits from Chris,** 7228 Asheville Highway.

**Kollege Inn,** Road 57 between I-85 and Cannons' Campground Road. Apparel.

**Kurtain Korners,** Asheville Highway (Ingles Shopping Center). Curtains and bedspreads.

**Ladies Factory Outlet,** Pinewood Shopping Center. (803) 585-9905.

**Lydia Fabrics,** I-85 at Bryant Road, Exit 76. (803) 578-2020.

**Manufacturer's Sample Shop,** 7144 Asheville Highway.

**Menswear Factory Outlet,** 1272 Asheville Highway. (803) 583-5341.

**Morgan's Discount Fashions,** SC-221 beyond Roebuck Lumber Co. Ladies' apparel.

**North 221 Outlet,** Chesnee Highway. Men's, ladies' jeans. (803) 578-7550.

**Outlet Park at Waccamaw:** 34 outlets, I-26 at New Cut Road, Exit 17, 1 mi. west of I-85.

**Pine Street Extension Cloth Shop,** 2363 S. Pine Street. Fabrics.

**Pine Street Ladies Outlet,** S. Pine Street Ext., on US-176 below Kohler Co.

## Outlets

**Pine Street Ladies Outlet,** S. Pine Street Ext., on US-176 below Kohler Co.

**Pinewood Ladies Factory Outlet,** N. Pine Street, SC-9. Apparel.

**Plej's Textile Mill Outlet,** 1300 Asheville Highway, same building as S-Mart.

**Raycord Factory Outlet,** N. Blackstock Road. Clothing. (803) 574-1175.

**Reeves Bros. Fairforest Remnant and Outlet Store,** US-29 west (turn at Reeves Bros. sign). Rainwear. (803) 576-9252.

**Richland Creek,** SC-176, 2 mi. past York Mills Outlet. Men's and women's clothing. (803) 474-2426.

**S & S Manufacturing Co.,** Broadcast Drive (Bypass 295). Ladies' and girls' blouses. (803) 585-0116.

**S-Mart,** 1300 Asheville Highway. Apparel.

**Shea's,** 3856 S. Pine Street and 993 Asheville Highway. Apparel.

**Simmons and Co.,** 1293 Asheville Highway. SC-56 east toward downtown, in Hodge Shopping Center. Ladies' fashions. (803) 573-9288.

**Smartn'up Wallpaper Outlet,** 1060 N. Church Street. Wallpaper supplies.

**Spartex, Inc.,** SC-295 Bypass, 851 E. Main Street. Cloth.

**The Children's Factory Outlet,** Rte. 7, SC-176, Ingles Shopping Center.

**The Pipe Rack,** 2034 Chesnee Highway. Ladies' clothing. (803) 583-6168.

**The Remnant Shop,** 653 N. Church Street, Northland Shopping Center. Fabrics.

**The Shoe Palace,** 1272 Asheville Highway. Ladies' shoes. (803) 585-6657.

**Wadsworth Industries,** Carver Mill Road. Apparel.

**Westgate Ladies Outlet,** 1413 W.O. Ezell Boulevard. Women's clothing. (803) 576-0434.

**Wholesale Wearhouse,** 980 Frontage Road, I-85, Exit 75 at SC-9. Family Clothing. (803) 582-4172.

**York Mills Factory Outlet,** SC-176, Rte. 11. Craft supplies. (803) 585-3329.

**\*STONE MOUNTAIN, GA.** **Showroom,** 5244 Memorial Drive. Women's apparel.
**Something Special,** 5205 Memorial Drive. Women's apparel.

**SWANNANOA, N.C.** **Bazaar:** collection of outlets under one roof, NC-70.
**Beacon Outlet Store,** 202 Whitson Avenue, just off I-40 at Exit 59. Linens, bedspreads, etc. (704) 686-5445.
**Valley Outlet Store,** US-70 off Exit 59. Bed and bath. (704) 686-5997.

**\*TAYLORS, S.C.** **Menswear Factory Outlet,** 4949 Wade Hampton Boulevard. (803) 877-0888.

**TOCCOA, GA.** **Champion Mills,** G-17 South. Family clothing.

**\*TRENTON, GA.** **Char-Del Shoes,** G-136. Shoes, handbags, etc.

**\*TUCKER, GA.** **Southern Mills Outlet,** 3972 Lawrenceville Highway. Linens.

**\*UNION, S.C.** **City View Fashions,** SC-176. Ladies' dresses, etc. (803) 427-6605.

**WAYNESVILLE, N.C.** **Gillani's Jeans Outlet,** downtown. Designer jeans and shoes. (704) 456-6864.

**\*WELLFORD, S.C.** **Famous Name Brand Shoes,** US-29, off I-85 at Exit 66, 1 mi. south on Highway 29. Ladies' shoes. (803) 439-3557.

**\*WOODRUFF, S.C.** **Enro Shirt Co. Outlet Store,** 369 Allen Street. Men's shirts.

# Parks: State, National and Private

The most spectacular and most visited park of them all is the Great Smoky Mountains National Park, straddling North Carolina and Tennessee. A smokelike blue haze envelops the peaks in this half-million-acre park that is a mix of forest wildlands and an outdoor museum of pioneer life. About 800 miles of trails link the waterfalls, coves, balds and rushing streams in the park where 1,400 kinds of flowering plants grow. Drive up to Clingmans Dome, the highest point in Tennessee at 6,643 feet, and then hike a half-mile to the summit and observation tower. Perhaps you will spot one of the estimated 400 to 600 black bears which live in the park.

Caesar's Head State Park, near the North Carolina border (30 miles from downtown Greenville, S.C.), offers breath-taking views from its rock cliffs. Caesar's Head Mountain rises 3,266 feet above sea level.

Oconee State Park, a restful retreat nestled in tall pines and hardwoods, is 12 miles northeast of Walhalla, S.C., in the Sumter National Forest. Its four-hour, 60-mile auto loop includes a fish hatchery, waterfalls, historic sites and a gorgeous view.

The Indians said that Table Rock Mountain was where a giant chieftain dined. Table Rock State Park in Pickens, S.C., has a 10-mile trail system. One trail leads to the top of Table Rock Mountain; another winds to the summit of nearby Pinnacle Mountain.

The newest park in the region is Lake Hartwell State Park, off I-85 in Oconee County, S.C. Plans call for the park to eventually offer a golf course, cabins and even a hotel.

Stumphouse Tunnel Park, north of Walhalla, S.C., features an unfinished railroad tunnel that was cut in the 1850s. Some 1,600 feet of the tunnel are open to the public. It rains every day down the shaft where the temperature is 50 degrees year-round, and the humidity is always 90 percent, no matter what the weather.

At Amicalola State Park near Dawsonville, Ga., a clear mountain creek plummets down the eastern side of a ridge in a series of sparkling cascades, creating Georgia's highest waterfalls at 729 feet. The name Amicalola is apt — it is an Indian word meaning tumbling waters.

For getting away from it all, for learning about Blue Ridge culture and history, for hiking and fishing and spectacular scenery, the state, national and private parks in the area are unbeatable.

**BLAIRSVILLE, GA.** **Vogel State Park,** 23 mi. northeast of Helen on US-19/129. Has 221 acres and a 17-acre lake with a a beach. Swimming, paddleboating and two 1-mi. nature trails. Rte. 1, Box 97, 30512. (404) 745-2628.

**CHATSWORTH, GA.** **Fort Mountain State Park,** 5 mi. east of Chatsworth on US-76. Contains 2,526 acres with a mysterious stone ruin on its highest peak. Miniature golf, picnicking, fishing, boating, hiking and cabins. Rte. 7, Box 1-K, 30705. (404) 695-2621.

**CLARKESVILLE, GA.** **Moccasin Creek State Park,** 25 mi. north of Clarkesville in Rabun County on G-197. The park covers 31 acres at an altitude of 1,850 feet on Lake Burton. Boating, fishing, picnicking, hiking and water skiing; 53 tent/trailer sites. Adjacent to the Georgia Dept. of Natural Resources Fish Hatchery. Route 1, 30523. (404) 947-3194.

**˙COMER, GA.** **Watson Mill Bridge State Park.** This park features the longest covered bridge in the state: 236 feet, over the Broad River. Picnicking, camping areas. To reach the park, go 3 mi. south of Comer on G-22. Contact: Watson Mill Bridge State Park, rte. 1, 30629. (404) 783-5349.

**DAHLONEGA, GA.** **Amicalola Falls State Park,** 20 mi. west of Dahlonega on G-52. Features the state's highest waterfall. Located near the southern end of the Appalachian Trail. Star Route, Dawsonville, Ga. 30534. (404) 265-2885.

    **Blackburn Park,** formerly a state park, now a private park. Activities include panning for gold, hiking and professional archery range. 9th District Opportunity, Inc. (404) 532-3191 or 864-3789.

**HARTWELL, GA.** **Hart State Park,** east of Hartwell on US-29 to the intersection with G-8; then north 7 mi. Swimming, boating, and fishing, easy access to all water sports. Hart State Park, 1515 Hart Park Road, 30643. (404) 376-8756.

**HELEN, GA.** **Unicoi State Park,** about 2 mi. northeast of Helen on G-356. Year-round activities on 1,023 acres. Known for its restaurant, conference facilities and cottages shaped like barrels. Boating, swimming, fishing, camping, courses in folk art, music and natural resources. Unicoi State Park, G-356, Box 256, 30545. (404) 878-2201.

    **Anna Ruby Falls,** off G-356 near Unicoi State Park. Has two falls. Surrounded by 1,600 acres. Picnic areas, restrooms and a pleasant hike of less than ½ mi. from the parking area to the falls.

**LAVONIA, GA.** **Tugaloo State Park,** 6 mi. north of Lavonia off G-328 via I-85. Bluegrass music, clogging, fishing year-round. Tugaloo State Park, Route 1, 30553. (404) 356-4362.

**MOUNTAIN CITY, GA.** **Black Rock Mountain State Park,** off US-23 and 441, it is the highest of the state parks with a maximum elevation of 3,800 feet. Wildlife tours, mountain music, craft demonstrations and historical presentations; 53 campsites and 10 cottages. Black Rock Mountain State Park, 30562. (404) 746-2141.

**ROYSTON, GA.** **Victoria Bryant State Park,** in the upper Piedmont section of Georgia. Fishing, swimming, golfing, camping. Easily accessible from Franklin Springs, north on G-327. Victoria Bryant State Park, Route 1, Box 257, 30662. (404) 245-6270.

**BLOWING ROCK, N.C.** **Blowing Rock Park.** A private park about 110 mi. north of Greenville-Spartanburg; two blocks off US-321 on Rock Road. A natural rock formation is the attraction: strong updrafts can return light objects which are thrown off. Gardens and an observation tower with spectacular views. April-October. Fee. (704) 295-7111.

**BRYSON CITY, N.C.** **Deep Creek.** Hiking trails, waterfalls, tubing center.

**CHEROKEE, N.C.** **Great Smoky Mountains National Park,** adjoins Cherokee Reservation; 514,093 acres lie in North Carolina. One of the world's finest wilderness sanctuaries. More than 800 square miles of streams, mountain peaks over 6,000 feet high, hiking trails, camping areas, abundant wildlife. Open year-round. Park's points of interest are:

   **Oconaluftee Visitor Center and Farmstead.** Information, publications, exhibits, living demonstrations of pioneer living. Four mi. north of Cherokee on US-441. Open daily. Year-round.

   **Mingus Mill.** Water-power turbine mill built in 1886. Corn ground daily. US-441 north of Cherokee. Easter-October.

**CHIMNEY ROCK, N.C.** **Chimney Rock Park.** A private park centered on a monumental granite tower with a spectacular 75-mi. view. Access is via a 150-step stairway to Pulpit Rock or by tunnel and taking a 25-story-high elevator ride, up a shaft blasted through the solid granite. The Park also contains beautiful Hickory Nut Falls, the highest in the eastern United States, with a drop of 404 feet; Moonshiners Cave, a deep cave with a year-round 60 degree temperature; several trails for hiking; restaurant and tourist shop on the Rock. March-November. About 50 mi. north of Greenville-Spartanburg, two mi. east of the intersection of US-74 and 64 and NC-9. P.O. Box 38, 28720. (704) 625-9204.

**\*GATLINBURG, TENN.** **Sugarlands.** Visitor Center, nature museum, nature trail. Open daily except Christmas. US-441.

**HENDERSONVILLE, N.C.** **Holmes State Forest,** 10 mi. west of Hendersonville on Route 1127 (Crab Creek Road). Equipped to explain the concept of forestry. The forest consists of rich bottomland, steep mountainsides, and a gently rolling mountaintop covered by typical mountain hardwoods mixed with white pine and hemlock. A ½-mi. forest walk along an easy grade explains forest use through audio stations. A 2-mi. forest demonstration trail climbs through several types of forest. The Forest Center has exhibits and displays and is surrounded by day-use recreational facilities. Write to Holmes State Forest, rte. 4, Box 308, 28739. (704) 692-0100.

**MT. MITCHELL, N.C.** **Mt. Mitchell State Park,** 35 mi. north of Asheville off the Blue Ridge Parkway. Contains the highest mountain in the East, the 6,684-foot Mt. Mitchell. The 1,469-acre park has 33 mi. of trails, campsites, nature museum, restaurant and gift shop.

**NEWFOUND GAP, N.C.** **Clingmans Dome Scenic Overlook,** a 7-mi. spur from Newfound Gap. Hike ¾ mi. to 6,642-foot elevation tower.

# South Carolina Parks

**CEDAR MOUNTAIN, S.C.** **Caesar's Head State Park.** Towers 3,208 feet above sea level, scenic views. Outcropping said to resemble the head of Caesar. Hiking, nature trail. On US-276 5 mi. north of SC-11. Open during daylight hours. Free. Contact: Caesar's Head State Park, 28718. (803) 836-6115.

**CLEVELAND, S.C. Pleasant Ridge State Park.** A small, restful park tucked away where the big hills begin. Cool mountain breezes, heavy woods. On South Carolina's most scenic highway. On SC-11, 22 mi. northwest of Greenville. Box 2, 29635. (803) 836-6589.

**°GREENVILLE, S.C. Paris Mountain State Park.** Three lakes and several streams are in this mountain park. Pleasant hiking trails wind through virgin forest. Fishing and swimming. Spectacular mountain view of beautiful Piedmont Valley. Six miles north of Greenville off US-276/SC-253. Contact: Paris Mountain State Park, rte. 2, Box 221, 29609. (803) 244-5565.

**°HARTWELL, S.C. Lake Hartwell State Park.** This new state resort lake is being developed on Lake Hartwell at the intersection of I-85 and SC-11 at the state line. It will feature facilities operated by both public and private interests. Camping, picnic area and water sports.

**PICKENS, S.C. Keowee-Toxaway State Park.** The history of the Cherokee Indians in South Carolina and their eventual removal is interpreted through the use of exhibits and an historic trail. Tues.-Sun. Off SC-178, north of Pickens. (803) 868-9748.

**Table Rock State Park,** on SC-11, 16 mi. north of Pickens; rte. 3, 29671. Against a background of high Appalachian peaks, the stream-cut park offers a variety of hill and valley trails. Spectacular view of countryside from atop Table Rock. Sparkling mountain streams and lake. Dense woodlands here are part of the world's largest coniferous forest.

**WALHALLA, S.C. Oconee State Park,** 12 mi. northwest of Walhalla on SC-107. Camping, swimming, fishing, nature trail, interpretive center, carpet golf, pedal boats, cabins, restaurant. Open during daylight hours. Free. (803) 638-5353.

**Stumphouse Mountain Tunnel Park,** on SC-107. In the 1850s the Blue Ridge Railroad began cutting 1½ mi. of tunnel through Stumphouse Mountain as a rail link in an effort to connect the port city of Charleston with the Midwest. The project failed when the contractor went bankrupt. You can walk 1,600 feet into the tunnel, picnic or camp near the tunnel and walk over to Issaqueena Falls, a beautiful splashing cascade falling 200 feet to the valley floor. Legend has it that the Indian maiden Issaqueena rode to a nearby fort to warn of a pending Indian attack. She then escaped from pursuing Indians by pretending to leap over the falls, but she really hid under the falls on a ledge. Open year-round during daylight.

## Resources and Information

### GEORGIA:

Parks, Recreation and Historic Sites Division
Georgia Department of Natural Resources
270 Washington Street. S.W.
Atlanta, Ga. 30334

North Georgia State Parks
Region I Office
Unicoi State Park
P.O. Box 148
Helen, Ga. 30345
(404) 878-2635

**NORTH CAROLINA:**

State Parks and Recreation
512 N. Salisbury Street
Archdale Building
Raleigh, N.C. 27611
(919) 733-4181

**SOUTH CAROLINA:**

Programs Section
Division of State Parks
1205 Pendleton Street
Columbia, S.C. 29201

**SMOKY MOUNTAINS:**

Copies of *Great Smoky Mountains National Park Handbook 112* are available at the park's visitor centers. To order a copy, send a check or money order for $6.50 (payable to the Superintendent of Documents) to:

Superintendent of Documents
U.S. Government Printing Office
Washington, D.C. 20402

*(See also Hiking chapter, resources, for a list of trail guides.)*

# Q

# Quilts and Quilting

In the Blue Ridge Mountains quilts displayed for sale on a clothesline under a pecan tree are as common as peaches in summer. But today quilts can be more than providers of warmth — they are an art form. So valued and guarded is the Smithsonian Institution's collection of antique American quilts in Washington, D.C., that it is shown only by appointment to no more than nine people on Tuesday mornings at 11 A.M. in a humidity- and temperature-controlled storeroom.

The quilting renaissance has brought some cheap imitations, of course, but it is possible to find high-quality quilts down a backroad or in a craft shop. Quality quilts are handmade and sewn with small, neat stitches, at least 10 per inch. Some new polyester-stuffed quilts made of cotton or cotton blends rival antique cotton-stuffed quilts.

Quilting is an ancient craft begun centuries ago in Egypt, China and Greece. Americans brought the skill from England and Holland. In Colonial times quilting was a necessity because blankets were scarce. The earliest quilts, called crazy quilts, used random pieces of fabric. Then pieced quilts came along and simple patterns developed. Names, such as Turkey Track, Churn Dash, Delectable Mountain, Lone Star and Double Wedding Ring, tell us something about the pioneer lifestyle and character.

Top contemporary quilters strive for originality and effective design. Some of their quilts resemble Picasso paintings or surrealistic fantasies. You can see the best of both traditional and contemporary designs at quilt shows such as those held in Aiken, S.C., and Hendersonville, N.C., and all over the Blue Ridge area. In Brasstown, N.C., the John C. Campbell Folk School quilters and the Hayesville Quilters Guild combine for one fall exhibit.

## Quilting Events

*(See also Craft Shops, Crafts, and Fairs and Festivals for more quilt sales outlets.)*

————May————

**FRANKLIN, N.C.  Smoky Mountain Quilters Guild,** at Macon County Community Facilities Building. First week. (704) 524-6728.

**HENDERSONVILLE, N.C.   N.C. Quilt Symposium,** Quilt Show and Merchants Mart, Kanuga Conference Center. Third week. (704) 692-5205.

**BLAIRSVILLE, GA.** **Mountain Settlers Quilt/Craft Sale**, Civic Center. By Historical Society. Quilts, crafts, music. Fourth week. (404) 745-5484.

————June————

**FRANKLIN, N.C.** **Spring Fling: Old-Time Quilting Bee.** Mountain kitchen, old fashioned mountain foods. Third week. (704) 524-3161.

————August————

**HIAWASSEE, GA.** **Georgia Mountain Fair**, Pioneer Village area. Quilting bee and demonstration. First week. Early August.

**HENDERSONVILLE, N.C.** **Quilt show**, at the armory. Fourth week.

————September————

**BRASSTOWN, N.C.** **The Mountain Quilt Show**, John C. Campbell Folk School. By the folk school and Hayesville Quilters Guild. Second week.

————October————

**GAINESVILLE, GA.** **Harvest Curb Market Quilt Show**, Green Street, downtown. Second week. (404) 535-9603 or 9600.

**HENDERSONVILLE, N.C.** **Quilt Show**, The Cedars. Second and third weeks.

————November————

**BLAIRSVILLE, GA.** **Mountain Settlers Christmas Quilting Craft Fair**, Union County Civic Center. First and second weeks. (404) 745-4744.

## Quilt Shops

**BLAIRSVILLE, GA.** **Pappy's Market Place**, US-19/129, 8 mi. south of town. Open weekends.

**CLAYTON, GA.** **The Fence Rail**, corner of Derrick and Church streets, downtown. (404) 782-3579.

**˚CRABAPPLE, GA.** **Crabapple Corners**, Crabapple Road, 5 mi. north of Roswell. Quilts for sale.

**DILLSBORO, N.C.** **The Country Mouse**, in the old school, US-441.

**FRANKLIN, N.C.** **Linda's Quilting Cabin**, 75 Porter Street, 28734. Complete line of quilting supplies. Custom-made quilts and log cabin crafts by Linda. (704) 369-8221.
  **Maco Crafts, Inc.**, Rte. 2, Box 1190, 28734. Complete line of crafts: quilts and custom-made furniture a specialty. Open Mon.-Sat. (704) 524-7878.
  **Tryphosa Quilt Center**, Andrea Potts, P.O. Box 361, Otto, N.C.; US-441, 12 mi. south of Franklin. Quilts, jelly, jams, crafts, gifts. (704) 369-9834.

**GAINESVILLE, GA.** **Georgia Craft Gallery, Inc.**, 311 Green Street, 1 block east of Georgia Mountains Center. Handcrafted traditional and contemporary works, wood furniture, quilts, weaving, wooden toys. (404) 534-4272.

**HAYESVILLE, N.C.** **Hayesville Quilters Guild**, community building. 26 members. Fourth Monday of each month.
  **The Misty Mountain Mountain Quilters Guild**, meets at Hayesville Community Building.

**˚MARIETTA, GA.** **Antique Store of Marietta**, 81 Church Street. Primitives, quilts. (404) 428-3376.

# R

## Restaurants — Blue Ridge Style

Bring your appetite, pull up a chair, and sit down to a table laden with juicy fried chicken, succulent trout, locally cured country ham, fresh squash, candied yams, just-picked okra, tender carrots and a multitude of other vegetables, biscuits and jam. Wash it down with Southern iced tea and top it off with a fruit cobbler.

That's the sort of meal that has made the classic mountain restaurants famous. Popular restaurants in the Blue Ridge area range from family-style establishments serving down-home food to those with an old-fashioned atmosphere, but serving gourmet or French foods as well as local favorites. Many of the restaurants and their buildings have a rich history.

Dillard House Restaurant in Dillard, Ga., has been serving bountiful spreads since the Dillard family first hosted itinerant ministers at the turn of the century. Today, it is known for meals featuring three meats, five or six vegetables, beverage and dessert at reasonable prices. The Tannery Restaurant in Buford, Ga., specializing in lobster tail and prime rib, was once the office headquarters of the Shadburn Brothers Tannery. The Sautee Inn in Sautee-Nacoochee, Ga., is a cozy old inn that serves a combination of fancy gourmet dishes such as beef Stroganoff and old-fashioned local vegetables — sort of a country gourmet. Smith House in Dahlonega, Ga., is a rustic, family-style restaurant where strangers sit at the same table and stuff themselves with two or three meats, 10 to 12 vegetables, fritters, homemade corn bread and rolls, and cobbler. It was built around 1890 over a rich gold vein. Dine in a grist mill more than 135 years old in Cedartown, Ga. The Old Mill Restaurant features fish and steak dinners.

Poor Richard's Summit Inn in Franklin, N.C., was built in 1898 as a private residence. It specializes in appetizers such as Oysters Rockefeller and entrees such as New York strip steak. The Railroad House in Saluda, N.C., built as a summer hotel for union members and their families, serves lots of seafood and non-countrified items such as moussaka. The Frog and Owl Cafe in Highlands, N.C., is next to a 100-year-old grist mill and is the place for escargot, rack of lamb and other fancy foods. Bryant McClure's near Otto, N.C., is set in a meadow by a creek. McClure cooks up American standards with his own special touches. In Dillsboro, N.C., dine at the Jarrett House, built in 1884, for family-style Southern specialties.

*Restaurants — Blue Ridge Style*
## Food Events

————March————
**TALLULAH, GA.  Annual (Big Pork) Tallulah Persimmon Bar-B-Que.** County Road 76. Sponsored by the fire dept. Third week.

————April————
**SYLVA, N.C.  Annual Ham Dinner,** Fairview Cafeteria. By Fairview PTA. First week.

**TOCCOA, GA.  Mrs. Geoghagan's Spaghetti Dinner,** Toccoa Elementary lunch room. By the PTA. First week.

————May————
**BREVARD, N.C.  Ham Supper.** Gwynn Valley Camp. By Dunn's Rock Community Club. Third week.

**WALHALLA, S.C.  Annual Lions Club Pancake Supper,** S. Pine Street Elementary School. By Walhalla Lions. Third week.

————July————
**RABUN GAP, GA.  July 4th Barbecue,** Hambidge Center.

**YOUNG HARRIS, GA.  July 4th Barbecue,** Young Harris Fire Dept. Country music, horse shoe contest.

**CASHIERS, N.C.  Fish Fry Dinner,** Cashiers Community Center. By community clubs for senior citizens. Second week.

**BLAIRSVILLE, GA  Annual Masonic Barbecue,** Georgia Mountain Branch Experiment Station. By Allegheny Lodge 114. Third week.

**GAINESVILLE, GA.  Mountain Food Festival,** Georgia Mountain Center. Late July, early August.

————August————
**HELEN, GA.  Georgia Mountain Eatin's and Squeezin's,** Unicoi State Park. "Area Folks" demonstrate the art of old-time food preparation. Third week.

————September————
**BLAIRSVILLE, GA.  American Legion Trout Dinner,** Georgia Mountain Branch Experiment Station. Third week.

**CLEMSON, S.C.  Annual Teacher Appreciation Dinner.** By Morrison PTO. Third week.

**LAKE LANIER ISLANDS, GA.  Country Food Festival.** Visitors sample and buy authentic country meals. Recipes, kitchen crafts; fruits and vegetables also sold. Third week.

————October————
**BREVARD, N.C.  Annual Transylvania Cattlemen's Assoc. Dinner,** Brevard High School. First week.

**BLAIRSVILLE, GA.  Union County Lions Club Annual Picnic,** Track Rock Campground. Music, hayrides. Second week.

**BLUE RIDGE, GA.  Mountain Harvest Sale,** Fannin County Homemakers Council. Second week. (404) 632-5223.

**WALHALLA, S.C.** Lions Barbecue. Oktoberfest. Third week.

**BREVARD, N.C.** **Strans Harvest Supper,** Strans School. By the PTO. Turkey dinner, bake sale, crafts, drawings. Fourth week.

**SENECA, S.C.** **Lions Barbecue,** Northside Elementary School. By Seneca Lions Club. Fourth week.

————November————

**ASHEVILLE, N.C.** **Annual Shriner's Ox Roast,** at the Shriner's ground on Rose Hill Road. Ox broiled over hickory coals; all-day event. Public invited. First week.

**TOCCOA, GA.** **Ham and Egg Supper,** National Guard Armory. By Pilot Club. First week.

**CASHIERS, N.C.** **Annual High Hampton Thanksgiving Houseparty.** Picnics, hayrides, barbecue, parties. Fourth week.

————December————

**CLEMSON, S.C.** **Wine and Cheese Social,** Sierra Club. First week.

**WALHALLA, S.C.** **Holiday Showcase.** By Oconee County Extension Homemakers Clubs. Recipes, items for sale. First week.

## Traditional Eating Establishments

**ASHEVILLE, N.C.** **Weaverville Milling Co.,** US-19/23 north, New Stock Road. Country food served family style. (704) 645-9000.

**BLAIRSVILLE, GA.** **Goose Creek,** US-19 and 129, near Vogel State Park. Home-style cooking. Daily, from April to November. (404) 745-5111.

**BLUE RIDGE, GA.** **Fannin Inn,** US-76 and G-5. Open daily. (404) 632-2005.
**Forge Mill Crossings,** US-76 and Forge Mill Road.

**BUFORD, GA.** **The Tannery Restaurant,** 625 Shadburn Avenue. Formerly the Shadburn Brothers Tannery. Evenings only. Closed Monday. (404) 945-7469.

**CHATSWORTH, GA.** **Fantastic Sunday Buffet,** Cohutta Lodge and Restaurant. Atop Fort Mountain. Daily. (404) 694-9601.

**CLARKESVILLE, GA.** **Charm House Dining Inn,** US-441. Elegant, Southern mansion (1907) in an historic setting. Daily. (404) 754-9347.
**LaPrade's,** Rte. 1, G-197. Family-style dining. Closed Wednesday. Reservations. (404) 947-3312.

**CLEMSON, S.C.** **Agricultural Sales Center,** in Newman Hall. Operated Mon.-Fri. by the University's Dept. of Agriculture. Famous for blue cheese and homemade ice cream. (803) 656-3242.

**CLEVELAND, GA.** **Gateway Inn,** US-129 and 75. Good, homey, Southern food is the specialty. Open daily. (404) 865-2023.

**DAHLONEGA, GA.** **The Smith House,** 201 S. Chesatee Street. Established early in this century. Serves family-style meals. Tues.-Sun. (404) 864-3566.

**DILLARD, GA.** **Dillard House,** overlooks Rabun Gap Valley, US-441. Begun in the early 1900s. Family style. No reservations.

**Moon Valley,** 3½ mi. west of Dillard off Betty's Creek Road. Open every night; by reservation only. (404) 746-2466.

**DILLSBORO, GA. The Jarrett House** (1884), US-441 and 23/19A. Country style. Open daily, April-October.

**FRANKLIN, N.C. Bryant McClure's Restaurant,** US-441, 6 mi. south of Franklin; turn at the Irish Farm House sign. Reservations. Gourmet meals. Herbs and spices grown there. (704) 524-7420.

**Poor Richard's Summit Inn,** East Rogers Street. Casual dining. Wood stove warms coffee and soup. Reservations appreciated. (704) 524-2006.

**HARTWELL, GA. Catfish Inn,** US-29. Formerly a church parsonage, built in 1918. Closed Monday. (404) 376-9313.

**HELEN, GA. Strudel Haus Restaurant and Strudel's Lounge,** in the center of town. Serves fresh beef which is flown from Chicago. Reservations. (404) 878-2332.

**HENDERSONVILLE, N.C. FO-FO-TH-BO,** on Main Street. An international cafe. Fresh and natural fruit juices, herbal teas, homemade biscuits and muffins, freshly ground coffee. Closed Monday.

**HIAWASSEE, GA. Deer Lodge,** G-17 and G-75, between Unicoi and Hiawassee. Home-style cooking. Trout a specialty. Open daily, April - late October. Evenings only. (404) 896-2181.

**HIGHLANDS, N.C. Frog and Owl Cafe,** Buck Creek Road. Open from late May until mid-October. Reservations. (704) 526-5500.

**Highlander Restaurant,** Main Street. Varied menu of home-cooked meals. Daily. (704) 526-3169.

**JASPER, GA. Woodbridge Inn,** G-5. Rainbow trout and onion soup are specialties. Closed Monday. (404) 692-6293.

**LAKE TOXAWAY, N.C. The Red Door,** US-64. Wed.-Sun. Reservations. (704) 966-4613.

**MOUNTAIN CITY, GA. The York House,** US-441 and 23. Since 1896. (404) 746-2068.

**PENDLETON, S.C. Farmer's Hall Tea Room and Restaurant,** Main Square. Closed Sun. and Mon. Reservations. (803) 646-7024.

**SALUDA, N.C. The Railroad House,** NC-176. Open Mon.-Sat.; also Sun. afternoon.

**SAUTEE, GA. Sautee Inn,** G-19 and 255. Famous for "Country Gourmet." Closed Tues. (404) 878-2940.

**TABLE ROCK, S.C. Table Rock Lodge Restaurant.** All you can eat, family-style dinner. Closed Mon.

**TOCCOA FALLS, GA. Gate Cottage,** entrance to Toccoa Falls. "A tradition in dining excellence." (404) 886-6831, ext. 230, or 886-4501 on weekends.

# Rockhounding

Being elbow-deep in mud can be fun — if you're searching for gold, sapphires or rubies in the hills of the Blue Ridge area. The lucky have something to show after a day's mining: amethysts, quartz, emeralds or one of the more than 300 other kinds of gems and minerals just waiting to be unearthed. More than 70 gem types have economic value and more than 50 are produced commercially.

Gem mining is especially entertaining, since someone else has already done the digging. A small fee entitles the fortune seeker to a bucket of dirt and gravel. Wash the dirt away and see whether there's anything that has possibilities. While most of the stones are small and imperfect, gem-quality stones of several hundred karats have been found.

Many mines are open on a daily basis from April 1 to late October. To provide a greater variety and abundance of minerals and gems, the mine operators add gem stones to those that occur naturally. These stones are called "enriched" stones.

Franklin, N.C., "The Gem Capital of the South," holds its annual Gemboree Festival the last weekend in July. Gem dealers sell and exhibit at the show, which is considered one of the top gem shows in the United States.

The excitement of the Gold Rush days lives in Dahlonega, Ga., where Benjamin Parks stumbled over a gold-veined rock while he was deer hunting in 1828 and started the rush. John Crisson's grandfather purchased a mine in Dahlonega in 1833, and in 1969 Crisson reopened it.

Although they're only soapstone, a group of rocks in the north Georgia mountains between Blairsville and Young Harris are valuable. The rocks in this area, known as Track Rock Gap, are etched with designs believed to be ancient. The carvings include human or animal footprints, bird tracks and other symbols. No one knows who made these stone carvings or why, but legends abound.

Whether you search for gems, gold or rocks, the pursuit can be fun and educational. Rock and mineral museums and rock shops add to the experience.

## Gem Mines

**BETHEL, N.C.** **Shovel Branch Mines,** US-276 south to NC-110. Sapphires — some tools needed. Facilities limited, attended. Fee.

**CANTON, N.C.** **Presley Mine** (Seth Woods Property), 19 mi. west of Asheville. Sapphires — pick and tools needed. No attendant or facilities. Fee.

**FRANKLIN, N.C.  Bonanza Ruby Mine,** Ruby Mine Road (SR-1343). Native and enriched stones. Daily. May 15-Oct. 31. (704) 524-6541.

**Caler Creek Mine,** Rte. 4, Box 415. Native stones. Daily. April 1-Oct. 31. (704) 524-7271.

**Cherokee Ruby Mine,** Rte. 4, Box 483. Native stones. Daily. April 1-Oct. 31. (704) 524-5684.

**Dale and Demko Mine,** County Road 1342, Rte. 4, Box 460. Native and enriched stones. April-October. Cottages and cabins. (704) 524-4310.

**Gem City Mine,** US-441 (1 mi. north of city). Native and enriched stones. May 15-Oct. 15. Open six days a week. July and August, open seven days a week. (704) 524-3967.

**Gibson Ruby Mine,** Rte. 4, Box 470. Native stones. May-October. Closed Sun. (704) 524-3546.

**Gregory's Ruby Mine,** Rte. 4. Native stones. Camping. April 1-Oct. 31. (704) 524-3552.

**Holbrook Ruby Mine,** Rte. 4, Box 438. Native stones. One of the original mines. April-October. Open daily. (704) 524-3540.

**Houston's Sapphire Mine,** Box 171, 28734. Sapphires, garnets.

**Jacob's Ruby Mine,** Rte. 4, Box 458A. Native stones. No digging. April 1-Oct. 31. (704) 524-7022.

**Jones Ruby Mine,** Rte. 3, Box 977. Native stones. No digging. April 1-Oct. 31. Closed Sun. (704) 524-5946.

**Laurel Valley Mine,** Rte. 8, Box 102. Native and enriched stones. April 1-October. (704) 524-4689.

**Mason's Ruby and Sapphire Mine,** Rte. 4, Box 151A. Native stones. April 1-Oct. 31. (704) 524-4239.

**McCook Rhodolite Mine,** NC-28 north. Rhodolite, sapphires.

**Mincy Mine,** 139 W. Main Street. Bronze, sapphires.

**Old Homestead Gem Mine,** Piney Grove Road, Rte. 8, Box 316. Native and enriched stones. May 1-October. (704) 524-7694.

**Rockhound Haven,** NC-28 north. Native stones.

**Rose Creek Mine, Campground and Stables,** Rte. 8, Box 370. Native and enriched stones. No digging. April 15-Oct. 31. (704) 524-5726.

**Sheffield Mine,** Rte. 4, Box 436AA. Native stones. April-October. (704) 369-8383.

**Shuler Ruby Mine,** Rte. 4, Box 479. Native stones. April 1-Oct. 31. (704) 524-3551.

**Youkon Ruby Mine,** Rte. 4, Box 452. Native and enriched stones. No digging. March 1-Dec. 31. Open year-round. Closed Christmas Day. (704) 524-6186.

**HIDDENITE , N.C.  Del-Ann Emerald Mine,** P. O. Box 229, 28636. Emeralds.

**LITTLE SWITZERLAND, N.C.  The Gemstone,** at Emerald Village, NC-226. Open daily. May 1-Oct. 31. Emeralds. (704) 765-MINE.

**SPRUCE PINE, N.C.  Bill Burleson Mine,** 13 mi. east on US-19 east; turn left on State Road 1132 for 1½ mi. Moonstone.

**Chalk Mountain Mine,** 2 mi. west on US-19 east; turn left on private road. Hyalite, autunite, garnet.

**Emerald Mine,** 5 mi. south on NC-226; turn right on Parkway to Switzerland; turn right on State Road 1100 to Church; follow State Road 1104. Emerald, tourmaline, mica, garnet. Fee.

**Harris Clay Mine,** 1½ mi. north on NC-226; turn right on State Road 1150. Hyalite, autunite, torbernite.

**International Minerals Mine,** 1½ mi. north on NC-226; turn right on State Road 1150. Hyalite, autunite, torbernite.

**Lawson Mine,** 2 mi. north on NC-226 to Minpro; turn right on private road. Autunite, torbernite, hyalite, garnet.

**McKinney Mine,** 5 mi. south on NC-226; turn right on Parkway to Switzerland; turn right and follow State Road 1100. Columbite, garnet, torbernite, calcite, fluorite, beryl.

**Old No. 20 Feldspar Mine,** 4 mi. west on US-19 east; turn left on State Road 1102, Crabtree Road, 3 mi.; turn right on State Road 1176, ½ mi. Hyalite, mica, uranium minerals.

**Olivine Mine,** 7 mi. west on US-19 east; turn right on State Road 80, ¼ mi. Olivine, chromite.

**Roan Mountain Flower Garden,** 12 mi. north on NC-226 to Bakersville; turn left on State Road 261, 12 mi. Unakite, epidote.

**Sullins Branch Mine,** 1 mi. north on NC-226; turn right on State Road 1146. Pitch-blend, garnet, autunite, thulite.

# Gem Events

**ASHEVILLE, N.C.** **Asheville Gem Festival,** National Guard Armory, Brevard Road, NC-191 South. Second week in October.

**BRYSON CITY, N.C.** **Nantahala Rock Swap,** Gorgama Park in the Nantahala Gorge, US-19, between Bryson City and Andrews. Second week in May, fourth week in August, first week in October.

**FRANKLIN, N.C.** **Macon County Gemboree,** Community Facilities Building, US-23-441 south. Dealers, exhibits, lectures, slides. Since 1965. Fourth week in July.

**HENDERSONVILLE, N.C.** **Henderson County Gem and Mineral Show Spectacular,** Immaculate School. First week in September.

**SPRUCE PINE, N.C.** **Mineral and Gem Festival,** Harris Middle School. Displays, field trips to local mines, exhibits, swap shops. First week in August.

# Gem Shops

**BLACK MOUNTAIN, N.C.** **My Blue Heaven,** McCoy Cove Road. Blue sapphire and kyanite crystals; feldspar, mica garnets.

**FRANKLIN, N.C.** **Cowee Valley Lapidary,** Rte. 4, Box 468. Cutting and mounting. (704) 524-2321.

**Franklin Gem Shop,** NC-28, P.O. Box 906. In business for 25 years. (704) 524-4554.

**Gem Creations Jewelry,** Clarks Chapel Community, P.O. Box 527. (704) 524-4869.

**Glass Barn and Rock Shop,** 3½ mi. south on US-441, Rte. 2, May-October

**Hykel's Gem and Lapidary,** Rte. 8, Box 63. (704) 524-7322.

**Ruby City Gems,** 44 E. Main Street. May-October. Billed as "largest and finest"; in business for 20 years. (704) 524-3967.

**Ruth and Bud's Cowee Gem Shop,** Ruby Mine Road, Rte. 4, Box 474. (704) 369-8233.

**Wood's Gem and Rock Shop,** 20 Palmer Street. (Wood's Motel). April-October. (704) 524-4403.

**Zebo's Gem Shop,** 39 Porter Street. Special exhibit of aquamarine crystal.

**HIGHLANDS, N.C.** **The Highlands Gem Shop,** "On the Hill." April 1-Jan. 1. (704) 526-2767.

# Gem and Mineral Museums

**ASHEVILLE, N.C.** **Colburn Mineral Museum,** lower level of Thomas Wolfe Auditoirum in the Civic Center Complex. Tues.-Sun. (704) 254-7162.

**˙ELBERTON, GA.** **Elberton Granite Museum and Exhibit,** G-72 and 17, near Elberton Civic Center, ½ mi. west of downtown Elberton. Open daily except Sat., Jan. 15-Nov. 15. (404) 283-2551.

**FRANKLIN, N.C.** **Franklin Gem/Mineral Museum,** 2 Main Street, 28734. Rock and mineral exhibits. May 15-Nov. 1, Mon.-Sat. No admission. (704) 524-7585, 524-3161.

**LITTLE SWITZERLAND, N.C.** **H. C. Mining Museum, Inc.,** P.O. Box 98, 28749. April 15-Nov.1.

**SPRUCE PINE, N.C.** **North Carolina Mineral Museum,** NC-226 and Blue Ridge Parkway, near Spruce Pine and Little Switzerland. Open daily, Easter-Thanksgiving weekend. Closed Tuesday and Wednesday in off season. (704) 765-2761.

**North Carolina Mining Museum.** Exit Blue Ridge Parkway at Little Switzerland and follow State Road 1100 2½ mi. Follow signs. From 4 mi. south of Spruce Pine on US-19 east, take State Road 1002 and 1100 5 mi. Museum is open May-October; Gemstone Mine open Memorial Day-Labor Day. Admission; pre-school is free if accompanied by adult. Group rates for 15 or more. Admission includes one bucket of gem-bearing material. Additional buckets may be purchased; price varies according to mineral contents of the bucket.


# Gold Attractions

**DAHLONEGA, GA.** **Crisson's Gold Mine,** 3 mi. south of city, Wimpy Mill Road. Camp, picnic, pan for gold. Mid-April-early November.

**Gold Hills,** ½ mi. from Town Square, G-50. Pan for gold; museum. Open weekends only, April, May and October. Open daily June-September.

**Gold Miner's Camp,** G-60 South, near city limits. (404) 864-6373.

**Gold Museum,** Town Square. History and exhibits. Audio-visual presentation of Gold Rush. (404) 864-2257.

**Gold Rush Days.** Third week in October, Tues-Sun. (404) 864-3711.

**DAWSONVILLE, GA.** **Blackburn Park,** Rte. 3, Box 160, 30534; Auroria Road Exit, off G-400 (9 mi. south of Dahlonega). Gold panning area.


# Miscellaneous Attractions

**CHIMNEY ROCK, N.C.** **Chimney Rock.** This giant granite landmark overlooks all Lake Lure. It took 8 tons of dynamite and 18 months to create a walking tunnel and elevator shaft. Trails lead to the highest waterfall in eastern America — Hickory Nut Falls — which drops 404 feet down a sheer granite cliff.

**MARION, N.C.** **Linville Caverns,** US-221, 15 mi. north of Marion and 3 mi. south of Linville Falls. Open all year. Guided tour of cavern takes 40 minutes. Admission; under 5 free. Group rates for 25 or more. (704) 756-4171.

**TATE, GA.** **Georgia Marble Company.** Quarry tours by appointment. (404) 688-2861.

**Marble Monumental Tours.** (404) 692-5600.

**YOUNG HARRIS, GA.** **Track Rock Gap,** between Blairsville and Young Harris, off G-180. Ancient designs carved into rock.

*Resources:*

*Appalachian Mineral and Gem Trails,* by June C. Zeitner. Lapidary Journal, Inc. San Diego, California 1968.

North Carolina Department of Natural Resources, Geological Survey Section, P. O. Box 27687, Raleigh, N.C. 27611. (919) 733-2423.

Museum of North Carolina Minerals, Blue Ridge Parkway, Milepost 331, Gillespie Gap, N.C.

Superintendent, Blue Ridge Parkway, 703 Northwestern Bank Building, Asheville, N.C. 28801.

# S

## Skiing

Many travelers love the Blue Ridge area in summer and fall when the hills are green or golden-red. What many don't realize is that it's a great place for snow skiing in winter.

Only two decades ago snow skiing was unheard of in Dixie. In 1961 Cataloochee at Maggie Valley, N.C., opened and showed it could be done. Due to innovative snowmaking methods, better grooming equipment, modern ski lift facilities, adaptable ski gear and fine resort accommodations, skiing has become a major industry in the South.

Many of the nation's 53 million skiers prefer the Southern mountain slopes over those to the West or Northeast. With the help of artificial snow the season begins as early as Thanksgiving at some resorts and lasts as late as March. Of course, "grass" skiing is available in summer to keep ski skills honed.

Whether you're a beginner just learning the joys of swooshing down a ski slope or an experienced skier looking for a challenge, there's a place for you. Many resorts such as Appalachian Ski Mountain in Blowing Rock, N.C., have slopes for novice, intermediate, advanced and expert skiers, as well as trails. The French-Swiss Ski College instructors there claim they can teach just about anybody to ski in one day. Every ski area has a ski school, and cross-country or Nordic skiing is also becoming popular.

More than two dozen ski areas in the Appalachian and Blue Ridge Mountains and resorts in Georgia, Tennessee and North Carolina provide something for everyone. The slopes are not as high as those in the Rockies, but the excitement is catching among the friendly skiers on the South's slopes. Accommodation reservations are a must. Write for the free Accommodations Directory (Travel and Tourism Division, 430 Salisbury Street, Raleigh, N.C. 27611). Package plans including fees, lessons and equipment are available. Joining a ski club can also defray some of the costs.

| Name | Slopes — Novice to: | Max. Run | Lodge | Night Skiing | Vert. Drop | Day Care | Number of Slopes |
|---|---|---|---|---|---|---|---|
| Appalachian Ski Mountain<br>P. O. Box 106<br>Blowing Rock, N.C. 28605<br>(704) 295-7828<br>Off US-221 between Boone<br>and Blowing Rock | Expert | 2,000 | Yes | Yes | 365 | No | 8 |
| Cataloochee<br>Route 1, Box 500<br>Maggie Valley, N.C. 28751<br>(704) 926-0285<br>4 mi. off US-19 at Maggie<br>Valley | Advanced | 5,300 | Yes | Yes | 740 | No | 8 |
| High Meadows<br>Box 222<br>Roaring Gap, N.C. 28668<br>(919) 363-2221<br>US-21 | Intermediate | 1,300 | Yes | Yes | 80 | No | 2 |
| Hound Ears<br>P. O. Box 188<br>Blowing Rock, N.C. 28605<br>(704) 963-4321<br>Off NC-105, 8 mi. southwest<br>of Boone | Intermediate | 1,200 | Yes | No | 107 | No | 2 |
| Mill Ridge<br>Rte. 1, Box 367<br>Banner Elk, N.C. 28604<br>(704) 963-4500<br>On NC-105, 8 mi. southwest<br>of Boone | Advanced | 2,500 | Yes | Yes | 225 | No | 3 |
| *Ober Gatlinburg<br>1001 Gatlinburg Parkway<br>Gatlinburg, Tenn. 37738<br>(615) 436-5423 | Intermediate | 4,900 | Yes | Yes | 800 | No | 4 |
| Peakes Resort (Under Con-<br>struction)<br>US-19-129 South<br>Blairsville, Ga. 30512 | | | | | | | |
| Sapphire Valley<br>P. O. Box 80<br>Sapphire, N.C. 28774<br>(704) 743-3441<br>On US-64, 20 mi. west of<br>Brevard | Expert | 1,500 | Yes | Yes | 425 | Yes | 4 |
| Scaly Mountain<br>Box 80<br>Scaly Mountain, N.C. 28775<br>(704) 526-3737<br>On NC-106, 7 mi. west of<br>Highlands | Advanced | 1,400 | Yes | Yes | 225 | No | 3 |

| | | | | | | | | |
|---|---|---|---|---|---|---|---|---|
| Seven Devils<br>Rte. 1 Box 256<br>Banner Elk, N.C. 28604<br>(704) 963-6561<br>Off NC-105, 6 mi. southwest<br>of Boone | Expert | 2,800 | Yes | Yes | 618 | No | 5 |
| Ski Beech<br>P. O. Box 1118<br>Banner Elk, N.C. 28604<br>(704) 387-2011<br>Off NC-194, south of Ban-<br>ner Elk | Advanced | 8,700 | Yes | No | 809 | Yes | 12 |
| Sky Valley<br>P. O. Box 1<br>Dillard, Ga. 30537<br>(404) 746-5301<br>Off US-441, on Ga.-N.C.<br>border | Intermediate | 2,200 | Yes | No | 250 | No | 5 |
| Sugar Mountain<br>P. O. Box 369<br>Banner Elk, N.C. 28604<br>(704) 898-5256<br>Off NC-194, southeast of<br>Banner Elk | Advanced | 7,920 | Yes | Yes | 1,200 | Yes | 15 |
| Wolf Laurel<br>Route 3<br>Mars Hill, N.C. 28754<br>(704) 689-2222<br>5 mi. off US-23, 27 mi.<br>north of Asheville | Expert | 3,500 | Yes | Yes | 700 | No | 11 |

# Ski Events

**BANNER ELK, N.C.   Equitable Family Ski Challenge Races,** Beech Mountain. Dates to be announced. Sundays during December and January. (704) 387-2011.

**Southern Star Pro-Am Classic,** Beech Mountain. First weekend in February. (704) 387-2011.

**Winterfest,** Beech Mountain. First ten days in February. (704) 387-2011.

**Grass Ski Races,** Beech Mountain. Third weekend in July. (704) 387-2011.

**BLACK MOUNTAIN, N.C.   Mt. Mitchell Ski Challenge,** Mt. Mitchell. First weekend in February. (704) 669-2052 or 669-2300.

# Sports

The Blue Ridge area has plenty of sports to offer both spectators and participants. Water sports, including canoeing, kayaking, rafting and even sailing and windsurfing are big. The Nantahala Outdoor Center, in Bryson City, is one of the top-rated places for instruction in kayaking, open canoeing and decked canoeing as well as for guided raft trips.

You can sail on your own or take classes at lakes in the area. Camping, fishing, water skiing and sunbathing are natural complements to sailing. Or, take wind surfing lessons from an instructor at Buckhorn Wind Surfing at Lake Lanier, Ga., and discover a sport that's cheaper than costly skiing.

Back on dry land, look up, and if it's late summer at Grandfather Mountain in Linville, N.C., you are likely to see hang gliders. They fill the skies at the annual Masters of Hang Gliding Championships there.

Want something out of the ordinary? Go to the Scottish Highland Games held each year in the summer when the Scottish clans gather at Grandfather Mountain for traditional sport, dances and music.

## Ballooning

**HELEN, GA.** Tarp Head Ballooning School, Box 28, 30545. (404) 865-3874.

## Hang Gliding

**CLAYTON, GA.** **Hang Gliders Heaven,** 3 mi. south of Clayton, Rabun Bald Mountain (4,663 feet). Training programs available for the novice.

**LAKE LANIER ISLANDS, GA.** **Blue Stratos Championships.** Hang-glider pilots compete in performance, duration and target landing events. Southern Air Time, Box 93701, Martech Station, Atlanta, 30318. First week in October. (404) 476-5446.

**LINVILLE, N.C.** **Masters of Hang-Gliding Championship,** southwest of Blowing Rock at Grandfather Mountain. The top 28 pilots in the world are invited to compete in this major international tournament. Admission. Mid-September. (704) 898-4720.

**'ROCK CITY, GA.** **Lookout Mountain Flight Park.** Gliders launch from McCarty's Bluff, 8 mi. south of Rock City on Scenic Highway and soar a thousand feet over the ridge. (404) 398-3549.

**'TRENTON, GA.** **Dade County Hang Gliding 22-mile Great Race** (American Cup), Lookout Mountain, Flight Park, US-11. Late October. (404) 398-3541 or (615) 867-4970.

# Sailing

**ANDERSON, S.C.    Hartwell Lake,** 204 Castlespring Road, 29621. The Western Carolina Sailing Club owns ten acres on a peninsula on Hartwell Lake. (803) 225-0423.

**LAKE LANIER, GA.    Lake Lanier Barefoot Sailing Club,** Box 1223, Atlanta, 30301. Contact: Bill Godsay, (404) 874-4679; Carol Emery, (404) 455-6872 or Caryl Carlson, (404) 325-4058. The club caters to racers and owners of small boats from Atlanta to Lake Lanier. All races held on weekends at Lake Lanier.

    **Buckhorn Wind Surfing,** 2341 Thompson Bridge Road. Boardsailing school lessons (surfboard with sail).

    **Lake Lanier Sailing Club.** A private club on 19 acres of land that includes campgrounds, beach, dock space and dry storage space on Lake Lanier near Flowery Branch. Membership limited to 205. Contact: Raymond Burke, (404) 767-1321.

*Sailing Resources: Sailing instruction information may be obtained from the Coastal Sailing Course, McKimmon Center, Division of Continuing Education, NCSU, P.O. Box 5125, Raleigh, N.C. 27610. (919) 737-2261. Or the Oriental School of Sailing, P.O. Box 127, Oriental, N.C. 28751. (919) 249-0960.*

# Sporting Events

**\*ATLANTA, GA.** For ticket or game information call: Atlanta Braves, (404) 577-9100; Atlanta Falcons, (404) 588-1111; Atlanta Hawks, (404) 681-3600; Atlanta International Raceway, (404) 946-4211; Omni Sport Coliseum, (404) 681-2100; Road Atlanta, (404) 881-8233.

————January————

**ASHEVILLE, N.C.    Annual University of North Carolina Asheville Collegiate Invitation Indoor Soccer Tournament,** Justice Gym. The 16-team World Cup format features top college teams from the Southeast. Fourth week.

————February————

**BLAIRSVILLE, GA.    Turkey Shoot,** Intersection US-19-129 and Haralson Drive. No sleeved guns. First week.

**HELEN, GA.    Turkey Hunters Weekend,** Unicoi State Park. Exhibits, movies, workshops, calling contests, banquet and sales of anything dealing with turkey hunting. First week. (404) 878-2201, ext. 232 or 283.

————March————

**SYLVA, N.C.    Annual Catamount Classic.** By Jackson County Recreation and Park Dept. Eight women's collegiate softball teams, ten games, double elimination tournament. Fourth week.

————May————

**BRYSON CITY, N.C.    Annual Spring Triathlon,** Nantahala Outdoor Center. Biking, running, canoeing. Second week. (704) 488-2175.

**\*HARTWELL, GA.    Tugaloo State Park Boat Show.** Boats on exhibit and demonstrations. Third week. (404) 356-4362.

## Sports

**BREVARD, N.C.** Natural Rock Slide, in the Sliding Rock Recreation Area in Pisgah National Forest. A 60-foot slide operated by the National Park Service is open through Labor Day. The Sliding Rock Recreation Area is located at Looking Glass Falls on US-276 south of Asheville.

——July——

**LINVILLE, N.C.** Annual Highland Games and Gathering of Scottish Clans, at Grandfather Mountain. Scottish clans and societies participate in traditional Scottish sports, dances and music. First week. (704) 898-4720.

**SUWANEE, GA.** Falcons' Football Practice, 30 mi. north of Atlanta, on I-85 N., exit 44. Call ahead for exact hours of training. Mid-July to August. (404) 588-1111.

**CULLOWHEE, N.C.** Horseshoe Tournament, Mark Watson Park. By Jackson County Recreation Dept. Fourth week. (704) 586-6333.

——August——

**CHEROKEE, N.C.** American Pepsi Challenge Doubles Championship, Magic Waters Park, US-19. First week.

**MURPHY, N.C.** Invitational Horseshoe Tournament, Murphy Fairgrounds. By Recreation Dept. Third week. (704) 837-6617.

**DAWSONVILLE, GA.** Bowhunter Rendezvous, Amicalola Falls. Fourth week. (404) 269-2885.

——September——

**BURNSVILLE, N.C.** Riverside Turkey Shoot, west of Riverside Bridge on 19E. Every Saturday, September-November, except Thanksgiving weekend.

**HIGHLANDS, N.C.** Turkey Shoot, at the Highlands Ballfield. Sponsored by the Lions Club. Mid-September to mid-November.

**BLAIRSVILLE, GA.** Turkey Shoot, at Jones Creek Motor Cross. Muzzle-loading rifle shoot out. Fourth week.

**BRYSON CITY, N.C.** Annual Fall Triathlon, at Nantahala Outdoor Center. Swim, run, canoe. Fourth week. (704) 488-2175.

——October——

**FRIENDSHIP, GA.** Turkey Shoot, at Myrick's Grocery Store, above Coneross Fish Lodge. First week. (404) 972-3773.

**WALHALLA, S.C.** Rotary Bowl, Memorial Field. Walhalla and Westminster Rotaries. Six football youth teams. First week.

**BLAIRSVILLE, GA.** Turkey Shoot. Wilderness Scouts. Second week. (404) 745-6166.
   Caravan Horseshoe Tournament, at Recreation Center. Second and third weeks. (404) 745-2743.

——December——

**CHEROKEE, N.C.** Turkey Shoot, Smoky Mountain Welcome Center on Jonathan Creek, across from KOA snack bar. First week. (704) 926-0101.

**\*ATLANTA, GA.** Peach Bowl Football, Atlanta Stadium; Peach Bowl, Box 1336, Atlanta 30301. Proceeds from this post-season college game go to the Lions Lighthouse for the Blind. (404) 525-2971.

# Tennis

What better place to play tennis than on a court served by cool mountain breezes. Courts are plentiful at resorts, public recreation centers and private tennis and racquet clubs throughout the Blue Ridge area.

Try entering one of the many local tournaments to test your skills, or go as a spectator. Consult the yellow pages in the phone directory to locate the nearest tennis courts in your area, or call the local Chamber of Commerce.

A big event for more than 50 years for tennis buffs in Asheville, N.C., is the annual city invitational tennis tournament for juniors and adults held at the Aston Park Courts in July. In June, Cullowhee, N.C., hosts the Jackson County American Cancer Society Tournament at Western Carolina University. Nearby Sylva, N.C., holds a tournament in May to benefit the Jackson County Heart Fund.

————March————

**TOCCOA, GA.** **Stephens County Open,** Henderson Falls Park. Third week. (404) 886-8288.

**˙HARTWELL, GA.** **Annual Northeast Georgia Junior Singles Tennis Championships,** Hartwell Recreation Dept. Courts. For 18-and-under division. By Hartwell Rotary Club. Fourth week.

————April————

**BREVARD, N.C.** **Glen Cannon Tennis Tournament,** at Glen Cannon Country Club and Brevard Racquet Club. Second week.

**ASHEVILLE, N.C.** **Annual Southeastern Indoor Tennis Championship,** Asheville Racquet Club, Hendersonville Road, US-25 south. Third week.

————May————

**SYLVA, N.C.** **Annual Jackson County Heart Fund Tennis Tournament.** By Jackson County Rec/Parks Dept. and N.C. Heart Assoc. Singles-doubles. Third week.

**BREVARD, N.C.** **Land of Waterfalls Adult Tournament,** at Brevard Racquet Club. USTA. Third week.

**ASHEVILLE, N.C.** **Land of the Sky Junior Tennis Championship Invitational,** at the Asheville Racquet Club on Hendersonville Road, US-25 south. Fourth week.

————June————

**CULLOWHEE, N.C.** **Cancer Society Tournament,** Western Carolina University courts. By Jackson County American Cancer Society. First week.

**BREVARD, N.C.** **The Brevard Racquet Club $1500 Professional Tennis Championship.** South Pro-tennis Assoc. Circuit. Second week.

# Tennis

**Lipton Iced Tea Mixed Doubles,** Glen Cannon Country Club. Open event. Fourth week.

**SYLVA, N.C. Open Tennis Tournament.** By Jackson County Rec/Parks Dept. Singles-doubles. Fourth week.

## ——July——

**ASHEVILLE, N.C. Annual Southern Pro Invitational,** Asheville Racquet Club. First week.

**CULLOWHEE, N.C. Catamount Tennis,** Western Carolina University Lower Courts. By Athletic Dept. Twenty events. First week.

**ASHEVILLE, N.C. Annual City of Asheville Invitational Tennis Championships,** at Aston Park Courts. Juniors and adults. Since 1930. Second week.

**HENDERSON FALLS, GA. Tennis Tournament.** By Northeast Georgia Tennis Assoc. Singles, doubles. Third week.

**PICKENS, S.C. Annual Tennis Invitational,** at Pickens County Country Club. STA/USTA. Third week.

**WAYNESVILLE, N.C. Annual Donnie Pankiw Memorial Tennis Championship,** Recreation Park. Adult, junior divisions. Third and fourth weeks.

## ——August——

**BLACK MOUNTAIN, N.C. Black Mountain Sourwood Tennis Tournament,** Black Mountain Recreation and Parks, 255 W. State Street, 28711. First week.

**WALHALLA, S.C. Walhalla Closed Tennis Tournament,** Recreation Dept. Singles and doubles. First week.

**SENECA, S.C. Oconee County Apple Festival Tennis Tournament,** S. Cove County Park. USTA/STA. Fourth week.

## ——September——

**CLEMSON, S.C. Clemson Tennis Tourney,** Clemson Recreation Dept. First-third weeks.
   **Pickens County YMCA Singles Tournament,** Easley Tennis Center. First week.

**SYLVA, N.C. Open Tennis Tournament,** Mark Watson Park. By Jackson County Recreation and Parks Dept. Fourth week.

## ——October——

**WALHALLA, S.C. Oconee County Closed Tennis Championships** by Walhalla Rec. Dept., P.O. Box AP, 29691. First week.

**CLEMSON, S.C. Mixed Doubles Tournament,** Clemson Park. Second and third weeks.

**CASHIERS, N.C. Fall Invitational Tennis Matches.** By Cedar Creek Racket Club and Carolina Mountain Bank. Third week.

**CORNELIA, GA. Habersham County Open Fall Doubles Tournament.** By Habersham County Recreation Dept. Third week.

**TOCCOA, GA. N.E. Singles Tournament,** Henderson Falls Park. Third week.

## ——November——

**EASLEY, S.C. Fall Doubles Tennis Classic.** By Easley Recreation Dept. Second week.

# Theater

Not all the drama in the hills is found in spectacular views or whitewater rapids. Plenty of drama unfolds on the stages of community and college theaters and at huge outdoor amphitheaters.

Summer brings acting, music and dance in outdoor dramas packed with history. *Unto These Hills* tells the story of the Cherokee Indian tribe's struggles before it was moved to Oklahoma. Cherokees act many of the parts in the play, which is held in Cherokee, N.C.

Boone, N.C., is the home of *Horn in the West*, which has told the story of Daniel Boone to thousands of outdoor theater-goers since it began in 1952.

Plays and musicals are staged at professional theaters such as the Southern Appalachian Repertory Theater at Mars Hill (N.C.) College Theater. North Carolina's Flat Rock Playhouse in Flat Rock is the official state theater. It provides a season of comedy hits from Broadway and London. Highlands Playhouse has a tradition of bringing fine performances of such plays as *South Pacific* and *Same Time, Next Year*. Parkway Playhouse, maintained by the University of North Carolina at Greensboro, provides summer stock theater in Burnsville.

Even smaller towns are not left out. Hayesville, N.C., for example, is the home of the thriving Licklog Players Community Theater. Cullowhee has the Western Carolina University Players.

In Asheville, N.C., the Montford Park Players bring Shakespeare alive in summer.

Habersham Community Theater in Tallulah Falls and Theater Young Harris at Young Harris College stage inexpensive summer treats for those visiting Georgia. Young Harris also is known for its madrigal productions.

Theater buffs should contact the specific theater or the area Chamber of Commerce about theater productions and dates and times.

## Outdoor Drama

**ASHEVILLE, N.C.** **Montford Park Players** "Shakespeare in the Park." Productions of Shakespeare on weekends, summer months. (704) 254-4540.

**Shakespeare in the Plaza,** City County Plaza. July and August. (704) 258-5222.

**\*BLACKSBURG, S.C. Kings Mountain National Park Outdoor Drama,** amphitheater. August; Thurs., Fri. and Sat. nights. Admission.

**BOONE, N.C.** *Horn in the West,* at the Daniel Boone Theater near the Blue Ridge Parkway. Portraying the struggles of the Appalachian mountain men led by Daniel Boone, the play focuses on their stands against the Cherokee warriors and the British militia during the Revolutionary War. Admission. June-August. (704) 264-2120 or 1 (800) 438-7500.

**CHEROKEE, N.C.** *Unto These Hills,* in the outdoor theater, US-441. A drama of the Cherokee Indian. It portrays N.C. history from the arrival of de Soto in 1540, through the tragic removal of this proud race to the West, over the infamous "Trail of Tears" in 1838. Every night except Sun. Late June-late August. Since 1949. Admission. (704) 497-2111 or 1-800-438-1613.

**FLAT ROCK, N.C.** **Rootabaga Stories,** Carl Sandburg Home National Historic Site. Sandburg's children's stories adapted to drama. Mon., Tues. First week in July to first week in August. (704) 693-4178.

**World of Carl Sandburg,** Carl Sandburg Home National Historic Site. Mon., Tues., Thurs., Fri. and Sat. Last week June to first week September. (704) 693-4178.

**HELEN, GA.** **Summer production,** in the pavilion on the banks of the Chattahoochee River. Admission. Tues.-Sat. Mid-July-mid-August. (404) 878-2155.

**Easter Passion Play,** in Helen's pavilion theater. A play about the life and teachings of Christ. Admission. Group rates available. (404) 878-2155 or 878-2184.

**\*KENANSVILLE, N.C.** *The Liberty Cart, Godspell.* Outdoor drama and religious rock musical. Wed.-Sun. Summer months. Admission. P.O. Box 470, 28349. (919) 296-0721.

**\*MANTEO, N.C.** *The Lost Colony,* at Waterside Theater. The nation's first and oldest outdoor drama. Dramatizes the settlers' struggles for survival and their mysterious disappearance. Mid-June-mid August. Admission. (919) 473-2127 or 3414.

**\*SNOW CAMP, N.C.** *The Sword of Peace,* outdoor drama. Portrayal of the new nation at war and struggles of patriots, Tories and Quakers. Admission. Late June-mid-August. (919) 376-6948.

**\*TOWNSEND, TENN.** **Smoky Mountain Passion Play,** US-321, 25 mi. from Gatlinburg. Admission. Mid-June-late August. (615) 448-2244 or 984-4111.

**\*VALDESE, N.C.** *From This Day Forward* historical drama, Old Colony Amphitheater. About Waldenses and their settling of what became the town of Valdese. Admission. (704) 874-0176.

*For more information contact N.C. Department of Cultural Resources, c/o Theater Arts Section, Raleigh, N.C. (919) 733-2111.*

## University Productions

**BLACK MOUNTAIN, N.C.** **Warren Wilson College,** Theater Department, Kittredge Theater. For reservations, call (704) 298-3325, ext. 260.

**BREVARD, N.C.** **Brevard Little Theater,** Brevard College Barn Theater. Summer productions.

**BURNSVILLE, N.C.** **Parkway Playhouse,** University of North Carolina (Greensboro). Summer repertory. July and August. (704) 682-6151.

**CLEMSON, S.C.** **Clemson Players,** Daniel Hall Annex at Clemson University. (803) 656-2461.

**Clemson Little Theater,** Central Cultural Center, Clemson University. (803) 656-2461.

**Performing Arts Series,** at Clemson University, Daniel Hall Auditorium. October, November, January, February, March. (803) 656-2461.

**CULLOWHEE, N.C.** **Western Carolina University Barter Theater Plays.** Speech and Theater Arts Dept. (704) 227-7491.

**Western Carolina University Little Theater Presentations.** Speech and Theater Arts. Dept., Stillwell Dept. Throughout the year. (704) 227-7365.

**Summer Theater,** Western Carolina University. Tues., Wed. and Thurs. Mid-June to mid-July. (704) 227-7365.

**DEMOREST, GA.** **Piedmont College Lyceum Program,** Jenkins Auditorium, Daniel Hall.

**GAINESVILLE, GA.** **Gainesville Junior College Theater Presentation.** Throughout the year.

**'GREENVILLE, S.C.** **Bob Jones University Classic Players Presentation.** Excellent religious productions held throughout the year.

**YOUNG HARRIS, GA.** **Young Harris College Theater Series.** Madrigal Dinner: October, November. Dinner Theater: February, April, May.

*Note: Refer to the Universities section for more information on college theater productions.*

# Theater

**ASHEVILLE, N.C.** **Asheville Community Theater,** 35 Walnut Street. For reservations, call (704) 253-4931 or 254-1320.

**Fine Arts Theater,** Inc., 36 Biltmore Avenue. (704) 252-7736.

**Four One Act Plays,** Old Newfound School. (704) 258-0710.

**Western North Carolina Montford Park Players.** (704) 254-4540.

**Southern Appalachian Repertory Theater.** (704) 689-1239.

**Theater University of North Carolina,** Belk Theater. (704) 253-5778.

**BUFORD, GA.** **Medieval Faire,** Lake Lanier Islands. Tom Graf, (404) 945-6701.

**BURNSVILLE, N.C.** **The Burnsville Little Theater,** a community theater group, stages three productions a year. (704) 682-2285.

**The Parkway Playhouse,** Drama Dept., University of North Carolina at Greensboro. A summer theater begun by local enthusiasts some years ago. (704) 682-6151.

**CENTRAL, S.C.** **Clemson Area Youth Theater of Pickens County,** Central Cultural Center. (803) 654-4602.

**CLAYTON, GA.** **Nacoochee Scrap Theater,** Laurel Ridge Road at Lake Burton, 3 mi. north of G-356 and G-197. Admission. Summer productions/puppets. (404) 947-3681.

**Rabun Theater Guild.** (404) 782-3513.

**FLAT ROCK, N.C.** **Flat Rock Playhouse,** N.C. State Theater. The oldest professional summer theater in the state. Since 1922. Late June to early September. (704) 693-0731.

**FRANKLIN, N.C.** **Nantahala Players.** Fine Arts Center at Franklin High School.

**'HARTWELL, GA.** **Hart County Community Theater,** Depot Street.

**HAYESVILLE, N.C.** **Licklog Players Community Theater.** (704) 389-3291.

**HELEN, GA.** **Stage Play,** Rathskeller Restaurant. Sat.-Tues. August-Labor Day.

**HENDERSONVILLE, N.C.** **Hendersonville Little Theater.**

**HIGHLANDS, N.C.** Highland Playhouse, P.O. Box 896. Summer theater Tues.-Sun. (704) 526-2695.

**LAKE BURTON, GA.** Nacoochee Scrap Theater, Laurel Lodge Road, G-197 North south end of Lake Burton. Fri., Sat., Sun. (404) 947-3681.

**LAKE LANIER ISLANDS, GA.** Medieval Faire, Gainesville, Lake Lanier Shakespearean events. (404) 945-6701.

**MARS HILL, N.C.** The Southern Appalachian Repertory Theater. This professional theater company stages dramas and musicals in its own 150-seat theater, makes performance tours to nearby communities and sponsors occasional art exhibitions and folk music performances. (704) 689-1203.

**MOUNTAIN CITY, GA.** Mountain City Playhouse, US-441, 3 mi. north of Clayton (404) 782-3882.

**MURPHY, N.C.** John C. Campbell Folk School Brasstown Players, community theater group. Seasonal productions. (704) 837-2775.

**SENECA, S.C.** Oconee Community Theater, 211 N. First Street. (803) 882-7700.

**TOCCOA, GA.** Toccoa-Stephens County Community Theater, Stephens County Junior High stage. Performances accompanied by Toccoa Symphony. (404) 886-2132. Children's Theater. (404) 882-7700.

**TRYON, N.C.** Children's Theater Festival. Professional productions for children (musicals, drama, dance, marionettes, story tellers, street performers). (704) 859-5428

# Town Names

See Rome and Athens without leaving Georgia. Rome, Ga., is built on seven hills as is ancient Rome, Italy; and Athens, Ga., has many beautiful Greek Revival houses. Just how they and the other towns in the Blue Ridge area were named reveals much about the area's history and culture.

Some towns still use the names the Indians gave them, such as Hiawassee and Dahlonega, Ga., and Cherokee, N.C. Other towns are named for colors, other states, months, seasons, mythical gods, politicians, prominent men, war heroes, things and objects, trees and plants.

Here's a look at some of these fascinating names.

**ASHEVILLE, N.C.**   Often referred to as "The Land of the Sky." The city was laid out in 1796, originally named Morristown, and later renamed in the honor of N.C. governor Samuel Ashe. A settlement established on the French Broad River about 1792 was incorporated in 1797 and renamed Asheville. In 1883 Asheville became a city and developed into a popular resort.

**ATHENS, GA.**   Named for Gen. Elijah Clarke who came to Wilkes County, Ga., from North Carolina in 1774 during the Revolutionary War. He signed treaties with the Cherokees in 1792 and with the Creeks in 1782 and 1785. Clarke County was created on Dec. 5, 1801. Athens was incorporated on Dec. 8, 1806. Athens was named after the great classical center in Greece. The wealthy built beautiful Greek Revival homes and mansions.

**\*ATLANTA, GA.**   Atlanta had two previous names in the early 1800s: first, Terminus, because of its railroad location, and then Marthasville, in honor of the governor's daughter. It became Atlanta in tribute to the Western and Atlantic railroad.

**BLACK MOUNTAIN, N.C.**   The small town in the Swannanoa and Black Mountains was originally called Gray Eagle but was later changed to Black Mountain by the railroad which was instrumental in its development. Hikers and the train people would always request to get off at the Black Mountain stop.

**BLAIRSVILLE, GA.**   Named after Capt. James Blair who served in the Ga. House of Representatives from 1810 to 1818 and 1826 to 1830. His efforts involved the settling of land lines between the Cherokees and Georgians and in keeping the peace. The town was incorporated Dec. 26, 1835. Union County was formed on Dec. 31, 1832 and named by John Thomas from his expression "call it Union, for none but Union men reside there."

**\*BRASELTON, GA.**   Named after the Braselton family who own 85 percent of the small town.

**BURNSVILLE, N.C.**   Named for Capt. Orway Burns (1755-1850), the legendary privateer whose ship, the *Snap-Dragon*, terrorized British merchant ships during the War of 1812.

**BURTON, GA.**   Unique history of a town which was flooded by Georgia Power Co. in 1920 (Lake Burton).

**CASHIERS, N.C.** In the spring of 1540, Hernando de Soto traveled through Cashiers Valley looking for valuable treasures. Cashiers Valley was settled by Col. John Zachary and James McKinney around 1830. In 1881 the name was shortened to Cashiers. This came from either a racehorse called "Cash" or maybe after the name of one of the original settlers.

**CHATSWORTH, GA.** Chatsworth was established in the 1870s as a rail stop for Spring Place. On Aug. 18, 1906, it was incorporated as a town. It was named either for a railroad official or a railroad official named it for an old fortified castle called Chatsworth in Chatsworth, England.

**CLARKESVILLE, GA.** Was chartered in 1823 and named after General and former Georgia governor John C. Clark.

**CLEVELAND, GA.** In honor of Gen. Benjamin Cleveland, a general in the war of 1812. The original village was called Mt. Yonah but was renamed in 1857 in honor of Gen. Cleveland.

**COOSA, GA.** The Cherokee name for an ancient Creek town.

**CORNELIA, GA.** Formerly known as Rabun Gap Junction. Judge Pope Barrow, a railroad attorney, renamed it after his wife, Cornelia, in 1882. Since the surrounding area developed into many apple orchards, the town in 1925 became known as the home of the Big Red Apple.

**DAHLONEGA, GA.** The county of Lumpkin was organized in 1833, but the county seat wasn't named until later. The name Dahlonega is believed to come from the Cherokee word of *Talonega*, meaning "gold."

**DEMOREST, GA.** Founded in 1889 by Demorest Mining and Improvement Co. to develop an industrial prohibition town. Named after the very popular prohibition orator, W. Jennings Demorest.

**DILLSBORO, GA.** Town built in 1882 and named after William Allen Dills; became a tourist town in 1886.

**EASLEY, S.C.** Named after Gen. W. K. Easley and chartered in 1874.

**FLAT ROCK, N.C.** Named for a large expanse of granite that had been a ceremonial ground of the Cherokee. This was one of the early small summer resort communities in western North Carolina. Early in the 1800s Flat Rock was a popular location with the rich S.C. plantation owners — thus the name "The Little Charleston of the Mountains." The beautiful homes built in the 1830s are historic landmarks.

**FLETCHER, N.C.** Named in honor of Dr. George Washington Fletcher, a practicing medical doctor. Dr. Fletcher built and operated an inn and shop to accommodate travelers going from Greenville, S.C., to Asheville, N.C.

**FRANKLIN, N.C.** Known as the "Sacred Town" in the Cherokee nation. In 1820, a state commissioner, Jesse Franklin, provided leadership in plotting the town and making it the seat of Macon County. Explorers in the area were: 1540 - Hernando de Soto, searching for gold; 1777 - William Bartram, noted botanist; 1871 - Jacob Silver and William Britton, first white settlers, who established a trading post.

**GAINESVILLE, GA.** There are two ideas on the origin of the name Gainesville: that it was named for a pioneer family named Gaines or named for Gen. Edmond Pendleton Gaines who was instrumental in treaty arrangements between the state and the Cherokees. Known as "Mule Camp Springs" in early days. Hall County was named for Dr. Lyman Hall and organized in 1818.

**'HARTWELL, GA.** Named after Nancy Hart, a Georgia Revolutionary War heroine who acted as a spy against the British Tories.

**HELEN, GA.** Named after a railroad executive's daughter, Helen. Became one of the largest sawmills in the eastern United States. The Bavarian town is now a popular tourist place.

**HIAWASSEE, GA.** Derived from an anglicized version of the Cherokee word ayuhwasi or ayuwasi, meaning "level land near a stream." Chartered in 1879. In 1733 the Indian village was known as Quanessee.

**HIDDENITE, N.C.** About 1880, William Earl Hidden, a New York mineralogist, was sent to North Carolina by Thomas A. Edison to search for platinum. Instead, he found near here the transparent emerald-green crystals now called hiddenite and for which the town was subsequently named.

**HIGHLANDS, N.C.** Laid out as a resort in 1875 by Samuel T. Kelsey and Charles Hutchinson of Kansas, who chose the site because it was the intersection of lines drawn from Chicago to Savannah and from Baltimore to New Orleans. Highlands is just what the name implies — the high lands of eastern America and "air conditioned by nature." Elevation: 3,834 feet.

**LANDRUM, S.C.** Named after a Dr. Landrum whose father provided land in 1880 for a railroad depot.

**LAURENS, S.C.** Named for Henry Laurens (1724-1792), Revolutionary War statesman.

**LITTLE SWITZERLAND, N.C.** Founded in 1910 and named for a resemblance of the surrounding mountains to the Swiss Alps.

**MAGGIE VALLEY, N.C.** Named for one of the daughters (Maggie, Mettie, Cora) of John Sidney Setzer, an unofficial postman, who rode horseback to deliver the neighbors' mail.

**MICAVILLE, N.C.** Named for the mineral mica that was once mined in the area.

**OLD FORT, N.C.** Named for Davidson's Fort, built in 1776, by militia under the command of Griffith Rutherford. For years it was the westernmost outpost on the N.C. frontier. Old Fort served as a refuge from hostile Cherokees and as a base for continued exploration and settlement of the Blue Ridge.

**PENDLETON, S.C.** Named for Judge Henry Pendleton, a Virginian who came to live in South Carolina and made a name for himself as a jurist.

**PICKENS, S.C.** Named after the distinguished Revolutionary soldier, Gen. Andrew Pickens.

**ROBBINSVILLE, N.C.** Named after the Robbins family, early settlers.

**ROBERTSTOWN, GA.** Named after a wealthy Englishman named Charles Roberts who died in 1907.

**SENECA, S.C.** Name was derived from a tribe of Cherokee Indians who roamed the hills of the area. Chartered in 1874.

**SHAKERAG, GA.** Named in the early days when strangers "did not let the sun set on them in town."

**SNAKE, GA.** Named after the reptile.

**TAMASSEE, S.C.**   Named for the Cherokee Fire Prophet.

**TIGER, GA.**   Named after mountain lions which were often called tigers.

**TOCCOA, GA.**   In Cherokee the word *toccoa* means "for the beautiful." Incorporated in 1874 and seat of Stephens County, named for Alexander Stephens, the vice president of the Confederate States.

**TOWNS COUNTY, GA.**   Named in honor of Gov. George M. Towns in 1856.

**TRYON, N.C.**   Named for Tryon Mountain, which bears the surname of William Tryon, British Governor of the colony of North Carolina in 1765. The town was incorporated on March 11, 1885. Some homes date back to the 1700s, and there are Polk County residents living on lands that have been in the family since granted by a deed from the King of England.

**'VANN'S VALLEY, GA.**   Named after David Vann, a mixed-blood Cherokee Indian.

**WEAVERVILLE, N.C.**   One of the first three settlements in North Carolina west of the Blue Ridge Mountains.

**WALHALLA, S.C.**   German settlers called it "Valhalla, a garden of the Gods."

Unusual town names in this area include Tell, Stop, Time, Fence, Talking Rock, Ball Ground and Flowery Branch in Georgia; Trust, Birdtown, Luck and Banner Elk in North Carolina; and Cheddar, Fair Play, Travelers Rest and Six Mile in South Carolina.

# Universities and Colleges

Where can you find cheap lodging, free art shows, sports facilities and possibly an idyllic setting for fall leaf viewing? Try a college or university. The hills are full of them.

Many, such as Appalachian State University in Boone, N.C., and Lees-McRae College in Banner Elk, N.C., rent dorm rooms to the general public in the summer at low rates.

Many other mountain campuses are worth a stop. You can stretch your legs and walk down beautifully landscaped walkways that lead to rose gardens, fountains, lakes, beautiful buildings, woods, or historic landmarks.

Programs such as Elderhostel provide low cost, short term residential academic programs. Designed for older adults, Elderhostel is found at more than 500 colleges, universities and other educational institutions. Programs have included courses in Southern history, Appalachian living, mythology and literature, music appreciation and bizarre psychological experiences. Some colleges such as Western Carolina University in Cullowhee, N.C., offer Camper College weekend summer courses in canoeing, clog dancing or spinner fishing.

Check each college for special programs. Brevard College in Brevard, N.C., for example, has an October in the Woods program featuring nature walks (afternoons) in the Gwynn Valley.

Whatever your interests, take advantage of the programs at these post-secondary schools. Call the nearest college and find out what's available there.

**ASHEVILLE, N.C. Asheville-Buncombe Technical College** (1963). Public, co-ed, two-year college. Technical education. Associates Degree/diploma. (704) 254-1921.

**Blanton's Business College.** Private, co-ed, two-year business programs.

**University of N.C. at Asheville** (1927). Public, co-ed, undergraduate, graduate, liberal arts. (704) 258-0200, ext. 250

**\*ATHENS, GA. Christian College of Georgia.** Private, church supported, Christian services program. (404) 543-3513.

**University of Georgia** (1785). Public, co-ed, undergraduate and graduate. First state granted and supported university. (404) 542-1473, 1421.

**BANNER ELK, N.C. Lees McRae College.** Private, co-ed, four years. (704) 898-5241.

**\*BOONE, N.C. Appalachian State University.** Public, state supported, co-ed, four year, graduate. (704) 262-3045.

**BREVARD, N.C. Brevard College** (1853). Private, co-ed, two year, liberal arts and fine arts, undergraduate, church supported. (704) 883-8292.

**CENTRAL, S.C. Central Wesleyan College.** Private, church supported, co-ed, four years.

**CLEMSON, S.C. Clemson University** (1889). Public, co-ed, land grant, undergraduate and graduate. Large variety of program offerings. (803) 656-2287.

**CLEVELAND, GA. Truett-McConnell College** (1946). Private, co-ed, liberal arts, church supported, four years. (404) 865-2139.

**CULLOWHEE, N.C. Western Carolina University** (1889). Multi-purpose state university: arts, sciences, business ed., health services. Co-ed, four year and graduate. (704) 227-7147.

**DAHLONEGA, GA. North Georgia College.** Public, co-ed, liberal arts, military college of Georgia, undergraduate, graduate, one of the "three" military colleges in the United States. (404) 864-3391.

**DEMOREST, GA. Piedmont College** (1893). Congregational Christian Churches of America. Co-ed, liberal arts, four year, graduate and undergraduate. (404) 778-8009.

**DUE WEST, S.C. Erskine College** (1839). Church supported, co-ed. South Carolina's first four year church-supported college. Undergraduate. (803) 379-8838.

**FLAT ROCK, N.C. Blue Ridge Technical** (1969). Public, technical education college, co-ed. Associate degree and diploma programs, certificates for short-term programs. (704) 692-3572.

**GAINESVILLE, GA. Brenau College.** Private, woman's college. Undergraduate four-year, graduate programs. Accept male students. (404) 532-4341.

   **Gainesville Junior College.** State-supported, co-ed. No housing. Two years. (404) 536-5226, ext. 202.

**MARS HILL, N.C. Mars Hill College** (1856). Private, Christian environment, co-ed. Unique Appalachian studies concentration program. Undergraduate. (704) 689-1201.

**MONTREAT, N.C. Montreat Anderson College** (1916). Church-related junior college. Two years, co-ed, liberal arts. (704) 669-8011.

**MURPHY, N.C. Tri-County Technical College.** Public, two years. (704) 837-6810.

**PENDLETON, S.C. Tri-County Technical College** (1963). Public, two year. Engineering, technical and industrial programs. Co-ed. (803) 646-3227.

**ROYSTON, GA. Emmanuel College** (1930). Private, two-year junior college. Church-supported, co-ed. (404) 245-6041.

**SPRUCE PINE, N.C. Mayland Technical College.** Public, state-supported, co-ed. Two years. (704) 765-7351.

**SYLVA, N.C. Southwestern Technical Institute.** Public, state-supported, co-ed. Two years.

**SWANNANOA, N.C. Warren Wilson College** (1890). Private, church-supported, co-ed. Liberal arts, four years. (704) 298-3325.

**TOCCOA, GA. Toccoa Falls College** (1907). Private Bible college. Undergraduate, general and professional programs. Four years. (404) 886-6831.

**TRYON, N.C. Isothermal Community College.** Adult learning center. Two years, co-ed. Carolina Drive. (704) 859-6744.

**YOUNG HARRIS, GA. Young Harris College** (1886). Church-supported, co-ed. Liberal arts, fine arts, mountain setting. (404) 379-3111.

## Dorm Accommodations Open To Non-Students:

| COLLEGE | TIME | ACTIVITIES |
|---|---|---|
| Lees McRae College<br>Banner Elk, N.C. 28604<br>(704) 898-5241 | June 1-Aug. 1 | Sightseeing, beautiful mountain area, campus facilities. |
| Appalachian State University<br>Boone, N.C. 28608<br>(704) 262-3045 | May 3-Aug. 7 | Guide to scenic areas in Appalachians. |
| Montreat-Anderson College<br>Montreat, N.C. 28757<br>(704) 669-8011, ext. 32<br>Summer Reservation Office | May 15-Aug. 14 | Hiking, horseback riding, tennis, swimming, square dancing, arts and crafts, boating, canoeing. |

## *Elderhostel Programs:*

| COLLEGE | APPROXIMATE DATES: |
|---|---|
| University of North Carolina at Asheville | First and fourth week, June; second week, July |
| Appalachian State University<br>Boone, N.C. | Second week, June; first week, August |
| Western Carolina University<br>Cullowhee, N.C. | Second week, June; first week, August |
| Piedmont College<br>Demorest, Ga. | Fourth week, June; first week, July |
| Brenau College<br>Gainesville, Ga. | Second week, June |
| Mars Hill College<br>Mars Hill, N.C. | First week, June, to first week, August |
| Warren Wilson College<br>Swannanoa, N.C. | First and second weeks, June |

# V

# Visitor Centers

How far is it to Greenville, S.C.? Where is the nearest outlet store? Where may my family camp? What is there to do around here? Visitor centers have the answers. They are scattered throughout the Blue Ridge area, usually just off interstate highways or near entrances to parks.

At the Brasstown Bald Visitor Information Center in the Chattahoochee National Forest near Blairsville, Ga., you can see a slide program, view exhibits such as "Man and the Mountain," hike or picnic. On a clear day four states are visible from the rooftop observation deck atop Brasstown Bald, at 4,784 feet, Georgia's highest mountain.

Terrora Park and Visitors Center in Tallulah Falls, Ga., is a 300-acre park including campgrounds, a swimming beach, pavilion, playground and picnic area, fishing pier, tennis courts, nature trails and a view of Tallulah Gorge. The center, owned by Georgia Power, contains exhibits on electricity and local history and provides free travel information.

The Keowee-Toxaway Visitor Center near Clemson, S.C., has exhibits that involve you in the history of the development of energy. You can handle a seam of coal, see solar panels, and so on. Owned by Duke Power Company, the center is adjacent to the Oconee Nuclear Station, one of the largest and best-run in the country.

See an old farmstead stir to life at the Oconaluftee Visitor Center and Pioneer Museum, 4 miles north of Cherokee, N.C. Visitors watch "pioneers" do their chores, from feeding the animals to running the spinning wheel and making soap.

*State Visitor Information Centers:*

GEORGIA

**Atlanta Airport Visitors Information Center**, Airport Branch, 30320. (404) 767-3231.

**Augusta Visitors Information Center**, I-20, Martinez, Ga., 30907. (404) 828-4610.

**Kingsland Visitors Information Center**, I-95, Kingsland, Ga., 31548. (912) 729-3253.

**Lavonia Visitors Information Center**, I-85, 30553. (404) 356-4019.

**Ringgold Visitors Information Center**, I-75, 30737. (404) 937-4211.

**Savannah Visitors Information Center**, I-95, 31403. (912) 964-5094.

**Tallapoosa Visitors Information Center**, I-20, 30176. (404) 574-2621.

## Visitor Centers

**Valdosta Visitors Information Center,** I-75, Lake Park, Ga., 31636. (912) 559-5828.

**West Point Visitors Information Center,** I-85, 31833. (404) 645-3353.

### NORTH CAROLINA

I-40, 10.5 mi. southwest of Tennessee line (near Waynesville).

I-85, 2 mi. south of Virginia line (near Norlina).

I-85, 2 mi. north of South Carolina line (near Kings Mountain).

I-26, 2 mi. north of North Carolina, South Carolina line (near Tryon, North Carolina).

I-95, ½ mi. south of Virginia line (near Roanoke Rapids).

US-64, ½ mi. south of Murphy city line.

### SOUTH CAROLINA

I-85, north of Georgia line (near Fairplay).

I-26, south of North Carolina, South Carolina line (near Landrum).

I-85, south of North Carolina line (near Blacksburg).

I-20, north of Georgia line (near Augusta).

US-301, north of Georgia line (near Allendale).

I-77, south of North Carolina line (near Little River).

I-95, north of Georgia line (near Hardeeville).

I-95, south of North Carolina line (near South of the Border).

### GREAT SMOKY MOUNTAINS NATIONAL PARK:

**Oconaluftee Center,** Cherokee, N.C. (704) 497-9146.

**Sugarlands Center,** Gatlinburg, Tenn. (615) 436-5615.

*Georgia Welcome Centers:*

**Athens Local Welcome Center,** 280 E. Dougherty Street. (404) 549-6800.

**Atlanta Local Welcome Center,** 3393 Peachtree Road, N.E., Lenox Square Mall, 30326. (404) 233-6767.

**Atlanta Local Welcome Center,** 233 Peachtree Street, N.E., Peachtree Center, 30303. (404) 523-6517.

**Clayton County Local Welcome Center,** 8712 Tara Boulevard, Jonesboro, Ga., 30236. (404) 478-6549.

**Dalton Local Welcome Center,** 524 Holiday Avenue, Dalton, Ga., 30720. (404) 278-7373.

**Gainesville Local Welcome Center,** 230 Sycamore Street, 30501. (404) 532-6206.

**Helen Welcome Center,** Main Street, 30545. (404) 878-2521.

**Rabun County Local Welcome Center,** US-441, Clayton, Ga., 30525. (404) 782-5113.

## Visitor Centers

**Rome Local Welcome Center,** Civic Center Hill, 30161. (404) 295-5576.

**Toccoa-Stephens County Local Welcome Center,** 907 E. Currahee Street, Toccoa, Ga., 30571. (404) 886-2132.

*Miscellaneous Visitors Centers:*

**BLAIRSVILLE, GA. Brasstown Bald Visitor Information Center,** on Brasstown Bald Mountain. Open daily, May 1-early November. (404) 896-2556.

**Georgia Mountain Branch Experiment Station,** 3 mi. south of Blairsville on US-19 and 129. Established in 1930. Has a diversified program in agricultural research and demonstrations. Mon.-Fri. Tours arranged. (404) 745-2655 or 745-6197.

**BURNSVILLE, N.C. Mt. Mitchell State Park,** NC-128. Observation tower, interpretive displays, listed on National Register of Natural Landmarks.

**CHEROKEE, N.C. Oconaluftee Visitor Center,** on US-441. A re-created mountain farm of 1900, 4 mi. north of Cherokee. Mid-June-Labor Day.

**SENECA, S.C. Keowee-Toxaway Visitors Center,** SC-130. Center operated by Duke Power Co. tells the story of energy with seven exhibit areas. Mon.-Sun. (803) 882-5620.

# W

## Wagon Trains

The wagon train was a necessity for early settlers who traveled the mountains carrying everything they owned, along with their dreams of a new life. Transportation has progressed but the spirit of those pioneer journeys lives today in the annual Western North Carolina Wagon Train.

Each year several hundred people, 300 to 400 horses, and about 75 covered wagons leave Andrews, N.C., in late June for a ten-day trek through Robbinsville, N.C.; Tellico Plains, Tenn.; Murphy, N.C., and back to Andrews. The event, including a Fourth of July parade, has attracted national attention. Along the way the travelers stop to cook, camp, sing and recuperate from the rough, bouncy ride.

It all started back in 1958 when the television show "Wagon Train" inspired a group of Southerners who decided a wagon train was just the thing to dramatize the need for a road betwwen Tellico Plains and Murphy. That first 45-mile wagon train of 64 covered wagons and 200 horses attracted thousands of greeters; wagon trains continued to roll every year. It wasn't until 1962 that the road the citizens wanted got under way. The road is now complete.

Chatsworth, Ga., celebrates in July with an Appalachian wagon train that takes one-day, 25-mile trips through Murray County and part of the Chattahoochee National Forest, returning to Chatsworth in late afternoon.

Whether you are a participant or a spectator, these wagon trains will vividly remind you what life was like when horses and wagons ruled the roads.

**ANDREWS, N.C.** Nation's oldest wagon train. From July 1 to July 4 each year, seekers after the pioneer spirit form a wagon train across the mountains from Tellico Plains, Tenn., to Murphy, N.C., along a trail first used in the late eighteenth century to bring out iron ore from Hanging Dog, Owl and Persimmon creeks and later to haul lumber out of the mountains on oxcarts. Participants, on wagons or horseback, are welcome. Write Western North Carolina Wagon Train, P.O. Box 805, Andrews, N.C., 28901.

**CHATSWORTH, GA.** Appalachian Wagon Train, July 10-19. Pioneer Wagon Train hits the trail at 8 A.M. for a parade through rural Murray County (this is really quite a spectacle, with as many as 200 wagons and 2,000 horseback riders participating). Admission. Murray County Saddle Club, located just east of Chatsworth on US-76, Chatsworth, 30705. (404) 695-2361 and 695-6060.

**CLAYTON, GA.** Wagon Train, Recreation Park. August 12 and 13. (404) 782-5226.

**HIAWASSEE, GA.** Georgia Mountain Fair Parade. Wagon parade on Saturday. Early August.

**LOVE VALLEY, N.C.** July 2-4 Frontier Weekend Rodeo: July 5-7 trail ride, wagon train. (704) 592-7451.

**WAYNESVILLE, N.C.** Western North Carolina Wagon Train, Waynesville Recreation Department. July 3-4. (704) 456-9541.

# Waterfalls

From cascading torrents to lacy wisps of water, the magic of water-falls captivates visitors in the Blue Ridge area. Some are roadside attractions with parking and recreational areas. Others are tucked away in remote forests. Some roar in an unchecked rampage, while others tumble playfully in ribbons of water.

The Brevard, N.C., area known as "Land of Waterfalls" attracts hundreds of waterfall watchers each year. You can drive under 120-foot-high Bridal Veil Falls near Highlands or view Looking Glass Falls and its massive towers of rock from your car, 8 miles north of Brevard. At Looking Glass there's a view of the 60-foot cascade, and you can take a swift cold ride down famous Sliding Rock. Whitewater Falls, at 411 feet, the highest cataract east of the Rockies, thunders near the North Carolina-South Carolina state line. Walk a quarter-mile to the overlook for an inspiring view from atop the falls. Non-hikers will like Dry Falls near Highlands. A short pathway near the parking area leads to a walk under the falls. Or, observe spectacular 123-foot Toxaway Falls from US-64 between Rosman and Cashiers.

Not to be outdone by the southwestern part of the state, northwestern North Carolina has plenty of tumbling falls, including Linville Falls in the Pisgah National Forest. Trails lead to both sides of Linville Falls and view of Linville Gorge, the "Grand Canyon of the South." Near Chimney Rock, is Hickory Nut Falls — well worth the short hike.

In north Georgia at DeSoto Falls Scenic Area in the Chattahoochee National Forest, a series of falls awaits hikers, who trek 2½ miles through a forest of hemlock trees and rhododendrons to the multi-tiered upper falls. Georgia's highest waterfall, Amicalola Falls, plunges 727 feet down the eastern side of Amicalola Ridge, south of Dahlonega. Near Helen, Duke's Creek Falls drops 300 feet, and the twin falls at Anna Ruby Falls plunge 50 and 153 feet. On the campus of Toccoa Falls College, the beautiful waters of Toccoa Falls leap from 186 feet, making the falls 16 feet higher than Niagara Falls.

Respect these natural wonders by obeying all signs and regulations. Some who have climbed over guard rails to try to get closer to the falls or who have taken other chances have not survived falls into the turbulent waters, or on the slippery rocks.

**AMICALOLA FALLS, GA.**   16 mi. northwest of Dawsonville via G-182, 52,263 acres; the highest waterfall in Georgia, plunging 729 feet. Accessible by car or hiking trail. (404) 265-2885.

**ANNA RUBY FALLS, GA.**   A 1,600-acre scenic area next to Unicoi State Park. Features twin waterfalls of 50 and 153 feet, an observation platform, fishing and hunting with permits, picnic facilities. A walking trail from the visitors' parking lot to the falls takes about 30 minutes. Open daily. Follow the signs from the entrance to Unicoi State Park. (404) 878-2201.

**BECKY BRANCH FALLS, GA.** Located 3 mi. east of Clayton, Ga., off Warwoman Road, directly across from Warwoman Dell Recreation Area. Round-trip hike from parking area is about 1/3 mi.; very steep.

**BRIDAL VEIL FALLS, N.C.** Over US-64 near Highlands, N.C. This picturesque falls cascades over the road. Cars drive under the falls. Height: 120 feet.

**CLEAR CREEK (SATULAH) FALLS, N.C.** Visible from NC-28; south from Highlands. Overlook 3 mi. south on NC-28 from intersection with US-64.

**CRABTREE FALLS, N.C.** Blue Ridge Parkway, N.C. Trail leads down from Crabtree Meadows.

**CULLASAJA FALLS, N.C.** On US-64 between Highlands and Franklin. Cascades about 250 feet.

**DE SOTO FALLS SCENIC AREA, GA.** Take US-19 and 129 south of Blairsville for 15. mi. or north from Cleveland for 15 mi. Beautiful views and several waterfalls. Clear streams, camping, fishing, wading and hiking.

**DOUGLAS FALLS, N.C.** Barnardsville, N.C. Craggy Mountain Scenic Area, Forest Road 74. Height: 70 feet.

**DRY FALLS, N.C.** 3 mi. west of Highlands, N.C., on US-64 is a thundering falls on the Cullasaja River. A pathway lets you stand safely beneath the falls as tons of water rush overhead.

**DUKES CREEK FALLS, GA.** Helen, Ga. Russell Scenic Highway, north of Helen. Dangerous path leads to scenic falls.

**GLEN FALLS SCENIC AREA, N.C.** Highlands, N.C.; NC-106, 2 mi. south. Three large falls drop 60 feet. Overlooks Blue Valley.

**HICKORY NUT FALLS, N.C.** Chimney Rock, N.C., US-74 and 64; ¾ mi. west of Chimney Rock parking area. Elevator landing on top of rock. More than 400 feet high. Admission.

**HOLCOMB CREEK FALLS/AMMONS CREEK FALLS, GA.** Clayton, Ga., 13 mi. east of Clayton off Warwoman Road. Just after Warwoman crosses the Chattooga River is Forest Service Road 86. Follow this road for about 7 mi. to a sign pointing to the falls. The first falls is Holcomb Creek, which drops about 200 feet. About ⅓ mi. beyond is Ammons Creek, which drops 150 feet. Round trip hike from parking area is about 3 mi.

**ISSAQUEENA FALLS, S.C.** Walhalla, S.C., near Stumphouse Mountain Tunnel Park. Named for an Indian maiden.

**KALAKALESKIES, N.C.** Highlands, N.C., off US-64 West. Series of small waterfalls.

**LEATHERWOOD/BOLD SPRINGS FALLS, N.C.** Hayesville, N.C., Forest Road 1244, 16 mi. north of Hayesville. Height: 100 feet.

**LINVILLE FALLS, N.C.** Off Blue Ridge Parkway and US-221, NC-105, 1.6 mi. Spectacular double-level falls and gorge. Milepost 316.4.

**MAIDEN HAIR FALLS, N.C.** Brevard, N.C., 4 mi. south; 1 mi. off US-276. Old water wheel. Private property. Height: 100 feet.

**MINNEHAHA FALLS, GA.** Clayton, Ga., 7 mi. west of US-23 and 441, south of Clayton. Make a left turn on the dirt road just below the Seed Lake Dam; follow for 2 mi. to the Forest Service sign pointing to the falls. Falls drop about 50 feet.

**PEARSON FALLS, N.C.** Tryon, N.C., 5 mi. north of Tryon, off US-176. A botanical sanctuary. Fee. (704) 859-6236.

**SATULAH FALLS, N.C.** Highlands, N.C., US-28. Upper Falls and Lower Falls (Clear Creek Falls).

**SOCO FALLS, N.C.** US-19 East, in Cherokee.

**TALLULAH FALLS, GA.** On US-23 and 441 in Tallulah Falls. Five falls in bottom of Tallulah Gorge. Main water flow has been diverted for the production of electricity. (404) 754-6036.

**TOCCOA FALLS, GA.** On the grounds of the Toccoa Falls Institute, 2 mi. northeast from Toccoa off G-17. Drops 186 feet.

**WALKER FALLS, N.C.** Forest Road 74, 10 mi. east of Barnardsville. Cascades 75 feet.

*Transylvania County, N.C., Area — "Land of Waterfalls":*

*Note: The following list provides information about the most "concentrated waterfall area" in the Blue Ridge region.*

**BEAR WALLOW FALLS.** US-64 southwest to Whitewater Road; turn left, 4½ mi. To reach the upper falls follow US-64 from Rosman for 13½ mi. or 1½ mi. west of Toxaway River Bridge. Bear Wallow Creek is probably the most rugged stream in this county.

**CATHEY'S CREEK FALLS.** From Brevard, US-64 about 3½ mi.; a short distance on left of State Road 1338. Falls are beautiful and easily accessible.

**CEDAR CREEK FALLS.** Near Cedar Rock Mountain, State Road 1338, right from US-64 at Cathey's Creek and on right from road a short distance from Cathey's Creek Road. Two falls.

**CONNESTEE FALLS.** About 100 yards from US-276, 8 mi. south of Brevard. Two falls are at the same location, Connestee and Baston creeks. Each is about 110 feet high.

**COURTHOUSE FALLS.** Right of State Road 1367, near Pinhook Gap in the Balsam Grove area. On Courthouse Creek, which is a tributary of the North Fork of the French Broad River; turn right 2 mi. west of Rosman on NC-215.

**COVE CREEK FALLS.** Right of Davidson River Road 3 mi. west of Pisgah National Forest Fish Rearing Station. Parking area near head of Davidson River Gorge, easily accessible from old Forest Service Road.

**DIAMOND CREEK FALLS.** Between the river's North Fork and West Fork near State Road 1322, outside Rosman.

**DISMAL FALLS.** On the west fork of the French Broad River, left of State Road 1308 near Jackson County line in Pisgah National Forest, Owens Gap Road. Obtain directions at Lake Toxaway.

**FLAT CREEK FALLS.** In the Quebec community to the right of State Road 1313. Other falls off State Road 1147, south of US-64.

**FROZEN CREEK SHOALS.** Near State Road 1139 in the Frozen Creek, Old Toxaway area. Only a very short hike to the bottom of the falls.

**GLEN CANNON FALLS.** One of these twin falls may be seen from the Glen Cannon golf course. A short hike is required to the top falls.

**HIGH FALLS** Near US-64 on Horsepasture River; turn left on Bohaney Road near Lake Sapphire between Toxaway and Cashiers. Height: 125 feet.

**KATHEY FALLS.** On Bear Wallow Creek about 1 mi. from Toxaway Falls Road or ¾ mi. from US-64. One of the most-visited falls.

**KIESEE FALLS.** In a hidden cove under the Pisgah Ledge near Pinhook Gap Road 1369. In the general area of Courthouse Falls.

**LAUGHING FALLS.** On Turkey Creek, 1 mi. off US-280, near State Road 1360 in Pisgah National Forest.

**LOOKING GLASS FALLS.** Adjacent to US-276, 5 mi. from the intersection of US-276, 280 and 64. One of the most scenic and best-known falls in the eastern United States. Park in area at falls.

**MILL SHOALS.** Adjacent to Owens Gap Road near Jackson County line. Two other falls may be visited in same area: Dismal and Still House Falls, left of State Road 1308.

**MOORE COVE FALLS.** Twin Falls about 1 mi. above Looking Glass Falls. Footbridge crosses creek from US-276 and falls are about 100 yards upstream.

**MT. TOXAWAY FALLS.** Probably the highest falls in the area. Turn right from US-64 on the road to Mt. Toxaway Lookout Tower.

**POUNDING MILL FALLS.** On the Middle Fork of the French Broad River near Eastatoe Gap. May be seen from US-178 or by turning on the road to lakes.

**RAINBOW FALLS** Near Whitewater Falls Road. On Horsepasture River ¼ mi. from State Road 1149. Driftwood Falls are passed before reaching Rainbow Falls. Height: 200 feet.

**RAVEN CLIFF FALLS.** Two mi. on right of US-276 before reaching Caesar's Head. A steep path leads to the bottom of the falls. Height: about 200 feet.

**SHOAL CREEK FALLS.** Crab Creek Road to Shoal Falls Farm Road, 4½ mi. from Penrose. On State Road 1911, ¾ mi. from Crab Creek Road.

**SLICK ROCK FALLS.** On Headwater Road between the National Fish Hatchery and the Pink Beds. The Forest Service Road offers a nice drive to US-276 with excellent view of John Rock and Looking Glass Rock.

**STAIRSTEP FALLS.** Near the headwaters of Lake Jocassee on Horsepasture River. Rough terrain but falls can be reached.

**STILL HOUSE FALLS.** Trail to falls from State Road 1308. Falls was named by Boy Scouts who found a liquor still behind the falls.

**TOXAWAY FALLS.** US-64 crosses the top of the falls, 20 mi. southwest of Brevard. Waterfalls, just below Lake Toxaway Dam, named Toxawa (Red Bird) by the Cherokee Indians. Height: 123 feet.

**TRIPLE FALLS.** Off State Road 1911. Almost inaccessible. There are many waterfalls in this area but most are on private property.

# Waterfalls

**WHITEWATER FALLS.** Off US-64 on an unpaved road near Oakland between Cashiers and Lake Toxaway; 10-mi. road from US-64 to Whitewater Falls. Four other falls. Two-level falls.

**WHITE OWL FALLS.** On headwaters of Thompson River left of Whitewater Falls Road 1149 in the Bohaynee area; between Rainbow and Whitewater Falls.

**WINDY FALLS.** On Horsepasture River between Rainbow and Stairstep Falls.

**WINTERGREEN FALLS.** On Toxaway River just above entrance of Bear Wallow Creek. One of the most beautiful waterfalls in the area.

*Waterfalls in Great Smoky Mountains National Park Region*
*(Within a short drive from Cherokee, N.C.):*

**FLAT CREEK FALLS.** Trailhead: Balsam Mountain Campground. Descends from Heintooga Overlook.

**INDIAN CREEK FALLS.** Trailhead: Deep Creek Road. Falls drop about 60 feet, forming a big base pool. Beyond campground on Deep Creek Road.

**JUNEYWHANK FALLS.** Trailhead: Deep Creek Road, ¼ mi. beyond Deep Creek Campground amphitheater.

**MINGO FALLS.** Trailhead: Big Cove Road. Follow Pigeon Creek Trail out of Mingo Falls Campground. Spectacular drop of 120 feet.

**TOMS BRANCH FALLS.** Trailhead: Deep Creek Road. On the Deep Creek Road, ¼ mi. beyond campground.

*Waterfall Information:*

*"Waterfalls in the Highlands Area"*
write:
U.S. Forest Service
Box 749
Highlands, N.C. 28741   (704) 526-3765

*"Land of the Waterfalls"* (map)
Send $.50 to:
Brevard Chamber of Commerce
Box 589
Brevard, N.C. 28712

For a free guide to the Boone, Blowing Rock waterfalls area including Linville Falls and Cascades, call: North Carolina High Country Host, 1 (800) 222-7575 inside N.C., or 1 (800) 438-7500 elsewhere in eastern U.S.

*"Streams and Waterfalls"*
Brochure of Smoky Mountains National Park. Available from Smoky Mountains Visitors Center at Oconaluftee and Sugarlands.

# Whitewater
## (Canoeing, Rafting, Tubing)

Tumbling down whitewater rapids in a bouncing rubber raft may be one of the most memorable vacation experiences you will ever have. It is a test of man against nature as the paddlers pit themselves against rapids rushing over perilous boulders.

From the threatening Chattooga River in North Georgia to the exciting but tamer Nantahala in North Carolina, the Blue Ridge area offers plenty of whitewater streams. Canoeing, kayaking and tubing are also popular sports.

Waters as diverse as cool mountain streams tucked away in a forest and mighty rivers such as the Chattahoochee are waiting for adventurers. Those willing to get wet and use their muscles may see some of the best scenery in the South. For help in deciding which rapids to conquer, find out how a river's rapids are rated. Rapids are classified by difficulty from I (novice) to VI (life-risking).

Making reservations with an experienced outfitter is a must when you are tackling true whitewater. Outfitters run scheduled trips using four- and six-man rubber rafts and provide guides, all equipment, transportation and lunch for trips that take most of the day. Guides teach you how to paddle and when, but do not do your work for you.

Most outfitters require children to be at least 10 years old and sometimes, 14, before allowing them on a rafting trip. Anyone who is in good physical condition should be able to handle a raft trip. However, an out-of-shape novice should avoid longer trips on the more awesome whitewater corridors.

Rates vary according to the length of the trip, number of guides, distance to drop-off site and the season. Weekday rates are usually cheaper. But the feeling when your heart leaps as the raft plunges down six feet, and the relief that follows when you are safe, are something money can't buy.

## Whitewater Events

————January————

**BRYSON CITY, N.C.** Canoe Races. Nantahala River. Winter races include slalom and wildwater races in all classes. First week.

————February————

**BRYSON CITY, N.C.** Nantahala Glacier-Breaker Race, Nantahala River. Race includes slalom and wildwater races in all classes. Fourth week.

——April——

**LAVONIA, GA.** **Paddle Your Own Canoe,** Tugaloo State Park. First week.

**BUFORD, GA.** **Dogwood Regatta,** Buford, Lake Lanier Islands. Second week.

**CULLOWHEE, N.C.** **Tuckasegee River Road Races.** Down-river, 9.9 mi. canoe race and 10-kilometer run. Second week.

**HELEN, GA.** **Annual Helen-Chattahoochee Championship** for canoes and kayaks, on Chattahoochee River. Slaloms on Sat.; sprints on Sun. Second week.

**BRYSON CITY, N.C.** **Dixie Division Open Canoe Championships,** Nantahala River. Nantahala Outdoor Center. Fourth week.

**\*ROYSTON, GA.** **Broad River Canoe Day,** Victoria Bryant State Park. Fourth week.

——May——

**BRYSON CITY, N.C.** **Dixie Division Open Canoe Championships,** Nantahala River. First week.

**CULLOWHEE, N.C.** **Tuckasegee River Races.** Open Canoe Championship, a 15-mi. river route, Class I and III. Day race, Sun., begins on Western Carolina University campus, University Center. First week.

**HELEN, GA.** **Annual Helen to Atlanta Race,** from the bank of the Chattahoochee River, leaving at 9 A.M. Fri., resuming 7 A.M. Sat., finishes Sat. afternoon at the Chattahoochee River Park on Roswell Road in Roswell. The 100-mile race is for experienced paddlers only. First week.

**BANNER ELK, N.C.** **Canoe five rivers in five days.** Edge of the World outfitters. Third week.

——June——

**BRYSON CITY, N.C.** **S.E. United States Canoe and Kayak Championship Races,** Nantahala River. Georgia Canoe Assoc. Second week.

**Open Canoe Slalom and Wildwater National Championship,** on the Nantahala River. Mid-June.

——September——

**HELEN, GA.** **Labor Day Triathlon,** Unicoi State Park, G-356. Includes swimming, canoeing and running. First week.

**BRYSON CITY, N.C.** **Triathlon Competition,** Nantahala River. Participants compete in a 1-mi. swim, a 4-mi. run, and an 8-mi. canoe race; individual and team competition. Fourth week.

## Tubing Events

**\*ATLANTA, GA.** **Great Rambling River Raft Race,** Chattahoochee River. Third Sat. in May.

**BLACK MOUNTAIN, N.C.** **Annual Flat Creek Tube Race,** Black Mountain Recreation and Parks, 225 W. State Street. Early August. (704) 669-2052.

**BRYSON CITY, N.C.** **Deep Creek Tube Center,** Deep Creek Road. Tubing on Deep Creek. (704) 488-6055.

**HELEN, GA.** **Great Helen Tube Race,** from Chattahoochee Restaurant to Bavarian Brook Tennis Club. Contestants man inner tubes for a 1-mi. race. Fee. Labor Day. (404) 878-2181.

**CHEROKEE, N.C.** **Deep Creek Campground Tubing,** in the Great Smoky Mountains National Park. Tubing down the river. (704) 488-3184.

**°LUGOFF, S.C.** **Water Tubing Festival,** Lugoff-Elgin High School. Regatta at the Wateree River. Country music, children's games, inner tube races. Third week in August. (803) 432-1453.

**ROBBINSVILLE, N.C.** **Water Slide,** Joyce Kilmer Slickrock Wilderness Area, 1 mi. north of town on US-129; 13 mi. east on local road, clearly marked. (704) 479-6431.

## Rafting Events

### ———May———

**°ATLANTA, GA.** **Great Rambling River Raft Race,** on the Chattahoochee River. The rest of the year you can bob down the river on an inner tube without being elbow to elbow to 250,000 rafters. Free. Water temperature is warmest from August to early October. The best stretch of river runs from Morgan Falls to the section that flows under US-41. Third Sat. in May.

### ———June———

**ASHEVILLE, N.C.** **French Broad River Race.** River rafting. By the Asheville Parks and Recreation Department. Mid-June.
**Rocking River Raft Race.** Raft down the French Broad River. Sponsored by the Buncombe Parks and Recreation Dept. Third week.

### ———September———

**ASHEVILLE, N.C.** **Annual French Broad River Week.** River rafting and canoeing. September.

**CLAYTON, GA.** **Chattooga River Whitewater Rafting.** Chattooga River Southeastern Expeditions. (404) 329-0433.

**LONG CREEK, S.C.** **Chattooga River Apple Festival,** at River Mountain Restaurant. By Wildwater Ltd. Third week.

## Outfitters

*NOTE: Consult travel directories, travel clubs, travel agencies and chambers of commerce for hotel, motel and campground accommodations.*

**ALMOND, N.C.** **Rolling Thunder River Co.,** P.O. Box 88. River outfitters. (704) 488-2030.

**ASHEVILLE, N.C.** **Bell's Outdoor Outfitters,** 1 Boston Way, Biltmore Village. (704) 274-2630.
**Black Canyon River Tours,** 502 Merrimon Avenue. Whitewater rafting. Put in at Poplar, N.C.; 9 mi., 5 hours. (704) 253-7656.

**°ATLANTA, GA.** **High Country Inc.,** 6300 Powers Ferry Road N.W., 30339. Reservations: all year. Chattahoochee River. Minimum age: 10 years. (404) 952-8562.

## Whitewater

**Mountain Ventures,** 918 Church Street, Decatur.

**Smoky Mountain Sports,** 2129 N. Decatur Road. Guided raft tours. (404) 325-5295.

**Southeastern Expeditions, Inc.,** 1955 Cliff Valley Way N.E., 30029. Reservations: all year. Minimum age: Ocoee, 12 years; Chattooga, 10-13 years. (404) 329-0433.

**BRYSON CITY, N.C.** **Fast River Rafts, Inc.** US-19, Nantahala River. (704) 488-2386 or 1 (800) 438-9251.

**Gorgarama Park,** Star Route, Box 70, 28713. Reservations: May-October. Minimum age: 7 years. Nantahala River. (704) 488-2325.

**Nantahala Outdoor Center,** Star Route, Box 68, 28713. Reservations: all year. Minimum age: Chattooga, 10-13 years; Nantahala, 7 years; Nolichuky, 13 years; Ocoee, 13 years. (704) 488-2175.

**CASHIERS, N.C.** **Smoky Mountain Sports,** NC-107 south, P.O. Box 443, 28717. (704) 743-9275.

**CHEROKEE, N.C.** **Luftee Outdoor Center,** Cherokee Funyack rentals on Oconaluftee River. (704) 497-9838.

**CLEMSON, S.C.** **Appalachian Trail Outfitters, Inc.,** SC-93. (803) 654-1737.

**CLERMONT, GA.** **Buckhorn Mountain Shop,** P.O. Box 68. Gainesville area. Whitewater programs: 2 day clinics, overnight clinics, 5 day programs, Ocoee River Whitewater rafting. (404) 536-0081 or 983-3768.

**˙DECATUR, GA.** **Georgia Outdoors,** 6518 Roswell Road N.E.; 4515 US-78; 1945 Candler Road.

**DILLARD, GA.** **Outdoor Ventures,** US-441, 12 mi. south of Franklin, N.C. P.O. Box 249, 30357. Guided hiking, canoeing and whitewater rafting trips. Guides, equipment, transportation and lunch. (704) 369-8910.

**˙DUCKTOWN, TENN.** **Ocoee Rafting, Inc.,** P. O. Box 461. Reservations: March-October. Min. age: 1. Ocoee River. (615) 496-2463.

**˙ERWIN, TENN.** **Nolichuky Expeditions, Inc.,** P.O. Box 484, 37650. Reservations: all year. Minimum age: French Broad River, 10 years; Ocoee, 12 years; Pigeon, 10 years; Watauga, 5 years. (615) 743-3221.

**HOT SPRINGS, N.C.** **Carolina Wilderness Adventures,** P.O. Box 488, 28743. Whitewater rafting trips on Nolichuky River and outfits raft trips on the French Broad and Pigeon rivers. Rock climbing and whitewater canoeing instruction available. (704) 622-7260.

**˙JEFFERSON, N.C.** **New River Outfitters, Inc.,** P.O. Box 433, 28640. Reservations: all year. Minimum age: 12 years. Nolichuky River. March-November. (919) 246-7711, (704) 264-1580.

**LONG CREEK, S.C.** **Chattooga Whitewater Shop,** US-76, 29658. Kayak, canoe, raft rentals; clinics. (803) 647-9083.

**Wildwater Ltd. Outdoor Adventures.** Reservations: Jan.-Oct. Minimum age: Chattooga, 12 and 13; Nolichuky, 13 years; Ocoee, 13 years. (803) 647-5336.

**˙OCOEE, TENN.** **Cherokee Rafting Service** US-64, 36361. Reservations: all year. Minimum age: 12 years, Ocoee River. (615) 338-5124.

**Ocoee Outdoors, Inc.,** P.O. Box 174, 37361. Reservations: March-October. Minimum age: 12 years. Ocoee River. (615) 338-2438.

**Sunburst Wilderness Adventures,** P.O. Box 238, 37361. Reservations: February-October. Minimum age: 12 years, Ocoee River. (615) 338-8388.

**\*ROSWELL, GA.** **Call of the Wild Outdoor Outfitters,** 425 Market Place. Rafting. (404) 992-5400.

**SYLVA, N.C.** **Eastern River Trippers,** P.O. Box 825, 28779. Offers raft and canoeing trips on the Nantahala, Tuckaseegee, French Broad, Ocoee and Nolichuky Rivers. Clinics also offered on the Chattooga River. (704) 586-6904.

# X

## X-tra, X-tra

Looking for something more mundane than majestic mountains? Had enough of the sound of rushing streams? Can't stand the sight of one more wonderful wildflower? Tired of invigorating hikes? Don't despair. There are plenty of weird, wacky, tacky and just plain strange things to do and see in the mountains.

On clear, moonless nights near Marion, N.C., you can look for the Brown Mountain Lights. These mysterious glowings, which some believe originate from UFOs, have scientists stumped. The lights at Beacon Heights off the Blue Ridge Parkway near Grandfather Mountain and at the former site of Cold Springs Lodge near Marion, have had people talking, looking and running since Indian days.

Or you might try dowsing. Demonstrations in the ancient art of how to use a divining rod are one of the many strange things that have been taught at Traveler's Rest State Historic Site in Toccoa, Ga.

Peculiar kinds of contests and exhibitions abound. Bring your earmuffs to the coon-dog barking contest held each year in Saluda, N.C. For real heart-stopping excitement, watch the Western North Carolina Checkers Tournament in Franklin, N.C., in May. Another action-packed contest is the annual pipe-smoking contest held in Helen, Ga., in the fall. The object is to see who can smoke a pipe the longest. You can test your skill with a chainsaw at a contest at Mountain Heritage Day in Cullowhee, N.C., in September.

Join the marchers in the first week of October who commemorate the defeat of the British soldiers at Kings Mountain, N.C., in 1780. They trek across the Overmountain Victory Trail winding through Marion, N.C., from Abbington, Va., to Kings Mountain, N.C.

End all toying with oddities by watching manmade Andrews Geyser shoot 200 feet into the air. Two miles west of Marion, N.C., the geyser was built about 1885 by the Southern Railroad as a scenic attraction for passengers who were bored with pure mountain views.

### Miscellaneous Events

*(Listed in alphabetical order by type of event.)*

**AIR SHOW,** Clemson, S.C. Fly-In, Oconee County Airport. Variety of planes. Third week in June.

**BOOK FAIR,** Franklin, N.C. Mountaineer Book Fair, Community Facilities Building, Macon County Public Library. Second week in July. (704) 524-3600.

**BOOK FAIR,** Gainesville, Ga. Annual sale held daily at Brenau College Book Building, Academy Drive on Brenau College campus. Sale of used paperbacks, children's books, encyclopedias. First week in October.

**DOG CONTEST,** Saluda, N.C.Coon Dog Barking Contest, 116 S. Jackson Street. In this contest judges award prizes for beauty and barking.

**DOG SHOW,** Asheville, N.C. All Breed Dog Show and Obedience Trial. AKC Approved. Asheville Kennel Club.

**DOG SHOW,** Black Mountain, N.C. Annual Dog Show. Fourth week in July.

**DOG SHOW,** Pine Creek, N.C.Bench Show and Field Trial. By Jackson and Macon County Fox Hunters Association. Second week in September.

**DOG SHOW,** Tryon, N.C. Annual Any and All Dog Show, Harmon Field. Tryon Riding and Hunt Club. Since 1932. First week in October.

**FIELD DAY,** Blairsville, Ga. PTA Field Day, Blairsville Chamber of Commerce. Parade, cart race, games, 4-mi. run, awards. Second week in May.

**FIELD DAY,** Central, S.C. Central Field Day. Third week in August.

**FIELD DAY,** Pendleton, S.C. Pendleton Field Day, Vet's Park. By American Legion Post. Second week in August.

**KITES,** Sylva, N.C. Krazy Kite Kontest. By Jackson County Recreation and Parks Dept. First week in April.

**PARADE,** Brevard, N.C. Children's Parade. Parade of families, school groups, scouts, churches, 4H. Third week in October.

**PARADE,** Ellijay, Ga. Apple Festival Pet Parade. First week in October.

**PARADE,** Westminster, S.C. Apple Festival Kiddie Parade, Ages 3 to 10 years. Second week in September.

**PULLING CONTEST,** Chatsworth, Ga. Mule Frolic. At the Murray County Saddle Club on US-76. C.W. Bradley, Rte. 1, Box 387, Chatsworth, 30705. Mules compete in pulling contests. Admission. First Friday in October.

**PULLING CONTEST,** Hartwell, Ga. Annual Tractor and Truck Pull. By Lake Hartwell Shrine Club. Hartwell Speedway. Fourth week in July.

**RAILROAD,** Atlanta to Toccoa, Ga. Round-trip train rides with a steam engine pulling 18 cars departs from Brookwood Station on Peachtree Street. Tickets available from Autumn Leaves Special, 1844 W. Rugby Avenue, College Park, 30337. Tickets must be ordered by mail before Oct. 16. Specify date desired and make check payable to AUTUMN LEAVES SPECIAL. Late October to early November.

**RAILROAD,** Hartwell, Ga. Hartwell/Bowersville railroad trip. A 2½-hour ride with arts and crafts shops at both ends of the line. Train runs several times daily; weekend schedule in the fall. Trip begins and ends in Hartwell. (404) 376-4901.

**RAILROAD,** Robbinsville, N.C. Bear Creek Railroad, US-129 south. Admission.

**RAILROAD,** Swannanoa, N.C. The Swannanoa railroad tunnel is 1,800 feet long, constructed by convict labor between 1877 and 1879 at a cost of $600,000 and 120 lives. Engineers made early use of nitroglycerin. A group of Swannanoa Tunnel songs grew up with many similarities to the John Henry work songs and ballads.

**RAILROAD,** Walhalla, S.C. The Blue Ridge Railroad began cutting a tunnel through Stumphouse Mountain in the 1850s but went bankrupt leaving a gaping hole of 1,600 feet. Off SC-107. Ask locally for directions.

**TALENT SHOW,** Blairsville, Ga. Kiwanis Talent Showcase, Junior High gym. Third week in March.

**TALENT SHOW,** Clayton, Ga. Annual Talent Show by Rabun County High School Council in the Auditorium. Second week in February.

**TALENT SHOW,** Westminster, S.C. Apple Festival Talent Show, College Street School. By Westminster Lions Club. First week in September.

**TRAVEL,** Cullowhee, N.C. WRGC's Annual Great Smokies Living Show, at the Reid Gym, Western Carolina University. Third week in May.

**TRAVEL,** Gainesville, Ga. Travel and Sports Fair, Georgia Mountain Center. Third week in March.

## Miscellaneous Events, Month by Month

———January———

**WINTER CARNIVAL,** Young Harris, Ga. Annual carnival, Student Center, Sharp Hall. By Dorcas Club YHC. Fourth week.

———February———

**TREE SALE,** Toccoa, Ga. Annual seedling sale. By Stephens County 4H Club. Second week.

———March———

**BANQUET,** Clayton, Ga. Annual Rabun County Star Student and Teacher Banquet. Rabun County High School. By the Chamber of Commerce. First week.

**SCOUT SHOW,** Clarkesville, Ga. Piedmont District show, Habersham County Fairgrounds. Exhibits and demos. Third week.

———April———

**SIDEWALK SALE,** Clayton Ga. Annual sale by Merchants Assoc. First week.

**BEACH OPENING,** Buford, Ga. Lake Lanier Islands. Third week. (404) 945-6701.

**SIDEWALK SALE,** Walhalla, S.C. By greater Walhalla Chamber of Commerce. Auction, barbecue, sale. Third week.

———May———

**DESIGN SHOW,** Asheville, N.C. Annual High Country Design Show. First week in May-second week in June.

**CHECKER TOURNAMENT,** Franklin, N.C. Western N.C. Checker Tournament, Macon County Facilities Building. Early May.

**SKY CON 4,** Asheville, N.C. Show and sale of comics, science fiction, Super Giant Books. 38 Wall Street. Second week.

**STRAWBERRIES,** Franklin, N.C. Double A. Farms (pick your own), 3 mi. south of Franklin, Clark's Chapel Community. May-June. (404) 369-9361 or 524-8245.

————June————

**DOLLHOUSE EXHIBIT/TOUR,** Blairsville, Ga. Thirty-room "Enchanted Palace." Six years to build and 30 years to furnish. US-129 south. June to October.

**HOMECOMING,** Rabun Gap, Ga. Annual Rabun Gap Nacoochee Homecoming at Rabun Gap N. School. Annual alumni meeting. Square dancing. Fourth week.

**SOFTBALL TOURNAMENT,** Sylva, N.C. Annual Tuckaseegee Class, sanctioned ASA men's softball tournament. Fourth week.

————July————

**DOWSING,** Toccoa, Ga. Traveler's Rest State Historic Site. Learn the history of dowsing and see demonstration. Fourth week.

**SUMMER PHOTO CONTEST,** Buford, Ga. Amateurs only. Lake Lanier Islands. Month of July.

————August————

**WNC OPEN DAIRY SHOW,** Asheville, N.C. Since 1943. At Western N.C. Agricultural Center. By N.C. Agriculture Extension Service. First week.

————September————

**AWARENESS DAY/HIAWASSEE RIVER,** Murphy, N.C. Stream watch committee. First week.

**C.B. JAMBOREE,** Seneca, S.C. By Appalachian C.B. Club, National Guard Armory. First week.

**PARADE,** Clemson, S.C. Annual Curb the Dawg. Downtown Clemson. By Pi Alpha Kappa. Football game vs. University of Georgia. Fall.

**CHAINSAW CONTEST,** Cullowhee, N.C. Mountain Heritage Days. Six award classes. Western Carolina University, Belk Building Field. Second week.

**STRONGEST MOUNTAINEER CONTEST,** Cullowhee, N.C. Also horseshoe pitch, tobacco spitting, chug contest. Third week.

————October————

**MARCH** (Along the Overmountain Victory Trail), Marion, N.C. Marchers dressed in the buckskin garb of mountain men and women 200 years ago, commemorate the defeat of the British soldiers at Kings Mountain on Oct. 7, 1780. First week.

**CHATTOOGA RIVER CLEAN UP,** Long Creek, S.C. To beautify Chattooga River. By U.S. Forest Service and Sierra Clubs and outfitters. Second week.

**PIPE SMOKING CHAMPIONSHIPS,** Helen, Ga. Second week.

**BEAUTIFUL BABY CONTEST,** Toccoa, Ga. Toccoa-Stephens County Jaycettes. Fourth week.

**BEST PUMPKIN CONTEST,** Brevard, N.C. By *Transylvania Times*. Fourth week.

————November————

**FALL CLEANUP WEEK,** Brevard, N.C. By Brevard Chamber of Commerce. Areas: Blue Ridge Parkway and Pisgah National Forest. First week.

## Miscellaneous Places, Etc.

**BALDWIN, GA.** Habersham Vineyards, G-365. Welcome Center. Premium winery. (404) 778-5845.

**CORNELIA, GA.** Big Red Apple Monument, downtown. Honors the area's apple-growing industry.

**DAHLONEGA, GA.** Yahoola Creek Farm, 5 mi. north of Dahlonega off US-19. Offers a 3-mi. hayride in and near the Chattahoochee National Forest. (404) 864-6735.

**LAKE LURE, N.C.** Whiteside's Pumpkin Center, Rte. 1, US-64 and 74. Piles of pumpkins. (704) 286-9438.

**MARION, N.C.** Andrews Geyser, west of Marion, 2 mi. off old US-70 on Mills Creek Road, built around 1885 by the Southern Railroad as a scenic attraction for passengers and to mark the railroad gateway to the Blue Ridge Mountains. The geyser shoots a stream 200 feet into the air.

Brown Mountain Lights, Beacon Heights off Blue Ridge Parkway near Grandfather Mountain or former site of Cold Springs Lodge on NC-18 or NC-105 near Marion. These mysterious glowings have stumped scientists and have been talked about since the time of the Indians. (704) 437-3021.

**MURPHY, N.C.** Fields of the Wood Park, on NC-294, west of Murphy. Display of religious symbols. Daily, sun-up to sundown.

**TATE, GA.** Tour of Georgia Marble Company. By appointment. Almost an unlimited supply is found here in the Long Swamp valley region.

**WALHALLA, S.C.** Sunken Springs Apple and Berry Farm, SC-11 north. Pick your own berries. (803) 944-1048 or 1085.

# Y

## You Wouldn't Believe . . .

While doing the research for this book, I came across an amazing number of "You Wouldn't Believe That" facts. The following information could be a miniature sort of *Guinness Book of World Records* or the beginning of a "trivial pursuit" game of the Blue Ridge Mountains area.

- The Southern Appalachian Mountain area is called the **"vegetation cradle of eastern North America"** by botanists.
- Fifteen million people visit the Southern Appalachian area each year. The area is accessible to more than one half the population of the United States within 1 day's travel by car.
- Holiday on Lake Lanier has the **world's largest "floating marina"** near Gainesville, Ga.
- The two woods which produce the most heat per cord are hickory and oak.
- Some old-timers say that if a bee-sensitive person will take a daily cup of confrey and golden-seal (also called yellow root) tea and eat or drink yogurt, kefir or acidophilus milk, the body will rid itself of built-up toxins and return to a natural bacterial state that enables it to better handle bee venoms.
- Hiawassee's annual (August) Georgia Mountain Fair has been named one of the three key Georgia events designated among the "Top Ten" tourism attractions in North America for 1983 by the American Bus Association.
- An average of about 490 people per hour slide down "Sliding Rock" near Brevard, N.C.
- Dry Falls, in the Cullasaja River Gorge near Highlands, N.C., is so named because you can walk under the falls, which is at an elevation of 3,365 feet.
- In 1921, hiking clubs began clearing the 2,000-mile Appalachian Trail, and by 1937 the trail was completed from Georgia to Maine, making it the **world's longest marked footpath.**
- The Cherokee County (N.C.) Courthouse is constructed of native "Regal Blue Marble," the only courthouse built of this material in the United States.
- Bob Jones University (Greenville, S.C.) has gained international recognition for its remarkable collection of more than 400 original paintings by the old masters, including early Flemish and Dutch.
- The McBee Chapel (Connestee, S.C.), built in 1841, is one of the few remaining octagonal churches in America.
- North Carolina offers more than 300 varieties of gems and minerals with emeralds, garnets and rubies being the most popular.
- Farriering, the process of fitting and placing shoes on horses and mules, is taught at Southwestern Technical College (Cullowhee, N.C.).
- The town of Elberton, Ga., is one of the world's largest suppliers of granite monuments.
- Galacking is a process of digging up the herb-type plant called galax. This plant was common in the Blue Ridge Mountains and was a large money crop in the early 1900s.
- The Indian word "Chattahoochee" is derived from two Creek Indian words — *chatto* (a stone) and *hoche* (flowered) — and means "flowered rock."

- The Indian mound (Helen, Ga.) near the intersection of G-17 and G-75 contained as many as 75 graves and numerous ceremonial artifacts, which were uncovered by experts from the Smithsonian Institution.
- The word Nacoochee (Georgia Valley) comes from the Cherokee words *nagu'tsi* or *nakushi,* meaning "little arrow."
- The Blue Ridge Mountains are considered to be among the oldest mountains in the world.
- Peaches were introduced in the United States in the early 1600s by China, and the first commercial peach shipment took place in Spartanburg County on July 21, 1924. Today, South Carolina produces almost 200 million pounds of peaches.
- The **oldest wagon train** still in existence in the United States today is sponsored by the Western N.C. Wagon Train Association and is held July 1-4 of every year (near Andrews, N.C.).
- Historic Harshaw Chapel built in 1869 (near Murphy, N.C.) supposedly includes the burial grave of Abram Enloe, the father of Abraham Lincoln, the 16th president of the United States.
- Lake Lanier Islands (Georgia) are four green islands that resulted from a math error when the overflow waters from Buford Dam flooded the area; engineers expected them to be covered by the lake.
- Tallulah Gorge (Georgia) is one of the nation's oldest gorges (2,000 feet deep).
- The Sosebee Cove Scenic Area (Blairsville, Ga.) is believed to contain more rare Dutchman Breeches (wildflowers) than any other area in the southern Appalachian Mountains.
- Toccoa Falls (Georgia) on G-17 is 186 feet high or 16 feet higher than Niagara Falls. The Cherokee word *toccoah* means "the beautiful."
- Georgia was the first state to charter a university, the University of Georgia (Athens), in 1785.
- In some of the Nacoochee Scrap Theater (Sautee, Ga.) puppet productions, the puppets are life-size or larger (5 feet tall).
- One of three factories in the United States that manufacture oak saddletrees (Western-style saddle frames) is in Demorest, Ga.
- The nation's **oldest (1926) and most colorful folk celebration** is the annual Mountain Dance and Folk Festival held at the Asheville Civic Center in early August.
- Horace King of LaGrange, Ga., was the man responsible for the building of most of the covered bridges in Georgia.
- The only Raft Guide School of its kind in the eastern United States is conducted by Wildwater Ltd. of Long Creek, S.C., during middle March.
- The **World's Largest Framed Oil Painting** depicts the interior of St. Peter's Cathedral (Athens, Ga.) and dominates the interior of the Greek Revival chapel of St. Peter's. It weighs over a ton and measures 17 by 23 ½ feet. The painting was completed in 1847.
- Franklin D. Roosevelt, our 32nd president, demonstrated a great deal of interest in the Smoky and Blue Ridge Mountains in various projects such as the T.V.A. (Tennessee Valley Authority), which provided electrical, commercial, recreational and environmental benefits; the Blue Ridge Parkway, a scenic drive from Virginia to the North Carolina Smoky Mountain area; and the Appalachian Trail (from Maine to North Georgia).
- Legend relates that dogwood was the timber used for Jesus's cross. The dogwood was so named because its odor when wet reminded people of the smell of a drenched dog.
- The **world's smallest daily newspaper** is the *Tryon (N.C.) Daily Bulletin,* printed Monday through Friday.
- The American beech tree (Fagas grandifolia) is unique, because it holds on to its tan-brown leaves in winter.

- The **Cullowhee lily** grows only in Cullowhee, N.C.
- Burt Reynolds has called Georgia his good luck charm because almost all of his big hits — **White Lightning, Gator, The Longest Yard** and **Deliverance** (Clayton, Ga.) — were filmed in Georgia.
- The city of Brevard, N.C., was named "Tree City U.S.A. — 1982" by the Arbor Day Foundation. Brevard has received this national award three times.
- **Hunkering** is the art of sitting without the use of a chair. It encompasses various positions of squatting down.
- Dr. Peter Witt, Swiss-born pharmacologist, has donated his personal collection of spider literature, valued at $2,500 and containing about 150 volumes of rare spider material, to Western Carolina University in Cullowhee, N.C.
- Approximately 45,000 snakebite incidents occur each year in the United States, but only 20 percent are from venomous or poisonous snakes.
- William Bartram, the famous naturalist, made his way into western North Carolina about the year 1875.
- The marble chosen for the Lincoln Memorial in Washington, D.C., came from the mountains of north Georgia. This marble is noted for its sparkling, crystalline beauty and amazing durability.
- The Japanese Paper Plant (Edgeworthia papyrifera), a native Japanese plant, may be seen in spring bloom along Wolf Creek in Rabun County, Ga.
- The Brevard Music Center (N.C.) is sometimes called the **"Summer Cultural Center of the South"** with its 1,000 young musical students in attendance.
- Sourwood honey is a delicacy of the mountains. True sourwood honey is delightfully sweet and extremely light.
- Loggers recently dragged a chestnut log out of the woods near Bryson City (N.C.) estimated to weigh 12 to 15 tons and containing about 1,450 board feet of lumber. It took two large wreckers and bulldozers to get it out.
- Asheville, N.C., was rated the **number one city** by Rand McNally's "The Place Rated Almanac" among cities in the United States under 125,000. It was also rated the best small city to retire in.
- Lake Hartwell is one of the largest man-made lakes east of the Mississippi with over 56,000 acres and a shoreline that covers nearly 1,000 miles. Lake Hartwell is the dividing line between Georgia and South Carolina.
- The Barak Norton Family Reunion, a reunion that has been held since about 1870 during late July in Highlands, N.C., is considered one of the oldest in western North Carolina.
- Evidence that America was visited in the distant past by Asian and European voyagers is evident around ancient stone ruins found in Georgia, specifically near Chatsworth in the Cohutta Mountains of northwest Georgia (Fort Mountain State Park).
- The Cherokee word *unicoi* (Unicoi Gap) means "white," so the gap may have been so named because in winter it was often white with snow.
- Kudzu, the creeping prolific vine that has spread over 400,000 acres in the Southeast, was introduced in the United States at the turn of the century by farmers anxious to rejuvenate nitrogen-deficient soils and provide forage for cattle.
- The **highest standard gauge railroad point in Eastern America** is at Balsam, N.C. (Jackson County).
- *Cataloochee* is a Cherokee word meaning "standing in rows."
- The Appalachian Mountains are the home of more than 1,500 species of flowering shrubs, trees and herbs.
- Georgia's 250th birthday was celebrated on Feb. 12, 1983, with the commemoration of the landing of James Oglethorpe and the colony's original settlers on Feb. 12, 1733.

- Two of the three nationally designated wilderness areas east of the Mississippi are Shining Rock Wilderness (south of Waynesville, N.C.) and Linville Gorge on the Linville River (N.C.).
- The Southern Highland Handicraft Guild has more than 600 members who live and work in the nine-state Southern Highland region. Their crafts are on view at the Folk Art Center near Asheville, N.C.
- The Vagabond Players at the Flat Rock Playhouse (N.C.) are rated one of the ten best summer theater companies in the United States.
- Carl Sandburg first came to the mountains of western North Carolina at Flat Rock in 1945 and spent the last 22 years of his life writing, reading, enjoying nature and raising Chikaminy goats.
- John Gilleland (Athens, Ga.) invented the famous but ill-fated double barrel cannon with its chained together cannon balls. The cannon was cast in an Athens, Ga., foundry in 1863 and was meant to fire the two balls simultaneously.
- The estimated black bear population in the Fires Creek Bear Sanctuary near Hayesville, N.C., is from 10 to 25 at any given time.
- Georgia has 19 **national champion trees**, trees that are the largest of their kind in the United States. The chestnut oak in the U.S. Forest Service District near Blairsville stands 133 feet tall, is 12 ½ feet in circumference, and has a crown spread of 58 feet.
- Baseball Hall of Fame's Johnny Mize was born and raised in Demorest, Ga. His career total was 359 home runs and a batting average of .312.
- The 90-foot-tall pine tree overlooking Helen, Ga., from Unicoi Hill is one of the largest outdoor, lighted Christmas trees in the southeastern United States.
- The Chattahoochee River, which forms 8 miles north of Helen, Ga., and continues 550 miles to the Gulf of Mexico, carries 56 million gallons of water daily through the town.
- The Mountain Regional Library at Young Harris (Ga.) contains the Appalachian Archives of Georgia, which consists of books, records, video tapes, cassettes and periodicals about southern Appalachian ways of life. Some 8,000 songs are included in the collection.
- Many kinds of flowering plants grow and thrive in the Blue Ridge Mountain region, more than are found on the continent of Europe.
- The South Carolina Canal and Railroad Line (SCCRL), built in 1824, was the first railroad in the world to carry mail and also the longest railroad, with 136 miles of track.
- Lake Jocassee (N.C.) is the home of the N.C. record-breaking brown trout.
- The Grace-Calvary Episcopal Church in Clarkesville, Ga., is the oldest unaltered Episcopal church building in the state of Georgia (1840).
- A large apple monument constructed of concrete and steel adorns the downtown area of Cornelia, Ga., which is known as the "Home of the Big Red Apple."
- The **"Tree That Owns Itself,"** corner of Finley and Dearing streets in Athens, Ga., is a white oak tree that was deeded a plot of land eight feet in radius from its trunk, by its former owner, Col. William H. Jackson, a professor at the University of Georgia, Athens, Ga.
- The Indians (Seneca) introduced the American settlers to the art of making dolls from apples, commonly called Applehead Dolls.
- The Cowee Valley mines near Franklin, N.C., are the only mines in the United States open to the general public solely for the purpose of ruby and sapphire mining.
- The first sawed plank house in the United States, constructed by Col. Joshua Sutton, is located in Batesville, Ga.
- Whiteside Mountain (between Highlands and Cashiers, N.C., on US-64) is the **highest sheer cliff in the eastern United States** at 4,930 feet.

- Jim and Hertha Flack, retired grandparents, hiked the 2,106-mile Appalachian Trail and wrote a book, *Ambling and Scrambling on the Appalachian Trail*, about their experiences.
- Gainesville, Ga., and the surrounding northeast Georgia area is the **poultry capital of the world.**
- The red clay soil of the Piedmont results from the presence of low-grade iron minerals such as hematite in the underlying rock. As the rocks eroded and weathered, the hematite and other iron compounds turned red and decomposed into fine particles, thus forming the red clay soils.
- The Cherokees thought that toothache was caused by a worm wrapping itself around the base of the tooth.
- The Cherokee written language contained 86 characters developed by Sequoyah, a jewelry maker, in 1821.
- The Cherokee word *talonega* (Dahlonega) means gold.
- Only two poisonous snakes, the timber rattler and the Southern copperhead, are found in the Appalachian Mountains.
- In 1828, settlers found gold on Duke's Creek, Ga., (near US-129) which was Cherokee land.
- The Biltmore Forestry School established in 1898 by Dr. Sheneck is **America's first forestry school.** Originally, it was part of the Biltmore Estate but now is part of the Cradle of Forestry Visitor Center (Brevard, N.C.).
- The Hiawassee Unit 2 pump-turbine, located at the Hiawassee Dam, N.C., has been named a National Historic Mechanical Engineering Landmark by the American Society of Mechanical Engineers. The unit, installed in 1956, was the **first integrated pump-turbine used in a power plant** in the country. It was the most powerful of its kind in the world at the time. The Tennessee Valley Authority owns and operates the Unit.
- The Coweeta Hydrologic Laboratory (Franklin, N.C.) is in the **highest rainfall zone east of the Pacific Coast.** Each year, 80 inches of rain will fall from about 128 storms.
- The Biltmore House in Asheville was named after Vanderbilt's forebears' Dutch town of Bildt and "more" from the English word for rolling, hilly country.
- Mountain folklore claims that if you throw the peel of a whole apple over your shoulder, it will form the initial of your "intended."
- The growing interest in reviving the art of blacksmithing is evident in the 40 charter members who founded the Artists Blacksmith Association of North America in Lumpkin County, Ga., in 1973.
- European and American craftsmen worked for five full years to build the two-hundred room Biltmore House, owned by the Vanderbilt family, in French chateau style planned by Richard Morris Hunt.
- Sky Valley, Ga., is the southern-most ski slope in the United States. However, a new resort center (The Peaks) is planned near Vogel State Park (Blairsville, Ga.).
- There are in excess of 5,000 natural springs in Rabun County, Ga.
- The Brasstown Bald Visitor's Center on top of Brasstown Bald Mountain (4,784 ft. elevation) was visited by 54,475 people from 40 foreign countries and 46 states during 1980.
- One of the first promotional activities for Tallulah Falls (Ga.) occurred in 1886 when Professor Leon walked across the gorge on a tightrope.
- The Chattahoochee United Methodist Church (1860) near Helen, Ga., was featured in the film *I'd Climb the Highest Mountain.*
- Frederic Law Olmsted, noted landscaper who designed New York's Central Park, created the original landscape design for the Biltmore Mansion in Asheville, N.C.
- The area in the vicinity of Black Mountain, N.C., is the largest Religious Conference Center in the world.

- NASA's Rosman (N.C.) Tracking Station is one of three such worldwide satellite tracking stations. The others are in Alaska and Australia.
- The Davidson River in the Pisgah National Forest of North Carolina is nationally famous for its superb rainbow trout fishing.
- Henderson County (N.C.) produces and supplies over 75 percent of North Carolina's apples each year.
- The nation's largest Episcopal Conference and camping center is the Kanuga Conference at Hendersonville, N.C.
- The town of Tryon (N.C.) has a very unusual climatic condition called the verdant zone: temperature inversions protect the area from freezing temperatures (always above 32 degrees F.).

- Rabun County (Ga.) is becoming a motion picture location: more than 90 films have been made there, including *Deliverance, Whiskey Mountain, The Million Dollar Dixie* and *Long Riders.*
- The Chief Vann House near Chatsworth, Ga., is the only historic mansion in America built by an American Indian.
- On the grounds of Traveler's Rest Plantation (Toccoa, Ga.) is one of the largest American holly trees in the state (on US-23, 6 miles north of Toccoa).
- Highlands, N.C., is known as the second highest incorporated town in the eastern United States. Beech Mountain, N.C., is now first.
- The mountain laurel was a special plant to the Cherokees — one of their sacred seven.
- The Georgia apple might have been a thing of the past had it not been for the research on black rot fungus by the Georgia Mountain Branch Experiment Station (University of Georgia, College of Agriculture).
- The archery range at Blackburn Park (Dahlonega, Ga.) is one of the few in north Georgia that is built to the National Archery Association specifications.
- Moccasin Creek State Park is north Georgia's smallest state park. Fishing is limited to senior citizens, children under 12 and handicapped people.
- The **second** highest point in Georgia is Rabun Bald, a 4,696-foot mountain in Rabun County.
- Clayton, Ga., was named one of the ten best retirement locations in the United States in 1981 by *Consumers Digest.*
- The Horticultural Gardens of Clemson University include one of the largest shrub collections in the eastern United States. Many of the sectional areas feature information marked in Braille along the Braille trail.
- The town of Pendleton (S.C.) has more than 40 points of historic interest. Most of them are private homes which have been restored by the present owners.
- The antebellum homeplace of John C. Calhoun, vice president of the United States, U.S. Senator, and secretary of war, is located at Fort Hill in Clemson, S.C. His son-in-law was Thomas G. Clemson, the benefactor of Clemson University.
- The former Long Creek (S.C.) Academy, now headquarters of Wildwater Ltd., was once featured in one of Walt Disney's television movies.
- The Chattooga River was designated a wild and scenic river by Congress on May 10, 1974.
- The Crawford W. Long Medical Museum (Jefferson, Ga.) covers the history of medicine with emphasis on the art of anesthetics. Dr. Long performed the first painless surgical operation using sulphuric ether in 1842.
- The Foxfire books written at Rabun Gap-Nacoochee School have motivated the younger generation to research, restore and remember the many mountain practices and philosophers. The books record facts and lore about mountain life in the Rabun Gap, Ga., area.

- Gainesville, Ga., was completely destroyed by fire in December of 1851 and was quickly rebuilt into a trade mill center and health resort (mineral waters).
- The South's first major, asphalt, Grand Prix-type road racing is at Road Atlanta (near Gainesville, Ga.).
- The Greenville County (S.C.) Museum of Art houses the largest collection of paintings by Andrew Wyeth outside of the artist's own holdings.
- The world's largest cross of Christ (150 feet long and 115 feet wide) and the largest Ten Commandments (letters 5 feet high and 4 feet wide) are at the "Fields of the Wood" outside Murphy, N.C.
- Haywood County (N.C.) has an abundant number of picturesque and weathered barns and is known as "Barn Country."
- The great Cherokee Chief Junaluska is buried within the city limits of Robbinsville, N.C.
- In 1889 you could buy a pound of coffee at the old Sautee Store (Ga.) for 25 cents.
- Karl Wallenda, the famous tightrope walker, made an historic walk across the Tallulah Falls Gorge (Ga.) on a 1,100-foot-long cable.
- The gold rush at Dahlonega, Ga., preceded the 1849 California gold drive by 20 years. A U.S. branch mint there was approved in 1835.
- Clingmans Dome, a 6,643-foot-high peak in the Smokies located in Swain County (N.C.) is the second highest in the eastern United States.
- Walhalla (S.C.) Fish Hatchery is one of the largest trout hatcheries in the United States with a yearly capacity of over 1 million trout.
- The largest private house in the world, the Biltmore House (Asheville, N.C.), includes 250 rooms, 32 guest suites, and a 75-foot-high banquet hall. The house is valued at $55 million.
- The state of Georgia is the largest state east of the Mississippi River. It includes about 58,914 miles of territory.
- The Appalachian Trail is called "the longest continuously marked footpath in the world" (2,000 miles from Springer Mountain, Ga., to Mt. Katadin, Maine).
- The nation's first garden club was founded in 1891 in Athens, Ga., with the name Ladies Garden Club of Athens.
- The "blue" haze which once made the Blue Ridge Mountains famous is being replaced by "white" haze due to the dominance of ammonium sulfate aerosols which defract light and change the colors from blue to hazy white through a chemical transformation.
- At Riverside Cemetery (Asheville, N.C.) you'll find the graves of authors Tom Wolfe (1900-1938) and O. Henry (1862-1910).
- On the 223 mountains that rise 5,000 feet or higher in western North Carolina, leaves get their fall colors earlier because the autumn chill comes sooner at higher altitudes. Peak coloration in higher altitudes generally occurs in the third week of October. Recommended areas are Great Smoky Mountains National Park, Linville Gorge, Joyce Kilmer National Forest, Snowbird Mountains, and the counties of Yancey and Madison.
- The Chattahoochee River provides water to nearly 33 percent of Georgia's population and 90 percent to the metropolitan Atlanta area.
- In the Cherokee National Forest you'll find 500 miles of hiking trails, including 190 miles of the Appalachian Trail — one of the finest trails in the United States. And the Ocoee River is one of the best whitewater rafting areas in the South.
- The *Horn in the West* outdoor drama in Boone, N.C., is the third oldest outdoor drama in the United States.
- The 12-by-27-foot frescoe entitled "The Mystery of Faith" (St. Mary's Church, Beaver Creek, N.C.) featuring the crucifixion of Christ is said to be the largest of its kind in the country.

- The world's second oldest river, the New River, flows north from the N.C. valley (Beaver Creek, N.C.) to the Ohio River.
- Joe E. Brown, one of Georgia's most famous governors, had his roots in the mountains of North Georgia. From his family home in the Gaddistown area near Suches, Brown went on to become governor of Georgia four times and served in that position during the Civil War.
- The Hamilton Rhododendron Garden on the Georgia Mountain Fairgrounds (Hiawassee, Ga.) is one of the largest in the Southeast with more than 400 varieties of rhododendron and more than 1,600 assorted rhododendron, azaleas and native plants.
- The oldest resort colony in western North Carolina is Flat Rock, N.C.
- The deepest cut in the earth's crust east of the Grand Canyon is the Linville (N.C.) Gorge, a National Wilderness Area (off the Blue Ridge Parkway).
- The National Climatic Center in Asheville, N.C., was established by the U.S. Dept. of Commerce in 1952 and keeps an eye on U.S. weather from Alaska to Puerto Rico and maintains all U.S. weather records.
- Georgia has the largest percentage of Indian names (people, towns, mountains, rivers, etc.) of any state in the United States.
- The Museum of N.C. Minerals (Spruce Pine, N.C.) contains exhibits of more than 300 kinds of minerals and gemstones found in North Carolina.
- The Great Smoky Mountains National Park is America's most popular national park, and one half of its land mass is in North Carolina.
- The steep sides of the Nantahala Gorge (Bryson City, N.C. area) allows only three hours of sunlight daily to enter the gorge during the winter months.
- Lake Lanier, (Ga.), a 37,000-acre impoundment, is known as the **spotted bass capital of the world.**
- Three towns in the Blue Ridge area have been acclaimed the best retirement places in the United States by authors R. Boyer and D. Savageau: Brevard, N.C.; Asheville, N.C.; and Clarkesville-Mount Airy, Ga.
- One of three marble sculptors in the United States, Jane Armstrong, works at her Spring Park Studio in Saluda, N.C.
- One of the largest rubies (163 carats) was found in Cowee Valley near Franklin, N.C.
- In 1969 a 1,438-carat emerald crystal was found in the Rist Mine (Hiddenite, N.C.) — largest ever found in North America.
- Tiffany owns the Carolina Emerald (13.14 carats), found in the Rist Mine near Emerald Valley, N.C., and valued at $700,000.
- The oldest known rock formations, about a billion years old, are found on the slopes of Grandfather Mountain (Linville, N.C.), according to the U.S. Geological Survey Bulletin.
- The Spruce Pine Mining District (N.C.) contains more than 40 minerals including mica, which the Cherokee Indians mined for more than 200 years before western North Carolina was settled by whites.
- Cabbage Patch Dolls were created by Xavier Roberts at Babyland General Hospital in Cleveland, Ga.
- Wolf Laurel Golf Club (N.C.) is the highest golf course east of the Mississippi with an elevation of 4,785 feet.
- The number 13 hole at Beaver Lake Golf Course (Asheville, N.C.) is said to be the world's longest par 5 hole (690 yards).
- The highest point in South Carolina is Sassafrass Mountain (3,548 feet) in Greenville County.
- The first cotton gin in the world to be operated by electricity was that of Oliver Bolt in Anderson County, S.C., during 1897.

- The private mint of Christopher Bechtler near Rutherfordton, N.C., produced the first gold dollar struck in the United States and minted more than 2 million dollars in gold during the period from 1831 to 1849.
- A ramp is a vegetable that grows in the cooler mountain regions of western North Carolina and is quite similar to an onion or scallion. A boy is initiated into manhood when asked to go along with the men to the ramp patch.
- The only elm tree in western North Carolina is near US-129 before the town of Robbinsville, N.C.
- Poultry Park in Gainesville, Ga., salutes the city's status as the **Broiler Capital of the World.**
- The **highest cross country ski event in Eastern America** is the Black Mountain-Mt. Mitchell (N.C.) Ski Challenge in February.
- The University of Georgia's Botanical Garden (Athens, Ga.), the Elizabeth Turner Memorial Rose Garden, has been accredited as a public rose garden by the All-American Rose Selection, Inc. It is one of 3 in Georgia and one of 100 in the United States. The garden includes 500 rose bushes representing about 50 cultivars.
- Asheville (N.C.) was known as the "tuberculosis capital" of the nation during the early 1900s.
- Carter's Lake (Ellijay, Ga.) is the deepest U.S. Army Corps of Engineers lake in Georgia.
- The first wagon train to cross the mountains in this century was initiated by Tennessee and North Carolina in 1957 (to spur interest in developing a road from Tellico).
- Bird watchers in the Blue Ridge Mountains can observe some 251 bird species.
- The Black Mountain Golf Club course (N.C.) claims the longest hole in the world: the 17th hole, par 6 at 745 yards.
- Archaelogical evidence suggests that the ancient stone ruins found near Fort Mountain (Chatsworth, Ga.) are related to the past visits of Asian and European voyagers.
- Georgia is number one in the nation in total poultry income and second in both egg and broiler production.
- The **World's Largest Bed** was constructed by craftsmen at MACO crafts in Franklin, N.C., for display at the World's Fair in Knoxville, Tenn. The bed, a four-poster oak measuring 18 feet wide and 22 feet long and standing 2 feet off the ground, took well over 1,000 manhours, 3,000 feet of oak and 125 two-by-fours. It made the *Guinness Book of World Records.*
- The U. A. Lawson Steeple of the William Price Memorial Administration Building on the North Georgia College campus in Dahlonega is covered in gleaming 24-karat gold leaf. The building sits on the foundation of a U.S. Mint that burned in 1878.
- The Stoval Covered Bridge is the shortest covered bridge (33 feet) in Georgia (off G-255 over the Chickamauga Creek northeast of Helen, Ga.) and was featured in the movie *I'd Climb the Highest Mountain.*
- The average yearly farm income in Union County, Ga., in 1937 was $50 from potatoes, $67.50 from beans and $25 from cabbage. Thus, the average cash income was $177.50. Source: Atlanta *Constitution,* Feb. 16, 1938.
- Since the Blue Ridge Parkway's opening 46 years ago, more than 300 million people have traveled it.
- North Georgia College (Dahlonega, Ga.) is the only co-educational, liberal arts, state-supported military college in the world. The 110-year-old institution is a member of the university system of Georgia and is one of four senior colleges classified as military colleges by the U.S. Army.
- One of the last remaining places where you can "ford a creek" on a state highway is Lovell Creek on G-197. Natives call it the "upside-down bridge."

- Fontana Dam (N.C.) is the highest hydroelectric dam in the eastern United States (480 feet high; 2,365 feet long), the largest dam in the TVA's system of lakes and the fourth-largest dam in the nation.
- The Blue Ridge Parkway has more than 100 overlooks along the scenic route with an average elevation of 3,000 feet. It is traveled by more than 6 million people each year.
- Franklin, N.C., claims to be the "**Quilt Capital of the World.**"
- The Blue Ridge Mountains contain approximately 130 different species of trees, 350 types of mosses and related plants, 2,000 species of fungi, and about 1,400 species of flowering herbs.
- There are about 1,500 varieties of wildflowers in the Great Smoky Mountains National Park.
- The nation's only Folk School is the John C. Campbell Folk School at Brasstown, N.C. It provides experiences in crafts, recorder, homesteading, folk dancing, and traditional music.
- Gilmer is Georgia's biggest apple-growing county and proclaims itself Georgia's Apple Capital.
- Amicalola, a Cherokee word which means "tumbling water," is one of the highest waterfalls in the Southeast, plunging in several cascades some 729 feet.
- The Farmer's Hall in Pendleton, S.C., is probably one of the oldest farmer's halls in continuous use in the United States. It has been used since the late 1820s.
- Lake Lanier Islands (Ga.) has the largest boat rental fleet in the Southeast and one of the world's largest floating marinas.
- According to the U.S. Army Corps of Engineers, Lake Lanier (Gainesville, Ga.), named after the poet Sidney Lanier, is the most popular and most-visited lake of all the 430 lakes the Corps owns.
- The first Indian newspaper, the *Cherokee Phoenix,* was printed in 1828 at New Echuta (Calhoun, Ga.). The paper was bilingual, containing both English and Sequoyan syllabary, the only known written North American Indian language.
- You can attend church on Sunday morning on the "Boat Church," a lake barge located between Hall's Boat House and Whitham's Point on Lake Rabun, Ga.
- What do John C. Calhoun, Thomas G. Clemson, Ulysses S. Grant and Robert S. Disney (father of Walt Disney) have in common? They were owners of gold mines in Dahlonega, Ga.
- Near the East Fork Creek at Walhalla National Fish Hatchery (S.C.) stand two state record trees: a white pine standing 165 feet (circumference of 12 feet, 6 inches) and a hemlock standing 148 feet.

# Z

## ZOOS

Zoos are not that plentiful in the Blue Ridge area, but there are some animal attractions that are worth the money and travel time to visit.

Soco Gardens Zoo in Maggie Valley, N.C., has a collection of animals, birds and reptiles from many parts of the world. Animals include deer, wild boar, badgers, bears, jaguars, leopards, parrots, monkeys, alligators, Asian birds, small mammals and snakes. Rattlesnake milking is featured on every tour. Continual tours are provided by guides from May to October.

The natural habitat area on Grandfather Mountain near Linville, N.C., includes native animals such as black bears and cubs, bald eagles, white-tailed deer and cougars (panther and mountain lion). Mildred the Bear's Environmental Habitat is acclaimed as one of the most beautiful and natural wild animal exhibits in the world.

Youngsters will enjoy the Pet Animal Park at Forge Valley Fun Park near Horse Shoe, N.C. It includes more than 100 animals of some 30 species. You can touch and feed the llamas, sheep, goats, cows, donkeys, horses and birds. Special attractions include the miniature animals (horses, cows, goats, sheep, bantams), Scotty the longhorn Scottish Highlander bull, Andrea the camel and a pair of giant anteaters.

Smaller children will enjoy the petting and feeding zoo on the grounds of Santa Land outside of Cherokee, N.C., from May to October, and also at Mt. Yonah Alpine Storyland near Sautee-Nacooche, Ga.

**ASHEVILLE, N.C.  Asheville Zoo,** in Recreation Park. Offers walking tours, a zoomobile, demonstration/workshops and film showings. (704) 298-1586.

**CHEROKEE, N.C.  Santa's Land Zoo,** US-19. Petting zoo. May-October. Admission. (704) 497-9192.

**HORSE SHOE, N.C.  Forge Valley Fun Park,** NC-280. The Pet Animal Park is open daily, May-October. Admission. (704) 891-3134 or 891-3241.

**LINVILLE, N.C.  Grandfather Mountain,** US-221 and Blue Ridge Parkway. America's great native animals; see and photograph them in beautiful natural habitats. Admission. (704) 733-4337.

**MAGGIE VALLEY, N.C.  Soco Gardens Zoo,** Rte. 1, Box 355. Animals, birds, reptiles. Admission. (704) 926-1746.

**SAUTEE-NACOOCHE, GA.  Mt. Yonah Alpine Storyland,** G-75 between Helen and Cleveland. Petting zoo includes imported and domestic animals. (404) 865-3613.

# Appendix A: State, Regional and Local Information Sources

*State Departments of Tourism:*

GEORGIA:

Department of Industry and Trade,
Tourist Communications Division
P.O. Box 1776
Atlanta, Ga. 30301

NORTH CAROLINA:

Travel & Tourism Division
Department of Commerce
430 N. Salisbury Street
Raleigh, N.C. 27611

SOUTH CAROLINA:

Division of Tourism
Room 30, Box 71
Columbia, S.C. 29202

## Georgia Chambers of Commerce

ATHENS AREA
P.O. Box 948
Athens, Ga. 30603
(404) 549-6800

ATLANTA CONVENTION & VISITORS
BUREAU
229 Peachtree-Cain Building
Atlanta, Ga. 30303
(404) 659-4270

BLUE RIDGE (FANNIN-COPPER
BASIN)
P.O. Box 875
Blue Ridge, Ga. 30513
(404) 632-5680

CHATSWORTH-MURRAY COUNTY
Box 327
Chatsworth, Ga. 30705
(404) 695-6060

CHEROKEE COUNTY
P.O. Box 757
Canton, Ga. 30114
(404) 479-8323

CUMMING-FORSYTH COUNTY
P.O. Box 711
Cumming, Ga. 30130
(404) 887-6461

DAHLONEGA-LUMPKIN COUNTY
P.O. Box 2037
Dahlonega, Ga. 30533
(404) 864-3711

DAWSON COUNTY
P.O. Box 105
Dawsonville, Ga. 30534
(404) 265-2616

ELLIJAY-GILMER COUNTY
P.O. Box 818
Ellijay, Ga. 30540
(404) 635-7400

GAINESVILLE AREA
P.O. Box 374
Gainesville, Ga. 30501
(404) 532-6206

HABERSHAM COUNTY
P.O. Box 366
Cornelia, Ga. 30531
(404) 778-4654

HART COUNTY
P.O. Box 793
Hartwell, Ga. 30643
(404) 376-8590

HELEN AREA
P.O. Box 192
Helen, Ga. 30545
(404) 878-2181

JASPER-PICKENS COUNTY
P.O. Box 327
Jasper, Ga. 30143
(404) 692-5600

LAVONIA AREA
Old Railroad Depot
Lavonia, Ga. 30553
(404) 356-8202

RABUN COUNTY
P.O. Box 761
Clayton, Ga. 30525
(404) 782-4812

TOCCOA-STEPHENS COUNTY
P.O. Box 577
Toccoa, Ga. 30577
(404) 886-2132

TOWNS COUNTY
Hiawassee, Ga. 33546
(404) 896-4191

UNION COUNTY
P.O. Box 727
Blairsville, Ga. 30512
(404) 745-5789

## Regional Associations — State of Georgia

GEORGIA CHAMBERS OF
COMMERCE
575 N. Omni International
Atlanta, Ga. 30335
(404) 524-8481

GEORGIA MOUNTAIN TOUR GUIDES
P.O. Box 979
Cleveland, Ga. 30528

NORTHEAST GEORGIA MOUNTAINS
REGION:
Georgia Department of Industry and
Trade
P.O. Box 887
Gainesville, Ga. 30503

SOUTHEAST REGION:
Chamber of Commerce
223 Perimeter Center East
Atlanta, Ga. 30346
(404) 393-0140

*RESOURCES:*

GEORGIA DEPT. OF INDUSTRY AND
TRADE
1400 N. Omni International
P.O. Box 1776
Atlanta, Ga. 30301
(404) 656-3553

GEORGIA DEPT. OF NATURAL
RESOURCES
270 Washington Street S.W.
Atlanta, Ga. 30334
(404) 656-3530

## North Carolina Chambers of Commerce

ASHEVILLE AREA
P.O. Box 1011
Asheville, N.C. 28801
(704) 258-3858 and (704) 258-5200

BEECH MOUNTAIN
P.O. Box 876
Beech Mountain, N.C. 28604
(704) 387-9283

BLACK MOUNTAIN-SWANNANOA
201 E. State Street
Black Mountain, N.C. 28711
(704) 669-2300

BREVARD AREA
35 W. Main Street
P.O. Box 589
Brevard, N.C. 28712
(704) 883-3700

BURNSVILLE CHAMBER
OF COMMERCE
No. 2 Town Square, Room 3
Burnsville, N.C. 28714
(704) 682-7413

CANTON CHAMBER OF COMMERCE
22 Park Street
P.O. Box 1026
Canton, N.C. 28716
(704) 648-2400

CASHIERS AREA
Box 238
Cashiers, N.C. 28717
(704) 743-5191

CHEROKEE TRIBAL TRAVEL AND PROMOTION
P.O. Box 465
Cherokee, N.C. 28719
(704) 497-9195; TOLL FREE: 1 (800) 438-1611

CHEROKEE COUNTY
115 U.S. 64 West
Murphy, N.C. 28906
(704) 837-2242

CHIMNEY ROCK
Box 39
Chimney Rock, N.C. 28720
(704) 625-4403

CLAY COUNTY
P.O. Box 386
Hayesville, N.C. 28904
(704) 389-3313

CULLOWHEE
Route 67, Box 112-H
Cullowhee, N.C. 28723
(704) 293-9648

FONTANA VILLAGE
Fontana Dam, N.C. 28733
(704) 498-2211

FRANKLIN
Box 180
180 Porter Street
Franklin, N.C. 28734
(704) 524-3161

GRAHAM COUNTY
P.O. Box 575
Robbinsville, N.C. 28771
(704) 479-3250

HAYWOOD COUNTY
Box 125
511 Walnut Street
Waynesville, N.C. 28786
(704) 456-3021 and (704) 456-6005

HENDERSONVILLE
330 N. King Street
Hendersonville, N.C. 28739-0489
(704) 692-1413

HIGHLANDS
P.O. Box 404
Highlands, N.C. 28741
(704) 526-2112

JACKSON COUNTY
18 N. Central Street
Sylva, N.C. 28779
(704) 586-2155

TOWN OF LAKE LURE
Box 255
Lake Lure, N.C. 28746
(704) 625-9396

MAGGIE VALLEY
Box 87
Maggie, N.C. 28751
(704) 926-1686

McDOWELL COUNTY
20 N. Logan Street
Marion, N.C. 28752
(704) 652-4240

POLK COUNTY
P.O. Box 146
Columbus, N.C. 28722
(704) 859-6236

SALUDA
Saluda, N.C. 28775
(704) 894-8236

SPRUCE PINE
150 Pine Bridge Center
Spruce Pine, N.C. 28777
(704) 765-9482

SWAIN COUNTY
P.O. Box 509
Bryson City, N.C. 28713
(704) 488-3681

TRYON
401 N. Trade Street
Tryon, N.C. 28682
(704) 859-6236

*Regional Associations:*

NORTH CAROLINA HIGH COUNTRY
600 N.C.-105 Extension
Boone, N.C. 28607

WNAC
Mountain Heritage Center
P.O. Box 2786
Cullowhee, N.C. 28723

In North Carolina motorists may call (800) 662-7956 for road condition information. For travel and tourist information, the number is (800) 334-1051.

*Resources:*

NORTH CAROLINA CITIZENS ASSOCIATION
Wake County Office Building
P.O. Box 2508
Raleigh, N.C. 27602
(919) 828-0758

NORTH CAROLINA HISTORIC SITES
109 E. Jones Street
Raleigh, N.C. 27611
(919) 733-7862

NORTH CAROLINA WILDLIFE RESOURCES COMMISSION
512 N. Salisbury Street
Archdale Building
Raleigh, N.C. 27611
(919) 733-7123

STATE PARKS AND RECREATION
512 N. Salisbury Street
Archdale Building.
Raleigh, N.C. 27611
(919) 733-4181.

## South Carolina Chambers of Commerce

CLEMSON AREA
P.O. Box 202
Clemson, S.C. 29633
(803) 654-1200

EASLEY AREA
P.O. Box 241
Easley, S.C. 29641
(803) 859-2693

GREATER PICKENS
P.O. Box 153
107 Court Street
Pickens, S.C. 29671

PENDLETON DISTRICT HISTORICAL AND RECREATION COMMISSION
P.O. Box 234
125 E. Queen Street
Pendleton, S.C. 29670
(803) 646-3782

SENECA AREA
P.O. Box 855
Seneca, S.C. 29679
(803) 882-2097

WALHALLA AREA
502 E. Main Street
P.O. Box 188
Walhalla, S.C. 29691
(803) 638-9585

*Regional Associations:*

DISCOVER UPCOUNTRY CAROLINA
ASSOCIATION
P.O. Box 3132
Greenville, S.C. 29602
(803) 233-2690

SOUTH CAROLINA CHAMBER OF
COMMERCE
Bankers Trust Tower, Suite 520
1301 Gervals Street
P.O. Box 11278
Columbia, S.C. 29211
(803) 799-4601

*Resources:*

NATIONAL FOREST SERVICE
U.S. DEPT. OF AGRICULTURE
1835 Assembly Street
Columbia, S.C. 29202
(803) 765-5222

SOUTH CAROLINA DEPT. OF AR-
CHIVES AND HISTORY
Attn: Research
1430 Senate Street
Columbia, S.C. 29201
(803) 758-5816

SOUTH CAROLINA DIVISION OF
PARKS
Edgar A. Brown Building
1205 Pendleton Street
Columbia, S.C. 29201
(803) 758-3622

SOUTH CAROLINA MUSEUM
COMMISSION
P.O. Box 11296
Columbia, S.C. 29211
(803) 758-8197

SOUTH CAROLINA DEPT. OF
WILDLIFE AND MARINE RESOURCES
P.O. Box 167
Columbia, S.C. 29202
(803) 758-0059

SOUTH CAROLINA DEPT. OF
HIGHWAYS AND PUBLIC
TRANSPORTATION
(Road Information and Maps)
P.O. Box 191
Columbia, S.C. 29202
(803) 758-3228

South Carolina travelers may call (803) 758-3228 for road information.

# Appendix B: Map Resources

**OFFICIAL STATE MAPS:**

**GA.**-Department of Transportation, 2 Capitol Square, Atlanta, Ga. 30334.

**N.C.**-N.C. Department of Transportation, Travel and Promotion Division, Department of Natural and Economic Resources, Raleigh, N.C. 27611.

**S.C.**-S.C. Department of Highways and Public Transportation, P.O. Box 191, Columbia, S.C. 29202.

**STATE TRAVEL PUBLICATIONS:**

**GA.**-Ga. Department of Tourism/Communications Division, P.O. Box 1776, Atlanta, Ga. 30301 (*Georgia - This Way To Fun*)

**N.C.**-N.C. Travel and Tourism Division, Department of Commerce, Raleigh, N.C. 27611. (*State Travel Guide*)

**S.C.**-S.C. Division of Tourism, Room 30, Box 71, Columbia, S.C. 29202. (*Come See South Carolina*)

**SPECIALTY MAPS**

For the hunter, fisherman, camper, outdoorsman, the following resource maps are available free of charge:

*Georgia*

*"Chattahoochee National Forest."* Forest Supervisor, U.S. Forest Service, Box 1437, Gainesville, Ga. 30501.
*"Chattahoochee-Oconee National Forest Recreation Areas."* Forest Supervisor, U.S. Forest Service, Box 1437, Gainesville, Ga. 30501.
*"Guide to North Georgia Wildlife Management Areas."* Atlantic Mapping, Box 7391, Marietta, Ga. 30065.
*"Hikers Guide to Chattahoochee National Forest,"* U.S. Forest Service, 1720 Peachtree Road. N.W., Atlanta, Ga. 30309.
National Park Service, S.E. Regional Office, Suite 800, 1720 Peachtree Road, N.W., Atlanta, Ga. 30309.
*"Wildlife Refuges."* Public Affairs Office, U.S. Fish and Wildlife Service, 75 Spring Street S.W., Atlanta, Ga. 30303.

*North Carolina*

*"National Forest Recreation Area in North Carolina."* Supervisor's Office, National Forests in North Carolina, P.O. Box 2750, Asheville, N.C. 28802.
*"Nantahala National Forest."* District Ranger, U.S. Forest Service, 201 Wood Drive, Murphy, N.C. 28906.
*"Appalachian Trail."* Forest Supervisor, Pisgah National Forest, National Forests of North Carolina, P.O. Box 2750, Asheville, N.C. 28802.
*"North Carolina State Parks."* P.O. Box 27687, Raleigh, N.C. 27611.

*South Carolina*

"Sumter National Forest." National Forest Service: U.S. Department of Agriculture, 1835 Assembly Street, Columbia, S.C. 29202.
Division of State Parks - South Carolina Dept. of Parks, Recreation and Tourism, 1205 Pendleton Street; Edgar A. Brown Building, Program Section, Columbia, S.C. 29201.

*Appalachian Trail*

"Appalachian Trail in Georgia, North Carolina and the Smokies." Appalachian Trail Conference, Box 236, Harpers Ferry, W.V. 25425.

*Topographic Maps*

Branch of Distribution, U.S. Geological Survey, 1200 South Eads Street, Arlington, Va. 22202.
Tennessee Valley Authority, Mapping Services Branch, 200 Haney Building, Chattanooga, Tenn. 37401.

*Chamber of Commerce Maps*

Contact the area Chamber of Commerce and request a free map of the specific area.

# Index

# East Woods Press Books

American Bed & Breakfast
  Cook Book, The
Backcountry Cooking
Berkshire Trails for Walking & Ski Touring
Best Bed & Breakfast in the World, The
Blue Ridge Mountain Pleasures
California Bed & Breakfast
Campfire Chillers
Campfire Songs
Canoeing the Jersey Pine Barrens
Carolina Curiosities
Carolina Seashells
Carpentry: Some Tricks of the Trade from
  an Old-Style Carpenter
Catfish Cookbook, The
Charlotte: A Touch of Gold
Complete Guide to Backpacking
  in Canada
Creative Gift Wrapping
Day Trips From Baltimore
Day Trips From Cincinnati
Day Trips From Houston
Drafting: Tips and Tricks on Drawing and
  Designing House Plans
Exploring Nova Scotia
Fifty Years on the Fifty:
  The Orange Bowl Story
Fructose Cookbook, The
Grand Old Ladies
Grand Strand: An Uncommon Guide
  to Myrtle Beach, The
Healthy Trail Food Book, The
Hiking from Inn to Inn
Hiking Virginia's National Forests
Historic Country House Hotels
Hosteling USA, Third Edition
How to Afford Your Own Log Home
How to Play With Your Baby
Indiana: Off the Beaten Path
Interior Finish: More Tricks of the Trade
Just Folks: Visitin' with Carolina People
Kays Gary, Columnist
Maine Coast: A Nature Lover's
  Guide, The
Making Food Beautiful
Mid-Atlantic Guest House Book, The
New England Guest House Book, The
New England: Off the Beaten Path
Ohio: Off the Beaten Path
Parent Power!
Parks of the Pacific Coast
Race, Rock and Religion
River Reflections
Rocky Mountain National Park Hiking Trails
Saturday Notebook, The
Sea Islands of the South
Separation and Divorce in North Carolina
South Carolina Hiking Trails
Southern Guest House Book, The

Southern Rock: A Climber's Guide
  to the South
Sweets Without Guilt
Tar Heel Sights: Guide to North Carolina's
  Heritage
Tennessee Trails
Toys That Teach Your Child
Train Trips: Exploring America by Rail
Trout Fishing the Southern Appalachians
Vacationer's Guide to Orlando and
  Central Florida, A
Walks in the Catskills
Walks in the Great Smokies
Walks with Nature in Rocky Mountain
  National Park
Whitewater Rafting in Eastern America
Wildflower Folklore
Woman's Journey, A
You Can't Live on Radishes


Order from:

**The East Woods Press**
**429 East Boulevard**
**Charlotte, NC 28203**

# You'll also enjoy these other guides...

**The Best Bed & Breakfast in the World,** 1984-1985, Sigourney Welles & Jill Darbey, $10.95 paper. More than 800 personally recommended establishments in Great Britain and Ireland with a special section on London and tear-out booking forms.

**Train Trips: Exploring America by Rail,** 1984-1985, William G. Scheller, $9.95 paper. Complete guide to U.S.'s Amtrak and Canada's Via Rail routes, with detailed visits to 52 major cities, including Houston.

**The Southern Guest House Book,** 1984-1985, Corinne Madden Ross, $7.95 paper. 107 lodgings in Alabama, Florida, Georgia, Louisiana, Mississippi, North Carolina, South Carolina, Tennessee, Virginia and the District of Columbia.

**East Woods Press Pak-books™** — Created with the outdoors in mind, these pocket-sized trail guides have sewn bindings, rounded outer corners and waterproofed and tear-resistant covers. From the Rocky Mountains to the East Coast, from hiking to campfire story-telling, they cover many regional outdoor activities. Send for a full description of these books in our free catalog.

Copies of these and other East Woods Press books are available from your bookseller or directly from The East Woods Press, 429 East Boulevard, Charlotte, N.C. 28203. (704) 334-0897. For orders **only**, call toll-free (800) 438-1242, ext. 102. In N.C. (800) 532-0476.

---

Please send me the following book(s)_____.
I am including $1.50 shipping and handling per book.
Enclosed is my check or use the Visa or MasterCard information below:

_____

Please send a complete catalog of East Woods Press books. ☐

Send to: _____

_____

_____

_____